FRAMING COMPLEXITY IN
FORMATIVE MESOAMERICA

FRAMING COMPLEXITY IN FORMATIVE MESOAMERICA

Edited by

LISA DELANCE AND GARY M. FEINMAN

UNIVERSITY PRESS OF COLORADO
Louisville

Published by University Press of Colorado
245 Century Circle, Suite 202
Louisville, Colorado 80027

 The University Press of Colorado is a proud member of
the Association of University Presses.

The University Press of Colorado is a cooperative publishing enterprise supported, in part, by Adams State University, Colorado State University, Fort Lewis College, Metropolitan State University of Denver, University of Alaska Fairbanks, University of Colorado, University of Denver, University of Northern Colorado, University of Wyoming, Utah State University, and Western Colorado University.

∞ This paper meets the requirements of the ANSI/NISO Z39.48–1992 (Permanence of Paper).

ISBN: 978-1-64642-287-6 (hardcover)
ISBN: 978-1-64642-288-3 (ebook)
https://doi.org/10.5876/9781646422883

Library of Congress Cataloging-in-Publication Data

Names: DeLance, Lisa L., editor. | Feinman, Gary M., editor.
Title: Framing complexity in Formative Mesoamerica / edited by Lisa L. DeLance and Gary M. Feinman.
Description: Louisville : University Press of Colorado, [2022] | Includes bibliographical references and index.
Identifiers: LCCN 2022017991 (print) | LCCN 2022017992 (ebook) | ISBN 9781646422876 (hardcover) | ISBN 9781646422883 (ebook)
Subjects: LCSH: Indians of Mexico—Social conditions. | Indians of Central America—Social conditions. | Indians of Mexico—Antiquities. | Indians of Central America—Antiquities. | Indigenous peoples—Mexico. | Indigenous peoples—Central America. | Excavations (Archaeology)—Mexico. | Excavations (Archaeology)—Central America.
Classification: LCC F1219.3.S57 F74 2022 (print) | LCC F1219.3.S57 (ebook) | DDC 972/.01—dc23/eng/20220504
LC record available at https://lccn.loc.gov/2022017991
LC ebook record available at https://lccn.loc.gov/2022017992

Cover illustration by Lisa DeLance

For Wendy, whose legacy endures.

Contents

Figures

Tables

Preface

This book began as a session for the 82nd Annual Meeting of the Society for American Anthropology designed to explore how crafting in Formative Mesoamerican communities illustrated differing processes of complexity. The idea of complexity as a process originated in discussions with the first editor's (Lisa DeLance) doctoral advisor, Dr. Wendy Ashmore, to whom this volume is dedicated. These discussions, often spontaneous intellectual exercises, were nearly always framed around deconstructing and probing the assumptions that have driven archaeological interpretation for the past century. These highly meaningful moments shaped Lisa's graduate school experience and fundamentally frame her approach to archaeological knowledge.

During one discussion, shortly before Wendy fell ill in 2017, I (Lisa) asked her one of the most complex questions yet to be answered: *How did we get here?* I was pondering the practical experience of a social group moving from an egalitarian to a highly stratified form of social organization. From that frankly absurdly abstract question came a series of discussions focused on the lived experience of social change in the present. How are certain types of leadership and certain

https://doi.org/10.5876/9781646422883.c000

qualities of leaders normalized, indeed idealized? How do cultural norms, standards, and values develop and change over time, such that they are experienced as natural? What is the impetus for change? How is it felt and negotiated at the micro-level? They are, indeed, complex questions.

Complexity has long fascinated archaeologists. Whether overtly explored or latently present in the interpretation of the past, issues of social complexity (the when, the why, the how) permeate our explorations of the human past. Complexity research, at its core, attempts to understand *how* and *under what circumstances* the similarities and divisions impacting our daily lived experience originated.

This is both a question that the larger public is grappling with in an increasingly polarized and uncertain time and a question that archaeologists have long attempted to answer. From the outset, this volume sought to explore complexity through a comparative lens and took a pan-Mesoamerican approach to facilitate the comparison of the emergence of unique social conditions and the circumstances in which they were experienced. We felt it important to bridge the scholarly gap in Mesoamerican research that tends to explore individual cultural groups as isolates rather than part of a contiguous system of interaction. The incorporation of data from Oaxaca, Central Mexico, the Yucatán, the Petén, and the eastern Maya Lowlands allows scholars to compare historical sequences of complexity and the establishment of group identity on a diverse scale throughout Mesoamerica.

Models of complexity in Mesoamerica are variable. Not only is there lack of consensus as to what specific social features illustrate complexity, there is also a general trend toward exploring complexity in the context of the "grandiose" rather than the "mundane." Models, by necessity, require researchers to employ typological classifications of specific social features and practically function as a set of "diagnostic criteria" for determining whether a society is complex. While the use of models of complexity is important in the generalizability of theories about complexity, they simultaneously disregard aspects of social differentiation that impact inter and intra-group relationships and the identities that develop from them.

This volume is guided by three fundamental questions: (1) How and when did social aggregations become more complex? What are the processes involved? In what way were they complex and how does that differ from other regions of Mesoamerica; (2) How and when did particular ethnic identities and affiliations emerge in the context of cultural affiliations; and (3) What are key aspects of regional and macroregional variability. Volume contributors address these questions as they apply to the development of complexity in Western and Central Mexico, the Yucatán, and the Maya Lowlands. The authors in this volume do not employ linear or uniform models in their analysis. Complexity in each case is explored as a process at a community level through the lens of evidence-based correlates to complex behavior in a local, regional, and supra-regional scales. We hope that as an example of the intellectual legacy of Wendy Ashmore, these chapters will elicit further exploration of novel approaches to long-standing archaeological questions.

This volume could not have been completed without the valued support and assistance of our editor, Darrin Pratt. Darrin and his team were welcoming, efficient, and insightful at all stages of this book's production, and we are grateful. The editors and the authors also owe a debt of gratitude to the local peoples who allowed us to investigate Mesoamerica's deep past on their lands and to the field and lab crews who assisted us in carrying out the research that we draw on here.

FRAMING COMPLEXITY IN FORMATIVE MESOAMERICA

1

Framing Complexity

LISA DELANCE

"How did we end up here?"

This is a question that many anthropologically trained archaeologists have attempted to grapple with throughout the history of the discipline. In many ways, this broad question frames our epistemological pursuits of the past as much as they condition how we understand our contemporary world. In times of increasing social and political upheaval where the complexity of our societies can seem overwhelming, humans often refer back to the past, partly out of the comfort of nostalgia but also as a way to understand and explain the turmoil of the present.

Scholars in multiple disciplines have explored the larger questions about why and how the social systems we rely on first arose in different parts of the world (Axelrod 1997; Barton 2014; Blanton and Fargher 2008; Carballo et al. 2014; Feinman 2012; La Porte 2015; Paynter 1989; Price and Feinman 2010; Stewart 2001; Tainter 2006). Rather than producing a coherent body of research illuminating what features indicate complexity, how complex social organization was constituted and reconstituted by communities in the past, and the forms that social complexity took, research on social complexity is as vast and complex as

https://doi.org/10.5876/9781646422883.c001

the various proposed definitions of the terms *social* and *complex*. In fact, there is relatively little agreement on what actually constitutes social complexity. Early attempts to define complexity sought to categorize social groups based on their power structures (Fried 1967; Sahlins and Service 1960; Service 1962). Other attempts focused on creating models based on the specific features a social group should have in order to be considered "complex" (Childe 1950; Redman 1979). This volume explores nascent social complexity in an attempt to answer broader social questions about egalitarian and transegalitarian prehispanic Mesoamerican cultural groups. In particular, the authors in this volume present multiple lines of evidence demonstrating the *process* of social complexity in an effort to explore the roots of the highly complex and grandiose Mesoamerican urban cities that characterized the Classic period.

COMPLEXITY IS COMPLEX

There is no standard definition for social complexity, and the definitions proposed are as varied as the archaeologists proposing them. For the purposes of this volume, complexity is considered to be a fluid *process* rather than a static state. It may be understood as the processes through which humans form more functionally differentiated societal units and groupings (Blanton et al. 1993), both within and between cultural groups. In prehispanic Mesoamerica, these processes occurred first as people coalesced in larger, semipermanent aggregations (Carballo et al. 2012) and as networks of individuals, who both competed and cooperated with each other in differing ways, elected to affiliate. Within the framework of cooperative relationships, individuals incur cost or risk associated with other individuals receiving benefits. In some cases, decisions made for the benefit of a community may harm certain individuals within this community. How these decisions are made and how individuals reconcile the cost and benefits of such decisions are grounded in the specific worldview of each cultural group. Essentially, archaeologists who study complex social organization seek "to understand how societies came to be differentiated, stratified, institutionalized, and multilayered" (Alt 2010, 2) It is variably influenced by individual agents within the community, complex networks of interpersonal and intergroup relationships, and the ability and willingness of communities to recursively adapt *and* develop political, social, economic, ideological, and environmental conditions. Processual complexity understands that each of these factors exists in relation to what has come before. In this sense, the process of complexity becomes exponentially more complex as communities integrate new intra- and inter-group considerations. Relationships and networks of interaction expand, contract, and shift in response to a variety of different factors, from isolated community-based concerns to larger, regional conditions.

What Makes a Society Complex?

In the most basic sense, complexity is seen when social groups develop more and larger webs of interpersonal social and economic relations. Complexity involves multiple (often overlapping) networks of social interaction, sometimes complementary, sometimes combative, that both define and condition our relationship to others. Complicating complexity even further, these networks of interaction exist on all levels of social aggregation, from the smallest family group to regional-scale webs of connectivity. Examples of these social components include (but are certainly not limited to) community-level religious belief, leadership activities and the establishment and maintenance of status differentiation within a community, the creation and consumption of non-utilitarian goods, and the establishment of long-distance trade networks.

What makes complexity particularly difficult to define is the fact that any social group may have any number of components interacting in a number of different ways to produce unique "flavors" of complexity. The variability in these "flavors" of complexity is sufficiently broad such that there is no definitive list—nor can there be—of complex societies or specific features that all complex societies should have (Lesure and Blake 2002). As Hepp notes (this volume), social complexity should not be exclusively thought of as unequal hierarchical relationships reflecting either ascribed or inherited status, or both. Indeed, this calls attention to the concept of heterarchy, that is, that interpersonal and intergroup relationships were multidimensional, recursive, and subject to ongoing negotiation (Crumley 1995, 2004; Feinman 2013). The variability in both size and structure of later Classic period Mesoamerican political and social complexity indicates that individual and community agency may have played a crucial role in the later development of high levels of social and political complexity. Political interaction, warfare, and competition for resources created the conditions for reimagining structures (thus allowing for both variability and the inherent instability necessary for social change) of prehispanic Mesoamerican groups (Carballo et al. 2012; Chase and Chase 1996; Demarest 1996; Foias 2013; Iannone 2002; Lucero 1999).

In reality, social organization in Mesoamerica, as in any other part of the world, involved interpersonal relationships between individuals and between groups. To understand the dynamics of Preclassic/Formative Mesoamerican (figure 1.1) communities as a whole, we must move beyond an elite focused understanding of a hierarchical social order and explore the sometimes nuanced ways in which people both acquiesced to and resisted different forms of power, both from above and from below, and how individuals as active agents in their social world created webs of interaction and obligation both within and between communities.[1]

---

1 The authors in this volume refer to either the Formative period or the Preclassic period, depending on the naming conventions for each particular region. For the purposes of this volume, both Formative period and Preclassic period refer to the same general chronological period.

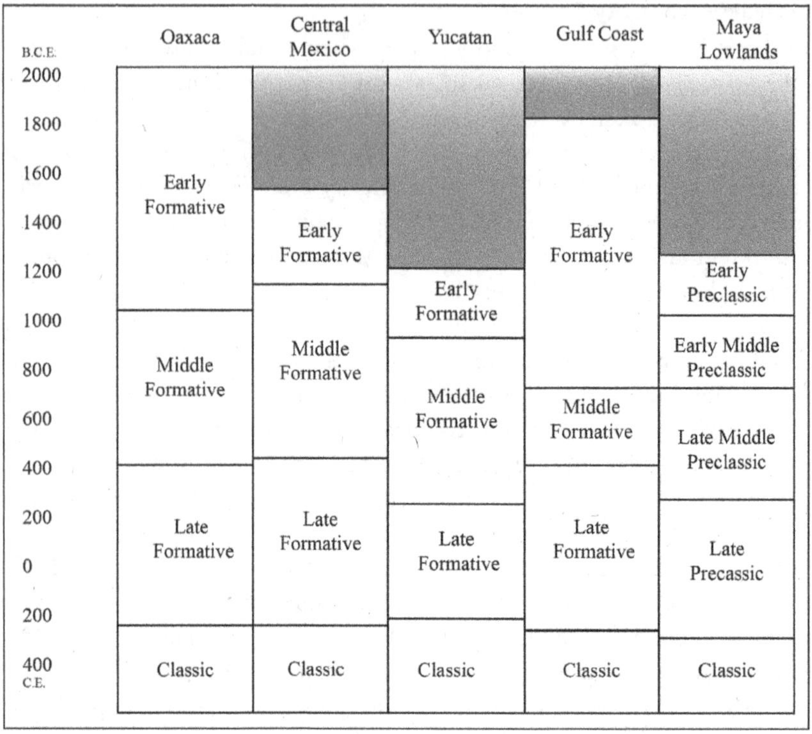

B.C.E.	Oaxaca	Central Mexico	Yucatan	Gulf Coast	Maya Lowlands
2000	Early Formative				
1800					
1600				Early Formative	
1400		Early Formative			
1200			Early Formative		Early Preclassic
1000	Middle Formative	Middle Formative			Early Middle Preclassic
800			Middle Formative	Middle Formative	
600					Late Middle Preclassic
400	Late Formative	Late Formative	Late Formative	Late Formative	Late Precassic
200					
0					
200					
400 C.E.	Classic	Classic	Classic	Classic	Classic

FIGURE 1.1. *Comparative regional chronology for Preclassic/Formative Mesoamerica.*

This volume explores social, political, economic, and architectural lines of evidence, in addition to craft specialization during the Preclassic/Formative period (figure 1.1) throughout Mesoamerica. In an attempt to synthesize similar trends in the development of complexity at various locations throughout Mesoamerica, the chapters in this volume explore three broad questions:

1. How and when did social aggregations become organized in more complex ways with larger and more differentiated segments and institutions?
2. How did particular ethnicities and cultural affiliations come about, and what was their relationship to community and regional cohesion?
3. What are some key aspects of regional and macroregional variability?

People were not simply passive actors in their social world; rather, they actively controlled, manipulated, and created circumstances and actions and thus created and maintained multilayered and interconnected relationships with one another. Individual relationships in the present are often complex and multifaceted, with differential power negotiations occurring simultaneously at multiple levels, and it is entirely reasonable to believe that interpersonal relationships in the past functioned similarly. From our earliest use of stone tools to the development of digital technology, human beings have a remarkable ability to adapt to our natural world. This adaptability extends to social interaction as well and contributes to the unique "flavor" of complexity that each social group has. There are many ways in which humans can solve social problems, and the extreme nature of human adaptability essentially ensures that different communities will experience complexity differently.

Complexity implies social networks with multiple, overlapping parts and can manifest along both horizontal and vertical orientations (Feinman, this volume). Horizontal complexity involves intra-community variation with little to no distinction in rank between individuals and subgroups, whereas vertical complexity entails ranked power, namely, ranked political power. Neither of these types of complexity exists in total on its own. Social groups can be horizontally complex in some ways and vertically complex in others. The specific characteristics of complexity vary depending on multiple factors, such as ecological management, proximity to other social groups, the prevalence of trade relationships, and access to resources to name a few.

When Did Social Aggregations become More Complex?

Throughout Mesoamerica, the Preclassic/Formative period is marked by the emergence of complex social aggregations and evidence for increasing social differentiation. While much of the research on intra-community complexity explores the emergence of elite status within communities, this type of differentiation generally comes after the social group has established a baseline collective identity. Rather than begin our discussion with the emergence of elite status, we have chosen to situate the discussions in this volume around the establishment of these collective identities vis-à-vis other social groups. The outset of the Preclassic/Formative period in Mesoamerica is generally measured by the creation of permanent settlements, and its end is marked by the appearance of publicly written records. These demarcations, however, are not entirely consistent for all cultural groups in Mesoamerica, a fact that directly contributes to the different flavors of complexity that develop between groups. The changes associated with the Preclassic/Formative period in Mesoamerica were the result of key transformations that took place over successive generations. Although we mark the Preclassic/Formative period through sedentism, the complexities that would eventually form during this period likely had their roots in much earlier modes of living associated with pre-sedentary Archaic peoples. Once Archaic peoples began to settle in villages and gain a larger population, the presence of population-based social problems began to appear, necessitating new strategies for dealing with conflict and new bases for cooperative action. As Feinman notes (this volume), the transition to sedentism involved more than a focus on agriculturally based subsistence; rather it was largely a social process that involved the creation and maintenance of overlapping webs of connectivity, complete with reciprocal obligations and expectations of members of the social group. The trade relationships that proliferated during the Preclassic/Formative period likely had their roots in earlier forms of inter-group communication and connective relationships.

This millennium length Preclassic/Formative period saw the rise of communities, cooperative action and competition, and the establishment of social and cultural identities that continue to define people into the present day. While many communities of identity arose during this period, they varied significantly in composition across Mesoamerica. Complexity did not emerge in the same way and at the same time in Central Mexico as it did in the Maya Lowlands.

Distinguishing between intra- and inter-community complexity is not always straightforward, as webs of relationships leading to complexity tend to be complicated and overlapping. Wolf and Silverman (2001) noted that "communities that form parts of a complex society can thus be viewed no longer as self-contained and integrated systems in their own right. It is more appropriate to see them as the local termini of a web of group relations that extend through intermediate levels from the level of the community to that of the nation" (Wolf and Silverman 2001, 125). This is not to claim that change comes from outside forced, rather, to advance the claim that complexity is relational, negotiated, and constituted by individuals and groups managing multiple layers relationships, that is, complexity is a *process*. The authors of this volume explore how complex social interactions arose in various parts of Mesoamerica, providing an avenue of comparison between different cultural groups that may or may not have been in contact with one another to explore consistent features and incongruities between social groups.

COMPLEXITY IN ARCHAEOLOGY

We cannot use a "checklist" of diagnostic criteria for complexity, because of the different forms it takes in different social groups. Archaeological studies of complexity tend to focus on larger questions of the formation and consistency of social groups, complete with overlapping layers of interaction that can be simultaneously complementary and combative, the formation and maintenance of multiple, overlapping levels of social interaction, the deployment of ethic signaling markers to differentiate social groups, and both intra- and inter-group axes of variability. Although institutional social complexity is marked by the emergence of marked hierarchical leadership and variable socioeconomic inequality (Feinman 2013), not all complexities are institutionalized. Indeed, community-based complexity is marked by dynamic and variable relationships based on the interplay between heterarchical and hierarchical relationships, kin altruism, cultural learning, and alliance building through cooperation (Feinman 2013).

The principle of interaction notes that the larger the size of groups, the greater the number of person-to-person contacts, hence the larger chance of disputes and the greater likelihood that leaders/administrators would arise to mediate, keep order, and prevent fission. Population size is sensitive to this complexity correlation, but population nucleation alone does not account for the variable types of complexity that arose in Formative/Preclassic Mesoamerica. The particular flavors of complexity that we see in the archaeological record were impacted by the cooperation and competition of individual networks and emerging power brokers. Social factors that condition our relationships with others include ideas of reciprocity, reputation or esteem, rewards and retribution, and so forth, and those factors intersect with one another in different ways with varying levels of importance (Feinman 2013).

Given the complex nature of "complexity," how, then, can archaeologists measure it? An important clue to the formation of complexity can be found in settlement studies. Close examination of settlements can lead to answers to larger questions, such as, When did social groups become differentiated? How did these aggregations of people come together to establish themselves as "different" than other communities? How did people cooperate and compete within their communities? How did they create a sense of belonging? How did community orientation change as populations grew? By exploring such questions at the nascent community level, archaeologists can begin to piece together the specific flavors of differentiation and identity that evolved within and between communities.

CHAPTER ORGANIZATION

Guy Hepp (this volume) suggests that the status differentiation in Formative period Oaxaca had its roots in the heterarchical relationships that developed as individuals within communities negotiated their roles and responsibilities vis-à-vis other community members. It is the creation of these heterarchical ties, complete with reciprocal social and economic obligations inherent in these ties, that is foundational to the establishment of at least some complex social organization in coastal Oaxaca. Exploring *how* these ties were created and maintained, Hepp challenges assumptions that complexity and hierarchy are interchangeable concepts.

Smyth argues (this volume) that control of water and water-based architecture became the impetus for elite control at Preclassic Xoch. The control of "the politics of water" became a significant component in elite authority, leading "to an extractive political economy involving coordinating major construction projects, performing major religious ceremonies, and implementing systems of taxation and tribute as well as the right to demand labor." For Smyth, elite-centric complexity emerged as community-based resources were co-opted by elites attempting to exert control over local populations.

Spenard et al. (this volume) discuss evidence of burgeoning complexity at the site of Pacbitun. In particular, they claim that during the Middle Preclassic, shell bead working was a community effort that took place within each household. By the end of the Preclassic, however, intra-community status differences become apparent, and the authors suggest that these differences are tied to the elite cooption of the production of shell beads. For Spenard et al., changes in the production of shell beads correlates with increasing social, political, and religious complexity with the emergence of inequality at Pacbitun.

DeLance and Awe (this volume) explore changes in figurine use and deposition during the Preclassic period at Cahal Pech, Belize. In particular, they note that fragmented ceramic figurines appear en masse in construction fill during the Middle Preclassic, however, by the Late Preclassic, the quantity of figurines found in construction fill was greatly reduced. Charting the rise of intra-community inequality, DeLance and Awe find a negative correlation between the deposition of fragmented figurines in construction fill and increasing inequality among the residents of Cahal Pech. The authors suggest that as Cahal Pech was becoming increasingly hierarchical, the practice of placing fragmented figurines within new constructions decreased such that by the Classic period, very few figurines were in use.

Elite Co-option

Archaeologists cannot deny that Classic period Mesoamerican communities were complex. However, over time, as complexity grew within these communities and larger regions, cultural and social mechanisms began to be co-opted by individuals within communities. These individuals, through a variety of mechanisms, eventually gained control of community-based resources leading to hierarchical inequality and exploitative relationships. While the purview of this volume is not state formation per se, many of the social and cultural features that would come to define a "state" originated during the Preclassic/Formative period, when social groups first began to aggregate. One feature of these aggregations is the development of cultural and ethnic affiliations that would come to define groups of people vis-à-vis others.

How Did Particular Ethnicities and Cultural Affiliations Come About and What Was Their Relationship to Community and Regional Cohesion?

The establishment of community-based identity supports the emergence of ethnic and cultural affiliations. The ethnic groups that today call Mesoamerica home had their roots in the Preclassic/Formative period. Through mechanisms of cooperation and competition and with the establishment of a concept of "us,"

cultural affiliation took root. This volume explores how this happened in different communities across Mesoamerica.

Identity can be difficult to conceptualize. As Voss (2008) writes, "to identify is
to establish a relationship of similarity between one thing or person and another,
and self-reflexively to position oneself in such an affinity with others. In this
sense, practices of identification call attention to perceived similarities and, in
doing so, achieve an erasure or elision of other kinds of variability." Identity,
then, is "embedded within social interactions because identities are relational
and depend on recognition and legitimation" (Voss 2008, 14). The establishment
of ethnic identity tends to be associated with population nucleation and the
establishment of sedentism. As community size increases, intra-group relationships tend to become complex while signaling ethnic identity in the context of
inter-group relationships becomes more salient.

Why It Is Important in the Present, and Why It Is Important in the Past

Today, we generally recognize the importance of the individual identities and
scholarly attention is paid to concepts of intersectionality and identity politics. Our
contemporary focus on identity, however, leads to the perilous assumption that
the social concept of individuality and identity to which we currently subscribe
is a human universal. Cultural anthropologists have long called attention to the
issue of the "cult of the individual" that permeates Western thought and have
noted that individualist orientation is not a universal phenomenon, nor is it a primary means by which most contemporary peoples identify. That being said, we
must be attentive to variability. Within the most communal of societies, people do
act out of selfish interest; however, the shape and form of those interests, along
with long-term consequences and the potential for collateral damage associated
with selfish interest, are variable and depend largely on community orientation.
Identity categories are cultural constructs, and as such, they are variable across
time and space. Just as we cannot assume that the contemporary Western notion
of individualistic identity is universal in the present, we cannot assume that these
notions were recognized in the past. "Our identity categories should continually
be evaluated so that we do not merely provide mirror images of what we might be
used to or what we think should exist in the past" (Insoll 2007, 5).

Even if we were able to completely eschew contemporary identity formulations, identity is as much an individual conception as it is a cultural one. How a
single person identifies themselves in the contemporary world is variously influenced by age, sex, sexuality, political environment, kin group, personal interest,
cultural norms and values, and so on, and it is important for archaeologists to
understand that these identity mechanisms may not have existed in their current
formulation for all people throughout the history of our species. "Without such
sensitivities, we run the risk of doing interpretive violence in representing the

people of the past and, by seamless extension, those imbricated in present-day struggles" (Meskell 2007, 23).

The experience of identity appears to be one of the few characteristics that most, if not all, humans share. We understand ourselves and our social world in relation to others. However, while the experience of identity seems to be a human universal, the manifestation and intersections of these identities varied across time and space. Indeed, although identity in relation to others seems to be a characteristic of all humans, the specific form that identity takes can vary across cultures and depend on multiple factors. The nature of archaeological data limits our ability to understand how individuals formulated and negotiated various identities. We can, however, explore continuity in behaviors that may lead to an understanding of certain aspects of group-based behavior.

Methods and Mechanisms for Studying Identity

Archaeologists are at a significant disadvantage when attempting to ascertain individual identity formulations in Formative / Preclassic Mesoamerica. Simply put, we cannot know the full minds and hearts of the people of the past in all of their complicated forms. Even sites with perfectly preserved material culture cannot give us these answers, because we cannot explore the internal lives of the people of the past. What we can study, however, is how social groups or communities set themselves apart from their neighbors. How and when did the concept of "us" take hold among the various social groups throughout Mesoamerica; that is, when is the first evidence for ethnogenesis? How did this concept of "us" variably influence individual communities and regional relationships?

Ethnogenesis

Merriam-Webster defines *ethnogenesis* as "the process by which a group of people becomes ethnically distinct: the formation and development of an ethnic group."[2] The creation of new cultural identities is the result of historical and cultural changes that mandate the use of new concepts of identification (Voss 2008, 1). In this way, ethnogenesis can be thought of as the creation of a group-based identity in which a social group seeks to differentiate itself in some way from other groups.

Much of the literature on ethnogenesis (Cipola 2017; Eriksen 2011; Hu 2013; Voss 2008; Weik 2014; among others) details the construction of group identity as a reaction to imposed external forces seeking to undermine or restrict social rights to certain identity-based groups. The formation of identity groups such as Latinx and Queer identity groups in the present has been conditioned by the experiences of those group members as a result of a social, economic, and political system built on oppression, and as such, they are deeply steeped in identity

---

2 *Merriam-Webster*, s.v. "ethnogenesis" (n.), accessed March 21, 2022, www.merriam-webster .com / dictionary / ethnogenesis.

FIGURE 1.2. *Map of Mesoamerica showing sites mentioned in this volume.*

as a reaction to conflict. While a significant portion of the anthropological literature focuses on conflict ethnogenesis, relatively little attention has been paid to cooperative ethnogenesis, that is, those community-based identities that are established as a way to differentiate groups of people from one another without the impetus of externally imposed conflict.

Such is the case with Formative/Preclassic Mesoamerica. None of the sites discussed in this volume (figure 1.2) had reached the level of "state" or even "nation" during the time period being analyzed. The ethnogenesis of different cultural groups in Mesoamerica came to the fore not as a result of conflict or the top-down imposition of categorization. People have and continue to express identity in multiple ways, regardless of the form of organization that a group takes. It is reasonable to assume that Archaic peoples expressed individual and group identities, however, the paucity of Archaic period material culture makes it difficult to ascertain the form or shape of these identities. During the Preclassic/Formative periods, ethnogenesis on the community level appeared to be connected to the establishment of an "us" in an increasingly integrated world, not necessarily through conflict between communities but because of cooperation, trade, and inter-group contact.

Brubaker et al. (2004) discuss the importance of human cognition in the development of ethnogenesis and ethnic-based identity. In the cognitive, subjective approach, Brubaker et al. (2004, 13) claim that ethnicity should be understood "in terms of the participants' beliefs, perceptions, understandings, and identifications." Cognitive perspectives hold that "ethnicity is not a thing *in* the world, but a perspective *on* the world" (Brubaker et al. 2004, 32). This perspective that any one individual has on the world can be understood to be the product of individual dispositions and negotiations in conjunction with established cultural norms and values. These cultural norms and values appear as expectations, myths, memories, narratives, and discourses. They come to communities through the establishment of traditions, through the stories that are passed on to younger generations, through the interaction that community members have with one another, and through an overall worldview of the place of the social group in the larger cosmos. "Cognitive perspectives suggest treating racial, ethnic, and national groups not as substantial entities but as collective cultural representations, as widely shared ways of seeing, thinking, parsing social experience, and interpreting the social world" (Brubaker et al. 2004, 45). Thus, the cognitive perspective suggests that community-based activities such as storytelling, myth making, spiritual development, social pressure, and craft specialization in their unique forms work to create a sense belonging, of shared history and a shared future for those who are part of the social group. This sense of shared history becomes even more important as inter-community communication and trade expand.

While ethnogenesis as a reaction to conflict and oppression is a significant domain of investigation in an increasingly diverse world steeped in identity politics, the type of conflict leading to ethnogenesis did not exist (at least in currently understood forms) at the outset of sedentism in Mesoamerica. Absent conflict, cultural and social activities themselves become the impetus for the establishment of a unique "us" as compared to "them." It seems highly likely that the types of community-based identity became a significant source of classification as trade relationships forced different social groups to interact.

The establishment of an "us," the creation of a sense of belonging (whether an individual wants to belong or not) influences the establishment of "ethnically specific behaviors" or "ethnic signaling" (Blanton 2015, 9177). Those behaviors not only serve to establish boundaries between groups, but they also reify the collectivity within groups. This collectivity is essential to group survival, as the group would need to come together for defense and resource management. The forms that this collectivity took were vast and depended on multiple factors, such as demographics, environmental conditions, resource procurement, trade relationships, and individual agency. Ethnic signaling may have been a significant component of the development of Formative/Preclassic Mesoamerican social groups in light of an expanding world that incorporated numerous other social groups in extended trade relationships.

The chapters in this volume explore ethnogenesis through the lens of community-based identity and belonging as evidenced by diachronic changes in pottery style and composition, the formulation and diffusion of religious iconography, the establishment and maintenance of very different cultural systems in close proximity, and evidence of an "us as distinct from them" mentality.

Brzezinski et al. argue that religious belief was intimately linked to group identity, and the spread of religious belief (as examined through iconography) indicates a community-based (bottom-up) imposition of religious iconography rather than an elite-centric (top-down) approach. The widespread adoption of religious iconography throughout the Lower Verde Valley by the end of the Formative period is not an example of aggrandizing elites controlling ritual for their own benefit but the result of a marked effort to expand religious identity throughout the region by both individuals and communities responding to "the communal nature of political authority and religious practice."

The formation of community identity is explored further in Rice and South's chapter. Exploring nascent complexity in the Petén Lakes area of the Maya Lowlands, Rice and South note that two different cultural groups established communities on opposite sides of the lakes. In fact, pottery, E Group construction, and settlement analysis provide evidence suggesting that two different communities with different roots occupied the same regional space. The maintenance of these distinct communities, even as they are in close proximity to one another, yields evidence of community-based identity formation in an increasing integrated and complex social world.

Exploring diachronic ceramic changes in the Yucatán, Stanton et al. chart the development of ceramic technology at Yaxuná. In particular, they note that not only did material quality and manufacturing change over the duration of the Preclassic but that these changes may be reflective of changing social and political priorities as seen through the medium of social bonding through food. Linking changes in ceramic technology to the adoption of sedentism and status differentiation, Stanton et al. effectively demonstrate how material culture can be used to explore inter and intra-personal relationships.

Stoner and Nichols explore diachronic changes in ceramics in the Basin of Mexico to argue that ceramic style was one type of group-signaling used in the Basin of Mexico as a marker of identity, including local cooperation and mutual interest. These signals may have been co-opted by elite authorities to further political interests while also contributing to an "us-versus-them" identity formation.

What Are Some Key Aspects of Regional and Macroregional Variability?

How did environmental and social adaptations of these webs of interaction contribute to the variability we seen among Mesoamerican cultural groups? The chapters in this volume explore different, and culturally distinct, social groups throughout Mesoamerica, including Oaxaca, Central Mexico, the Maya Lowlands, and the Yucatán Peninsula. Each of these microclimates had different resources and differing landscapes and required different configurations of cooperation and competition to develop the unique flavors of complexity that are found in each location.

Within the Belize River Valley, Rawski and Brown call attention to foundational architectural landscape modification by the earliest settlers at the site of Xunantunich. In particular, they note that the dramatic and labor-intensive initial construction, such as the leveling of paleosol and bedrock may have served as a community-based cooperative event rather than one controlled by the elite. Through the symbolism of a community-based ritual space, Rawski and Brown ultimately argue that the settlers of Early Xunantunich may have been attempting to distinguish themselves from their nearby counterparts. It was not until the end of the Preclassic that dominant political and economic elites began coopting this communal space.

CONCLUDING THOUGHTS

Complexity is a complex process. As the chapters in this book demonstrate, developmental trajectories of complexity take different forms in different communities. This volume frames the discussion of complexity through three overarching themes. Exploring the emergence of complex, overlapping social aggregations in different parts of Mesoamerica provides archaeologists with the tools to expand their notions of complexity to include the mundane aspects social organization. An integral part of complexity is the understanding of similarity and differences between individuals and groups. How, then, did particular ethnicities and cultural affiliations that signaled distinctions between groups develop? What are the markers of difference? How did each of these communities develop within the specific environmental context that they did?

This volume attempts to answer these questions by reframing understandings of complexity, that is, to explore emergent complexity from a "bottom-up" processual perspective by paying special attention to the creation and maintenance of difference by people surviving on the landscape and the cooperation and competition that people negotiated to create enduring communities.

Acknowledgments. I would like to extend my gratitude to Claire Ebert, Amy Gillaspie, Felicia Beardsley, Thomas Patterson and Gary Feinman for their editorial advice and guidance.

REFERENCES

Alt, Susan. 2010. *Ancient Complexities: New Perspectives in Pre-Columbian North America.* Logan: University of Utah Press.

Axelrod, Robert. 1997. *The Complexity of Cooperation: Agent-Based Models of Competition and Collaboration.* Princeton, NJ: Princeton University Press.

Barton, C. M. 2014. "Complexity, Social Complexity, and Modeling." *Journal of Archaeological Method and Theory* 21 (2): 306–24.

Blanton, Richard E. 2015. "Theories of Ethnicity and the Dynamics of Ethnic Change in Multiethnic Societies." *Proceedings of the National Academy of Sciences* 112 (30): 9176–81.

Blanton, Richard, and Lane Fargher. 2008. *Collective Action in the Formation of Pre-Modern States*. New York: Springer.

Blanton, Richard E., Stephen A. Kowalewski, Gary M. Feinman, and Laura M. Finsten. 1993. *Ancient Mesoamerica: A Comparison of Change in Three Regions*. Cambridge, UK: Cambridge University Press.

Brubaker, Rogers, Mara Loveman, and Peter Stamatov. 2004. "Ethnicity as Cognition." *Theory and Society* 33:31–64.

Carballo, D. M. 2012. "Cultural and Evolutionary Dynamics of Cooperation in Archaeological Perspective." In *Cooperation and Collective Action: Archaeological Perspectives*, edited by D. M. Carballo, 3–34. Boulder: University Press of Colorado.

Carballo, D. M., P. Roscoe, and G. M. Feinman. 2014. "Cooperation and Collective Action in the Cultural Evolution of Complex Societies." *Journal of Archaeological Method and Theory* 21 (1): 98–133.

Chase, Arlen, and Diane Z. Chase. 1996. "The Organization and Composition of Classic Lowland Maya Society: The View from Caracol, Belize." In *The Eight Palenque Round Table, 1993*, edited by Merle Robertson, Martha Macri, and Jan McHargue, 213–22. San Fancisco: Pre-Columbian Art Research Institute.

Childe, V. Gordon. 1950. "The Urban Revolution." *Town Planning Review* 21:3–17.

Cipolla, Craig N. 2017. *Native American Diaspora and Ethnogenesis*. Oxford Online. www .oxfordhandbooks.com / view / 10.1093 / oxfordhb / 9780199935413.001.0001 / oxfordhb -9780199935413-e-69.

Crumley, Carole L. 1995. "Heterarchy and the Analysis of Complex Societies." *Archaeological Papers of the American Anthropological Association* 6 (1): 1–5.

Crumley, Carole L. 2004. "Contextual Constraints on State Structure." In *Alternativity in Cultural History: Heterarchy and Homoarchy as Evolutionary Trajectories, Third International Conference Hierarchy and Power in the History of Civilizations*, edited by Dmitri M. Bondarenko and Alexandre A. Nemirovskiy, 3–22. Moscow: Center for Civilizational and Regional Studies of the RAS.

Demarest, Arthur A. 1996. "Closing Comment: The Maya State: Centralized or Segmentary?" *Current Anthropology* 37:821–24.

Eriksen, Love. 2011. "Nature and Culture in Prehistoric Amazonia: Using GIS to Reconstruct Ancient Ethnogenetic Processes from Archaeology, Linguistics, Geography, and Ethnohistory." PhD diss., Lund University.

Feinman, Gary M. 2013. "The Emergence of Social Complexity: Why More than Population Size Matters." In *Cooperation and Collective Action: Archaeological Perspectives*, edited by D. M. Carballo, 35–56. Boulder: University Press of Colorado.

Fried, Morton H. 1967. *The Evolution of Political Society*. New York: Random House.

Foias, Antonia E. 2013. *Ancient Maya Political Dynamics*. Gainesville: University Press of Florida.

Hu, Di. 2013. "Approaches to the Archaeology of Ethnogenesis: Past and Emergent Perspectives." *Journal of Archaeological Research* 21 (4): 371–402.

Iannone, G. 2002. "Annales History and the Ancient Maya State: Some Observations on the 'Dynamic Model.'" *American Anthropologist* 104:68–78.

Insoll, Timothy. 2007. *The Archaeology of Identities: A Reader*. New York: Routledge.

La Porte, T. R. 2015. *Organized Social Complexity: Challenge to Politics and Policy*. Princeton, NJ: Princeton University Press.

Lesure, Richard G., and Michael Blake. 2002. "Interpretive Challenges in the Study of Early Complexity: Economy, Ritual, and Architecture at Paso de la Amada, Mexico." *Journal of Anthropological Archaeology* 21 (1): 1–24.

Lucero, Lisa J. 1999. "Classic Lowland Maya Political Organization: A Review." *Journal of World Prehistory* 133:211–63.

Meskell, Lynn. 2007. "Archaeologies of Identity." In *The Archaeology of Identities: A Reader*, edited by Timothy Insoll, 23–43. New York: Taylor and Francis.

Paynter, R. 1989. "The Archaeology of Equality and Inequality." *Annual Review of Anthropology* 18 (1): 369–99.

Price, T. D., and G. M. Feinman, eds. 2010. "Social Inequality and the Evolution of Human Social Organization." In *Pathways to Power*, 1–14. New York: Springer.

Redman, Charles L. 1979. *The Rise of Civilization: From Early Farmers to Urban Society in the Ancient Near East*. San Francisco: W. H. Freeman.

Sahlins, Marshall D., and Elman R. Service, eds. 1960. *Evolution and Culture*. Ann Arbor: University of Michigan Press.

Service, Elman R. 1962. *Primitive Social Organization*. Ann Arbor: University of Michigan Press.

Stewart, P. 2001. "Complexity Theories, Social Theory, and the Question of Social Complexity." *Philosophy of the Social Sciences* 31 (3): 323–60.

Tainter, J. A. 2006. "Social Complexity and Sustainability." *Ecological Complexity* 3 (2): 91–103.

Voss, Barbara L. 2008. *The Archaeology of Ethnogenesis: Race and Sexuality in Colonial San Francisco*. Berkeley: University of California Press.

Weik, Terrance M. 2014. "The Archaeology of Ethnogenesis." *Annual Review of Anthropology* 43:291–305.

Wolf, Eric. R, and Sydel Silverman. 1999. *Pathways of Power: Building an Anthropology of the Modern World*. Berkeley: University of California Press.

2

Heterarchy and the Emergence of Social Complexity in Early Formative Period Coastal Oaxaca, Mexico

GUY DAVID HEPP

INTRODUCTION

Since early in the history of the discipline, archaeology has exhibited a bias toward the grandiose. Mesoamericanist research is one example, but by no means the only example, of this phenomenon. Much of the initial systematic work in the Maya region, for instance, focused on monumental architecture and noble lineages (e.g., Kidder 1937, 1945; see also Taylor 1948, 49, 55–56; Willey and Sabloff 1993). The first major projects in Oaxaca, Mexico, orbited around the gravitational mass of Monte Albán (Alfonso Caso 1932; 1969; Alfanso Caso, Bernal, and Acosta 1967; Blanton 1978; Santley 1980; Winter 1974) and later around other highland centers such as Mitla (Alfonso Caso and Rubín de la Borbolla 1936) and Monte Negro (Acosta and Romero 1992). In the Old World (Childe 1925), as in the New (Adams 1966; Childe 1950), the archaeology of the Holocene has traditionally focused on urban centers, with more recent research emphasizing social identities, households, relationships between urban and pastoralist groups, and object biographies (e.g., Banning 2011; Blomster 2009; Carballo 2011; R. A. Joyce 2002; Lesure 1997; Mendelsohn 2018; Meskell 2004; Stein 1999).

https://doi.org/10.5876/9781646422883.c002

The study of the origins of sociopolitical complexity in Mesoamerica has followed this trend of emphasizing the spectacular. One concept central to this research has been that of hereditary, hierarchical inequality. In studies focused on social organization, the concept of complexity has often been tacitly conceived of, or even explicitly defined, as consisting of this type of inequality (e.g., Blake and Clark 1999; Blanton et al. 1996; Clark 1991; Flannery and Marcus 2012). The notion that other modes of political organization are "middle-range" steppingstones toward hierarchy seems built into the "band, tribe, chiefdom, state" model (Sahlins and Service 1960; Service 1962) that remains a common theoretical conceit despite decades of critique (e.g., Fried 1967; A. T. Smith 2003). Even as incipient inequality has been traced further back in time (i.e., to the Early Formative period [2,000–1,000 BCE] in some regions), questions remain regarding how ostensibly "egalitarian" groups became "transegalitarian," or shifted toward permanent inequalities. The transition from the supposed egalitarianism of the Archaic (7,000–2,000 BCE) to the well-demonstrated hierarchies of later prehispanic history provides an opportunity to problematize the conventions I have outlined. Attempts to model "transegalitarian" societies are examples of that endeavor (Blake and Clark 1989; Hayden 1995, 2011, 2014).

In this chapter, I join a few other researchers (Crumley 1995, 2004, 2015; DeMarrais 2013; Pauketat and Emerson 2007) in suggesting that heterarchical distinctions were foundational to more commonly recognized modes of complexity in Mesoamerica. In particular, I present several lines of evidence for interpreting social organization at the Early Formative period village of La Consentida, located on the western coast of Oaxaca, Mexico. This supporting information comes from the study of ceramic figurines, remnants of jewelry and tools for producing clothing, patterns of mortuary treatment, evidence of feasting, and earthen architecture. I conclude that distinctions in attire and specialized knowledge at La Consentida suggest one avenue through which egalitarian peoples laid the foundations of the well-known hierarchies of later Mesoamerican history. I also suggest that La Consentida bore the seeds of hereditary inequalities, as demonstrated in part by stratigraphic evidence of increasingly organized communal labor. In my concluding thoughts, I propose that the search for the origins of Mesoamerican hierarchies must include scrutiny of late Archaic and Early Formative period complex heterarchies.

THEORETICAL CONTEXT

Archaeological and ethnohistoric evidence indicates that the social organization of the Middle Formative through early Colonial periods included hierarchical inequality inherited according to lineage or familial affiliations. Distinctions between nobles and commoners and interaction between nobles in different regions promoted a rich elite culture exemplified by monumental constructions and intricate political systems during these times (Adams 1966; Drennan 2009; Ensor 2013; Feinman and Marcus 1998; Feinman and Nicholas 1989; A. A. Joyce 2000, 2010; Kowalewski 1990; Lesure and Blake 2002; Sanders and Nichols 1988; Sousa 1998; Spores 1997; W. B. Taylor 1979; Terraciano 2000, 2001). Due to the pervasive influence of commoner/elite distinctions established by the Late Formative period (400 BCE—250 CE), and because of the evolutionist models frequently used to explain them, emergent complexity of the Early Formative has long been discussed in terms of ascribed hierarchies (e.g., Blake and Clark 1999; Clark 2004; Clark and Cheetham 2002; Flannery and Marcus 2003; MacNeish 1992; Parsons 1974; Sanders and Nichols 1988; Sanders and Webster 1978).

I propose that a quest to identify the advent of social complexity by revealing the earliest instances of ascribed hierarchy is problematic in that it potentially represents a logical fallacy: it is a search for the origins of a circumstance through identifying its earliest discernable traces rather than the conditions that *produced* it. As Lesure and Blake (2002) pointed out, early iterations of complexity in Mesoamerica are difficult to recognize, given that they likely took hold in various aspects of economies, ideologies, subsistence strategies, and settlement practices throughout diverse regions. As many researchers (e.g., Arnold 1996; Crumley 1995, 2004; McGuire 1983; Pauketat and Alt 2003; Pauketat and Emerson 2007) have recognized, inherited inequality is but one type of complexity, which may also take the form of heterarchical specialization without formal hierarchy. To propose that specific late Archaic and initial Early Formative period communities were *heterarchically* complex is not the same as reciting the facile truism that "all human groups are complex." Instead, communities with marked socio-economic specialization, despite a relative lack of hierarchy, have *different* modes of organization (perhaps in degree rather than kind) than do other egalitarian groups (see Arnold 1996; Crumley 1995, 2015; Fried 1967; McIntosh 1999; Pauketat and Emerson 2007; Vega-Centeno Sara-Lafosse 2007).

It is worth noting here that since the late 1990s, there have been attempts to break down a simple dichotomy between heterarchically and hierarchically organized societies. In other words, hierarchy and heterarchy need not be mutually exclusive but can operate together or regardless of one another. Seeing hierarchy and heterarchy as two potentially coexisting axes of diversity in social organization may help to explain the incredible diversity in the forms of complexity researchers have identified. Also, several researchers (e.g., Blanton et al. 1996; Fargher, Blanton, and Heredia Espinoza 2010; Feinman and Carballo 2018) have pointed out that there is not just one mode of hierarchy but rather that different forms of hierarchy can be more or less centralized in the hands of individual rulers, lineages, or institutions. In particular, these approaches have focused on ways to nuance the study of complex polities and not merely discuss states as the most elaborate form of social organization in a ranked evolutionist scheme from lesser to greater sophistication.

Rather, these scholars look for meaningful categories within the broader concept of "states" or complex polities. Blanton and colleagues, for example (1996), highlighted "corporate" and "network" political strategies in complex polities. Within Mesoamerica, Blanton and coauthors (1996, 8, 12) identified the Olmec horizon and some of the Maya city-states as evidence of ruler-aggrandizing "network" societies wherein power was consolidated among elites who exchanged exotic goods with allied or competing polities as a marker of their authority. Teotihuacán, for these authors (Blanton et al. 1996, 7, 9–10), served as an example of a "corporate" polity wherein authority was vested in a small ruling class of decision-makers holding considerable cumulative power and yet operating within social structures deemphasizing the aggrandizement of individual rulers. In an interesting update to this approach, Fargher and colleagues (2010) explored how an almost democratic form of collective action, which included the promotion of rulers from within the ranks of a warrior class, provided the Postclassic era Tlaxcaltecan society with a structural resistance to Aztec conquest. These concepts have also been applied to the Valley of Oaxaca at the end of the Classic period (250–900 CE), where the site of Lambityeco evidently saw the consolidation of hierarchical power within aggrandized noble lineages following centuries of more collective hierarchical control at the nearby Zapotec capital of Monte Albán (Feinman and Nicholas 2019). Such studies offer a useful set of criteria for exploring diversity *within* hierarchically complex polities. In fact, in a recent study, Feinman and Carballo (2018) proposed a model for examining the impact of "collaborative" versus "competitive" political strategies. These authors identified a pattern suggesting that more collaborative societies enjoyed greater longevity and resiliency to key threats experienced in prehispanic Mesoamerica, including "periodicities in production related to adequate land and water for agriculture" (Feinman and Carballo 2018, 15).

Though these collective action studies are useful for understanding the diversities of social organization in large-scale "state" polities, their focus is not on the complexity found among groups first adopting sedentism and agriculture, or indeed on the actual origins of hierarchical complexity itself. Put simply, we need to address multiple dimensions of complexity, with the horizontal differentiation of heterarchy conceptually distinct from vertical inequality, even if the two are often coexisting or even correlated. This distinction has been applied to the Mesoamerican Formative period with promising results (e.g., Carballo 2009, 496; Lesure 1999b), but it is nonetheless often overlooked in studies of emergent complexity. In a sense, we seem stuck on *complexity* being synonymous with *hierarchy*. Furthermore, both vertical and horizontal social distinctions may be negotiated, contested, and variable throughout not only the history of a polity but also individual lifetimes and negotiated according to age, gender, specialized knowledge, roles enacted in ritual cycles, and myriad social affiliations (Brumfiel 2003, 2006; R. A. Joyce 1999, 2000, 2002; McGuire 1983; Stockett 2005).

Together, these dimensions of social organization imply a staggering degree of variability in the material traces we should expect from a nascent complex society. Given both the emphasis hierarchical complexity has already received in Mesoamerica and the nature of the evidence I am presenting, my focus here will be on heterarchy, which I define as the differentiation of specialized social roles without necessarily implying hierarchical inequality. Material evidence of complex heterarchy might include anthropomorphic iconography indicative of discrete and specialized social roles (see R. A. Joyce 2000; Lesure 1997, 1999a, 2011), evidence of diverse identities displayed via clothing or attire, and grave goods and other funerary practices suggesting that community members occupied diverse social positions or possessed special crafting, environmental, or ritual knowledge (see Carr 1995; Gillespie 2001; Hepp, Sandberg, and Aguilar 2017).

If complex heterarchies did help lay the groundwork for later Mesoamerican hierarchies, that is another transition (in addition to the emergence of complex heterarchy itself) deserving examination. Transegalitarian society may represent a key theoretical bridge between egalitarian and ranked groups, which are too often viewed as diametrically opposing (Blake and Clark 1989; 1999; Clark 2004; Hayden 1995, 18). Such societies may leave material traces associated with competitive feasting, exchange of prestige goods, public architecture, procurement of surpluses, ancestor veneration, burial offerings indicating a transition from achieved to ascribed status, population nucleation, and differences in house structures (Hayden 1995, 41–42, 49–50, 60–61). Productive refinements of the transegalitarian model have stressed collective agency, gender complementarity, and unintended consequences (Carballo 2012; R. A. Joyce 2004).

REGION AND SITE BACKGROUND

One of the earliest known villages on Mesoamerica's Pacific Coast (figure 2.1), La Consentida was rediscovered by archaeologists in the 1980s (A. A. Joyce 1991, 116–17; 2005; Winter 1989). The site has been the focus of intensive investigations since 2008 (Hepp 2015, 2019b). Nine Early Formative period AMS radiocarbon samples (2020–1510 cal BC) from secure contexts such as hearths sealed between fill layers, burned food adhering to a jar fragment from a midden, plant charcoal representing chronological "bookends" from early and termination strata within a feasting midden, and human bone collagen processed with XAD purification demonstrate the site's early occupation relative to other Mesoamerican villages (Hepp 2019c; Powell 2020, 10, 30).[1] La Consentida has produced evidence of early

---

1 AMS radiocarbon calibration performed with IntCal 20 curve by OxCal v.4.4 and rounded to ten-year increments. Dates presented here include two new samples not previously published (Powell 2020) and differ slightly from those listed elsewhere (e.g., Hepp 2015, 5; Hepp, Sandberg, and Aguilar 2017) due to the use of a new calibration curve. Unless otherwise stated, all calibrations are reported with 2σ probability (Reimer et al. 2020).

FIGURE 2.1. *Map of Mesoamerica with key sites mentioned in the text.*

pottery (represented by the recently defined Tlacuache phase), a transition to sedentism, and a mixed diet incorporating maize (Hepp 2019a, 2019b; A. A. Joyce et al. 2017). Mortuary deposits include diverse but modest offerings, with one adult male exhibiting a possibly achieved elevated status (Hepp, Sandberg, and Aguilar 2017). Earthen stratigraphy suggests increasingly organized communal labor over time (Hepp 2019b). Based on the evidence of attire, adornment, and specialized social roles, I will argue here that heterarchical distinctions were key components of the transition to village life in coastal Oaxaca. I suggest that specific forms of heterarchy were, in this case, fundamental building blocks of later hierarchical inequality. They probably began as diverse but unranked aspects of identity within late Archaic and Early Formative period communities, only later to be hierarchically categorized during the later Formative period and thereafter.

ATTIRE

To date, excavations at La Consentida have recovered portions of over 250 ceramic figural artifacts. These finds occur in the full range of excavated deposits, including fill, burials, middens, domestic areas, and a ritual cache.[2] The figurines (and related artifacts such as musical instruments and masks) were hand formed of medium or coarse brown paste, and most are solid bodied. A few examples were likely pendants. Size varies considerably, and evidence exists of larger statuary. The majority

---

2 Although I refer here to some contexts that produced La Consentida's figurines, more detailed information can be found elsewhere (Hepp 2019b).

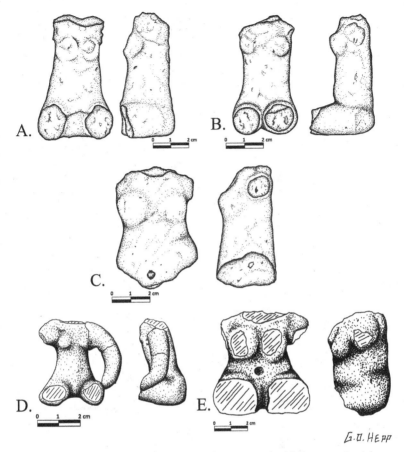

G.D.HEPP

FIGURE 2.2. *Female anthropomorphs from La Consentida: (a) From near burial B2-I3; (b) From near burial B2-I3; (c) From early fill near a dated hearth (3358 ± 43 [AA92454; carbon-rich sediment; δ¹³C, −25.2], or 1750–1510 cal BCE) and burials; (d) From domestic structure floor; (e) From near domestic structure.*

of the artifacts are anthropomorphic, with the primary exception being bird effigy aerophones. Even in the earliest fill layers, where redeposited artifacts likely date to initial occupations, humanoid figurines bear a variety of head garments and hairstyles. Some have generalized or schematic features, while others are more individualized. Previous research in the region has found that varied facial styles suggest some Formative period anthropomorphic artifacts represented specific individuals while others referred to generic categories such as "ancestor," "deity," or "spirit" (Barber and Hepp 2012; Hepp, Barber, and Joyce 2014).

Based on visible secondary sexual characteristics of hips, waists, and breasts, as well as traditionally gendered elements such as elaborate hairstyles, La

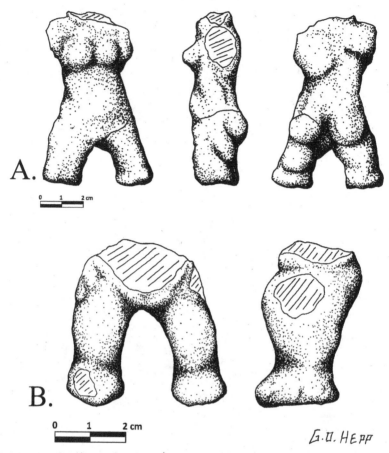

A.

B.

G.D. HEPP

FIGURE 2.3. *Standing anthropomorphs: (a) From fill with burials; (b) From domestic area.*

Consentida's anthropomorphs tend to represent women or feminine characters (Cyphers Guillén 1993; Blomster 2009; Hepp and Joyce 2013; R. A. Joyce 2000; Lesure 1997; Marcus 1998, 2018). As demonstrated in figure 2.2, these figures are often depicted nude or nearly nude. The figurines shown in figure 2.2A and 2.2B, for example, are nearly identical female torsos that were recovered near the burial of an adult male, suggesting that mortuary offerings need not reflect interred individuals in an anatomical sense. As with most of the La Consentida figurines, these examples appear intentionally broken (often at their thickest points), likely as part of a termination ritual (R. A. Joyce 2009, 416; Shafer and Taylor 1986, 51; L. Smith 1932). When anthropomorphs are more complete (figures 2.2a, 2.2b, 2.2d, and 2.2e) it is clear that they often depicted characters in a seated position. Others portray standing figures (figure 2.3). These objects also exemplify an interest in representing full-figured, even corpulent, bodies. As Guernsey and

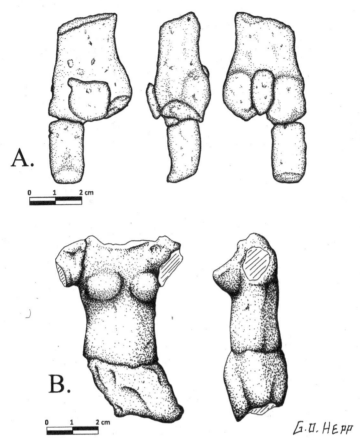

FIGURE 2.4. *Anthropomorphs with indications of clothing: (a) From fill with burials; (b) Likely associated with Burial B12-I14.*

others have discussed, seated figures with big bellies suggest elevated status in some Formative period contexts (Guernsey 2012, 121–22; Lesure 1999a).

Though many of La Consentida's anthropomorphs are nude, others wear minimal clothing such as skirts or loincloths (figure 2.4). While we cannot be certain these garments represent actual clothing worn by members of the community, archaeological, ethnohistoric, and ethnographic research has recorded similar outfits in Mesoamerica from ancient through modern times (e.g., Altman and West 1992; Brumfiel 2006, 866, 868; King 2003, 81–82, 217–22, 301–3; Klein 1997; Stephen 1991, 107–8; Urcid and Joyce 2001). Systematic studies of anthropomorphic imagery in coastal Oaxaca have indicated correspondence between outfits shown on figurines, stelae, and other media and the people they represented (Hepp and Rieger 2014; Jennings 2010). As was the case later in the Formative period in coastal Oaxaca, fancy hairstyles and headgear were more often depicted with female or feminine

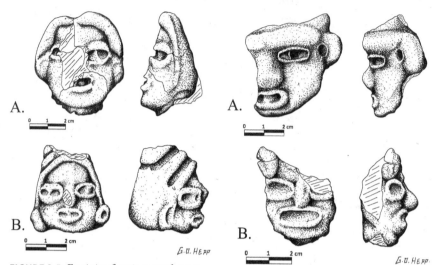

FIGURE 2.5. *Feminine figurines emphasizing hairstyles: (a) From deep fill interface; (b) From burial B5-I6.*

FIGURE 2.6. *Anthropomorphic heads: (a) From near burials B6 and B7; (b) From burial B8–10.*

characters than with masculine, male, or gender-neutral ones. Specifically, when figurines are complete enough to show both secondary sexual characteristics and fancy hairstyles or headgear, they usually represent women. This association between representations of biology and cultural accoutrements thus implies that the latter were gendered feminine. This correspondence has also been identified in highland Oaxacan Formative period contexts, sometimes with enough specificity as to permit inferences not only of gender but also of lifecycle stages (Marcus 1998, 4; 2018, 2–3). While figurines and stelae suggest that men in Formative period coastal Oaxaca wore pendants more often than women, some accoutrements, such as ear spools, crosscut gender categories. Ubiquitous recovery contexts of figural artifacts indicate that portraying the human body was not restricted by social status or to the domestic sphere during the Formative period (Hepp and Rieger 2014, 123, 133–34). Late in the Formative period and thereafter, depictions of the human body and other forms of figural representation became more controlled and constrained to particular contexts (such as to ostensibly public spaces) than they had been during the more communal days of the Early and Middle Formative (Guernsey 2020).

Figurine heads at La Consentida were often loci for diverse appliques and personalizing details (figures 2.5–2.8). The artifact pictured in figure 2.5a, for example, shows a good deal of attention paid to the hair. Recovered from the interface between two deep fill strata, this artifact was likely redeposited and therefore dates to very early in site occupation (Hepp 2015). The depiction of

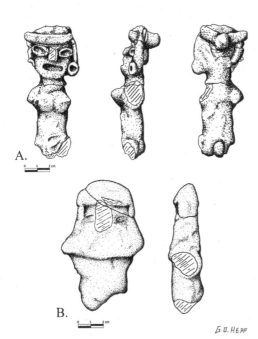

A.

B.

G.U. HEPP

FIGURE 2.7. *Figurines with diverse attire: (a) Female anthropomorph from fill with burials; (b) Eroded feminine anthropomorph with cowl and* quechquemitl-*like garment from dense ceramic deposit atop architectural fill.*

individualized identity or at least of femininity was thus a long-standing tradition at La Consentida. The artifact pictured in figure 2.5b also bears an elaborate hairstyle and is one of several figurines found with burials. The artifacts shown in figures 2.5b and 2.6a were both found face-down near prone burials, further suggesting associations between figurines and funerary practice at the site.

Several of La Consentida's anthropomorphic figurines are complete enough to suggest that accoutrements signified key aspects of identity. The artifact displayed in figure 2.7a, for example, demonstrates how even the simplest torsos could be connected to detailed heads. This artifact's hairstyle, ear spools, and knotted headband have later analogs in the region that appear to correlate with identity (Hepp and Joyce 2013; Hepp and Rieger 2014). Artifacts from other contexts also represent diverse attire and adornment. The figurine shown in figure 2.7b, though badly eroded, appears to depict a feminine character wearing a hood attached to an upper-body garment reminiscent of a *quechquemitl*. This artifact was recovered from a dense ceramic deposit atop architectural fill. It has been refitted along an ancient break. That the two fragments were found together is suggestive of intentional artifact retirement before interment with the ceramic deposit. The figurine depicted in figure 2.8a, especially when compared to others such as those shown in figures 2.8b and 2.8c, exemplifies the variability of headdresses and headgear in the collection.

Even the styles of anthropomorphic faces themselves are remarkably diverse at La Consentida (for instance, contrast figure 2.6a with figures 2.7–2.10). Despite

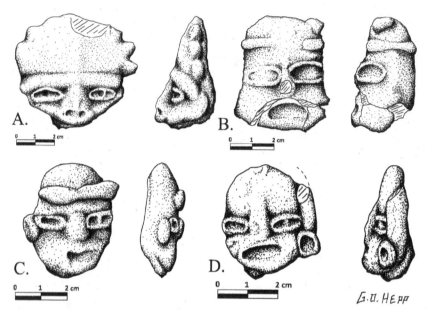

FIGURE 2.8. *Examples of diverse head accoutrements among figurines: (a) From fill near domestic structure; (b) From domestic structure; (c) From fill with burials, possibly associated with B8-I10; (d) From fill with occupation surface.*

this variety, two items from different contexts appear to reference a similar and peculiar facial expression (figures 2.9a and 2.9b). These objects are likely fragments of different types of artifacts (an effigy vessel and a figurine, respectively) and were recovered from different parts of the site. Mesoamerican artistic conventions related to half-lidded eyes suggest that these objects may be referencing death (e.g., Guernsey 2010). This interpretation is borne out by the grimacing mouths, which seem reminiscent of the way the lips might pull back from the teeth of a putrefying human corpse. The attention to detail of the artifacts shown in figure 2.9, in general, also contrasts with the more nondescript features of those displayed in figure 2.10.

Other figurine fragments may refer to specific social roles that community members occupied at La Consentida (figure 2.11). The artifact shown in figure 2.11a appears to combine human and animal features. This artifact is similar to later Formative period coastal Oaxacan figurines that have been termed "transformational," and which appear to reflect the abilities of some ritual practitioners to transform into animals or hybrid beings (Hepp and Joyce 2013, 266–67). Mesoamerican ethnographic and ethnohistorical evidence, when combined with archaeological data, has demonstrated the long-held traditions of nagualism and tonalism likely behind such representations (Foster 1944; Kaplan 1956; Rojas 1947). In conjunction with a ritual cache from the site (see discussion below), this artifact

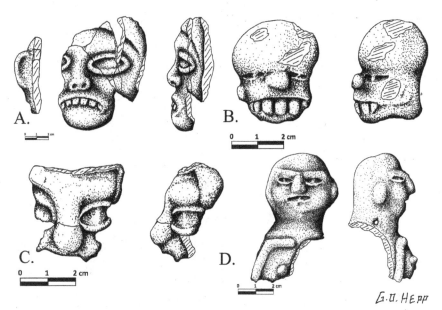

FIGURE 2.9. *Unique figural artifacts from La Consentida: (a) Probable effigy vessel fragment from domestic area; (b) From feasting midden; (c) From feasting midden; (d) From dated hearth or burning feature (3435 ± 44 [AA101269; carbon-rich sediment; $\delta^{13}C = -25.5‰$], or 1890–1620 cal BCE) in feasting midden.*

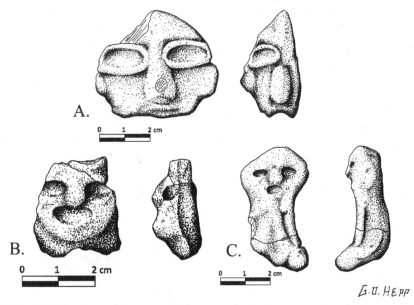

FIGURE 2.10. *Examples of elementary anthropomorphs: (a) From occupational debris and fill; (b) From domestic building; (c) From domestic building.*

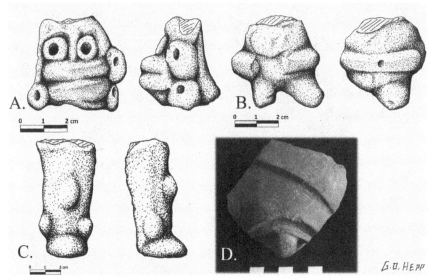

FIGURE 2.11. *Figural artifacts suggesting specialized social roles: (a) From surface on Platform 1; (b) From feasting preparation midden; (c) From burial B8-I10; (d) Probable mask fragment from midden with decorated ceramics.*

suggests the presence of ritual practitioners with specialized knowledge. In a related vein, the artifact pictured in figure 2.11b appears to represent a ballplayer wearing a thick belt. Other authors (e.g., Blomster and Salazar Chávez 2020; Hill and Clark 2001) have emphasized the important role of Mesoamerican ball games in the emergence of social complexity. Although no ballcourts have been identified at La Consentida, this artifact suggests that the community was aware of ball games and of the iconographic traditions used to represent players. Another figurine fragment (figure 2.11c) appears to show a human leg adorned with dancing bells. The burial with which this artifact occurred (B8-I10) was also accompanied by a musical instrument, perhaps suggesting that the adolescent male was a musician or dancer for his community. Like musical instruments, mask fragments (figure 2.11d) also suggest that dancing and public performance were part of social life at the site (Hepp et al. 2020). Although these few artifacts can only be taken as evocative of broader patterns of social organization rather than as concrete evidence for them, the artifacts displayed in figure 2.11 suggest that La Consentida's residents may have occupied, at least part of the time, specialized roles such as "ballplayer," "dancer or musician," and "ritual practitioner" capable of nagualistic transformation. In a general sense, La Consentida's figurines confirm the deep prehispanic history of using attire to denote social status in coastal Oaxaca.

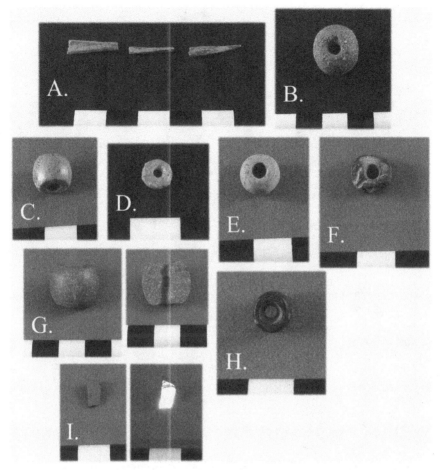

FIGURE 2.12. *Evidence of adornment and clothing: (a) Probable bone needle from near burial B12-I14; (b) Ceramic bead from burial B5-I6; (c) Greenstone bead from domestic structure; (d) Shell bead from fill or shell dump; (e) Greenstone bead from fill/resurfacing context; (f) Black stone bead from feasting midden; (g) Two views of partial greenstone bead from near burials B6 and B7; (h) Black stone bead from the wrist of burial B12-I14; (i) Two views of possible hematite mirror fragment from near domestic structure.*

JEWELRY, CLOTHING, AND SPECIALIZED RITUAL KNOWLEDGE

Though few elements of Early Formative period attire preserve beyond the medium of ceramic figurines, some tantalizing clues about the clothing worn at La Consentida do remain (figure 2.12). Beads, often of fired clay, but sometimes of shell, black stone, or greenstone, are fairly common at the site. These occur in fill, domestic contexts, and burial offerings. Like figurines, the beads suggest that

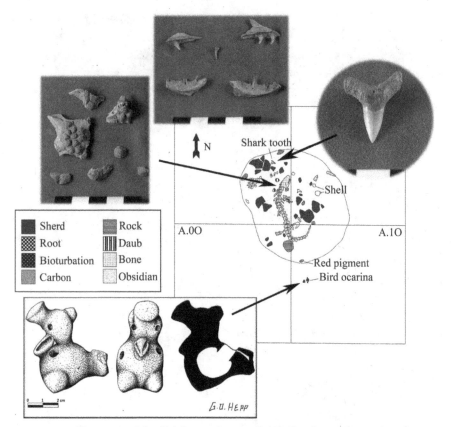

FIGURE 2.13. *Plan map and detailed close-up images of a ritual cache near human burials.*

community members distinguished themselves through attire. Furthermore, specialized goods such as delicate shell beads (see Powell 2020, 46–49) and imported greenstone denote the role of craft specialization in displaying identity (Carballo 2009). Other artifacts provide secondary evidence of clothing. Probable bone needles (figure 2.12a) imply sewn fabrics or skins. A tiny piece of a possible hematite mirror (figure 2.12i) may be more directly related to status distinction. Several researchers (Ashmore 2004, 184–85; Blomster 2004, 85, 186; Clark 1994, 126; Heyden 1991, 195; Saunders 2001) have argued that mirrors and headdresses were associated with an elevated social status in Mesoamerica. Such links between dress and social distinction have been inferred for later Formative coastal Oaxaca, as well (Barber and Olvera Sánchez 2012; Hepp and Rieger 2014).

Another intriguing piece of evidence of social diversity is a ceremonial cache found near several burials at La Consentida (figure 2.13). This feature included the complete skeleton of a venomous reptile (*Heloderma horridum*), a playable ceramic bird ocarina (one of the oldest known musical instruments in Mesoamerica), the possibly fossilized tooth of a bull shark, pottery sherds, and other mineral and faunal remains (Hepp, Barber, and Joyce 2014; Hepp 2019b, 153–55). Many Mesoamerican groups saw the world as organized into four cardinal directions associated with sacred colors and patron deities (Beekman 2003; Pugh 2001; Stross 1994; Taube 2010). The Aztecs, for instance, related the north and west with the underworld and with Tezcatlipoca and Quetzalcóatl, respectively. The flayed god Xipe Totec was associated with fertility and rejuvenation coming from the east with the rising sun. The south was the dominion of Huitzilopochtli, the hummingbird warrior god (Carmack et al. 2016, 99–101). Similar directional associations (i.e., watery symbolism to the north and west and aerial symbolism to the south) appear in the La Consentida cache. The question of temporal depth of these cosmological themes aside, this cache is of note here because its recipe of symbolism suggests the work of a ritual practitioner with specialized knowledge and thus likely a discrete social identity, at least concerning special religious events. Coupled with the other evidence from La Consentida, this cash suggests that the possession of specialized ritual knowledge defined one of a set of discrete social identities in the community without implying hierarchy, per se.

MORTUARY TREATMENT

The use of mortuary data to infer elements of social organization has a long history in archaeology (Binford 1971; Gillespie 2001; R. A. Joyce 1999; Saxe 1971; Spencer and Redmond 2004; Whalen 1983; Winter 2002). Critiques of traditional mortuary studies (e.g., Carr 1995; Love 2007), have focused on a lack of understanding regarding the social value placed on particular offerings or mortuary treatments in the past. Despite these valid critiques, it would be an oversight not to consider mortuary treatment as one line of evidence of social organization in the community that produced those burials. To date, fourteen or perhaps fifteen sets of human remains have been identified in twelve burials uncovered in two excavation areas (Ops. LC09 B and LC12 A) at the site (Hepp, Aguilar, and Sandberg 2020). Both of these mortuary contexts are away from known domestic structures. This discrete spatial patterning and consistency in body orientation and positioning (with individuals extended, in a southwest/northeast orientation, and often prone), suggest the presence of early cemeteries. The burials are accompanied by fewer offerings than are later examples in coastal and highland Oaxaca (Barber et al. 2013; Higelin Ponce de León and Hepp 2017; A. A. Joyce 1991, 718–87; Marcus and Flannery 1996, 97–106). The burials also come in the form of relatively simple primary inhumations rather than the secondary interments seen later in Oaxaca (Levine 2011, 192–94) or elaborate tombs. Although several burials were accompanied by pottery, figurines, or stone tools, they show relatively little differentiation in the number and type of offerings.

One individual (B2-I3, a male aged forty to fifty years) was buried with a few more offerings than others at the site. These items included figurines (figures 2.2a and 2.2b), a tabular stone atop the pelvis, a mano, a chert knife (figure 2.14a), a ceramic bottle (figure 2.14b), and a probable crocodilian mandible tool (Hepp, Aguilar, and Sandberg 2020, cuadro 1). Although it may be tempting to attribute these offerings to an elevated and ascribed social status, accomplishments during life, rather than status given at birth, could explain them. Another individual (B12-I14, a female aged forty-five to fifty years) was found with only a single black stone bead at her wrist (figure 2.12h). This burial, directly dated to 1690–1530 cal BCE, appears stratigraphically early in the sequence of known adult burials at the site, which may indicate that the semi-formalized mortuary contexts discovered to date were produced fairly late in site occupation.[3] The early relative chronological position of this burial, the individual's age or gender, or some other aspect of her social identity may explain the relative paucity of offerings. Another burial (B8-I10) of a young adult male (aged fifteen to eighteen years) was accompanied by figurine fragments, a partial ocarina, pottery, and a carbonized seed (Bérubé, Hepp, and Morell-Hart 2020). As discussed above, one figurine fragment from the chest area of this individual (figure 2.11c) appears to depict bells worn on the leg of a dancer. The ocarina fragment, meanwhile, was found near the young man's pelvis. This combination of artifacts related to music and dance underscores the importance of public performance in mortuary rites or perhaps the specialized role of the deceased.

Some child burials at La Consentida also included offerings. Some of the site's only complete ceramic vessels, for instance, occurred as offerings with two children interred in separate events in the Op. LC12 A mortuary area. These individuals (B9-I11, aged three to four years, and B11-I13, aged two to four years) were buried early in the site's history. Collectively, they were accompanied by two ceramic grater bowls (figures 2.14c and 2.14d), a collared ceramic jar that was likely suspended (figure 2.14e), other pottery fragments, green and black minerals, and lithics (see Acuña 2018, 111–13). A recent paleoethnobotanical study has indicated the processing of maize and wild beans in one of the grater bowls (figure 2.14c), as well as maize in the collared jar (figure 2.14e) from B9-I11 (Bérubé, Hepp, and Morell-Hart 2020). Although it is unclear whether most children at the site were interred with offerings, at least one other child (B1-I2, aged one to two years) apparently was not.

---

3 Extracted collagen from the femur of B12-I14 was dated twice (Cummings 2017; Hepp 2019c, 440). When these two samples are calibrated together using the R_Combine command in OxCal v.4.4, the result is 3337 ± 20 (PRI-5423A/B [H6]; human bone) or 1690–1530 cal BCE. This dating process employed XAD purification, a technique designed to remove background carbon from bone and produce more reliable radiocarbon dates (Stafford et al. 1991; Waters et al. 2015).

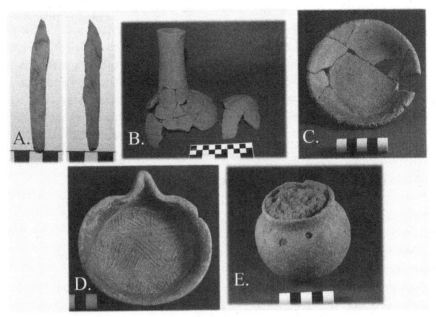

FIGURE 2.14. *Examples of La Consentida's burial offerings: (a) Two views of a chert knife from B2-I3; (b) Partially reconstructed ceramic bottle from adult male burial B2-I3; (c) Nearly complete grater bowl from child burial B9-I11; (d) Complete grater bowl with spout from child burial B11-I13; (e) Small collared jar (photographed while still containing sediment) from child burial B9-I11. (Images [a] courtesy of David T. Williams.)*

As discussed above, a ritual cache suggesting the presence of specialized religious knowledge (figure 2.13) was uncovered just a few centimeters from burials in Op. LC12 A. This close association suggests that ritual practice and mortuary treatment may have been closely related at the site. As is also discussed above, the burials at La Consentida appear to represent a very early establishment of formal cemeteries on the Pacific Coast. Early Formative cemeteries are also known from highland Oaxaca (Cervantes Pérez, Mijangos García, and Andrade Cuautle 2017; Whalen 1981; 2009, 78). Unlike in the highlands, however, the people of La Consentida seem not to have buried children and infants under the floors of houses, at least based on the evidence available to date. Cemeteries went on to become common at later Formative period sites in coastal Oaxaca (Barber et al. 2013; A. A. Joyce 2010, 181–85; Mayes et al. 2020). What the mortuary contexts from La Consentida suggest in terms of social organization, I think, is a community of people fulfilling different social roles despite little hierarchical distinction. Although one individual (B2-I3) may have enjoyed an elevated social position (based primarily on the number of offerings), that might easily have been due to his accomplishments in life rather than some inherited status. The other known burials, both of males and females, of adults and children, often were accompanied by a few offerings but generally shared much in common in terms of body orientation, offerings, and body treatment. In addition to reflecting aspects of the social lives of the deceased, however, one must remember that cemeteries are made by the living. As such, they form but a partial picture of a community's activities and do not directly indicate the self-identified roles of the deceased. In the next section, I will consider other evidence of group activities that suggest elements of social organization at the site.

FEASTING AND COMMUNAL LABOR

Public events at La Consentida are evinced by midden deposits uncovered at the site. These contexts contained well-preserved faunal remains, decorated pottery likely used for serving, and utilitarian vessels such as cooking jars. Two middens, in particular, (excavated in Ops. LC12 E and LC12 H) suggest feasting. The ceramics of the Op. LC12 H midden comprised about 94 percent utilitarian jars. These vessels were mostly undecorated, globular jars with out-curving necks. The vessels were deposited quickly, as indicated by several well-preserved (and thus not likely redeposited) and refitting fragments from up to 60 cm apart in depth. This circumstance suggests that the ceramics represent just one or very few depositional events. That such an event related to the preparation for a large community gathering rather than for a domestic meal is suggested by very large jars (up to 53 cm in rim diameter) in the sample. Burned food from the interior of one jar fragment in this midden returned an AMS radiocarbon date of 3419 ± 36 (AA104836; carbonized food; $\delta^{13}C$, -15.5) or 1880–1610 cal BCE. The Op. LC12 E midden was also deposited quickly but contained a wider variety of ceramics, and relatively more decorated vessels, than did the Op. LC12 H midden. Many of the vessel fragments recovered from the Op. LC12 E midden were from serving wares such as bowls (26 percent of diagnostic fragments) and bottles (12 percent of diagnostic fragments). Of the Op. LC12 E midden ceramics, 9.5 percent were decorated, compared to only 1.9 percent from Op. LC12 H.[4] The Op. LC12 E midden produced a high percentage of marine animal remains (about 90 percent fish, by NISP), the highest of any excavated context at the site (Hepp 2019b, 105–12; see also Powell 2020).

Numerous archaeologists have considered public events such as feasts to be important venues for social maneuvering (Blake and Clark 1999; Clark and Blake 1994; Hayden 1990; 2011, 2014; Hill and Clark 2001). "Aggrandizers" displaying prestige goods such as exotic imports or decorated pottery at such occasions, as well as establishing lasting relationships of indebtedness with their neighbors, may have

---

4 This comparison is calculated by the total weight of ceramics recovered, to help correct for the extremely friable nature of the sherds (Hepp 2015, 476–77).

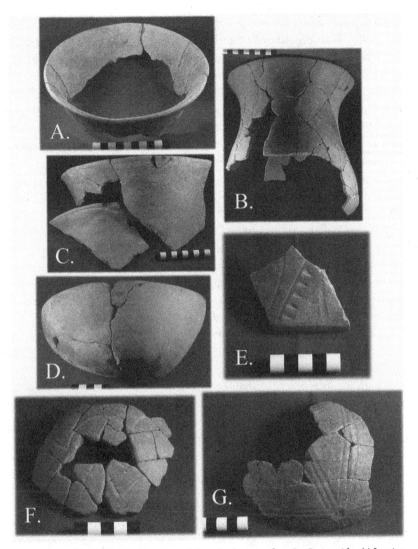

FIGURE 2.15. *Examples of utilitarian and decorated pottery from La Consentida: (a) Jar rim from LC12 H midden; (b) Partially reconstructed jar from LC12 H midden; (c) Jar rim from LC12 H midden; (d) Partial hemispherical bowl from LC12 H midden; (e) Decorated conical bowl fragment from LC09 B midden; (f) Decorated partial bottle from LC12 E midden; (g) Decorated probable bottle fragment from eroded/redeposited midden.*

been one of the main catalysts for shifting social organization in transegalitarian communities (Blake and Clark 1989; Hayden 1995, 2009). Feasts could also have been one of several settings for the solidarity-promoting activities of social collectives in addition to more exclusionary forms of social organization (R. A. Joyce

2004; R. A. Joyce and Henderson 2007, 2010). According to Kuijt (2009, 643; see also Twiss 2008), "Feasting occurs in the social context of coexisting integrative and competitive processes, not just competition." The presence of decorated ceramics in La Consentida's middens suggests that community members had an interest in displaying prestige items and implies increasing craft specialization. Shellfish remains identified in the Op. LC12 E midden likely represent seasonal feasting rather than a dietary staple (Powell 2020). The presence of other artifacts such as masks (figure 2.11d) in these middens further suggests that feasting was interwoven with other forms of public ritual and performance (Hepp et al. 2020).

Earthen architecture may provide another measure of La Consentida's social organization. As discussed elsewhere (Hepp 2019b, 86–91), a population averaging about eighty people (see Feinman 1991; Feinman and Nicholas 1990, 1992; Nicholas 1989), with perhaps twenty-five to fifty community members doing most of the physical labor, likely produced the site's approximately 150,000 m³ of earthen architecture in 250–300 years, a span that fits well within the site's duration of occupation when the carbon dates are reported with 1σ probability (410 years, or 1950–1540 cal BCE). Although it is unclear if individual strata represent consistent annual events, assessments of the building phases of Platform 1 and its substructures (see Hepp 2019b, fig. A1.8) indicate significant variation in the volume of these strata and in the labor they required. Initial layers (e.g., LC12 A-F19) tended to be thinner than some later deposits, an observation that is consistent with the interpretation that the first occupants may have only seasonally occupied the site (figure 2.16). Also, at least some of the substructural mounds were under construction from early in the site's occupational history, indicating that they were planned from an early date. Later construction layers (e.g., LC12 A-F10-s1, A-F4-s1, and A-F2) became relatively uniform in thickness. One explanation for this increasing uniformity is that group labor projects became a routine occurrence, taking place in distinct but regular (perhaps even seasonal) intervals when subsistence interests permitted. These explanations for variation in earthen fill may also suggest increasing organization of labor, and thus perhaps the first glimmers of social hierarchy at the site. Beginning with sporadic construction episodes, the community developed more consistent architectural practices. As suggested by the early production of substructural mounds (see stratum LC12 A-F11-s1), however, certain aspects of communal labor organization may have been in place from early in site occupation (figure 2.16).

CONCLUSION

Rather than focusing on evidence of emerging hierarchy, I have striven here to consider the evidence for specialized social roles and practices at La Consentida as independent of a ranked hierarchy. Some of the clearest evidence of social distinctions at the site comes from small-scale iconography. The presence of seated,

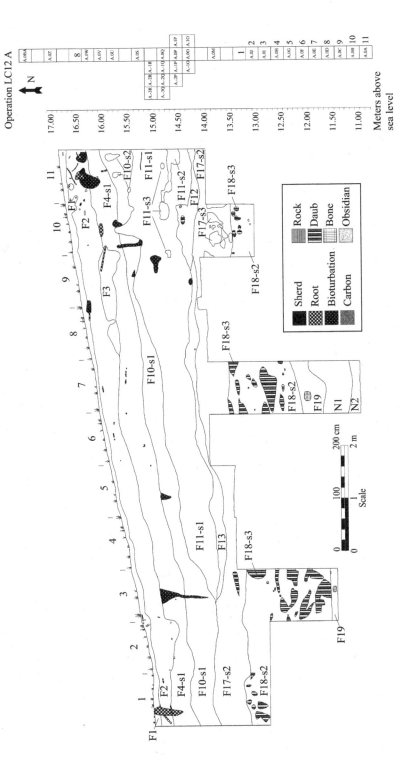

FIGURE 2.16. Excavation profile showing layers of earthen architectural construction at Op. LC12 A.

big-bellied, and headdress-wearing figurines is consistent with diverse social roles, likely associated with age and gender, that in later Mesoamerican contexts are considered indicative of elevated status (Guernsey 2012, 108, 121–22; 2020, 154; Hepp and Rieger 2014; Lesure 1999a, 121). Remnants of actual jewelry and a possible mirror fragment further suggest personal adornment and divination associated with elites in later Mesoamerican contexts. Although the attributes of figural artifacts may at times indicate prescribed social ideals rather than actual dress and comportment, they nonetheless provide one of our best records of how ancient people saw themselves, their communities, their ancestors, and their deities. In the absence of journals and photographs, iconography, traces of funerary practices, and human remains themselves provide us our best snapshots of these past lives.

As Lesure and Blake (2002) discussed, identifying emergent social complexity is difficult because it is to be expected in discontinuous and regionally variable patterns. Although I have emphasized iconography in this chapter, evidence of actual adornment, specialized knowledge resulting in a ritual cache, and differential burial treatment all suggest that La Consentida was heterarchically complex. Diverse social roles at the site included communal labor organizers, dancers, musicians, ballplayers, feasting facilitators, and ritual specialists. Given indications of the significance of these roles in later Mesoamerican hierarchies, I argue that their presence at La Consentida suggests that the community bore the seeds of such inequalities. In fact, one of the benefits of aggrandizer models (e.g., Clark and Blake 1994; Hayden 2011) for Early Formative period social developments is that they help us explore how relative egalitarianism articulated with collective modes of political interaction among formally hierarchical societies (Blanton et al. 1996; Fargher, Blanton, and Heredia Espinoza 2010; Feinman and Nicholas 2019). Viewed from that perspective, it is the aggrandizing "network" strategies, for example of Middle Formative Olmec and Classic period Maya polities, that stand as something of an unstable outlier among Mesoamerican political organizations (Feinman and Carballo 2018). Unfortunately, most research regarding Mesoamerican social complexity has focused on identifying formalized hierarchies rather than on understanding social distinctions in the egalitarian and transegalitarian societies that presaged them (though see Arnold 1996; Crumley 1995; McGuire 1983; Paynter and McGuire 1991). Because such hierarchies developed within societies that were traditionally egalitarian, however, the burden of proof for identifying modes of social organization should not be on those suggesting heterarchy but rather on those suggesting the more derived form of social interaction in human history: hierarchy. I have suggested here that heterarchical social distinctions of the Early Formative period were fundamental in the eventual establishment of hierarchies. Rather than trying to understand social complexity by searching for the first evidence of hierarchy, I have employed the archaeology of La Consentida as an example of an Early

Formative period community in which hierarchy may have emerged in the context of complex social heterarchy likely originating in the late Archaic period. Moving forward, I suggest that the role of heterarchical complexity should be a major research agenda of Mesoamerican archaeology, at least as it relates to the Early Formative period.

Acknowledgments. This research was made possible by funding from the National Science Foundation (Grant #: BCS-1213955), a Fulbright-García Robles scholarship (Grantee ID: 34115725), the Colorado Archaeological Society, and the University of Colorado Boulder. California State University, San Bernardino, supported the completion of this manuscript. I am grateful to the Instituto Nacional de Antropología e Historia for permitting the fieldwork and laboratory studies and to the people of coastal Oaxaca for their participation. I thank Lisa DeLance and Gary Feinman for inviting me to participate in this volume and for their feedback. I also thank Gary for providing comments that helped me think in a more nuanced way about hierarchies. Finally, I thank the anonymous reviewers who provided comments useful in revising this chapter.

REFERENCES

Acosta, Jorge R., and Javier Romero. 1992. *Exploraciones en Monte Negro, Oaxaca: 1937–38, 1938–39 y 1939–40.* Mexico City: Instituto Nacional de Antropología e Historia.

Acuña, Julian Eduardo. 2018. "Early Formative Period Exchange, Crafting and Subsistence: An Analysis of La Consentida's Chipped Stone Assemblage." Master's thesis, California State University, San Bernardino.

Adams, Robert McCormick. 1966. *The Evolution of Urban Society: Early Mesopotamia and Prehispanic Mexico.* Chicago: Aldine Publishing Company.

Altman, Patricia B., and Caroline D. West. 1992. *Threads of Identity: Maya Costume of the 1960s in Highland Guatemala.* Los Angeles: Fowler Museum of Cultural History.

Arnold, Jeanne E. 1996. "The Archaeology of Complex Hunter-Gatherers." *Journal of Archaeological Method and Theory* 3 (1): 77–126.

Ashmore, Wendy. 2004. "Classic Maya Landscapes and Settlement." In *Mesoamerican Archaeology,* edited by Julia A. Hendon and Rosemary A. Joyce, 169–91. Malden, MA: Blackwell.

Banning, E. B. 2011. "So Fair a House: Göbekli Tepe and the Identification of Temples in the Pre-Pottery Neolithic of the Near East." *Current Anthropology* 52 (5): 619–60.

Barber, Sarah B., and Guy David Hepp. 2012. "Ancient Aerophones of Coastal Oaxaca, Mexico: The Archaeological and Social Context of Music." In *Studien zur Musikarchäologie VIII: Sound from the Past: The Interpretation of Musical Artifacts in an Archaeological Context,* edited by R. Eichmann, J. Fang, and L-C. Koch, 259–70. Rahden/Westf.: VML.

Barber, Sarah B., Arthur A. Joyce, Arion T. Mayes, and Michelle Butler. 2013. "Formative Period Burial Practices and Cemeteries." In *Polity and Ecology in Formative Period Coastal Oaxaca*, edited by Arthur A. Joyce, 97–133. Boulder: University Press of Colorado.

Barber, Sarah B., and Mireya Olvera Sánchez. 2012. "A Divine Wind: The Arts of Death and Music in Terminal Formative Oaxaca." *Ancient Mesoamerica* 23 (1): 9–24.

Beekman, Christopher S. 2003. "Fruitful Symmetry: Corn and Cosmology in the Public Architecture of Late Formative and Early Classic Jalisco." *Mesoamerican Voices* 1:5–22.

Bérubé, Éloi, Guy David Hepp, and Shanti Morell-Hart. 2020. "Paleoethnobotanical Evidence of Early Formative Period Diet in Coastal Oaxaca, Mexico." *Journal of Archaeological Science: Reports* 29:102047. https://doi.org/10.1016/j.jasrep.2019.102047.

Binford, Lewis R. 1971. "Mortuary Practices: Their Study and Their Potential." *Memoirs of the Society for American Archaeology* 25:6–29.

Blake, Michael, and John E. Clark. 1989. "The Emergence of Hereditary Inequality: The Case of Pacific Coastal Chiapas, Mexico." Paper presented at the Circum-Pacific Prehistory Conference, Seattle, WA.

Blake, Michael, and John E. Clark. 1999. "The Emergence of Hereditary Inequality: The Case of Pacific Coastal Chiapas, Mexico." In *Pacific Latin America in Prehistory: The Evolution of Archaic and Formative Cultures*, edited by Michael Blake, 55–73. Pullman: Washington State University Press.

Blanton, Richard E. 1978. *Monte Albán: Settlement Patterns at the Ancient Zapotec Capital.* New York: Academic Press.

Blanton, Richard E., Gary M. Feinman, Stephen A. Kowalewski, and Peter N. Peregrine. 1996. "A Dual-Processual Theory for the Evolution of Mesoamerican Civilization." *Current Anthropology* 37 (1): 1–14.

Blomster, Jeffrey P. 2004. *Etlatongo: Social Complexity, Interaction, and Village Life in the Mixteca Alta of Oaxaca, Mexico.* Belmont, MA: Wadsworth/Thomson Learning.

Blomster, Jeffrey P. 2009. "Identity, Gender, and Power: Representational Juxtapositions in Early Formative Figurines from Oaxaca, Mexico." In *Mesoamerican Figurines: Small-Scale Indices of Large-Scale Social Phenomena*, edited by Christina T. Halperin, Katherine A. Faust, Rhonda Taube, and Aurore Giguet, 119–48. Gainesville: University Press of Florida.

Blomster, Jeffrey P., and Víctor E. Salazar Chávez. 2020. "Origins of the Mesoamerican Ballgame: Earliest Ballcourt from the Highlands Found at Etlatongo, Oaxaca, Mexico." *Science Advances* 6 (11): eaay6964. doi:10.1126/sciadv.aay6964.

Brumfiel, Elizabeth M. 2003. "It's a Material World: History, Artifacts, and Anthropology." *Annual Review of Anthropology* 32 (1): 205–23.

Brumfiel, Elizabeth M. 2006. "Cloth, Gender, Continuity, and Change: Fabricating Unity in Anthropology." *American Anthropologist* 108 (4): 862–77.

Carballo, David M. 2009. "Household and Status in Formative Central Mexico: Domestic Structures, Assemblages, and Practices at La Laguna, Tlaxcala." *Latin American Antiquity* 20 (3): 473–502.

Carballo, David M. 2011. "Advances in the Household Archaeology of Highland Mesoamerica." *Journal of Archaeological Research* 19 (2): 133–89.

Carballo, David M. ed. 2012. *Cooperation and Collective Action: Archaeological Perspectives.* Boulder: University Press of Colorado.

Carmack, Robert M., Janine Gasco, Marilyn A. Masson, and Michael E. Smith. 2016. "Late Postclassic Mesoamerica, 2nd edition" In *The Legacy of Mesoamerica*, edited by Robert M. Carmack, Janine Gasco, and Gary H. Gossen, 78–119. New York: Routledge.

Carr, Christopher. 1995. "Mortuary Practices: Their Social, Philosophical-Religious, Circumstantial, and Physical Determinants." *Journal of Archaeological Method and Theory* 2 (2): 105–200.

Caso, Alfonso. 1932. "Monte Albán, Richest Archaeological Find in America." *National Geographic Magazine* 62 (4): 487–512.

Caso, Alfonso. 1969. *El Tesoro de Monte Albán, Memorias del Instituto Nacional de Antropología e Historia 3*. Mexico City: Instituto Nacional de Antropología e Historia.

Caso, Alfonso, Ignacio Bernal, and Jorge R. Acosta. 1967. *La Cerámica de Monte Albán. Vol. 12*. Mexico City: Instituto Nacional de Antropología e Historia.

Caso, Alfonso, and Daniel F. Rubín de la Borbolla. 1936. *Exploraciones En Mitla, 1934–1935*. Mexico City: Talleres Gráficos de La Ofi. de Pubs. y Prop. de La SAyF 21.

Cervantes Pérez, José Manuel, Tito Cuauhtémoc Mijangos García, and Augustín E. Andrade Cuautle. 2017. "Collective Memory in San Sebastián Etla, Oaxaca: Bioarchaeological Approaches to an Early Formative Period (1400–1200 BCE) Mortuary Space." *Journal of Archaeological Science: Reports* 13:737–43.

Childe, V. Gordon. 1925. *The Dawn of European Civilization*. London: Kegan Paul, Trench, Trubner.

Childe, V. Gordon. 1950. "The Urban Revolution." *Town Planning Review* 21 (1): 3–17.

Clark, John E. 1991. "The Beginnings of Mesoamerica: Apologia for the Soconusco Early Formative." In *The Formation of Complex Society in Southeastern Mesoamerica*, edited by William R. Fowler Jr., 13–26. Boca Raton, LA: CRC Press.

Clark, John E. 1994. "The Development of Early Formative Rank Societies in the Soconusco, Chiapas, Mexico." PhD diss., University of Michigan, Ann Arbor.

Clark, John E. 2004. "Mesoamerica Goes Public: Early Ceremonial Centers, Leaders, and Communities." In *Mesoamerican Archaeology: Theory and Practice*, edited by Julia A. Hendon and Rosemary A. Joyce, 43–72. Malden, MA: Blackwell.

Clark, John E., and Michael Blake. 1994. "The Power of Prestige: Competitive Generosity and the Emergence of Rank Society in Lowland Mesoamerica." In *Factional*

Competition and Political Development in the New World, edited by Elizabeth M. Brumfiel and John W. Fox, 17–30. Cambridge. UK: Cambridge University Press.

Clark, John E., and David Cheetham. 2002. "Mesoamerica's Tribal Foundations." In *The Archaeology of Tribal Societies*, edited by William A. Parkinson, 278–339. Ann Arbor, MI: International Monographs in Prehistory.

Crumley, Carole L. 1995. "Heterarchy and the Analysis of Complex Societies." *Archaeological Papers of the American Anthropological Association* 6 (1): 1–5.

Crumley, Carole L. 2004. "Contextual Constraints on State Structure." In *Alternativity in Cultural History: Heterarchy and Homoarchy as Evolutionary Trajectories, Third International Conference "Hierarchy and Power in the History of Civilizations,"* edited by Dmitri M. Bondarenko and Alexandre A. Nemirovskiy, 3–22. Moscow: Center for Civilizational and Regional Studies of the RAS.

Crumley, Carole L. 2015. "Heterarchy." In *Emerging Trends in the Social and Behavioral Sciences: An Interdisciplinary, Searchable, and Linkable Resource*, edited by Robert A. Scott and Marlis C. Buchmann, 1–14. Wiley Online.

Cummings, Linda Scott. 2017. *Bone Collagen Extraction, XAD Purification, and AMS Radiocarbon Age Determination of Samples from La Consentida, Oaxaca, Mexico*. Golden, CO: PaleoResearch Institute.

Cyphers Guillén, Ann. 1993. "Women, Rituals, and Social Dynamics at Ancient Chalcatzingo." *Latin American Antiquity* 4 (3): 209–24.

DeMarrais, Elizabeth. 2013. "Understanding Heterarchy: Crafting and Social Projects in Pre-Hispanic Northwest Argentina." *Cambridge Archaeological Journal* 23 (3): 345–62.

Drennan, Robert D. 2009. "Religion and Social Evolution in Formative Mesoamerica." In *The Early Mesoamerican Village: Updated Edition*, edited by Kent V. Flannery, 345–68. Walnut Creek, CA: Left Coast Press.

Ensor, Bradley E. 2013. *Crafting Prehispanic Maya Kinship*. Tuscaloosa: University of Alabama Press.

Fargher, Lane F., Richard E. Blanton, and Verenice F. Heredia Espinoza. 2010. "Egalitarian Ideology and Political Power in Prehispanic Central Mexico: The Case of Tlaxcallan." *Latin American Antiquity* 21 (3): 227–51.

Feinman, Gary M. 1991. "Demography, Surplus, and Inequality: Early Political Formations in Highland Mesoamerica." In *Chiefdoms: Power, Economy, and Ideology*, edited by Timothy Earle, 229–62. Cambridge, UK: Cambridge University Press.

Feinman, Gary M., and David M. Carballo. 2018. "Collaborative and Competitive Strategies in the Variability and Resiliency of Large-Scale Societies in Mesoamerica." *Economic Anthropology* 5 (1): 7–19.

Feinman, Gary M., and Joyce Marcus, eds. 1998. *Archaic States*. Santa Fe, NM: School of American Research Press.

Feinman, Gary M., and Linda M. Nicholas. 1989. "The Role of Risk in Formative Period Agriculture: A Reconsideration." *American Anthropologist* 91 (1): 198–203.

Feinman, Gary M. and Linda M. Nicholas. 1990. "Settlement and Land Use in Ancient Oaxaca." In *Debating Oaxaca Archaeology*, edited by Joyce Marcus, 71–113. Ann Arbor: University of Michigan Anthropological Papers.

Feinman, Gary M. and Linda M. Nicholas. 1992. "Human-Land Relations from an Archaeological Perspective: The Case of Ancient Oaxaca." In *Understanding Economic Process*, edited by Sutti Ortiz and Susan Lees, 155–78. New York: University Press of America.

Feinman, Gary M. and Linda M. Nicholas. 2019. "Civic-Ceremonial Transition at Lambityeco, Oaxaca, Mexico." In *Historical Ecologies, Heterarchies and Transtemporal Landscapes*, edited by Celeste Ray and Manuel Fernández-Götz, 248–64. New York: Routledge.

Flannery, Kent V., and Joyce Marcus, eds. 2003. *The Cloud People: Divergent Evolution of the Zapotec and Mixtec Civilizations*. New York: Percheron Press.

Flannery, Kent V., and Joyce Marcus. 2012. *The Creation of Inequality: How Our Prehistoric Ancestors Set the Stage for Monarchy, Slavery, and Empire*. Cambridge, MA: Harvard University Press.

Foster, George M. 1944. "Nagualism in Mexico and Guatemala." *Acta Americana* 2:85–103.

Fried, Morton H. 1967. *The Evolution of Political Society: An Essay in Political Anthropology*. New York: Random House.

Gillespie, Susan D. 2001. "Personhood, Agency, and Mortuary Ritual: A Case Study from the Ancient Maya." *Journal of Anthropological Archaeology* 20 (1): 73–112.

Guernsey, Julia. 2010. "Rulers, Gods, and Potbellies: A Consideration of Sculptural Forms and Themes from the Preclassic Pacific Coast and Piedmont of Mesoamerica." In *The Place of Stone Monuments: Context, Use, and Meaning in Mesoamerica's Preclassic Transition*, edited by Julia Guernsey, John E. Clark, and Barbara Arroyo, 207–30. Washington, DC: Dumbarton Oaks.

Guernsey, Julia. 2012. *Sculpture and Social Dynamics in Preclassic Mesoamerica*. Cambridge, UK: Cambridge University Press.

Guernsey, Julia. 2020. *Human Figuration and Fragmentation in Preclassic Mesoamerica: From Figurines to Sculpture*. Cambridge, UK: Cambridge University Press.

Hayden, Brian. 1990. "Nimrods, Piscators, Pluckers, and Planters: The Emergence of Food Production." *Journal of Anthropological Archaeology* 9 (1): 31–69.

Hayden, Brian. 1995. "Pathways to Power: Principles for Creating Socioeconomic Inequalities." In *Foundations of Social Inequality*, edited by T. Douglas Price and Gary M. Feinman, 15–86. New York: Plenum Press.

Hayden, Brian. 2009. "The Proof Is in the Pudding: Feasting and the Origins of Domestication." *Current Anthropology* 50 (5): 597–601.

Hayden, Brian. 2011. "Big Man, Big Heart? The Political Role of Aggrandizers in Egalitarian and Transegalitarian Societies." In *For the Greater Good of All: Perspectives on Individualism, Society, and Leadership*, edited by Donelson R. Forsyth and Crystal L. Hoyt, 101–18. London: Palgrave Macmillan.

Hayden, Brian. 2014. *The Power of Feasts: From Prehistory to the Present.* Cambridge, UK: Cambridge University Press.

Hepp, Guy David. 2015. "La Consentida: Initial Early Formative Period Settlement, Subsistence, and Social Organization on the Pacific Coast of Oaxaca, Mexico." PhD diss., University of Colorado, Boulder.

Hepp, Guy David. 2019a. "Interaction and Exchange in Early Formative Western and Central Mesoamerica: New Data from Coastal Oaxaca." In *Interregional Interaction in Ancient Mesoamerica,* edited by Joshua D. Englehardt and Michael D. Carrasco, 51–82. Louisville: University Press of Colorado.

Hepp, Guy David. 2019b. *La Consentida: Settlement, Subsistence, and Social Organization in an Early Formative Mesoamerican Community.* Louisville: University Press of Colorado.

Hepp, Guy David. 2019c. "Radiocarbon Evidence for Initial Early Formative Period Occupation in Coastal Oaxaca, Mexico." *Latin American Antiquity* 30 (2): 437–44.

Hepp, Guy David, José Aguilar, and Paul A. Sandberg. 2020. "Contextos Mortuorios en la Consentida, Oaxaca, durante el Formativo Temprano." *Anales de Antropología* 54 (1): 57–69.

Hepp, Guy David, Sarah B. Barber, Jeffrey S. Brzezinski, Arthur A. Joyce, and Rachael L. Wedemeyer. 2020. "The Symbolism, Use, and Archaeological Context of Masks in Formative Period Coastal Oaxaca, Mexico." *Cambridge Archaeological Journal* 30 (2): 257–74.

Hepp, Guy David, Sarah B. Barber, and Arthur A. Joyce. 2014. "Communing with Nature, the Ancestors, and the Neighbors: Ancient Ceramic Musical Instruments from Coastal Oaxaca, Mexico." *World Archaeology* 46 (3): 380–99.

Hepp, Guy David, and Arthur A. Joyce. 2013. "From Flesh to Clay: Formative Period Ceramic Figurines from Oaxaca's Lower Río Verde Valley." In *Polity and Ecology in Formative Period Coastal Oaxaca,* edited by Arthur A. Joyce, 256–99. Boulder: University Press of Colorado.

Hepp, Guy David, and Ivy A. Rieger. 2014. "Aspects of Dress and Ornamentation in Coastal Oaxaca's Formative Period." In *Wearing Culture: Dress and Regalia in Early Mesoamerica and Central America,* edited by Heather Orr and Matthew Looper, 115–43. Boulder: University Press of Colorado.

Hepp, Guy David, Paul A. Sandberg, and José Aguilar. 2017. "Death on the Early Formative Oaxaca Coast: The Human Remains of La Consentida." *Journal of Archaeological Science: Reports* 13:703–11.

Heyden, Doris. 1991. "Dryness before the Rains: Toxcatl and Tezcatlipoca." In *To Change Place: Aztec Ceremonial Landscapes,* edited by Davíd Carrasco, 188–204. Louisville: University Press of Colorado.

Higelin Ponce de León, Ricardo, and Guy David Hepp. 2017. "Talking with the Dead from Southern Mexico: Tracing Bioarchaeological Foundations and New Perspectives in Oaxaca." *Journal of Archaeological Science: Reports* 13:697–702.

Hill, Warren D., and John E. Clark. 2001. "Sports, Gambling, and Government: America's First Social Compact?" *American Anthropologist* 103 (2): 331–45.

Jennings, Sarah. 2010. "Mold-Made Figurines of the Lower Río Verde Valley, Oaxaca, Mexico: Insights into Popular Ideology in the Classic and Early Postclassic." Master's thesis, University of Colorado.

Joyce, Arthur A. 1991. "Formative Period Occupation in the Lower Río Verde Valley, Oaxaca, Mexico: Interregional Interaction and Social Change." PhD diss., Rutgers University, New Brunswick.

Joyce, Arthur A. 2000. "The Founding of Monte Albán: Sacred Propositions and Social Practices." In *Agency in Archaeology*, edited by Marcia-Anne Dobres and John Robb, 71–91. London: Routledge.

Joyce, Arthur A. 2005. "La Arqueología del Bajo Río Verde." *Acervos: Boletín de Los Archivos y Bibliotecas de Oaxaca* 7 (29): 16–36.

Joyce, Arthur A. 2010. *Mixtecs, Zapotecs, and Chatinos: Ancient Peoples of Southern Mexico.* Malden, MA: Wiley-Blackwell.

Joyce, Arthur A., Sarah B. Barber, Guy David Hepp, Matt Sponheimer, Michelle Butler, Sarah Taylor, Michelle Goman, Aleksander Borejsza, Raymond G. Mueller, and Paul A. Sandberg. 2017. "Landscape and Dietary Change in Formative Period Coastal Oaxaca." Paper presented at the 82nd Annual Meeting of the Society for American Archaeology Annual Conference, Vancouver, BC.

Joyce, Rosemary A. 1999. "Social Dimensions of Pre-Classic Burials." In *Social Patterns in Pre-Classic Mesoamerica*, edited by David C. Grove and Rosemary A. Joyce, 15–47. Washington, DC: Dumbarton Oaks.

Joyce, Rosemary A. 2000. *Gender and Power in Prehispanic Mesoamerica.* Austin: University of Texas Press.

Joyce, Rosemary A. 2002. "Beauty, Sexuality, Body Ornamentation, and Gender in Ancient Mesoamerica." In *In Pursuit of Gender: Worldwide Archaeological Approaches*, edited by Sarah M. Nelson and Myriam Rosen-Ayalon, 81–92. New York: Altamira Press.

Joyce, Rosemary A. 2004. "Unintended Consequences? Monumentality as a Novel Experience in Formative Mesoamerica." *Journal of Archaeological Method and Theory* 11 (1): 5–29.

Joyce, Rosemary A. 2009. "Making a World of Their Own: Mesoamerican Figurines and Mesoamerican Figurine Analysis." In *Mesoamerican Figurines: Small-Scale Indices of Large-Scale Social Phenomena*, edited by Christina T. Halperin, Katherine A. Faust, Rhonda Taube, and Aurore Giguet, 407–425. Gainesville: University Press of Florida.

Joyce, Rosemary A., and John S. Henderson. 2007. "From Feasting to Cuisine: Implications of Archaeological Research in an Early Honduran Village." *American Anthropologist* 109 (4): 642–53.

Joyce, Rosemary A., and John S. Henderson. 2010. "Forming Mesoamerican Taste: Cacao Consumption in Formative Period Contexts." In *Pre-Columbian Foodways:*

Interdisciplinary Approaches to Food, Culture, and Markets in Ancient Mesoamerica, edited by John Edward Staller and Michael Carrasco, 157–73. New York: Springer.

Kaplan, Lucille N. 1956. "Tonal and Nagual in Coastal Oaxaca, Mexico." *Journal of American Folklore* 69 (274): 363–68.

Kidder, A. V. 1937. "A Program for Maya Research." *Hispanic American Historical Review* 17:160–69.

Kidder, A. V. 1945. "Excavations at Kaminaljuyu." *American Antiquity* 11:65–75.

King, Stacie Marie. 2003. "Social Practices and Social Organization in Ancient Coastal Oaxacan Households." PhD diss., University of California, Berkeley.

Klein, Kathryn. 1997. *The Unbroken Thread: Conserving the Textile Traditions of Oaxaca*. Los Angeles: Getty Conservation Institute.

Kowalewski, Stephen A. 1990. "The Evolution of Complexity in the Valley of Oaxaca." *Annual Review of Anthropology* 19 (1): 39–58.

Kuijt, Ian. 2009. "What Do We Really Know about Food Storage, Surplus, and Feasting in Preagricultural Communities?" *Current Anthropology* 50 (5): 641–44.

Lesure, Richard G. 1997. "Figurines and Social Identities in Early Sedentary Societies of Coastal Chiapas, Mexico, 1550–800 B.C." In *Women in Prehistory: North America and Mesoamerica*, edited by Cheryl Claassen and Rosemary A. Joyce, 227–48. Philadelphia: University of Pennsylvania Press.

Lesure, Richard G. 1999a. "Figurines as Representations and Products at Paso de La Amada, Mexico." *Cambridge Archaeological Journal* 9 (2): 209–20.

Lesure, Richard G. 1999b. "On the Genesis of Value in Early Hierarchical Societies." In *Material Symbols: Culture and Economy in Prehistory*, edited by John Robb, 23–55. Carbondale: Center for Archaeological Investigations, Southern Illinois University.

Lesure, Richard G. 2011. *Interpreting Ancient Figurines: Context, Comparison, and Prehistoric Art*. Cambridge, UK: Cambridge University Press.

Lesure, Richard G., and Michael Blake. 2002. "Interpretive Challenges in the Study of Early Complexity: Economy, Ritual, and Architecture at Paso de La Amada, Mexico." *Journal of Anthropological Archaeology* 21 (1): 1–24.

Levine, Marc N. 2011. "Negotiating Political Economy at Late Postclassic Tututepec (Yucu Dzaa), Oaxaca, Mexico." *American Anthropologist* 113 (1): 22–39.

Love, Michael W. 2007. "Recent Research in the Southern Highlands and Pacific Coast of Mesoamerica." *Journal of Archaeological Research* 15 (4): 275–328.

MacNeish, Richard S. 1992. *The Origins of Agriculture and Settled Village Life*. Norman: University of Oklahoma Press.

Marcus, Joyce. 1998. *Women's Ritual in Formative Oaxaca: Figurine Making, Divination, Death and the Ancestors*. Ann Arbor: University of Michigan Press.

Marcus, Joyce. 2018. "Studying Figurines." *Journal of Archaeological Research* 27:1–47.

Marcus, Joyce, and Kent V. Flannery. 1996. *Zapotec Civilization: How Urban Society Evolved in Mexico's Oaxaca Valley*. London: Thames and Hudson.

Mayes, Arion T., Sarah B. Barber, Arthur A. Joyce, and Michelle M. Butler. 2020. "Cambio social en el Bajo Río Verde, Oaxaca, México: Una perspectiva bioarqueológica." *Anales de Antropología* 54 (1): 71–79.

McGuire, Randall H. 1983. "Breaking Down Cultural Complexity: Inequality and Heterogeneity." *Advances in Archaeological Method and Theory* 6:91–142.

McIntosh, Susan K., ed. 1999. *Beyond Chiefdoms; Pathways to Complexity in Africa*. Cambridge, UK: Cambridge University Press.

Mendelsohn, Rebecca R. 2018. "The Formative to Classic Period Transition at Izapa: Updates from the Izapa Household Archaeology Project." *Ancient Mesoamerica* 29 (2): 309–31.

Meskell, Lynn. 2004. *Object Worlds in Ancient Egypt: Material Biographies Past and Present*. London: Berg.

Nicholas, Linda M. 1989. "Land Use in Prehispanic Oaxaca." In *Monte Albán's Hinterland. Part 2, The Prehispanic Settlement Patterns in Tlacolula, Etla, and Ocotlán, the Valley of Oaxaca, Mexico*, edited by Stephen A. Kowalewski, Gary M. Feinman, Laura M. Finsten, Richard E. Blanton, and Linda M. Nicholas, 449–505. Ann Arbor: Museum of Anthropology, University of Michigan.

Parsons, Jeffrey. 1974. "The Development of a Prehistoric Complex Society: A Regional Perspective from the Valley of Mexico." *Journal of Field Archaeology* 1 (1/2): 81–108.

Pauketat, Timothy R., and Susan M. Alt. 2003. "Mounds, Memory, and Contested Mississippian History." In *Archaeologies of Memory*, edited by Ruth M. Van Dyke and Susan E. Alcock, 151–79. Malden, MA: Blackwell.

Pauketat, Timothy R., and Thomas E. Emerson. 2007. "Alternative Civilizations: Heterarchies, Corporate Polities, and Orthodoxies." In *Alternativity in Cultural History: Heterarchy and Homoarchy as Evolutionary Trajectories, Third International Conference "Hierarchy and Power in the History of Civilizations" June 18–21 2004, Moscow. Selected Papers*, edited by Dmitri M. Bondarenko and Alexandre A. Nemirovskiy, 107–17. Moscow: Center for Civilizational and Regional Studies of the RAS.

Paynter, Robert, and Randall H. McGuire. 1991. "The Archaeology of Inequality: Material Culture, Domination, and Resistance." In *The Archaeology of Inequality*, edited by Randall H. McGuire and Robert Paynter, 1–27. Oxford: Blackwell.

Powell, Steven. 2020. "Like Listening to a Seashell: A Midden Analysis from La Consentida, Oaxaca, Mexico." Master's thesis, California State University, San Bernardino.

Pugh, Timothy W. 2001. "Flood Reptiles, Serpent Temples, and the Quadripartite Universe: The Imago Mundi of Late Postclassic Mayapan." *Ancient Mesoamerica* 12 (2): 247–58.

Reimer, Paula J., William E. N. Austin, Edouard Bard, Alex Bayliss, Paul G. Blackwell, Christopher Bronk Ramsey, Martin Butzin, et al. 2020. "The IntCal20 Northern Hemisphere Radiocarbon Age Calibration Curve (0–55 Cal KBP)." *Radiocarbon* 62 (4): 725–57.

Rojas, Alfonso Villa. 1947. "Kinship and Nagualism in a Tzeltal Community, Southeastern Mexico." *American Anthropologist* 49 (4): 578–87.

Sahlins, Marshall D., and Elman R. Service. 1960. *Evolution and Culture*. Ann Arbor: University of Michigan Press.

Sanders, William T., and Deborah L. Nichols. 1988. "Ecological Theory and Cultural Evolution in the Valley of Oaxaca [and Comments and Reply]." *Current Anthropology* 29 (1): 33–80.

Sanders, William T., and David T. Webster. 1978. "Unilinealism, Multilinealism, and the Evolution of Complex Societies." In *Social Archaeology: Beyond Subsistence and Dating*, edited by Charles L. Redman, Mary J. Berman, Edward V. Curtin, William T. Longhorn Jr., Nina M. Versaggi, and Jeffrey C. Wanser, 249–302. New York: Academic Press.

Santley, Robert S. 1980. "Disembedded Capitals Reconsidered." *American Antiquity* 45 (1): 132–45.

Saunders, Nicholas J. 2001. "A Dark Light: Reflections on Obsidian in Mesoamerica." *World Archaeology* 33 (2): 220–36.

Saxe, Arthur A. 1971. "Social Dimensions of Mortuary Practices in a Mesolithic Population from Wadi Halfa, Sudan." *Memoirs of the Society for American Archaeology* 25:39–56.

Service, Elman R. 1962. *Primitive Social Organization*. New York: Random House.

Shafer, Harry J., and Anna J. Taylor. 1986. "Mimbres Mogollon Pueblo Dynamics and Ceramic Style Change." *Journal of Field Archaeology* 13 (1): 43–68.

Smith, Adam T. 2003. *The Political Landscape: Constellations of Authority in Early Complex Societies*. Berkeley: University of California Press.

Smith, Ledyard. 1932. "Two Recent Ceramic Finds at Uaxactun." *Contributions to American Archaeology* 2 (5): 1–25. No. 436. Washington, DC: Carnegie Institution of Washington.

Sousa, Lisa. 1998. "Women in Native Societies and Cultures of Colonial Mexico." PhD diss., University of California, Los Angeles.

Spencer, Charles R., and Elsa M. Redmond. 2004. "Primary State Formation in Mesoamerica." *Annual Review of Anthropology* 33:173–99.

Spores, Ronald. 1997. "Mixteca Cacicas: Status, Wealth, and the Political Accommodation of Native Elite Women in Early Colonial Oaxaca." In *Indian Women of Early Mexico*, edited by Susan Schroeder, Stephanie Wood, and Robert Haskett, 185–98. Norman: University of Oklahoma Press.

Stafford, Thomas W., Jr., P. E. Hare, Lloyd Currie, A. J. T. Jull, and Douglas J. Donahue. 1991. "Accelerator Radiocarbon Dating at the Molecular Level." *Journal of Archaeological Science* 18 (1): 35–72.

Stein, Gil. 1999. *Rethinking World-Systems: Diasporas, Colonies, and Interaction in Uruk Mesopotamia*. Tucson: University of Arizona Press.

Stephen, Lynn. 1991. *Zapotec Women*. Austin: University of Texas Press.

Stockett, Miranda K. 2005. "On the Importance of Difference: Re-envisioning Sex and Gender in Ancient Mesoamerica." *World Archaeology* 37 (4): 566–78.

Stross, Brian. 1994. "Maize and Fish: The Iconography of Power in Late Formative Mesoamerica." *Anthropology and Aesthetics* 25:10–35.

Taube, Karl A. 2010. "Where Earth and Sky Meet: The Sea in Ancient and Contemporary Maya Cosmology." In *Fiery Pool: The Maya and the Mythic Sea*, edited by Daniel Finamore and Stephen D. Houston, 202–19. Salem, MA: Peabody Essex Museum.

Taylor, Walter W. 1948. *A Study of Archaeology*. Carbondale: Southern Illinois University Press.

Taylor, William B. 1979. *Drinking, Homicide, and Rebellion in Colonial Mexican Villages*. Stanford, CA: Stanford University Press.

Terraciano, Kevin. 2000. "The Colonial Mixtec Community." *Hispanic American Historical Review* 80 (1): 1–42.

Terraciano, Kevin. 2001. *The Mixtecs of Colonial Oaxaca: Nudzahui History, Sixteenth through Eighteenth Centuries*. Stanford, CA: Stanford University Press.

Twiss, Katheryn C. 2008. "Transformations in an Early Agricultural Society: Feasting in the Southern Levantine Pre-pottery Neolithic." *Journal of Anthropological Archaeology* 27 (4): 418–42.

Urcid, Javier, and Arthur A. Joyce. 2001. "Carved Monuments and Calendrical Names: The Rulers of Río Viejo, Oaxaca." *Ancient Mesoamerica* 12 (2): 199–216.

Vega-Centeno Sara-Lafosse, Rafael. 2007. "Construction, Labor Organization, and Feasting during the Late Archaic Period in the Central Andes." *Journal of Anthropological Archaeology* 26 (2): 150–71.

Waters, Michael R., Thomas W. Stafford Jr., Brian Kooyman, and L. V. Hills. 2015. "Late Pleistocene Horse and Camel Hunting at the Southern Margin of the Ice-Free Corridor." *PNAS* 112:4263–67.

Whalen, Michael E. 1981. "Excavations at Santo Domingo Tomaltepec: Evolution of a Formative Community in the Valley of Oaxaca, Mexico." *Memoirs 12 Museum of Anthropology*. Ann Arbor: University of Michigan Press.

Whalen, Michael E. 1983. "Reconstructing Early Formative Village Organization in Oaxaca, Mexico." *American Antiquity* 48 (1): 17–43.

Whalen, Michael E. 2009. "Zoning within an Early Formative Community in the Valley of Oaxaca." In *The Early Mesoamerican Village*, edited by Kent V. Flannery, 75–79. updated ed. Walnut Creek, CA: Left Coast Press.

Willey, Gordon R., and Jeremy A. Sabloff. 1993. *A History of American Archaeology*. 3rd ed. New York: Freeman.

Winter, Marcus. 1974. "Residential Patterns at Monte Albán, Oaxaca, Mexico." *Science* 186 (4168): 981–87.

Winter, Marcus. 1989. "Excavaciones En La Consentida, 1988." Mexico City: Report submitted to the Instituto Nacional de Antropología e Historia.

Winter, Marcus. 2002. "Monte Albán: Mortuary Practices as Domestic Ritual and Their Relation to Community Religion." In *Domestic Ritual in Ancient Mesoamerica Monograph 46*, edited by Patricia Plunket, 67–82. Los Angeles: Cotsen Institute of Archaeology.

3

Pottery and Society during the Preclassic Period at Yaxuná, Yucatán

TRAVIS W. STANTON, SARA DZUL GÓNGORA,
RYAN H. COLLINS, AND RODRIGO MARTÍN MORALES

INTRODUCTION

Despite the fact that there is no correlation between pottery and complex forms of social, political, and economic structures, the appearance of ceramic technology is often used by Mesoamerican archaeologists as one of the hallmarks to mark the emergence of "complexity" in this part of the world. One of the reasons for this interpretational link is that the first appearance of pottery in Mesoamerica coincides relatively closely with other evidence of increasingly sedentary lifeways and more clearly marked inequality. Thus, it is often used as part of a cluster of data that signify the gradual coalescence of a "Mesoamerican identity" marking the process toward the emergence of state societies. The lowland Maya region is no exception to this trend, although the appearance of ceramics occurs several centuries after they are first dated in neighboring societies (e.g., Clark and Cheetham 2005). Regardless of its "origins," understanding the role of pottery in early sedentary societies in the Maya Lowlands is of keen interest to archaeologists. After it was adopted, we want to understand the changing contexts of how and why it was used. In this paper, we discuss the appearance and transformation of Preclassic

https://doi.org/10.5876/9781646422883.c003

period ceramics from the E Group at Yaxuná, Yucatán. The stratigraphy of the plaza is composed of at least eleven Preclassic floors and contains several features and substructures allowing for more detailed analysis of the changes in ceramic forms and technology than is available from other published contexts across the northern Maya Lowlands. Radiocarbon assays indicate that the plaza complex was first established in the earliest portion of the Middle Preclassic and was largely abandoned by the end of the Late Preclassic, when Yaxuná was the center of a polity approximating a state level development. We discuss the changes in ceramics and their social implications from two perspectives. First, we focus on changes in attributes, in particular ceramic forms, from an archaeological perspective. Second, we discuss the implications of material and technological changes from a perspective we term ceramic ethnoanalysis.

POTTERY AND "COMPLEXITY"

While pottery technology is known to have been used by some fairly mobile groups throughout the world (Strum et al. 2016), it is much more common among more sedentary societies. In the case of Mesoamerica, the first development of ceramic technology roughly correlates with other evidence for substantial shifts to more sedentary lifeways and emerging inequality, leading some scholars to discuss its role in the development of more complex social and political structures (Clark and Blake 1994). Given the morphological variability of ceramic objects afforded by the great degree of plasticity present during the manufacturing process, when pottery was adopted by a society it could be well tailored to meet a range of needs perceived by ceramic producers and consumers. Correspondingly, the variability of ceramic forms throughout the world is quite high, including drains, pipes, architectural features, figurines, personal adornments, musical instruments, and a vast array of cooking, serving, and storage vessels, among others. Given its durability and substantial frequency in some societies like that of the Preclassic Maya, tracking the spatiotemporal patterns of ceramic attributes such as forms, design styles, and tempers can provide valuable information concerning human behavior in the past and can inform us of social processes leading to increasingly hierarchical social systems associated with complexity in the past. In this paper, it is not our goal to equate the appearance of pottery with the emergence of complexity, although the earliest pottery technology in the Maya Lowlands coincides with the same general time as the first identifiable public architecture (e.g., Inomata et al. 2015). Instead, we focus more on the changes in pottery from its initial adoption near the beginning of the Middle Preclassic to the end of the Late Preclassic, when clearly more hierarchical social and political systems existed.

Over the past several decades, early Maya social and political structures have come under increasing scrutiny (Brown and Bey 2018). New data for the transition from a more mobile lifestyle characterizing the Archaic period to one characterized by the increasing reliance of maize in the subsistence system, permanent public architecture like early E Groups, and initial sedentary lifeways generally place this transition around 1200–900 BCE across the lowlands. During this time, it is widely believed that emergent Maya societies had relatively low degrees of social inequality but that the foundations of social hierarchy were already in place (e.g., Hammond 1999). Early public architecture like E Groups may have been gathering places for still relatively mobile groups (Inomata et al. 2015; Stanton and Collins 2017) where more community-level activities such as calendrical celebrations were performed. However, much like arguments for more precocious neighboring societies (Reilly 1994), it is hypothesized that ritual specialists had begun to leverage their ability to perform rituals and access sacred knowledge into increasingly more social clout, leading the Maya down the path to the type of political system based on divine kingship that characterized the Classic period.

By the last centuries BCE, Maya society had transformed to a great degree. For example, demographically, there appear to have been many more people on the landscape (e.g., Glover and Stanton 2010; Tourtellot 1988); people who were largely sedentary and even organized in substantial urban centers (Hansen 1998). Figurine use in households in certain communities decreased, indicating shifts to more state-sponsored ritual activities (e.g., DeLance 2016). More restrictive public architecture such as triadic groups appeared (e.g., Stanton and Collins 2021). The first tombs were located in sacred centers (e.g., Pellecer 2005; Saturno et al. 2017), suggesting the acceptance of a new practice whereby certain ancestors of high rank could be integrated as part of the sacred geography, and images of divine rulers appeared at places like San Bartolo (Taube et al. 2010) and Loltún (Andrews 1981). Thus, within the span of a millennium complex hierarchical social structures that we might call "state-level" appear to have been firmly entrenched throughout the lowlands. The question we pose in this work is, Do changes in ceramic objects, as well as some other material markers articulate with and inform us of these societal transformations, and if so, how? To address this question, we turn to the ceramic data from the E Group at Yaxuná.

BACKGROUND AND METHODS

Research at Yaxuná's E Group was undertaken over the course of four field seasons (2013–2016) by the Proyecto de Interacción Política del Centro de Yucatán (PIPCY). First tested by George Brainerd (1958; see also Stanton et al. 2010; Tiesler et al. 2017) during the early Carnegie Institution work in the northern Maya Lowlands, the E Group and other monumental architecture at Yaxuná have been long known to demonstrate an important early occupation of Yucatán. While other early sites have been reported since Brainerd's work (e.g., Andrews and Ringle 1992), Yaxuná still remains just one of a handful of sites in the northern lowlands to have been identified with an E Group complex (Stanton 2017), a much more common form of early architectural expression to the south in Petén and Belize (Freidel et al. 2017).

E Groups are considered to have been spaces for important community-wide rituals associated with calendrics (Freidel et al. 2017). Importantly, many of the well-researched examples of E Group complexes have very early phases, some of which are argued to be among the earliest examples of public architecture in the Maya Lowlands (Inomata et al. 2015). Further, these groups generally have long sequences of construction with multiple building episodes spanning, in some cases, over a millennium. Their tendency to have substantial stratigraphic sequences makes them ideal for investigating questions of change over time.

Research at the Yaxuná E Group by PIPCY was undertaken to understand questions of the origins of Maya society in the northern lowlands and to refine the chronological sequence for the Preclassic at Yaxuná (Stanton and Collins 2017; Stanton et al., in press). Substantial excavations were performed across the plaza, measuring roughly 80 × 100 m in its final phase, but were concentrated in the center and eastern portions of the plaza (figure 3.1). Additionally, the central portion of the eastern range structure (Str. 5E-2, heavily damaged by Classic period stone robbing) and an earlier version of the range structure located in the plaza (Str. 5E-6) were also explored. In total, 12,566 sherds and three relatively whole vessels were recovered in the excavations, which were performed in 20 cm maximum vertical levels following the cultural and natural stratigraphy within maximum horizontal units of 2 × 2 m. Geophysical survey, in particular ground-penetrating radar, was also performed and informs us of some possible stratigraphic features in areas of the plaza not excavated.

The ceramic material recovered from the E Group was first subjected to type-variety analysis to understand chronological changes using the classificatory system widely utilized by archaeologists in this area of Mesoamerica (see Andrews 1988; Smith 1971). All the ceramic rim sherds were then drawn and measured for orifice diameter. Using comparative collections from the Ceramoteca at Centro INAH Yucatán, vessel shapes and forms were assigned (Stanton et al., forthcoming).

A smaller sample of materials, representative of the rims found in association with each of the floors, was then subjected to analysis by a local potter familiar with raw materials and their functional capabilities in Yucatán. While this chapter is not the forum in which to discuss in detail this method, in brief, we do not consider this research to be ethnoarchaeology but instead have termed the work "ethnoanalysis." As defined by Gremion and her colleagues (2014, 467) ceramic ethnoanalysis is the collaboration between local potting experts and archaeologists in the direct analysis of archaeological ceramics and/or in the experimentation with modern ceramic materials that results in a more

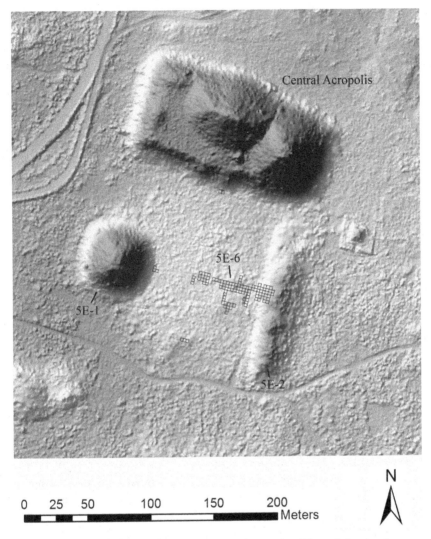

FIGURE 3.1. *Lidar image of the E Group and Central Acropolis of Yaxuná showing the area of excavations.*

informed understanding of archaeological ceramics. The fact that this method is collaborative sets it apart from traditional ethnoarchaeology and presents the opportunity to create research that is mutually beneficial. In our approach, data are not extracted from ethnographic contexts to be employed in academic contexts. Rather, the barrier of the "ethnographic context" is eliminated and local potters work directly with archaeologists and archaeological data and/or modern materials for experimentation. To date, we have performed experimental work (such as tensile stress and porosity tests among others) on 580 test tiles using local raw materials. These tests, along with Martín Morales' participation in the macroscopic analysis of the E Group materials, among other Preclassic period collections from Yucatán, guide our discussion of technological change and raw material selection choices.

With all this combined information in hand, we compared the data from each floor in the Yaxuná E Group to understand how the ceramics changed over time. To assign ceramics to floors, we took the ceramics from below the first stratigraphic evidence of the floor to the surface of the next substantial stratigraphic break (floor or bedrock); materials associated with features such as cuts in floors were subjected to a Harris Matrix analysis to assign their stratigraphic position. The great majority of the ceramic materials come from fill contexts and few materials were noted in direct association with the floor surfaces. While some of our colleagues might call attention to this fact, correctly pointing out that the ceramic material might have come earlier chronological contexts prior to being transposed as fill, there is evidence that at least some broken artifacts were intentionally deposited as infill during building construction in the Maya Lowlands (DeLance 2016), and we must remain open to the idea that much of the material might be in a relatively correct chronological order. With this in mind, at worst we have a situation where some of the material dated to the floors might be from earlier contexts. We analyzed the materials with this potentiality in mind and did not come across much glaring evidence (e.g., later Flaky Ware fabrics were in the upper levels, earlier wash surface treatments were generally in the lower levels, etc.) of chronological mixing, and attributes generally followed the general progression of ceramic changes published in the current literature. Further, the carbon samples used for radiometric dating also came from fill contexts, and the dates from these samples get progressively younger farther up in the stratigraphic sequence. With that said, we acknowledge the potential for chronological mixing and have omitted from consideration clearly early material in later contexts (e.g., pre-Mamom Huchim Burnished in upper strata clearly associated with Late Preclassic material). Finally, we complemented this fine-grained analysis with knowledge of ceramics from Preclassic contexts from other parts of Yaxuná that are not as stratified.

THE E GROUP STRATIGRAPHY

In the western two thirds of the plaza, we encountered the most complex stratigraphy, and a minimum number of eleven floors were identified (figure 3.2). We have organized these floors into four general construction phases that coincide with Yaxuná's early development. In this section, we summarize the stratigraphy by phase and provide chronological information based on type-variety and radiometric dating (table 3.1).

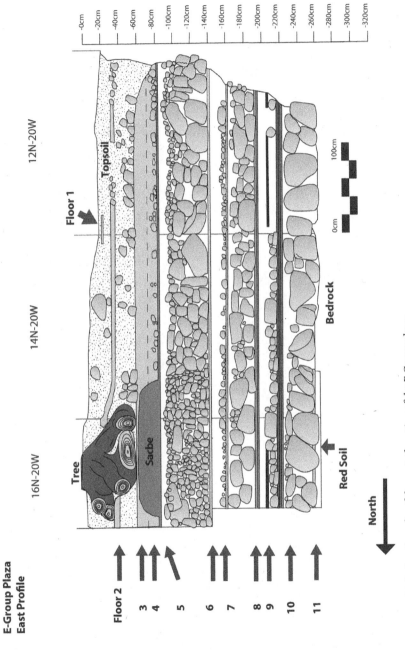

FIGURE 3.2. *Stratigraphy of the central portion of the E Group plaza.*

TABLE 3.1. Calibrated radiocarbon dating results.

Lab Code	Provenience	δ13C value	14C age BP	δ14C age	calibrated 2s	Notes	Cons. Phase	Floor #
YU-5484	YAX152.2A_12N-22W_10.1	-23.709	2691	21	896–807 BCE (95.4%)	From within the Earthen Floor in the center of the Plaza	I	10
AA104919	YAX152-2A, 16N-20W_9.1	-25.1	3,001	32	1381–1344 BCE (7.9%), 1306–1124 BCE (87.5%)	Plaza Center: Fill 5cm below Floor 9. Old Carbon.	I	9
YU-5494	YAX152.1B_12N-4W_11.1	-26.300	2537	21	796–746 BCE (52.5%), 686–666 BCE (11.6%), 643–553 BCE (31.3%)	Floor 9 A, first layer of three-part floor	I	9
YU-5498	YAX152.1B_12N-4W_10.1	-26.933	2503	21	778–728 BCE (20.6%), 714–710 BCE (0.4%), 694–542 BCE (74.4%)	Floor 9 B, second layer of a three-part floor.	I	9
YU-5500	YAX152.1B_12N-4W_9.1	-27.823	2498	20	774–728 BCE (19.0%), 718–707 BCE (1.4%), 695–541 BCE (75.0%)	On Floor 9 C, third and most recent layer of three-part floor.	I	9
YU-5487	YAX152.2A_12N-22W_9.1	-25.419	2532	21	795–745 BCE (44.6%), 686–666 BCE (12.9%), 644–552 BCE (37.8%)	Sample 1: Taken from the burning coinciding with the destruction of Floor 9.	II	8
YU-5488	Scraping of Vessel	-23.388	2442	20	748–685 BCE (26.3%), 666–641 BCE (8.1%), 588–580 BCE (0.8%), 560–410 BCE (60.1%)	Vessel in hole # 1 of Str. 5E-6 Phase G, this hole was left exposed for some time.	II	8
YU-5491	YAX152.1B_12N-6W_8.1	-23.415	2490	21	770–701 BCE (22.3%), 696–540 BCE (73.1%)	Carbon on Floor 9 inside of circular structure foundation area.	II	8
YU-5493	YAX152.2B_Feature 1_9.1	-27.191	2482	21	768–536 BCE (95.4%)	In intentional cut hole of Floor 10	II	8

continued on next page

TABLE 3.1.—continued from previous page

Lab Code	Provenience	δ¹³C value	¹⁴C age BP	δ¹⁴C age	calibrated 2s	Notes	Cons. Phase	Floor #
AA104923	YAX152-3A, 16N-26E_5.1	-27.8	2,754	32	979 BC—825 BCE (95.4%)	On bedrock, west of Str. 5E-2 Sub: Large burned-wood fragment beneath Floor 7. The date is most likely associated with Floor 10 or 11, although the lowest floor in the stratigraphy here is Floor 7.	II	7
AA104925	YAX152-1-16N-16E-9.1	-27.3	2,720	35	930–806 BCE (95.4%)	On bedrock east of Str. 5E-6: In rubble matrix on potential flagstones under Floor 7. The date is most likely. associated with Floor 10 or 11, although the lowest floor in the stratigraphy here is Floor 7.	II	7
AA104917	YAX152-2A, 14N-22W_8.1	-25.3	2,543	59	814–481 BCE (94.9%), 442–434 BCE (0.5%)	Plaza Center: Floor surface of level 7, S. Central border of unit.	II	6
AA104920	YAX152-2A, 12N-60W_8.1	-24.1	4,084	38	2863–2806 BCE (17.8%), 2760–2717 BCE (7.8%), 2710–2559 BCE (61.0%), 2536–2491 BCE (8.8%)	East of Str. 5E-1: Sample 1; provenance on lot form. Old carbon.	II	6
AA104922	YAX152-3A, 16N-26E_4.1	-24.7	2,590	38	830–748 BCE (80.3%), 685–667 BCE (4.0%), 641–587 BCE (8.5%), 581–556 BCE (2.5%)	West of 5E-2 Sub: Carbon under Floor 6 surface on smooth subsurface	II	6
YU-5496	YAX152.1B_14N-4W_7.1	-26.897	2209	19	361–303 BCE (95.4%)	Carbon from dry fill under Floor 5	III	5
YU-5497	YAX152.1B_12N-6W_7.1	-25.357	2282	21	401–357 BCE (77.8%), 285–235 BCE (17.6%)	Carbon from dry fill under Floor 5	III	5
AA104921	YAX152-2A, 14N-24W_6.2	-25.9	2,499	28	781–538 BCE (95.4%)	Plaza Center: Level chich fill below floor surface 5; Old carbon?	III	5

continued on next page

TABLE 3.1.—continued from previous page

Lab Code	Provenience	$\delta^{13}C$ value	^{14}C age BP	$\delta^{14}C$ age	calibrated 2s	Notes	Cons. Phase	Floor #
YU-5490	YAX152.1B_14N-16E	-25.445	2183	21	358–278 BCE (59.3%), 259–177 BCE (36.1%)	Carbon on Floor 6, dirt fill after strata	III	5
YU-5492	YAX152.2B_Feature 1_8.1	-26.594	2211	20	362–336 BCE (13.5%), 330–204 BCE (81.9%)	Layer 3.1. of feature 1.	III	5
YU-5499	YAX152.1B_16/14N-14E_6.2	-26.619	2243	22	386–350 BCE (26.1%), 311–209 BCE (69.3%)	In compact earthen floor matrix, representing Floor 5, unique to the area east of Str. 5E-6.	III	5
AA104918	YAX152-2A, 14N-60W_4.2	-29.7	post-bomb		1956 CE—1957 CE, 2009 CE	Contamination.	III	4
AA104926	YAX152-1-16N-16E-4.3	-26	2,259	49	401–203 BCE (95.4%)	East of 5E-6: In the soil matrix fill under dry core boulders, on top of compacted earth layer (Floor 5?), at least 30 cm and above floor 6.	III	4
YU-5485	YAX152.2A_12N-60W_4.2	-24.243	13777	40	14,952–14,479 BCE (95.4%)	Early Carbon from a late fill layer east of Str. 5E-1.	III	4
YU-5486	YAX152.2A_16N-24W_5.1	-26.585	2187	18	359–277 BCE (62.2%), 260–186 BCE (33.2%)	5 cm down in the Chacbe, a sascab causeway feature of Floor 5.	III	4
YU-5495	YAX152.1B_14N-6E_3.2	-28.210	2203	19	360–202 BCE (95.4%)	Excavations of an architectural floor west of Str. 5E-6's Old Wall.	III	4
YU-5489	YAX152.1B_12/14N-4/8W_3.1	-22.563	2188	19	359–275 BCE (61.7%), 261–192 BCE (33.7%)	Inside ceramic vessel of Floor 4 (SD #1), associated to Floor 3 construction.	III	3

Phase I

The earliest identifiable floors, 9, 10, and 11, compose Phase I. It is during this phase where we see the earliest activities occurring at Yaxuná; to date, no other occupational deposits date to Phase I across the site, although some scattered pre-Mamon material has been found in a few later contexts in other areas of the site core. From radiometric testing, we situate the dating for this early period between some time before 900 BCE and 700 BCE; the earliest carbon sample (dated to the ninth century BCE) was associated with Floor 10. Construction during Phase I is limited to the extensive plaza floor, spanning 60 m east-west and at least 40 m north-south. In part, floors 9–11 are grouped because of their composition, being distinctive mixtures of tamped earth and clay, a building tradition that is a sign of great antiquity in the Maya Lowlands (Brown 2003). Floor 11 was composed of a white mixture of tamped earth and marl that was laid directly over bedrock, with little to no fill separating the layers. The subsequent Floor 10 was constructed in three layers of tamped earth, the earliest being orange, the second being red, and the final appearing brown with small sascab inclusions, a sandy material of calcite origin (Littman 1958). Construction fill between Floors 11 and 10 consisted of large limestone cobbles, raising the overall height of the plaza by roughly 40 cm though some ceramic sherds and beads were scattered in this matrix. Floor 9, where preserved, was placed 10 cm above Floor 10, separated only by small limestone cobbles. Curiously, Floor 9 was visibly fragmented and burned leading to its poor preservation especially on the eastern side of the plaza.

Investigations of architecture during Phase I have reached only the initial phase of Str. 5E-6, the earliest range structure, and early floors in the plaza, although we suspect that Str. 5E-1, the western pyramid, likely has its origins during this period as well because of stratigraphic evidence demonstrating that Floors 9–11 extend under the surface architecture of this building. Str. 5E-6's first phase though is not defined by masonry construction but instead through a small natural rise in bedrock, standing at a height but one meter above the earliest floor surfaces. We believe that this natural bedrock feature is like the early marl pyramid and range strange structure observed at Cival (Stanton and Collins 2021). With Floor 10's construction, Str. 5E-6 was reduced to about half of its previous height though it remained a significant feature on the landscape.

On Str. 5E-6, four intentional holes roughly 25 cm in diameter, and one natural, were found sealed and extending into a possible cave system. In the central hole a short neck jar of the pre-Mamon type Chel Burnished (see Boucher and Palomo 2005) was found resting on a ledge. We understand this feature as sharing some commonalities with the famous quadripartite feature at Cival, Cache 4, which also contained water jars (Estrada-Belli 2006). A carbon sample recovered from a scraping the inside of the jar yielded a range of 748–410 BCE However, because this feature was sealed with the construction of Floor 8, we assume that it dates to the transition to Phase II. A second primary context containing ceramic sherds, likely of a single eroded vessel, was found in a feature that was subsequently replicated throughout the entire sequence of floor constructions in the plaza. The first iteration of this feature observed on Floor 11 was a small natural aperture in the bedrock sealed with a removable limestone top in an area we calculate to be the center of the plaza during this period. Subsequent floors replicate this feature with small circular stone alignments that we interpret as a fire altar (Stanton et al. n.d.).

We understand Phase I as representing a more egalitarian time at Yaxuná. No prestige wares have been recovered from this phase, there is no evidence of architectural specialization, and long-distance exchange goods are also absent. Like Ceibal, no residences are visible during this early period, and we believe that the earliest inhabitants of Yaxuná were likely more mobile although transitioning toward a sedentary lifestyle (Stanton and Collins 2017, 2021).

Phase II

During Phase II of the E Group, substantial changes are seen at Yaxuná in the form of early residences, new construction techniques, monumental architecture, prestige goods, and some non-local items (Stanton and Ardren 2005; Stanton et al. 2010). The E Group plaza was also expanded eastward by 20 m, potentially allowing for the accommodation of a larger populace. Together each of these factors suggests a general increase in complexity at the site coinciding with a fully sedentary lifestyle. In the E Group plaza, evidence of such changes is present on Floors 6, 7, and 8, a period with an AMS range between 700 and 400 BCE.

Unlike the floors of Phase I, Floors 6–8 are all composed of mixtures of sascab and earth, with increasingly more sascab in each consecutive floor. To make sascab or other limestone into stucco requires intensive burning, suggesting much more preparation and evolving technologies toward the stucco industry that characterized the Late Preclassic. This is most apparent by Floor 6 which is composed of a 20 cm layer of extremely durable sascab. The fill between each of the floors in Phase II is generally composed of small limestone cobbles, with some ceramics scattered throughout.

Architecturally, Phase II is marked by three transformations to Str. 5E-6, the early range structure. The first modification to Str. 5E-6 coincided with the laying of Floor 8 and is represented by the construction of a small platform of relatively squared limestone cobbles on top of the bedrock outcrop. With Floor 7, there is a visible shift to architecture of grander proportions and by the time Floor 7 was buried, Str. 5E-6 was raised to a height of two meters; the stones for final construction phase associated with Floor 7 were all smoothly shaped, suggesting an increase in time and resources. The earliest phase of Str. 5E-2, the second range structure standing four meters tall and representing an expanded boundary to the plaza, is also contemporary with Floor 7. The masonry stones composing Str. 5E-2 are stylistically the same as the smoothed stones previously mentioned for Str. 5E-6.

We also recorded several isolated patches of burning and two intentional cuts into Floor 7 on the eastern portion of the east-west centerline of the plaza. The features suggest ritual activity and mark the earliest observed appearance of intentionally deposited materials aside of the central feature and the cuts into the bedrock surface of Str. 5E-6's first phase discussed above. Within the cuts, several materials were found, notably a large ceramic rim sherd and a polished fragment of non-local magnetite, a form of iron ore typically mined in Oaxaca and found among roughly contemporaneous Gulf Coast sites (Flannery and Winter 1976). Along with contemporary deposits containing malachite at Str. 6E-32 (Stanton 2017), part of the first identifiable domestic context at Yaxuná and contemporaneous with Phase II, the magnetite marks some of the earliest non-local prestige items to be observed at Yaxuná.

Floor 6 was extended over the entire plaza of the E Group and was constructed in three phases. First, a layer of small-fill limestone cobbles was tightly laid over Floor 7, as was customary in this phase. Second, a 10 cm thick layer of course sascab with small, gravel-like limestone inclusions was poured. Finally, a second 10 cm layer of durable sascab was poured and smoothed to an incredibly well-preserved finish, making it the most durable surface to date.

Phase III

Phase III marks the transition to the Late Preclassic at the E Group. Radiocarbon dates from the Floors 5, 4, and 3 of this phase have a range between 400 and 200 BCE. It is during this time that the site underwent what is perhaps its largest transformation. Several new monumental groups were initiated at Yaxuná during this period and arranged along the cardinal axes, with the E Group in the center (Stanton and Freidel 2005). Additionally, this is the period when we see hinterland growth at Yaxuná, with the neighboring site of Tzacauil established and linked to the site via an extensive causeway (Hutson et al. 2012). It is during this period that Stanton and Collins (2021) believe that Yaxuná took on many of the characteristics of a city and perhaps those developing toward that of a state. Exemplifying this is material evidence of increased stratification, population growth, monumental construction, concerted specialization, and access to new long-distance resources.

The floors of Phase III are remarkably consistent in composition and visually distinct from all other phases. Floors 5–3 are composed of a distinctly reddish orange sascab and are much thinner than previous phases, being only around 3–5 cm in thickness. The latest phase, Floor 3, is even coated in a thin veneer of stucco, a material that would have aided in the floor's water resistance, which is characteristic of Yaxuná's floors during the later Classic period.

The planning of Phase III was literally etched into the surface of Floor 6, where the path of a causeway placed in association with Floor 5 was incised into the surface of this previous floor. When thinking of complexity, the notion of planning, especially in an urban context, is often thought to coincide with a centralized authority and with increased hierarchy (Smith 2007). On Floor 6, four sets of incised lines were documented. With some overlap between features, the purpose for the lines varied from civic planning, the marking spaces of continued social significance (collective memory), and the incorporation of external traditions. The line features to note here specifically are rectangular and span the entirety of the east-west central axis of the plaza. Patterned in 160 cm squares, the lines were remarkably well crafted, with each segment being a consistent length. Between the lines, small stone cobbles were compactly fitted together, being fixed by sascab in certain areas. Outside the lines, a different fill pattern was observed of large limestone blocks, which created a visible difference. When the sascab of Floor 5 was being laid over the fill, the area of small compact cobbles, resting directly over the incised lines, was treated differently. This space was coated in a deep red-orange sascab and raised to a height of 25 cm above the plaza floor, establishing a small causeway directly linking structures 5E-1 to 5E-6. It is possible that the small causeway served as a performative stage or procession for an individual of political or religious significance, potentially like the depictions found on the San Bartolo murals (Taube et al. 2010) and/or that the causeway was placed over some large patolli board that covered the plaza. Additionally, several patterned post holes were found along the edge of the causeway, potentially representing a scaffold, while in the center of the plaza, three posts were found, mirroring the sacrificial altars also depicted on the San Bartolo murals. Taken together, the planning and construction of causeway, its potential function as a stage-like procession, its associated features, and parallels to the imagery depicted on the San Bartolo murals are suggestive of the beginnings of more centralized authority at Yaxuná.

Nothing with Phase III was done haphazardly. While the fill between Floors 6 and 5 was patterned to accommodate the construction of new architectural features, it was also used to conceal portions of Str. 5E-6, reducing its height to one meter above the plaza surface. This reduction in height for Str. 5E-6 coincided with the largest single phase of construction for Str. 5E-2, which was raised to a height of seven meters (not accounting for the height of the poorly preserved superstructures), and 5F-1 (the Central Acropolis), which now reached upward of 20 m (Stanton et al. 2010). Additionally, the masonry stones of this phase were carved with precision, with sharp edges that locked in place with prepared foundations on the ground.

The choice of color with the floors of Phase III also marks a significant shift in aesthetics from a cream-like white to a reddish orange. On a cross-section of the causeway, we observed that the materials composing the sascab varied in color, while the outside veneer was always finished in reddish orange. This observation shows intent to emphasize the reddish orange color of the final product.

While the depositing of whole ceramic vessels was rare in the E Group at Yaxuná (given that we excavated along the centerline where we would expect such deposits to occur, we do not believe this is an issue of sampling), a Ciego Composite bowl containing a single greenstone bead was found in the purely sascab fill between Floors 4 and 3 in the plaza. To deposit the bowl, a circular area of about 25 cm in diameter, at a depth roughly 15 cm, was cut into Floor 4. The sascab mixture of Floor 3 was later poured directly over the feature. This bowl was significantly placed in an area that had been marked on previous spaces, suggesting a continuity of activities within this space.

Phase IV

The final period of building in the E Group occurred in Phase IV. The dating of this phase is difficult to determine, as no sealed contexts were recovered from the plaza during this period. This phase began sometime after 200 BCE, but it is unclear when the plaza was abandoned except to note that none of the E Group plaza floors appear to date past the end of the Preclassic. Phase IV, composed of the poorly preserved Floors 2 and 1, saw some minor modification to Str. 5E-6 though nothing monumental in scale or proportion, and while some Flaky Ware ceramics have been recovered, the typical bichromes of the Terminal Preclassic are absent. Scattered materials from the Late and Terminal Classic periods are found in the upper layers in contexts not sealed by floors, but none of these materials appear to date known construction phases, and it is known that Yaxuná was a thriving center until at least 900 CE (Suhler et al. 1998).

In the E Group's waning years, the complex was subject to less investment from political authorities, who shifted the focus of monumental construction to the much more restricted and less public monumental groups (Stanton and Collins 2021). This shift signifies a sense of further stratification at Yaxuná during the latter portion of the Late Preclassic. Like many other sites throughout the central lowlands, the shift away from the public E Group to a more private triadic acropolis group appears intentional and likely related to the advent of dynastic rulership (Saturno et al. 2017).

Termination events mark the visible end of reverent cultural activities to take place within the E Group, bringing about an end to a continuity of events, traditions, and memory that spanned roughly a thousand years of occupation. The plaza's original center, where continuity was present on every single floor phase present in the area, was deeply cut into, penetrating three phases of floors in an area two meters in diameter. This aperture was then filled with centrally aligned large and compacted fill stones, which were then coated in a light layer of earth.

Str. 5E-6 was subject to similar happenings, with the final phase's floor being cut into, covered with large stones, and eventually coated with ash, marl, and a thin layer of dirt. While it is unclear if the other buildings in the complex were subject to similar activities, Str. 5E-2 was subject to stone looting for other masonry projects, and a nearly complete Flor Cream vase was left exposed at the base of the centerline area associated with the final construction phase. Together, these factors showcase a final shift away from the more egalitarian foundations of the E Group to a more stratified organization that characterizes the Classic period. Now we turn to a discussion of the ceramic data.

CERAMIC ANALYSIS

Phase I

The ceramics from Phase I can generally be considered belonging to a pre-Mamom Middle Preclassic complex, which we now refer to as the Laapal Complex (see Stanton et al., in press). This complex is divided into two facets: Early Laapal (?-900 BCE, primarily coming from a trash pit dating prior the construction of Floor 11); and Late Laapal (900–700 BCE), which shares burnished and wash surface treatments, although the first true slips and certain surface colors (e.g., Almeja Burnished Gray) begin to appear only by the Late Laapal (see Stanton et al., in press). Little has been published concerning such materials in the northern lowlands, although there has been some consensus reached that some of the materials in Andrews (1988; see also Boucher and Palomo 2005) Ek Complex at Komchén date to this early time. Without doubt, these are among the earliest ceramics in the northern Maya Lowlands, but considerable regional work is still needed to better understand temporal and regional variability among these early materials in this area of the lowlands. With that said, we appear to see some stratigraphic variability in the Yaxuná samples from the E Group units. For example, burnishing and wash surface treatments appear to be exclusive to the earliest deposits (the pre-Mamom Early and Late Laapal Complexes, 84% of the material exhibits this surface treatment), while some slips, particularly in brown and orange (although some cream-colored examples are also present) appear toward the end of the phase (only 0.02% of the total complex). The burnished patterning reported by Brainerd for the Yotolín Group was virtually absent in the collection; while there were some possible small sherds with potential burnished patterning, none was identified with certainty.

In general, these ceramics are not particularly well fired, suggesting that firing technologies were somewhat rudimentary and could not reach the higher temperatures of later periods, possibly indicating open-pit firing (figure 3.3a). While burnishing (Chel burnished brown [Boucher and Palomo 2005], Huchim rosy burnished [Boucher and Palomo 2005], and Almeja burnished gray [Andrews 1988]) and unslipped light striations or impressions (possible textile or fibrous

FIGURE 3.3A. *Photo of Laapal Complex ceramics.*

materials such as palm fibers, a the type called Kanxoc Striated [Stanton et al., in press]) were the most common surface treatments, washes, specifically in brown color (Hunukú brown burnished wash) but also in black and possibly cream colors, appear fairly early in the Yaxuná sequence as the first steps toward a slip technology. By the end of the Laapal Complex, the brown washes evolve into a slip (Dzeal brown) that does not appear to adhere particularly well to the walls of the fabric but seem to be moving toward the Dzudzuquil Group of the following Hok'ol Complex (corresponding to the Early Nabanché Complex defined by Andrews [1988] at Komchén), and waxy-like finishes, possibly a result of using *jabonoso* clays, are present. Better-made orange slips that are well within the color range of the Kin Group also appear. As Stanton and Ardren (2005) note, Juventud Group ceramics tend more toward orange tones in older deposits, and while Juventud and Kin group materials can be separated in older Early Nabanché deposits, they share a common technological origin with these early orange pre-Mamom Kin Group ceramics, the primary technological difference most likely being the amount of dilution of the clay for the slips when applied.

One of the most striking features of these early materials is the fabric composition. In general, there is a substantial amount of crypto-crystalline temper (termed *ji* by Yucatecan potters [Thompson 1958]). Further, this temper, as well as other tempering elements, is not found to be in a very fine state but tends to be rather course compared to the following Hok'ol Complex ceramics. While not used much today, *ji* has been traditionally used in Yucatán to temper cooking vessels. As our experimental work with *ji* has demonstrated, in certain amounts, *ji* increases the resistance of pottery to catastrophic failure due to direct exposure to fire (Stanton and Gremion 2011). Macroscopic and petrographic analysis confirms that *ji* is almost always found in short-necked jars (such as those of the Achiotes, Yokat, Tipikal, Unto, and Pisté groups), where use-wear analysis indicates substantial frequency of burning toward the bases of vessels. However, the occurrence of *ji* during pre-Mamom times seems to be independent of vessel form, and the rather course grain sizes indicates that it may have been present in the clays. *Ji* forms through the process of water filtration in limestone. While it can be found in small solution cavities near the surface, it is heavily present in caves. Flowstone and speleothems in caves throughout the Maya Lowlands are composed of *ji*; in fact, the common way for potters in Ticul to collect *ji* in the mid-twentieth century was to build a fire on the wall of a cave to spall it off. We know that the Maya were entering caves during pre-Mamon times, as caves are the locations where archaeologists most commonly encounter the bottle-shaped vessels of the Brainerd's (1958; see also Smith 1971) Yotolín Group; we argue that this ceramic group has now been effectively rendered useless by the creation of the Chel, Huchim, and Almeja groups (see Stanton et al., in press) and will not use it here. The Maya at this time may have been using the caves to collect water and/or for ritual purposes, but they may have also noted a rather obvious fact: caves are prime locations for clay development off weathering limestone (Uc 2004, 2006), locations that are easier to identify and mine than most others such as the famous mines of Yokat (Arnold and Bohor 1977). The presence of coarse *ji* suggests that the pre-Mamom Maya were using clay from caves, which had a high content of cryptocrystalline inclusions, or that they were collecting and coarsely grinding materials from the cave walls and/or other features. In any event, these Maya do not seem to have been exploiting harder-to-find sources, and their choice of temper seems to have been rather rudimentary.

Finally, the suite of vessel forms during this period was very limited (figure 3.3b). The pre-Mamom ceramics from the E Group are primarily short-necked

FIGURE 3.3B. *Profiles of Laapal Complex ceramics.*

jars, sometimes thought to be water jars by researchers but that as mentioned above were also used as cooking pots. Baskets may have been used for boiling food prior to ceramics (and quite likely somewhat after as well), yet despite fire-cracked rock being reported with some frequency in the Maya area, little is known about baskets and their uses in this area of the world. Some large (30–36 cm diameter) everted flat-bottom bowls are also in the collection, although their numbers pale in comparison to the jars (making up over 90% of the collection). In Classic period iconography, such bowls are depicted as serving vessels, often shown containing tamales (Taube 1989). In general, the size of these kinds of bowls is quite large during the Preclassic, although as we will discuss below, smaller sizes appear with increasing frequency during the Late Preclassic. The large size of serving bowls may indicate that food was served in a communal setting at this time and that by the Classic period, the structure of food consumption had changed and individual serving vessels were the norm. Additionally, very few *cuencos*—small, thin-walled, round-bottom bowls—and bottles were recovered in the excavations. Incurving bowls, or *tecomates*, while present at this time, are rare throughout the entire Yaxuná sequence, a notable pattern for the early periods given their relatively frequent occurrence among early semi-sedentary societies elsewhere in Mesoamerica (Arnold 1999). Decorative designs were limited in the collection, restricted to post-firing incised hatching on flat-bottom bowls and some jars, as has been reported at other sites in Yucatán (Andrews 1988; Ceballos and Robles 2012), although these decorations appear closer to the transition to Hok'ol Complex contexts than at the beginning of the Laapal Complex sequence.

Phase II

Phase II ceramics correspond to the Hok'ol Complex at Yaxuná (700–300 BCE), related to the broader Mamom phenomenon and the better known Early Nabanché

Complex from Komchén in the northern lowlands (Andrews 1988). In contrast to the Phase I ceramics, Phase II ceramics are much better made. Their increased hardness indicates advances in firing technology that allowed for higher temperatures. Changes in tempering materials and their preparation likely increased the durability of the ceramics at this time as well. In particular, finely ground sascab was adopted as the primary tempering material, although other tempers, such as *ji*, were still utilized in particular vessel forms such as jars. Interestingly, the appearance of sascab tempering material coincides with the first attempts at sascab floors at the E Group, suggesting that sascab mining first took place in earnest at the beginning of Mamom times. Other technological changes in the ceramics from this period can also be noted, including the use of white clay under-slips that help adhere other "flaky clays," such as many of the red and black tones, to the vessel walls. Monochrome and bichrome slip treatments are common during this period in tones of black, cream-to-buff, red, and orange. Some of the black tones appear to be slips, while others are clearly the result of placing vessels into burning vegetation, fixing the smoke particles to the vessel walls. Decorative techniques include pre-slip and post-slip incisions, fluting, and chamfering, as well as some occasional black trickle and simple negative line designs.

As with Phase I materials, Phase II materials lack some of the common vessel forms found later in the sequence (figure 3.4). Basins, for example, are conspicuously absent, and the primary forms found in Phase II continue to be short-necked jars and large everted flat bottom bowls (30–53 cm diameter), the latter found with increasing frequency. As noted by other scholars, the relative frequency (still under 1.0% of the total collection at Yaxuná) of fluted and chamfered designs indicates a desire to replicate gourds, likely the preferred containers for holding and consuming liquids prior to this time; gourds are never fully replaced, but ceramics seem to be preferred in certain contexts beginning at the outset of the Mamom times. Some very fine thin-walled jars and bowls also appear. A few spouted vessels, argued to be "chocolate-pots" (e.g., Powis et al. 2002), are also found during this period, although they are rare (under 0.1% of the collection). Regardless, the suite of forms during Phase I indicates the same types of uses for ceramics as Phase I: storing and serving liquids, cooking, and serving food.

Phase III

Phase III materials correspond to the Ka'nal Complex (300 BCE–1 CE), Yaxuná's version of the Chicanel Sphere ceramics of the Late Preclassic. As Anderson (2014) and others have noted, most Chicanel types are in some way a continuation of Mamom types in terms of their surface treatment and decoration, and at times it can be difficult to distinguish fragmentary ceramics from one period to another. With that said, probably the most striking changes between the ceramics from the two periods are in the vessel forms (figure 3.5).

FIGURE 3.4. *Profiles of Hok'ol Complex ceramics.*

FIGURE 3.5. *Profiles of Ka'nal Complex ceramics.*

Besides minor changes to rim shapes such as less everted lips, there is more variety of general shapes within the Yaxuná collection. While jars and large flat-bottom bowls still dominate, jars are more restricted to unslipped ceramic groups such as Sabán, Achiotes, and Chancenote; the Flor Group is an exception to this trend, with fairly high frequencies of jars, making up over a third of the sherds from this type. The highly popular and slipped Sierra and Ucú group forms, however, are dominated by large flat-bottom bowls. Within the Sierra Group, we do see more diversity, though. For instance, some of the bowls are smaller, resembling Classic period bowls, and some have composite shapes with straight everted rims and round bases. Yet one of the more telling changes is the appearance of basins and "buckets." While not particularly large (18–32 cm diameter) and still quite rare in the collection, we argue that these shapes represent a set of activities, such as storage and fermentation, that hint at higher levels of permanence at particular places on the landscape. While the "bucket" shapes would eventually disappear, basins increase in frequency and size at Yaxuná during the Classic period and would be a hallmark for practices that reflect a highly sedentary agricultural lifestyle.

Phase IV

Phase IV ceramics are the most difficult to assess, as the last two floors associated with this phase are close to the surface and not very well preserved. Bioturbation and the mixing of later materials deposited when the E Group was in ruins are issues. With that said, the current data suggest that this phase also dates to the Ka'nal Complex, and we did not notice major differences in the ceramics when compared to Phase III. Some Flaky Ware ceramics were present in these upper strata, suggesting that the switch to light-colored clays prominent during the Terminal Preclassic in the central portion of the peninsula had begun (see Glover and Stanton 2010), but their frequencies were minimal in the collections.

DISCUSSION

The ceramics at Yaxuná changed over time in many important ways. Yet perhaps no change was more significant for understanding the profound shifts of lifeways experienced by Maya populations over the course of the Preclassic period as that in vessel forms. The relative lack of variety of vessel forms during pre-Mamon and Mamon times is telling of a lifestyle still heavily rooted in the idea of mobility. As Inomata and his colleagues (2015) have cogently argued, pre-Mamon E Groups served as fixed spatial points on a landscape for relatively mobile peoples to gather, exchange ideas and goods, socialize, and engage in ritual practices, all leading to the creation, maintenance, and transformation of community identities. The early focus on short-necked jars and, slightly later, large everted flat-bottomed bowls during the Laapal Complex suggests a focus on food preparation and consumption, much as has been argued in other early Mesoamerican contexts (Clark and Blake 1994). Further, we argue that the lack of later forms such as basins used for diverse activities such as fermentation and storage indicates a society still in transition to a sedentary life. The very low numbers of *tecomates*, however, might indicate that by the time Yaxuná was founded, this form, often associated with more mobile populations (e.g., Clark and Cheetham 2005), was already phased out of the northern lowland "container complex" (Nelson 2001) or alternatively that it was not reproduced in pottery and instead, gourds continued to be used for these kinds of restricted-mouth bowls. In any event, Laapal Complex pottery forms suggest a semi-sedentary lifestyle.

While Laapal pottery is fairly well shaped, there are indicators that would suggest a fairly simple production process compared to later periods. First, this early pottery appears to have been fired at relatively low temperatures, indicating that firing technologies were not well developed. Although pottery kilns have not been well reported in the Maya Lowlands, this does not mean that fairly complex kilns did not exist. Seligson and his colleagues (2017) have now reported kilns for lime production in the Puuc region, and traditional ceramic kilns in towns like Mama and Ticul would not leave much of a surface trace beyond a small pile of unfinished stones and perhaps some preserved daub. However, as we argued previously, we believe that the range of temperatures that Laapal Complex pottery was fired most likely fits into the range appropriate for simple pit-firing, not a technology that would require much specialization. Further, if we are correct in our inference that the temper could have existed in the clays (possibly coming from cave contexts) as natural inclusions, then this would support the idea that the production sequence was much simpler than it was in later periods, when specific tempers were sought and, in many cases, ground to much more specific sizes. We suggest that these data indicate that while Laapal pottery production required some specialized knowledge, it was not at a level of specialized craft production that would characterize later periods, which not surprising given the level of mobility that still may have typified Laapal times.

During Hok'ol times, pottery production appears to have become more complex, with specific tempers being targeted. As we mentioned, the fact that sascab tempers and floors appear around the same time suggests that both ceramic and stucco technologies were tied to the mining of this material around or after 700 BCE. Stucco technologies took some time to develop into the rock-hard prepared surfaces that are found in Ka'nal times, but the use of sascab as temper had an immediate impact on the craftsmanship of pottery, aiding in the production of more durable ceramic vessels. It is difficult to assess the implications of sascab mining in Middle Preclassic Maya society. While it could have occurred on a part-time basis, easily conducted by non-specialists, the amount of sascab consumed was considerable when taking into account known stucco features (the floors, although it is possible that other stucco features such as masks and facades still lie hidden and/or have been obliterated by the elements) and ceramics; there are substantial stucco floors in both the E Group and the 6E-30 group, and nearly all of the Middle Preclassic ceramics have sascab as temper. In any event, we suggest that it is possible that the development of these sascab-based technologies indicate changes in production systems whereby some members of the society became increasingly specialized in the working of certain materials. Potters in Yucatán today do not often mine the sascab themselves but hire others to excavate and transport this material to their workshops. While we might not know if the organization of labor was similar in the past, the fact there was a lot of experimentation with sascab in both ceramic and stucco media that resulted in substantial increases in the functional performance of these materials by the end of the Middle Preclassic would suggest that much more time was being spent by individuals on tasks associated with their production. By the Late Classic period, both stucco and ceramics appear to be produced by specialists (e.g., Reents-Budet et al. 2000; Seligson et al. 2017) and potentially to have been distributed in a market system (e.g., King 2015). While the origins of a market system in the Maya area are still unclear, data suggesting increasing specialization in material classes such as ceramics as well as the potential of early E Group complexes serving a regional nexuses for exchange systems (Inomata et al. 2015; Stanton and Collins 2017) may indicate that substantial changes in the organization of Maya economies occurred around the time when evidence for "divine" kingship in the Maya Lowlands becomes more apparent (e.g., Andrews 1981; Saturno et al. 2005).

Hok'ol pottery also includes some vessel forms that indicate changes in consumption practices. In particular, the appearance of spouted vessels, which have been linked to chocolate consumption elsewhere in the Maya Lowlands (Powis et al. 2002), and thinner and more finely made drinking forms suggest that the consumption of prestige drinks was occurring at this time, if not before (we are unaware of any residue studies of pre-Mamom pottery to indicate the consumption of chocolate-based beverages during this early period in the Maya Lowlands). Much has been made of the consumption of cacao in elite contexts (especially during the Classic period), and it has been argued that cacao beans could function as a fungible resource (papers in King 2015). Given the presence of these forms, we infer that cacao was likely consumed during Hok'ol times. Yet it is not just that cacao was consumed but the ceramic forms in which it was consumed that draw our attention. The introduction of finely made specialized drinking vessels suggests that the consumption of prestige items was now more formalized, indicating a further elaboration of ideas concerning wealth and prestige occurred at this time, just several centuries prior to the Late Preclassic, when formal images of divine kings appear in the Maya Lowlands

(Andrews 1981; Saturno et al. 2005). This formalization may indicate the use of consumption to create and maintain social bonds not just among smaller corporate groups but among more distant groups of emerging elites, who may have viewed their identities along more recent class divisions than tied directly to specific places on the landscape. Interestingly, cacao is linked to market economies during later periods (e.g., King 2015), making us wonder how early cacao might have been used as a fungible resource in the Maya Lowlands. As Inomata and his colleagues (2015; see also Doyle 2013; Stanton and Collins 2017) have proposed, E Groups were gathering places during the Middle Preclassic, where still relatively mobile populations could come together to participate in social, political, ritual, and economic activities. E Group plazas may have been the first formalized architectural spaces where exchange took place, functioning as a sort of antecedent to later marketplaces (Stanton 2017). Much like other places throughout the world where mobile populations come together for exchange on a seasonal cycle, very early E Groups may have provided the physical space for exchange on a specific calendrical timetable much like has been proposed for markets linked to pilgrimage centers in the Late Postclassic (Ringle et al. 1998). The appearance of spouted and finely made drinking vessels, then, may indicate a change in attitudes toward exchange and how Maya economies functioned. While this is a difficult proposition to test, it is food for thought.

By the Late Preclassic, the Maya were more firmly committed to adapting their daily practices to a more spatially fixed agricultural lifestyle and, by that time, the attempts at urbanism and state formation that would come with it. During Ka'nal Complex times, we begin to see ceramic evidence for the changes to a more sedentary way of life, and ceramic forms became more diversified. The appearance of basins and "buckets" happens during the Late Preclassic and may indicate significant changes concerning storage and possibly food preparation. We also see an increase in smaller bowls, possibly indicating that serving food began to happen more regularly on an individual basis rather than in communal settings. It is tempting to think that this change might have something to do with a shift in the role of kin groups given that the Late Preclassic is likely a time that lowland Maya society was undergoing increased stratification. This is a difficult hypothesis to test, however, since the kinds of iconographic and epigraphic data concerning pottery available for the Classic period (e.g., Houston et al. 1989) are virtually nonexistent for the Preclassic.

One last pattern of note is something that we have not mentioned up to this point—the complete lack of ceramic figurines. At Yaxuná, and for the northern lowlands in general, figurines are not at all common. There are no figurines reported from Preclassic contexts at Yaxuná in over thirty years of relatively sustained research at the site. Given the occurrence of Preclassic figurines elsewhere in the Maya Lowlands, as well as how common they are in other parts of Mesoamerica (e.g., DeLance 2016; Halperin 2014; Halperin et al. 2009; Lesure 1997), we find this pattern striking. Much has been made of figurines and their potential roles in ancestor worship and kin relations for this early period. Were such images just made out of perishable materials in the early north? Did other kinds of objects fill the roles of figurines? These are difficult questions to answer given the data available. Yet it is clear that while ceramics played an important role in the changes that northern lowland Maya societies experienced throughout the Preclassic period, ceramic figurines do not seem to have played a part.

In sum, the ceramics from the E Group at Yaxuná indicate several notable patterns over time that can relate them to changes in complexity. First, from pre-Mamom to Late Preclassic times, the data suggest an increase in specialized knowledge for production. Pre-Mamom materials were not well made in comparison to later materials from the Mamom and Chicanel spheres. By the beginning of the Hok'ol Complex, the ubiquitous and large-scale use of sascab in both ceramic and stucco materials suggests that perhaps specialized mining occurred. Further, it is likely that more formal kilns were constructed to manufacture these materials at the quality we see them in the material record. The appearance of the first formal households at Yaxuná during Hok'ol times indicates that the increasing quality of materials like ceramics was done in a social context of increasing residential sedentism and that ideas of being fixed on the landscape had an impact on the ability of certain craft-workers to invest more time and energy to producing higher quality products.

Second, there are substantial changes in the vessel forms between the Middle and Late Preclassic. In particular, the appearance of basins that could have functioned as storage vessels may indicate that the Late Preclassic is when the Maya at Yaxuná more fully embraced a sedentary lifestyle. Further, the increase in smaller, more individual serving vessels may indicate changing attitudes concerning food consumption in the context of social bonding. While we are cautious about going too far with the interpretations of this last pattern, it could possibly be linked to the partial fraying of kin-group bonds with the formation of new social and political relationships that accompanied the more stratified social contexts that appear to have existed at this time. In any event, it is clear that while there is still much more work to be done on this subject, data concerning craft production have much to offer to our understandings of how more complex social, political, and economic structures emerged and transformed over time.

Acknowledgments. We thank the Consejo de Arqueología of the Instituto Nacional de Antropología e Historia for granting the permits to conduct this research; all data are cultural patrimony of Mexico. This research was generously supported by the Fundación Roberto Hernández, Fundación Pedro y Elena Hernández, the Selz Foundation, and Jerry Murdoch. This paper benefited from discussions with George Bey and Teresa Ceballos, although the final product is the sole responsibility of the authors. Finally, we thank the community of Yaxuná for allowing us to conduct research in their ejido.

REFERENCES

Anderson, David S. 2014. "The Pottery of Xtobó, Yucatán, Mexico: A Case Study of Maya Pottery Analysis." In *The Archaeology of Yucatán: New Directions and Data*, edited by T. W. Stanton, 123–44. BAR International Series. Oxford: Archaeopress.

Andrews, Anthony P. 1981. "El guerrero de Loltún: Comentario analítico." *Boletín de la Escuela de Ciencias Antropológicas de la Universidad de Yucatán* 48–49:36–50.

Andrews, E. Wyllys, V. 1988. "Ceramic Units from Komchen, Yucatan, Mexico." *Cerámica de Cultura Maya* 15:51–64.

Andrews, E. Wyllys, V, and William M. Ringle. 1992. "Los mayas tempranos en Yucatán: investigaciones arqueológicas en Komchen." *Mayab* 8:5–17.

Arnold, Dean E., and Bruce F. Bohor. 1977. "The Ancient Clay Mine at Yo' K'at, Yucatan." *American Antiquity* 42:575–82.

Arnold, Phillip J., III. 1999. "*Tecomates*, Residential Mobility, and Early Formative Occupation in Coastal Lowland Mesoamerica." In *Pottery and People: A Dynamic Interaction*, edited by J. M. Skibo and G. M. Feinman, 157–70. Salt Lake City: University of Utah Press.

Boucher, Sylviane, and Yoly Palomo. 2005. "Cerámica del Preclásico Medio y Tardío en depósitos sellados del sitio de Tzubil, Yucatán." *Temas Antropológicos* 27:153–88.

Brainerd, George W. 1958. *The Archaeological Ceramics of Yucatan*. Anthropological Records, Vol. 19. Berkeley: University of California.

Brown, M. Kathryn. 2003. "Emerging Complexity in the Maya Lowlands: A View from Blackman Eddy, Belize." PhD diss., Southern Methodist University.

Brown, M. Kathryn, and George J. Bey III, eds. 2018. *Pathways to Complexity: A View from the Maya Lowlands*. Gainesville: University Press of Florida.

Ceballos Gallareta, Teresa, and Fernando Robles Castellanos. 2012. "Las etapas más tempranas de la alfarería maya en al noroeste de la península de Yucatán." *Ancient Mesoamerica* 23:403–19.

Clark, John E., and Michael Blake. 1994. The Power of Prestige: Competitive Generosity and the Emergence of Rank Societies in Lowland Mesoamerica. In *Factional Competition and Political Development in the New World*, edited by E. M. Brumfiel and J. W. Fox, 17–30. Cambridge, UK: Cambridge University Press.

Clark, John E., and David Cheetham. 2005. Cerámica del Formativo de Chiapas. In *La producción alfarera en el México antiguo I*, edited by B. L. Merino Carrión and A. García Cook, 285–433. Mexico, DF: Instituto Nacional de Antropología e Historia.

DeLance, Lisa. 2016. "Enchaining Kinship: Figurines and State formation at Cahal Pech, Cayo, Belize." PhD diss., University of California, Riverside.

Doyle, James A. 2013. "The First Maya 'Collapse': The End of the Preclassic Period at El Palmar, Petén, Guatemala." PhD diss., Brown University.

Estrada-Belli, Francisco. 2006. "Lightning, Sky, Rain, and the Maize God: The Ideology of Preclassic Maya Rulers at Cival, Petén, Guatemala." *Ancient Mesoamerica* 17 (1): 57–78.

Flannery, Kent V., and Marcus C. Winter. 1976. "Analyzing Household Activities." In *The Early Mesoamerican Village*, edited by K. V. Flannery, 34–47. New York: Academic Press.

Freidel, David A., Arlen F. Chase, Anne S. Dowd, and Jerry Murdock, eds. 2017. *Early Maya E-Groups, Solar Calendars, and the Role of Astronomy in the Rise of Lowland Maya Urbanism.* Gainesville: University of Florida Press.

Glover, Jeffrey B., and Travis W. Stanton. 2010. "Assessing the Role of Preclassic Traditions in the Formation of Early Classic Yucatec Cultures." *Journal of Field Archaeology* 35:58–77.

Gremion, Daniela, Travis W. Stanton, and Rodrigo Martín Morales. 2014. "Etnoanálisis, arqueología experimental y la cerámica maya de Yucatán: Resultados de la resistencia tensil." In *The Archaeology of Yucatán: New Directions and Data*, edited by T. W. Stanton, 467–76. BAR International Series. Oxford: Archaeopress.

Halperin, Christina T., 2014. *State and Household: The Sociality of Maya Figurines.* Austin: University of Texas Press.

Halperin, Christina T., Katherine Faust, Rhonda Taube, and Aurore Giguet, eds. 2009. *Mesoamerican Figurines: Small Scale Indices Large Scale Phenomena.* Gainesville: University Press of Florida.

Hammond, Norman. 1999. "The Genesis of Hierarchy: Mortuary and Offertory Ritual in the Pre-Classic at Cuello, Belize." In *Social Patterns in Pre-Classic Mesoamerica*, edited by D. C. Grove and R. A. Joyce, 49–66. Washington, DC: Dumbarton Oaks.

Hansen, Richard D. 1998. "Continuity and Disjunction: The Pre-Classic Antecedents of Classic Maya Architecture." In *Function and Meaning in Classic Maya Architecture*, edited by S. D. Houston, 49–122. Washington, DC: Dumbarton Oaks.

Houston, Stephen D., David Stuart, and Karl A. Taube. 1989. "Folk Classification of Classic Maya Pottery." *American Anthropologist* 91:720–26.

Hutson, Scott R., Aline Magnoni, Travis W. Stanton. 2012. "'All That Is Solid . . .': Sacbes, Settlement, and Semiotics at Tzacauil, Yucatan." *Ancient Mesoamerica* 23:297–311.

Inomata, Takeshi, Jessica MacLellan, Daniela Triadan, Jessica Munson, Melissa Burham, Kazuo Aoyama, Hiroo Nasu, Flory Pinzón, and Hitoshi Yonenobu. 2015. "The Development of Sedentary Communities in the Maya Lowlands: Co-existing Mobile Groups and Public Ceremonies at Ceibal, Guatemala." *PNAS* 112 (14): 4268–73.

King, Eleanor M., ed. 2015. *The Ancient Maya Marketplace: The Archaeology of Transient Space.* Tucson: University of Arizona Press.

Lesure, Richard G. 1997. "Figurines and Social Identities in Early Sedentary Societies of Coastal Chiapas, Mexico, 1550–800 B.C." In *Women in Prehistory: North America and*

Mesoamerica, edited by Cheryl Claassen and Rosemary A. Joyce, 227–48. Philadelphia: University of Pennsylvania Press.

Littman, Edwin R. 1958. "Ancient Mesoamerican Mortars, Plasters, and Stuccos: The Composition and Origin of Sascab." *American Antiquity* 24:172–76.

Nelson, Kit R. 2001. "The Container Complex: Ethnographic and Environmental Patterning." PhD diss., Southern Methodist University.

Pellecer Alecio, Mónica. 2005. "El Grupo Jabalí: Un complejo arquitectónico de patrón triádico en San Bartolo, Petén." In *XIX Simposio de Investigaciones Arqueológicas en Guatemala*, edited by J. P. Laporte and H. Escobedo, 937–48. Guatemala: Museo Nacional de Arqueología y Etnología.

Powis, Terry G., Fred Valdez Jr., Thomas R. Hester, W. J. Hurst, and S. M. Tarka. 2002. "Spouted Vessels and Cacao Use among the Preclassic Maya." *Latin American Antiquity* 13:85–106.

Reents-Budet, Dorie, Ronald L. Bishop, Jennifer T. Taschek, and Joseph W. Ball. 2000. "Out of the Palace Dumps." *Ancient Mesoamerica* 11:99–121.

Reilly, F. Kent, III. 1994. "Visions to Another World: Art, Shamanism, and Political Power in Middle Formative Mesoamerica." PhD diss., University of Texas, Austin.

Ringle, William M., Tomás Gallareta Negrón, and George J. Bey III. 1998. "The Return of Quetzalcoatl: Evidence for the Spread of a World Religion During the Epiclassic Period." *Ancient Mesoamerica* 9:183–232.

Saturno, William A., Boris Beltrán, and Franco D. Rossi. 2017. "Time to Rule: Celestial Observation and Appropriation among the Early Maya." In *Early Maya E-Groups, Solar Calendars, and the Role of Astronomy in the Rise of Lowland Maya Urbanism*, edited by D. A. Freidel, A. F. Chase, A. S. Dowd, and J. Murdock, 328–60. Gainesville: University of Florida Press.

Saturno, William A., Karl A. Taube, and David Stuart. 2005. *The Murals of San Bartolo, El Peten, Guatemala. Part 1, North Wall*. Ancient America 7. Barnardsville, NC: Center for Ancient American Studies.

Seligson, Kenneth, Tomás Gallareta Negrón, Rossana May Ciau, and George J. Bey III. 2017. "Burnt Lime Production and the Pre-Columbian Maya Socio-economy: A Case Study from the Northern Yucatán." *Journal of Archaeological Science* 48:281–94.

Smith, Michael E. 2007. "Form and Meaning in the Earliest Cities: A New Approach to Ancient Urban Planning." *Journal of Planning History* 6:3–47.

Smith, Robert E. 1971. *The Pottery of Mayapan*. Papers of the Peabody Museum of Archaeology and Ethnology, Vol. 66. Cambridge, MA: Harvard University Press.

Stanton, Travis W. 2017. "The Founding of Yaxuná: Place and Trade in Preclassic Yucatan." In *Early Maya E-Groups, Solar Calendars, and the Role of Astronomy in the Rise of Lowland Maya Urbanism*, edited by D. A. Freidel, A. F. Chase, A. S. Dowd, and J. Murdock, 450–79. Gainesville: University of Florida Press.

Stanton, Travis W., and Traci Ardren. 2005. "The Middle Formative of Yucatán in Context: The View from Yaxuná." *Ancient Mesoamerica* 16:213–228.

Stanton, Travis W., and Ryan H. Collins. 2017. "Los orígenes de los mayas del norte: Investigaciones en el Grupo E de Yaxuná." *Arqueología Mexicana* 145:32–37.

Stanton, Travis W., and Ryan H. Collins. 2021. "The Role of Middle Preclassic Place-making in the Creation of Late Formative Yucatecan Cities: The Foundations of Yaxuná." In *Early Mesoamerican Cities: Urbanism and Urbanization in Formative Period Mesoamerica*, edited by M. Love, 99–120. Cambridge, UK: Cambridge University Press.

Stanton, Travis W., Sara Dzul Góngora, Ryan H. Collins, and Donald A. Slater. Forthcoming. "The Early Laapal Complex at Yaxuná: Early Middle Preclassic Ceramics from the E Group." In *Exploring an Unnamed Era: Pre-Mamom Pottery in the Maya Lowlands*, edited by D. S. Walker. Boulder: University Press of Colorado.

Stanton, Travis W., and David A. Freidel. 2005. "Placing the Centre, Centring the Place: The Influence of Formative Sacbeob in Classic Site Design at Yaxuná, Yucatán." *Cambridge Archaeological Journal* 15:225–49.

Stanton, Travis W., David A. Freidel, Charles K. Suhler, Traci Ardren, James N. Ambrosino, Justine M. Shaw, and Sharon Bennett. 2010. *Excavations at Yaxuná, 1986–1996: Results of the Selz Foundation Yaxuná Project*. BAR International Series 2056. Oxford: Archaeopress.

Stanton, Travis W., and Daniela Gremion. 2011. "Thermal Shock Tests to Understand the Role of Calcite Crystal Temper in Clay Cooking Pots from the Late-Terminal Classic Northern Maya Lowlands." Paper presented at the 76th Annual Meeting of the Society for American Archaeology, Sacramento, CA.

Stanton, Travis W., Karl A. Taube, and Ryan H. Collins. Forthcoming. "Domesticating Time: Quadripartite Symbolism and Rituals of Foundation at Yaxuná." In *Telling Time: Myth, History, and Everyday Life in the Ancient Maya World*, edited by D. A. Freidel, A. F. Chase, A. S. Dowd, and J. Murdock. Gainesville: University Press of Florida.

Strum, Camilla, Julia K. Clark, and Loukas Barton. 2016. "The Logic of Ceramic Technology in Marginal Environments: Implications for Mobile Life." *American Antiquity* 81 (4):6 45–63.

Suhler, Charles K., Traci Ardren, and Dave Johnstone. 1998. "The Chronology of Yaxuna: Evidence from Excavation and Ceramics." *Ancient Mesoamerica* 9: 176–82.

Taube, Karl A. 1989. "The Maize Tamale, *wah*, in Classic Maya Epigraphy and Art." *American Antiquity* 54:31–51.

Taube, Karl, David Stuart, William A. Saturno, and Heather Hurst. 2010. *The Murals of San Bartolo, El Petén, Guatemala. Part 2, The West Wall*. Ancient America 10. Barnardsville, NC: Center for Ancient American Studies.

Thompson, Raymond H. 1958. "Modern Yucatecan Maya Pottery Making." Memoirs of the Society for American Archaeology, No. 15. Washington, DC: Society for American Archaeology.

Tiesler, Vera, Andrea Cucina, Travis W. Stanton, and David A. Freidel. 2017. *Before Kukulkán: Maya Life, Death, and Identity at Classic Period Yaxuná*. Tucson: University of Arizona Press.

Tourtellot, Gair, III. 1988. "Excavations at Seibal, Department of Peten, Guatemala: Peripheral Survey and Excavation Settlement and Community Patterns." Memoirs of the Peabody Museum of Archaeology and Ethnology, Vol. 16. Cambridge, MA: Harvard University.

Uc González, Eunice del Socorro. 2004. La obtención del barro en grutas de la región Puuc y sus implicaciones culturales. Licenciatura thesis, Facultad de Ciencias Antropológicas, Universidad Autónoma de Yucatán, Mérida.

Uc González, Eunice del Socorro. 2006. "La utilización del barro de las cavernas del Puuc en tiempos prehispánicos." In *Los mayas de ayer y hoy: Memorias del Primer Congreso Internacional de Cultura Maya*, Tomo I, edited by A. Barrera Rubio and R. Gubler, 524–41. Mérida: Eugenia Montalván Proyectos Culturales SCP.

4

The Emergence of Complex Imagery on Late Terminal Formative Gray Ware Pottery from Coastal Oaxaca, Mexico

JEFFREY S. BRZEZINSKI, SARAH B. BARBER,
AND ARTHUR A. JOYCE

INTRODUCTION

Decorated pottery is one of a few ubiquitous classes of material culture through which Mesoamerican archaeologists can reconstruct complex social life in the past. Studies of decorated pottery from precolumbian Oaxaca have informed research on a wide range of topics, including interregional interaction (Elson and Sherman 2007; Joyce 2003; Levine 2013; Spencer et al. 2008; Workinger and Joyce 2009), domestic ritual (Forde 2016; Levine et al. 2016), identity formation (Levine 2013), political economy (Feinman 1985; Feinman and Nicholas 2007; Joyce et al. 2001; Levine 2011), and religious worldview (Brzezinski 2011; Caso et al. 1967; Marcus and Flannery 1996). For scholars of Indigenous groups that lacked formal writing systems, iconographic analyses of ceramic decorations provide insights into the worldviews held by the people who crafted them. In this paper, we examine the spread of religious belief as an aspect of social complexity reflected through iconographic pottery. We focus on a distinctive set of iconographic motifs carved on gray ware serving vessels from the lower Río Verde Valley of Pacific coastal Oaxaca, Mexico. The corpus is chronologically

https://doi.org/10.5876/9781646422883.c004

sensitive, co-occurring with the emergence of the region's first regional "polity" centered at the urban site of Río Viejo during the late Terminal Formative period Chacahua phase (100–250 CE). The end of the Formative was also characterized by political turbulence, as the Río Viejo polity collapsed at ca. 250 CE, and the region's settlements shifted toward the piedmont.

In traditional models of social complexity, religious belief is often thought to be imposed by elites as a form of ideology (Balkansky 1998; Chase and Chase 1996; Marcus and Flannery 1996; Redmond and Spencer 2006). From this top-down perspective, the political authority that characterizes early complex societies is constituted through leaders' specialized access to the divine realm (Schele and Freidel 1990). However, as some Mesoamerican archaeologists have argued, the emphasis on leaders' primary role in religion has limited consideration of the ways in which other collectivities (e.g., commoners, outlying communities, cults, etc.) may have negotiated the terms of political authority (Joyce and Barber 2015a; Lohse 2007; McAnany 1995). Moreover, research has shown that a number of important religious beliefs and practices originated among commoners and were only later appropriated by the nobility (Lucero 2003; Robin 2002).

Given the lack of formal writing in the region, iconographic pottery provides an ideal medium to examine social complexity near the end of the Formative in coastal Oaxaca. Based on an analysis of 457 pieces of iconographic pottery from seventeen lower Verde sites, we argue that religious themes associated with agricultural fertility, particularly the life cycle of maize and ritual petitioning for precipitation, became increasingly formalized toward the end of the Formative period. While archaeologists in other regions of Mesoamerica have documented the distribution of iconographic ceramic vessels—and the religious beliefs they referenced—as emanating from rulers at political centers (e.g., Elson and Sherman 2007; Rosenswig 2012), we do not see the emergence of the lower Verde iconographic corpus as occurring in the same manner. Rather, we see the widespread adoption of religious imagery during the late Terminal Formative as part of ongoing social negotiations between various collectivities, during which people shared in the sustenance provided by deities in return for acts of sacrificial offerings. Incipient leaders at Río Viejo may have attempted to marshal these religious themes to their advantage by scaling up local ceremonial practices like ritual feasting at the site's ceremonial center. The tensions created by drawing people away from their local communities may have ultimately contributed to the collapse of the nascent Río Viejo "polity" (Joyce 2010; Joyce and Barber 2015a; Joyce et al. 2016).

LATER FORMATIVE PERIOD CERAMICS IN THE LOWER VERDE

The Terminal Formative period (150 BCE–250 CE) in the lower Río Verde Valley witnessed population growth and nucleation as well as the culmination of political complexity with the emergence of the urban center of Rio Viejo, the region's political seat (Joyce 2010). Río Viejo increased in size from 25 hectares in the Late Formative Minizundo phase (400–150 BCE) to 225 hectares by the early Terminal Formative Miniyua phase (150 BCE–100 CE). During the late Terminal Formative Chacahua phase (100–250 CE), construction was completed on the massive Mound 1 acropolis, the civic ceremonial center of the site, which occupied an estimated volume of 455,050 m³ (Joyce et al. 2013). Regional population also grew throughout the valley, with the occupational area of sites reaching approximately 1,138 hectares by the Chacahua phase (Hedgepeth Balkin et al. 2017). Other large communities also developed, including Charco Redondo, Cerro de la Virgen, Tututepec, and San Francisco de Arriba, all of which ranged in size from sixty to seventy-two hectares.

During this period of increasing social complexity, a significant reorganization of ceramic production occurred, marked by the adoption of gray wares across the valley (Joyce 1991; Levine 2013). Late Formative Minizundo phase ceramics in the lower Verde were characterized by coarse- and fine-tempered wares made in an oxidizing environment that resulted in brown or reddish-colored pastes. These wares were decorated with slips, paint, and incision (Joyce 1991). Gray ware ceramic technology, relying on reduced firing at a higher temperature than lower Verde oxidized wares, developed in different regions of Oaxaca at different times. They appeared in the Mixteca Alta during the Early Formative (1900–1000 BCE) and the Valley of Oaxaca in the Middle Formative (1000–400 BCE) (Blomster 2004; Feinman et al. 1989; Flannery and Marcus 1994; Marcus and Flannery 1996). Imported gray wares first appeared in the lower Verde during the Minizundo phase, and potters began to make local versions during the early Terminal Formative Miniyua phase (Joyce 1991). Miniyua phase potters eschewed slips and paint, instead adorning gray ware serving vessels with abstract geometric designs, the most elaborate of which potters carved on the exteriors of composite silhouette bowls (Joyce 1991; Levine 2013). Elaborate icons were rare, although animal effigy designs occasionally occurred on rim tabs with impressed line decorations (Joyce 1991, 156).

Though the symbolic connotations of decorated composite silhouettes remain obscure for the Miniyua phase, Levine (Levine 2013, 254) argues that the bowls may have held a privileged role in practices of social negotiation. Many decorative patterns have been found at numerous sites, suggesting that they transcended personal expression and likely referred to larger social affiliations. Large enough for a single serving of food or drink, the bowls may have been part of the necessary "equipment" needed to "lubricate interactions characterized by negotiation," such as ritual feasting (Levine 2013, 255). Levine also sees the adoption of gray ware technology in the lower Verde as a means of emphasizing connections with exchange partners, but not in the sense that it was promulgated or mandated by elites. Ethnographic data from Mesoamerica broadly demonstrates that potters were often low-status individuals, and because gray ware pottery is found in both elite and commoner contexts, Levine (2013, 255) suggests that lower Verde people "became people who 'ate and drank from gray bowls' like many of their peers throughout Oaxaca."

Gray wares completely replaced fine brown wares as the dominant paste type for serving vessels during the Chacahua phase (Joyce 1991, 160–66). A small percentage of gray ware vessels were undecorated, while the majority had plastic decorations that were significantly more complex than previously seen in the region. Ceramic iconography depicted an array of common Formative period Mesoamerican themes such as vegetation, climatic phenomena, sacred landmarks, and anthropomorphic and zoomorphic figures (Brzezinski 2011). Although data are not available on the production of gray ware serving bowls during the Chacahua phase, archaeological evidence indicates that the vessels were widely available. They have been found in contexts indicative of mortuary ceremonies, ceremonial offerings, and ritual feasts, as well as in quotidian domestic practices of elites and commoners (Barber 2013; Brzezinski 2015; Joyce 2010).

During the Chacahua phase, people from across the valley contributed to communal construction projects and brought their gray ware serving bowls to participate in large-scale feasts at the Río Viejo acropolis. While these data might suggest top-down communal organization centered at Río Viejo, evidence from outlying communities suggests that practices of affiliation that focused on Río Viejo and its rulers did not transcend or replace those at the level of the local community (Joyce et al. 2016, 77–79). Regional idiosyncrasies relating to site orientations, construction techniques, ceremonial caching, and perhaps mortuary practices distinguished community identity (Barber 2005, 2013; Barber et al. 2014; Brzezinski 2019; Brzezinski et al. 2017; Joyce and Barber 2015a; Joyce et al. 2016; Workinger 2002). The collapse of the Río Viejo "polity" at circa 250 CE was accompanied by changes in ceramic production during the Early Classic Coyuche phase (250–500 CE). People burned many sections of the Río Viejo acropolis at the end of the Formative, suggesting that the structure was ritually terminated and abandoned (Joyce et al. 2013). Incised gray wares continued to be produced into the Early Classic, but the religious iconographic themes of the preceding Chacahua phase disappeared. In the next section, we briefly discuss the archaeological context and geographic distribution of Chacahua phase gray wares, identifying general patterns in decorative methods and consumption of the vessels across the valley.

THE CONTEXT OF CHACAHUA PHASE GRAY WARES

The Chacahua phase iconographic corpus includes 457 gray ware sherds and partial vessels compiled in a non-random sample of collections recovered from 1986 to 2009 (Brzezinski 2011). Sites occupying every level of the regional settlement hierarchy were sampled, spanning all geographic areas in the lower Verde, including the piedmont, coastal estuaries, and the floodplain to the east and west of the Río Verde (figure 4.1) (Barber 2005; Joyce 1991; Joyce and Barber 2011; Joyce and Levine 2009; Workinger 2002; Workinger and Joyce 1999). Only artifacts with elaborate plastic decorations were included in the sample. As such, the sample is not representative of all Chacahua phase gray ware pottery but rather a subset of decorated serving wares. Primary deposits were preferred, but secondary deposits (e.g., redeposited construction fill) and surface collections were also sampled and dated according to the established regional typology (Joyce 1991, 121–171).

Most gray wares with complex decorations were serving bowls ($n = 421$; 92%), followed by jars ($n =18$; 4%), and indeterminate vessel types ($n = 18$; 4%). To create the decorations, potters used a small, rounded implement to incise decorative lines into the paste while it was leather-hard, prior to firing. Occasionally, potters excised portions of the clay with a flat-headed tool, creating parts of the design in low relief. Decorated gray wares tended to be semispherical, incurving wall, or conical bowls, though a few examples of cylindrical and composite silhouette bowls were recorded. On average, incurving-wall bowls tended to be small with rounded bases and convergent walls, some of which had slightly restricted openings. Conical bowls were generally larger, with flat bases and out-leaning or out-curving walls. Decorations were placed in locations that enhanced visibility (Brzezinski 2011, 44–53).

People used iconographic gray wares in public and domestic settings. Artifacts with secure provenience primarily came from public buildings and features. To date, only one domestic midden dating to the Chacahua phase has been excavated (Barber 2005, 262), from which ten gray wares were included in the iconographic corpus. At Río Viejo, the only communal practice involving elaborately decorated serving bowls was ritual feasting. Evidence from ten refuse deposits on the south and west sides of acropolis indicates that gray wares were used and discarded in abundance during large-scale feasting events (Joyce et al. 2016). Five of the middens were internally stratified, suggesting that they were formed over an extended period by multiple events (Joyce and Barber 2015b). People likely cooked some of the food for feasts in a large earth oven located at the base of Structure 2 on the acropolis, the refuse from which contained ash as well as burned rocks and sherds utilized to retain heat (Brzezinski et al. 2012; Joyce et al. 2016).

Finely carved pottery has also been found in more mundane settings at Río Viejo. Excavations carried out by Joyce (1991, 384–85) at Mound 9 uncovered a 35 cm thick deposit of ceramics, many of which contained elaborate iconographic decorations, overlying the sterile bedrock. Based on sherd weights and the lack of other items such as shell, bone, ash, and charred plant remains, Joyce (1991, 384–85) interpreted the feature to represent a ceramic dumping ground rather

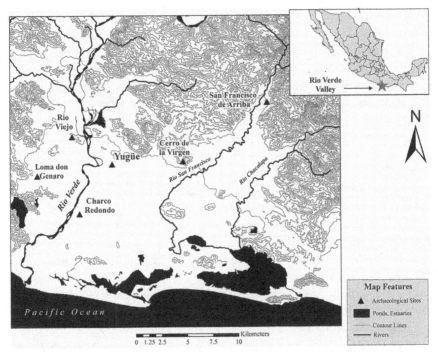

FIGURE 4.1. *Map of the lower Río Verde Valley with sites mentioned in the text. (Map courtesy of Jessica Hedgepeth Balkin.)*

than a midden. The deposit resembles deposits of sherds placed in shallow pits on the acropolis at the end of the Terminal Formative as termination offerings (Brzezinski et al. 2012). However, because the Mound 9 deposit was placed directly on bedrock, it was probably not involved in ritual termination.

Gray wares were intimately involved in practices associated with public buildings and spaces at the 9.75-hectare Terminal Formative community of Yugüe, located on the floodplain to the east of the Río Verde. A public space at the summit of the site's mixed-use platform, Substructure 1, was the setting for mortuary ceremonialism in the form of a communal cemetery, the placement of coarse brown ware cylindrical vessels as communal offerings, and ritual feasts. Archaeological evidence indicates that a late Terminal Formative sheet midden from Substructure 1 containing a significant number of fancy gray ware bowls was likely the result of one or a small number of feasts (Barber 2005, 2013).

Several other large communities were also the setting for communal practices involving iconographic gray wares. At the sixty-hectare hilltop site of Cerro de la Virgen, located in the piedmont 11 km east of Río Viejo, evidence of both feasting and caching rituals involving iconographic gray wares were associated with the site's ceremonial center, located around a large public plaza (Brzezinski 2015; Joyce et al. 2016). Near the top of the hill at the southeastern edge of the civic ceremonial center is Terrace 1, which supports a high-status domestic complex (Residence 1). A small domestic midden associated with the earliest construction phase of the terrace contained predominantly coarse brown ware cooking vessels, as well as bone fragments, figurine sherds, worked stone, and some iconographic gray ware serving bowls (Barber 2013). At Complex A, located below Terrace 1 on the northeastern edge of the plaza, evidence for ceremonial activities involving gray wares comes from a large cache of 260 ceramic vessels in the complex's northern patio. Interspersed with the vessels were thin granite slabs oriented vertically, some of which formed "compartments" for the vessels (Brzezinski 2019; Joyce et al. 2016). While the majority (93.7%) of vessels were coarse brown wares, nine gray wares were recovered, one of which was placed in a stone compartment. However, these vessels lacked complex imagery.

Better evidence of iconographic gray wares placed in ritual caches comes from the 64.5-hectare secondary center of San Francisco de Arriba, a piedmont site located at the northeastern edge of the valley. Although it experienced a drop in population during the transition between the Late and Terminal Formative periods, several occupational levels from the site's monumental acropolis dated to the late Terminal Formative period. Excavations conducted by Workinger (2002, 192–96) uncovered offering 99F-F36, which included nine miniature gray ware jars, one of which contained zoomorphic decorations of a possible bird deity. The offering was deposited in a pit excavated into construction fill dating to the Chacahua phase and included 356 greenstone beads, 27 crystal beads, and 109 beads of an unidentified lower-quality stone.

Together, the diversity of public settings containing the remains of iconographic pottery reflects the ubiquity of these materials in communal practices across the valley. Not only were fancy gray wares available to denizens of the urban center of Río Viejo; they were also used by residents of smaller, hinterland communities. In the next section, we provide an in-depth description of the most salient icons that appear in the corpus, drawing on iconographic interpretations from other regions of later Formative period Mesoamerica.

CHACAHUA PHASE ICONOGRAPHY

The most prevalent and recognizable imagery from the Chacahua phase depicts a range of concepts associated with the divine realm. Our analysis relies on iconographic interpretations from other regions of Mesoamerica, particularly the Valley of Oaxaca, the Basin of Mexico, and the Mixteca Alta. Our interpretations also draw on semiotic concepts of iconicity and indexicality, or the idea that some forms of visual media can be affected and constrained by the physical world in a way that is not completely arbitrary (Hodder 1989; Preucel and Bauer 2001). A decoration may be iconic in that it formally resembles the thing (i.e., concept, object, etc.) to which it refers and therefore is recognizable by observers who may lack embedded cultural knowledge of semasiographic practices (Preucel 2006). A decoration is an index if it actively "points" to the idea or object to which it refers by resembling something physically or ontologically related to it (e.g., billowing smoke indexes fire). In our analysis, we rely on interpretations of symbolic media from other regions of Mesoamerica but also leave open the possibility that certain icons physically resembled the concepts that they referenced. Table 4.1 presents the most prominent designs, motifs, and icons that appear in the Chacahua phase sample, each of which is described and interpreted below.

TABLE 4.1. Frequency of main icons in the Chacahua phase sample.

Icon	Number	Percentage (%)
Trefoil	59	12.9
Lazy-S	80	17.5
U Motif	44	9.6
Stepped Fret	2	0.4
Zig Zags	16	3.5
Anthropomorph	5	1.1
Zoomorph	11	2.4
Spirals	58	12.7
Unidentified, rectilinear	110	24.1
Unidentified, curvilinear	65	14.2
Crosshatch	7	1.5
Total	457	100.0

Life Cycle of Maize

One of the defining decorative motifs of the Chacahua phase was the trefoil, named for its outline of three lobes with smaller, linear designs on the interior of the icon. The trefoil appeared at 11 of 17 (65%) of the sites in the gray ware sample, in addition to one artifact that lacked provenience. The general form of the icon is relatively consistent, though some potters created the outline with a single incised line, in relief, or a combination of the two. Based on fifty-eight artifacts with trefoil icons, we identify three variants of the motif, each characterized by the configuration of the interior decorative component (figure 4.2). Type 1 exhibits an interior component consisting of one or two incised lines ending in one or two curls. The interior of Type 2 is like Type 1 but lacks a curl, containing instead one or two straight lines. Type 3 exhibits an elongated rectangular shape extending out from the base of the tri-lobed outline. Occasionally, potters adorned vessels with a combination of trefoil forms in various patterns.

The trefoil motif in its three configurations represents vegetation, more specifically, the growth cycle of the maize plant. Agricultural imagery in precolumbian Mesoamerican art has tremendous time depth, appearing in Olmec iconography by the Middle Formative period (Covarrubias 1946; Reilly 1990; Sellen 2002, 2007; Taube 1996, 2000; Urcid 2002). The Olmec Maize God is depicted on jadeite

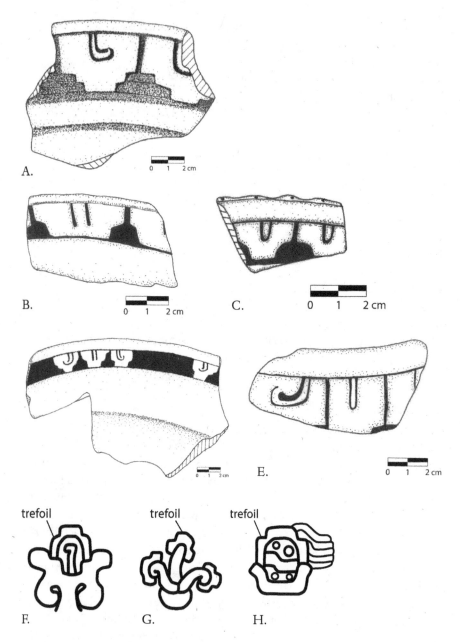

FIGURE 4.2. *Variants of trefoil icon motif: (a) Lower Verde trefoil Type 1; (b) Lower Verde trefoil Type 2; (c) Lower Verde trefoil Type 3; (d) Lower Verde trefoil Types 1 and 2; (e) Lower Verde trefoil Types 1 and 3; (f) Depiction of the life cycle of maize on Zapotec effigy vessel of Cociyo (Dolores Olmeda Museum, Cat. 32) as germinated kernel, (g) flowered plant, and (h) ear of corn (redrawn from Sellen 2002, fig. 8).*

celts from numerous Olmec sites, many of which depict a cob of corn with a tripartite design growing out of the cleft of the deity's head (Taube 1996). The trefoil appears in the Valley of Oaxaca by as early as the Middle Formative, incorporated into calendrical glyph J, which Urcid and Winter (2003) identify as the physical depiction of the maize plant. During the Classic period (300–800 CE), trefoils occurred in a variety of forms on ceramic effigy vessels. Sellen (2011, 75–76, figs. 4–6) has described two particular types: one with a trefoil shape with two ends that curl under the base and another variation in which the top of the trefoil is split open, revealing "a hooked element on an oval frame." While Caso and Bernal (1952) interpreted the glyph to be a flower, Shaplin (1975, 116) identified the symmetrical imagery of the glyph to represent "foliage of corn" in a variety of forms. Boos (1966) also recognized that the glyph varied in its representation. Building on Shaplin's and Boos's interpretations, Sellen (2011, 76) argues that the glyph represents maize in "distinct moments of growth," depicting a maize kernel in its simpler trefoil form and a germinated seed in the form that spreads open to reveal a hook. The maize glyph most often appears with Cociyo, the commander of climatic forces and provider of agricultural fertility in Zapotec cosmology (Caso et al. 1967; Sellen 2007, 2011). Sellen (2011, 77) details the ontogenetic progression of maize displayed in the headdresses of Cociyo effigy vessels where the maize grain is swollen with moisture and a stem germinates in the first stage, the second stage shows the growing plant, and the third stage displays a fully developed ear of maize (figure 4.2f–h).

The three categories of Lower Verde trefoil configurations likely represent maize at different growth stages, including the germinated seed, the growing or matured stalk, and the developed corncob. The inner component of Type 1 may represent a germinated maize seed or a growing stalk with a leaf growing from a node on the side. The shorter, straight lines that appear in the Type 2 version of the trefoil may represent spikelets that grow during the initial reproductive stages of the maize growth cycle or a fully grown maize prior to the germination of cobs. Finally, the elongated shape of the Type 3 trefoil resembles a fully grown maize cob but lacks the additional stylized designs found on Zapotec effigy vessels (Taube 1996; Urcid 2009).

Sky, Lightning, Water, and "Bringers" of Rain

Pre-Columbian artistic motifs that reference religious themes such as agricultural fertility are commonly associated with the pan-Mesoamerican rain deity complex (Estrada-Belli 2011; Schaafsma and Taube 2006; Sellen 2007; Thompson 1970). The lower Verde Chacahua phase is no exception to this trend (Barber and Olvera Sánchez 2012; Brzezinski 2011; Brzezinski, Joyce, and Barber 2017; Joyce et al. 2016). In addition to vegetation, several lower Verde ceramic icons that appear frequently on iconographic gray wares depict "climatic" manifestations of the rain deity complex, particularly as clouds, lightning, and water. We trace and interpret the semiotic implications of these themes by referencing pan-Mesoamerican iconographic crossties. Further, we speculate that, in some instances, lower Verde potters combined certain "climatic" elements into more complex imagery that may have depicted the concept of the sacred mountain, which many scholars have implicated as a cosmological source of rain and an essential locus for petitioning the divine realm for agricultural fertility (Joyce 2000; López Austin and López Luján 2009; Markens 2013).

The Lazy-S motif is one of the most common ceramic decorations in the Chacahua phase gray ware assemblage, appearing on 80 of 457 (18%) artifacts sampled. The motif first appears in the lower Verde on gray ware composite silhouette bowls dating to the early Terminal Formative Miniyua phase, on which a small curvilinear line design is repeated around the entire vessel. By the Chacahua phase, the form of the design changed to a more elongated, curvilinear horizontal line or group of lines that curled slightly downward on one side of the motif and upward on the opposite side (figure 4.3a). Based on iconographic analyses of a variety of artistic media from the Middle Formative to the Classic period (see below), we interpret the Lazy-S motif to be an abstract representation of clouds and sky (Orr 1994, 2001; Reilly 1996a). Decorative themes depicting the sky-related elements are prevalent in Mesoamerican art, appearing by as early as the Middle Formative period at Chalcatzingo in the Basin of Mexico (Grove 1987, 2000; Reilly 1996a) and San Lorenzo on the Gulf Coast (Coe and Diehl 1980, 312). Chalcatzingo Monument 1, a relief sculpture depicting a human figure seated on a throne within the cavernous maw of the "cave monster," demonstrates the central role of the Lazy-S motif within the rain-vegetation artistic complex. In the upper section of the scene, three sets of triple-layered clouds expel curtains of heavy rain that morph into exclamation-point-shaped raindrops. Vegetation sprouts from the falling water, which Reilly (1996a, 3) suggests may depict the maize plant. The scrolls of smoke or mist that emerge from the cave monster's open mouth have been interpreted as emerging clouds, the source of the falling rain. The human figure, seated on a throne adorned with the Lazy-S motif, has been interpreted as a ritual specialist, perhaps a community leader, imbued with the ability to traverse the boundary between the physical and divine worlds to petition for agricultural fertility (Grove 2000).

Reilly (1996a) has argued convincingly that a direct iconographic substitution can be made between the tri-layered clouds in the scene from Monument 1 and the more abstract Lazy-S symbols depicted in other monuments from Chalcatzingo. For example, Monument 31 depicts a feline creature, identified as supernatural by its flamed eyebrow and stylized ear symbol, dismembering a human body (figure 4.3b; Reilly 1996a, 5). Above the feline at the top of the monument is a Lazy-S symbol, from which three exclamation-point-shaped rain drops fall. A

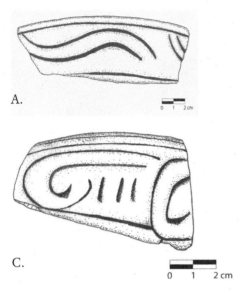

FIGURE 4.3. *(a) Conical bowl from Río Viejo with Lazy-S motif; (b) Monument 31, Chalcatzingo, Mexico; (c) Incurving wall bowl from Río Viejo with half Lazy-S motif and rain drops.*

similar iconographic element has been identified in the epigraphic corpus of the Classic period Maya (Reilly 1996a). The T632/muyal glyph shares a similarly curled, S-form shape as the Middle Formative example, appearing in the Dresden Codex in several instances above the rain deity, Chaac, on whom raindrops can be seen falling. Taube (2009, 29; also see Covarrubias 1946) has also noted several instances in which the motif appears in the headdress of Chaac, the Maya rain deity. Several sherds in the Chacahua phase corpus depict a half Lazy-S, from which three raindrops fall in a similar fashion as seen in Chalcatzingo Monument 1 (figure 4.3c). In addition to the Lazy-S, the U-shaped motif is also associated with clouds and rainfall. The design is characterized by two deeply incised, downward-facing U-shaped lines that enclose a singular dot. Curved lines typically emanate from the motif, likely representing falling rain similar to the clouds that adorn the upper register of Chalcatzingo Monument 1 (figure 4.4). The U-shaped design occurs almost exclusively on the everted rim of semispherical gray ware bowls with little to no additional decorations.

Despite some subtle differences in the composition of the motif, we argue that the lower Verde Lazy-S iconically references the concept of clouds in a similar fashion as the Middle Formative Olmec and Classic Maya examples. The

FIGURE 4.4. (a) The U-shaped motif carved into the everted rim of a Chacahua phase semispherical bowl from Barra Quebrada; (b) Icon depicting a cloud and rainfall from Chalcatzingo Monument 1. (Redrawn after Reilly 1996a, fig. 3.)

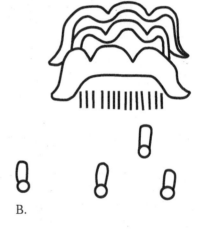

motif in the lower Verde tends to be more elongated, lacking the tightly coiled curls of the Olmec Lazy-S and the Classic Maya T632/muyal glyph. Iconically, the lower Verde Lazy-S may occupy a semiotic space between the sheets of rain depicted in the triple-layered cloud motif and the more stylized Lazy-S in the Chalcatzingo corpus. In the Valley of Oaxaca, Zapotec artists often coupled S-form icons with raindrop motifs in imagery associated with Cociyo (Orr 1994; Sellen 2007, 12). Caso and Bernal (1952, figs. 74–77) note its presence on several carved urns depicting Cociyo from the highland sites of Tlacochahuaya and Zaachila, each figure exhibiting a prominent pectoral element displaying Zapotec Glyph C, the sign for the calendrical day name "Water," below which a Lazy-S motif hangs within a border banded with circular and curvilinear decorations. Further iconographic references to celestial/climatic phenomena can be seen in a stucco frieze known as the *viborón*, located at the North Platform of the Main Plaza at Monte Albán (Acosta 1965, 816; Urcid 1994, 64–65). Dating to the Pe phase (300–100 BCE), the *viborón* exhibits a sky band with S-shaped scrolls surrounding serpentine, goggle-eyed figures resembling

FIGURE 4.5. *Spiral motif carved on incurving-wall gray ware bowls from Río Viejo (left) and Yugüe (right).*

Cociyo (Orr 1997; Reilly 1996b, 36). Rain flows from the figures' mouths, further demonstrating the connection between S-shaped icons and precipitation.

In addition to the Lazy-S, lower Verde potters also depicted a common Meso-american motif associated with lightning, depicted in the form of a descending zigzag design. The lower Verde zigzag motif is comprised of rectilinear line segments oriented at right angles that form descending steps, typically beginning near the vessel's upper framing line and ending in the middle of the panel. The motif was recorded on 18 vessels (4%), predominantly on large, flat-bottomed conical bowls with out-leaning or out-curving walls and occasionally on small, incurving-wall bowls. In the Valley of Oaxaca, descending zigzags were most commonly associated with Cociyo, iconically representing the real world manifestation of the deity as lightning shooting through the sky (Caso and Bernal 1952; Caso et al. 1967; Elson and Sherman 2007). By as early as the Terminal Formative Nisa phase (100 BCE–200 CE), Zapotec artisans painted and carved simple geometric zigzag designs on the exterior of cylindrical serving vessels (Caso et al. 1967: Laminas IX, Xa and Xc). In an examination of Nisa phase pottery production and consumption at Monte Albán, Elson and Sherman (2007, 271–74) argue that crema ware serving bowls were manufactured to display lightning in the form of zigzag motifs, which played a vital role in "petitioning or thanking Cociyo for agricultural prosperity" through abundant rainfall.

Rainfall is intertwined with a broader set of associations in Mesoamerican belief and iconography that also includes wind, water (more generally), mountains, and serpents. The key iconographic motif in this complex is the spiral, which has broad geographic and temporal depth in Mesoamerica (Markens 2013, 2014; Russo 2005), and also appeared on Chacahua phase pottery. Spirals occurred on 58 (12.7%) vessels in the Chacahua phase sample in the form of a wide, curled element carved in low relief, typically accompanied by a thin, shallower accent line running through the center (figure 4.5). The motif was represented broadly throughout the lower Verde at thirteen of the seventeen sites sampled and occurred on incurving-wall and conical bowls.

In ancient Mesoamerica, spiral motifs often reference moving air, appearing in imagery denoting music, song, and the sacred speech or "flowery" breath of elites, venerated ancestors, and deities (Barber and Olvera Sánchez 2012; Houston and Taube 2000; Taube 2001). Evidence in the lower Verde for spirals as spoken, moving air is best represented by a carved bone flute recovered from the site of Yugüe that dates to the Terminal Formative period (Barber and Olvera Sánchez 2012; Barber, Sánchez Santiago, and Olvera Sánchez 2009). The flute's decorative iconography displays a flying human figure, probably a ritual specialist, with a spiraled scroll emanating from its mouth (Barber and Olvera Sánchez 2012, 15). Trefoils emblazon the loincloth and speech scroll of the figure, who is wearing a buccal mask, situating it among other rain and wind deity complexes in precolumbian Mesoamerica (Jansen and Pérez Jiménez 2007; Masson 2001; Sellen 2007). In addition to speech and breath, the movement of air as wind is entangled in the relational ontologies of ancient Mesoamerican religion as one of many manifestations of the life-giving force that animates the cosmos (Monaghan 1995, 127–28; Vogt 1969, 369–71).

The spiral motif as an icon for water is evident in a series of Indigenous maps from the central highlands of Mexico dating to the early Colonial period (1519–1600 CE). As documented by Markens (2014, 70–71), though the spiral was not universally employed in map imagery, its use was so frequent that it could be counted as a basic element in the broader repertoire of signs for rivers. In the *Historia Tolteca-Chichimeca*, a map of Cholula depicts the Atoyac River running from the northeast to the south of the community with spirals included at various points (Lind 2012, 91). Another map of Cholula from the *Relación Geográfica de Cholula* depicts a similar river (Oudijk 2008, fig. 3.3). Russo (2005, 132) documents several examples of the spiral denoting flowing rivers in early colonial documents, including a map of the Río Nautla, Misantla, and Tecolutla in the hinterland surrounding Hueyetepec, Veracruz. Markens (2014, 70) suggests that the spiral may represent the eddies that occur in turbulent rivers and streams when flowing water swirls, creating a suddenly slackened or reverse current.

Spiral designs were often found together with stepped frets in more complex icons, exemplified by the *xicalcoliuhqui* motif (Caso et al. 1967; Markens 2013, 2014). Markens (2013, 2014) has argued that the *xicalcoliuhqui* demonstrates the relationship between the pan-Mesoamerican serpent-deity complex and sources of water. Mesoamerican scholars have attributed the stepped fret motif to represent a wide range of concepts, including deities such as Quetzalcóatl of central Mexico (Piña Chan 1977), natural phenomena such as wind, ocean waves (Palmer 2007), place names (Kubler 1962), and the nobility (Hernández Sánchez 2008). In the modern-day Indigenous town of San Mateo Macuilxóchitl, Oaxaca, residents describe a feathered serpent that inhabits Cerro Danush, a large hill located next to the town (Faulseit 2011; Markens 2013; Markens et al. 2008). Offerings are placed at the base of the hill once a year, just before the arrival of the first rains that mark the growing season (Markens 2013). The association between the feathered serpent and natural landforms such as Cerro Danush is important because it provides an example of liminal spaces between the world of humans and the divine realm.

Described by many anthropologists as "mountains of creation," these landforms and their associated non-human actors, such as the feathered serpent that lives inside Cerro Danush, are active members of the community and sources of life-giving rain (Albores and Broda 1997; Joyce 2010; López Austin and López Luján 2009). In the same sense, monumental buildings were often conceived as mountains of sustenance. Several prominent buildings exhibit snake imagery in their exterior adornments, including the Temple of Kukulkán and the Temple of the Sacerdote at Chichén Itzá, the Temple of the Feathered Serpent at Teotihuacan, the Pyramid of the Niches at Tajín, and perhaps the *viborón* at Monte Albán. Ethnographic and ethnohistoric accounts from Zapotec, Mixtec, and Mixe communities of the highlands (Lipp 1991; Monaghan 1995; Parsons 1932) and Huave communities of the Isthmus of Tehuantepec (De la Cruz 2007; Signorini 1997) demonstrate that the water serpent was responsible for unleashing wind, floods, and other forms of climatic destruction. This force was balanced by the fire serpent, which returned the water to its sacred resting place in the mountain.

Citing the resemblance in the *xicalcoliuhqui* between the stepped element and the serpent and between the spiral and water, Markens (2013) identifies the combination of motifs as iconic of the mountain of creation (figure 4.6a). A particular pattern of lower Verde ceramic icons resembles the *xicalcoliuhqui* and likely references sacred natural landforms or human-built structures. We call attention to two examples in the Chacahua phase gray ware sample as possibly reflecting a worldview similar to what Markens describes. The first artifact, a fragment of a conical bowl recovered from a small sherd deposit on the Río Viejo acropolis, depicts a series of seven stepped icons carved in low relief on the vessel's exterior (figure 4.6b–c). In the center of the fragment, a curled element similar in style to the Type 1 trefoil emerges from the base of a stepped icon, which may indicate a reference to maize. To the right, a spiral design runs through the center of another stepped icon. Unlike the lower Verde trefoil, the stepped icons on the vessel fragment contain additional tick marks at the apex and base, suggesting the motif refers to an alternative concept, most likely architecture. In the second example, a small gray ware plate recovered from a Chacahua phase midden on the Río Viejo acropolis, a similar set of stepped elements with tick marks at the base repeats around the edge of the vessel. Although limited to two artifacts, the intersection of agricultural fertility imagery and sacred landscapes

A.

B.

C.

FIGURE 4.6. *(a) Carved* xicalcoliuhqui *motif from side wall of antechamber to Tomb 1, Zaachila, Oaxaca; (b) Small gray ware "plate" from Yugüe with architectural motif on interior; (c) Gray ware conical bowl Río Viejo with stepped-fret motifs on the exterior panel. (Photograph [a] by Robert Markens; photographs [b] and [c] by Jeffrey Brzezinski.)*

underscores the importance of sacred spaces in the ritual economies of the Terminal Formative period.

Death and Sacrifice

While the life cycle of maize and the process of petitioning for rain were much more prevalent themes depicted on iconographic gray wares, limited evidence from the Chacahua phase sample indicates that other religious concepts such as death and sacrifice were also referenced. We distinguish sacrifice from death by associating the latter with the "sacred covenant," a fundamental tenet of Mesoamerican religious belief. The covenant entails a transactional relationship between humans and the divine wherein humans give sacrificial offerings to the gods in return for the privilege of practicing agriculture (Hamann 2002; Joyce 2000; Monaghan 1990). Death in Native American ontologies implies the transcendence of the human life force to another plane of existence, whereas the sacred covenant could be invoked by practices other than death or human sacrifice. These practices may include auto-sacrifice (e.g., bloodletting) and the placement of offerings of other-than-human materials such as copal incense, maize dough, jade, quetzal feathers, and stone objects (Brzezinski et al. 2017; Freidel et al. 1993; Joyce and Barber 2015a; López Luján 2005; Monaghan 1990, 2000).

Images of skulls and dead humans, especially on anthropomorphic gray ware vessel appliques and on ceramic and carved stone figurines, suggest the important role of death, and perhaps sacrifice, in precolumbian religion of coastal Oaxaca (Barber et al. 2013; Brzezinski 2011, 105; Brzezinski et al. 2017, 517–19; Hepp and Joyce 2013, 277–79). Skull designs carved on a conical bowl recovered from Cerro de la Cruz may indicate that iconographic gray wares were used in mortuary ceremonialism (figure 4.7a). In another example from Yugüe, a ritual specialist was depicted on the exterior of a semispherical bowl recovered from an offering in an exclusive public building. The scene depicts a human face with a long speech scroll emanating from the figure's mouth (figure 4.7b). The figure wears the mask of a saurian creature with a long, upturned snout, which is likely a regional variant of the Zapotec *xicani* or the Mixtec *yahui*, a high-status sacrificial specialist who wears a similar style of mask (Hermann Lejarazu 2009).

Decorations of bird zoomorphs may also reflect themes of death and sacrifice in the iconographic gray ware corpus. Bird imagery on Chacahua phase gray wares is abstract and exceedingly rare, appearing on only two artifacts in the sample—an elaborately carved miniature gray ware jar from San Francisco de Arriba and a decorated basal support from Yugüe. The miniature jar from San Francisco de Arriba depicts the head of a bird with a downturned pointed beak, above which is a flared carbuncle (figure 4.7c). Curvilinear decorations are displayed behind the bird's head, possibly representing wings, moving air, or both. We link the Chacahua phase bird imagery to the Principal Bird Deity Complex

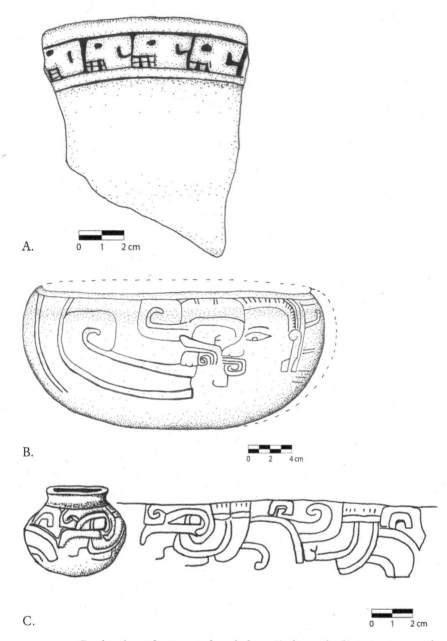

A.

B.

C.

FIGURE 4.7. *Death and sacrifice imagery from the lower Verde sample: (a) Gray ware conical bowl from Cerro de la Cruz with skull imagery incised on interior of vessel; (b) Gray ware incurving-wall bowl from Yugüe with religious specialist carved on exterior; (c) Drawing and rollout of a carved miniature gray ware vessel from San Francisco de Arriba possibly depicting the principal bird deity.*

of the Maya (Bardawil 1976, 196; Guernsey 2006) and the Zapotec wide-billed bird deity (Caso and Bernal 1952, 344). Among the Maya, the deity was associated epigraphically with human sacrifice and kings' accession to power in the Classic period (Taube 1987, 5). Urcid (2005, 41–42, 54) has also identified Zapotec Glyph "U" as a representation of the wide-billed bird deity that was restricted to iconography found in tombs of the elite. Urcid's (2005, 62–63) analysis of carved stelae at Monte Albán suggests that avian imagery and death were closely associated, with the practice of bird sacrifice perhaps involved in certain rituals such as tomb reopening ceremonies that honored deceased ancestors.

DISCUSSION

We may situate the Chacahua phase iconographic corpus within the broader ritual and political economy of the lower Río Verde Valley by illustrating the intersection of religious themes referenced on gray wares and the communal practices during which they were used, consumed, and discarded. Based on their relative ubiquity in domestic, public, and ritual assemblages, decorated gray wares were employed in quotidian and ceremonial practices. Their appearance in both ritual caches and feasting middens may have invoked the sacred covenant—as offerings given to the divine realm, perhaps in return for the sustenance provided by deities and ancestors that was consumed during feasts.

Public buildings and spaces in ancient Mesoamerica were receptacles for offerings such as caches of objects and burials of human bodies that embodied the social ties that constituted local communities (Hendon 2000, 42–46). Caches placed in public buildings in the lower Verde were designed to animate these structures and their associated ancestors and deities (Barber 2013; Brzezinski et al. 2017; Joyce et al. 2016). In this way, public buildings were active agents within Formative period communities, indicated by the placement of ceremonial offerings during the initial dedication and ritual closure of these structures (Brzezinski et al. 2017; Joyce and Barber 2015a). Many of the most impressive caches were placed over extended periods and intended to feed and nurture animate buildings and their associated divinities (Joyce and Barber 2015a).

The prevalence of iconographic gray wares in feasting contexts may indicate that food was recontextualized as a means by which the covenant could be invoked. For example, offerings at Yugüe included large vessels containing estuarine mussel shells, which raises the possibility that vessels such as those in the offerings at Cerro de la Virgen and San Francisco de Arriba contained perishable food items as well. Given the ubiquity of agricultural, climatic, and sacrificial themes carved on Chacahua phase gray wares, people may have been referencing the sacred covenant as they participated in these commensal practices. They likely carried their serving bowls with them when attending large-scale feasts, such as those that occurred at the Río Viejo acropolis. This may partly explain why the diversity of vessel types and icons at Río Viejo exceeds all other sites sampled (Brzezinski 2011, 72–73).

While the depositional contexts of gray wares were diverse, statistical comparisons of decorations suggest that the types of icons that appeared on gray wares did not vary significantly. Chi-square analyses were conducted to compare iconographic assemblages from each site that contributed thirty or more artifacts to the sample, including Barra Quebrada, Cerro de la Cruz, Río Viejo, San Francisco de Arriba, and Yugüe. Unknown rectilinear and curvilinear designs were not included in these comparisons. Yates's correction was applied to the chi-square analysis to ensure a conservative statistical test. From these comparisons, the only assemblage that varied to a statistically significant degree from at least one other was from Barra Quebrada ($p = 0.03$). This anomaly was likely due to the comparatively larger number of conical vessels with a Lazy-S motif in the Barra Quebrada sample.

Religious imagery became more formalized during the Chacahua phase, but current evidence does not support a scenario in which leaders at the political center of Río Viejo sponsored their manufacture and distribution. Archaeological evidence indicates that leaders at Río Viejo attempted to expand their influence by drawing some people away from their local communities to participate in communal practices at the political center, including the construction of monumental buildings such as the Mound 1 acropolis (Barber and Joyce 2007; Joyce et al 2016; Joyce et al. 2013). The acropolis almost certainly would have required labor from beyond Río Viejo itself because large segments of the structure were built all at once rather than via accretion. Excavations on the acropolis indicate that the Terminal Formative construction methods varied considerably from unconsolidated basket loads of sediment to structured fill, characterized by unfired adobe blocks and occasionally fired bricks of various sizes (Joyce et al. 2013). Joyce and colleagues have identified at least four types of structured fill, none of which provided a structural advantage over the others. These likely represented variable construction methods used by teams of workers from different communities in the valley.

People from across the valley contributed to communal construction projects and participated in large-scale feasts at the acropolis, but evidence from outlying communities suggests that practices of affiliation focused on Río Viejo, and its rulers did not transcend those at the level of the local community (Joyce et al. 2016, 77–79). Research over the past two decades has shown regional idiosyncrasies among outlying communities in site orientations and construction techniques, as well as ceremonial caching and mortuary practices in public buildings (Barber 2005, 2013; Barber et al. 2014; Brzezinski et al. 2017; Joyce and Barber 2015a; Joyce et al. 2016; Workinger 2002). Río Viejo was a powerful political center, but current evidence suggests that ceramic production was organized at the local level, perhaps by households. The lack of centralized production of pottery follows a broader pattern outlined by Feinman (1999, 81), who argues that specialized craft production in precolumbian Mesoamerica "generally took place in domestic contexts." At El Palmillo, products produced by craft specialists circulated from house to house rather than through tributary institutions controlled by leaders at Monte Albán (Feinman et al. 2002). Currently, there is no evidence for markets in the lower Verde at the end of the Formative, suggesting that ceramic production and distribution was locally controlled.

To date, lower Verde researchers have found no evidence of kilns or large deposits of misfires that would indicate mass production of pottery subject to exclusive control by the site's leaders, such as those discussed by Elson and Sherman (2007; also see Martínez Lopez and Markens 2004) for the Main Plaza at Monte Albán. We also do not suspect that the conquest of neighboring regions provided leaders with external resources. Further, there is little evidence for foreign influence on the adoption of gray ware imagery. Levine's (2013) research on Miniyua phase gray wares suggest ideas were exchanged between communities on the coast and in the highlands of Oaxaca, but this was likely indirect communication. Evidence suggests that there was a disruption in long-distance trade between the coast and highlands during the Chacahua phase, perhaps prompted by warfare in the highlands (Joyce 1993, 74; Spencer and Redmond 2001). A relative scarcity of imported ceramic vessels exemplifies this decrease in trade (Joyce 1993). Typological evidence also indicates that Chacahua phase gray ware styles developed locally (Joyce 1991).

CONCLUSION

The Chacahua phase iconographic corpus represents fundamental Mesoamerican religious principles related to agriculture, rain, and sacrifice, which may explain why they were easily understood and adopted. Ceramic styles of the Terminal Formative period, including those of the earlier Miniyua phase, spread incrementally as a result of daily interactions between neighbors. During the Chacahua phase, iconographic gray wares were widely available and used in day-to-day domestic activities as well as in ceremonial practices such as commensal feasting and the placement of offerings and grave goods. More importantly, they employed a widely shared suite of beliefs that focused on the fertility of a broadly beneficial staple crop and the rain that facilitated its growth.

As a collective practice, feasting would have brought people together to share ideas and worldviews, and iconographic gray wares perhaps served as a portable and available artistic medium to express them. The portability of decorated gray wares could have been a point of departure for ruling elites who may have tried to marshal the religious principles to their advantage by scaling up communal practices like feasting that were historically local in scale. It is possible that the widely available iconographic ceramics materialized a religious worldview that legitimated the central role of leaders in religious belief and practice in the lower Verde, but there is no evidence suggesting that leaders controlled the production and distribution of the vessels. Rather, we suggest that the wide distribution of iconographic gray wares could have been an outgrowth of the communal nature of political authority and religious practice at the end of the Formative. If authority was constituted more by consensus than by decree, then the spread of the Chacahua phase icons was likely driven by the interactions of people at communal events rather than due to elites imposing them on the broader population.

While traditional models of social complexity tend to conceptualize religious belief as imposed on commoners by elites as a form of ideology, current evidence suggests that fundamental ideas concerning the sacred covenant may have spread as a combination of both the commensal acts of the populace and through the ideological projects of the elite. The power vested in local elites around the valley was predicated more on long-standing, communal forms of authority and identity, rather than self-aggrandizement and exclusionary authority. Clearly, this was not a top-down process; however, it was not entirely bottom-up either. In many cases, local elites were scaling up communal rituals to build a larger network of affiliates who aided in growing the scale of public construction across the valley. Leaders at Río Viejo may have co-opted the widely shared suite of beliefs to attract people from outlying communities to the center for ritual and feasting, but there is no evidence that they actively controlled the production or distribution of these goods. What remains important is that the ritual symbolism communicated through ceramic iconography focused on the fertility and life cycle of maize, the benefits of which could be collectively organized among collectivities at multiple levels of power and authority.

In addition to semiotic and iconographic analyses, researchers in the lower Verde must also address where serving vessels were made and ultimately consumed through archaeometric analyses such as instrumental neutron activation analysis. Locating and broadly sampling class sources on the coast must also be carried out for petrographic analyses. Together, these analyses have the potential to further our understanding of the dynamism of social and political life on the coast of Oaxaca at the end of the Formative period.

REFERENCES

Acosta, Jorge R. 1965. "Preclassic and Classic Architecture of Oaxaca." In *Handbook of Middle American Indians*, edited by R. Wauchope and G. Willey, 814–36. Austin: University of Texas Press.

Albores, B., and J. Broda, eds. 1997. *Graniceros: Cosmovisión y meteorología indígenas de Mesoamérica*. El Colegio Mexiquense, AC: Instituto de Investigaciones Histoicas, UNAM, Zinacantepec.

Balkansky, Andrew K. 1998. "Origin and Collapse of Complex Societies in Oaxaca (Mexico): Evaluating the Era from 1965 to the Present." *Journal of World Prehistory* 12 (4): 451–93.

Barber, Sarah B. 2005. "Heterogeneity, Identity, and Complexity: Negotiating Status and Authority in Terminal Formative Coastal Oaxaca." PhD diss., University of Colorado, Boulder.

Barber, Sarah B. 2013. "Defining Community and Status at Outlying Sites during the Terminal Formative Period." In *Polity and Ecology in Formative Period Coastal Oaxaca*, edited by Arthur A. Joyce, 165–92. Boulder: University Press of Colorado.

Barber, Sarah B., and Arthur A. Joyce. 2007. "Polity Produced and Community Consumed: Negotiating Political Centralization through Ritual in the Lower Río Verde Valley, Oaxaca." In *Mesoamerican Ritual Economy: Archaeological and Ethnological Perspectives*, edited by E. Christian Wells and Karla L. Davis-Salazar, 221–44. Boulder: University Press of Colorado.

Barber, Sarah B., Arthur A. Joyce, Arion T. Mayes, and Michelle Butler. 2013. "Formative Period Burial Practices and Cemeteries." In *Polity and Ecology in Formative Period Coastal Oaxaca*, edited by Arthur A. Joyce, 97–134. Boulder: University Press of Colorado.

Barber, Sarah B., and Mireya Olvera Sánchez. 2012. "A Divine Wind: The Arts of Death and Music in Terminal Formative Oaxaca." *Ancient Mesoamerica* 23 (1): 9–24.

Barber, Sarah B., Gonzalo Sánchez Santiago, and Mireya Olvera Sánchez. 2009. "Sounds of Death and Life in Mesoamerica: The Bone Flutes of Ancient Oaxaca." *Yearbook for Traditional Music* 41:94–110.

Barber, Sarah B., Andrew Workinger, and Arthur A. Joyce. 2014. "Situational Inalienability and Social Change in Formative Period Coastal Oaxaca." In *Inalienable Possessions in the Archaeology of Mesoamerica*, edited by Brigitte Kovacevich and Michael G. Callaghan, 38–53. Washington, DC: American Anthropological Association.

Bardawil, Lawrence W. 1976. "The Principal Bird Deity in Maya Art—An Iconographic Study of Form and Meaning." In *The Art, Iconography and Dynastic History of Palenque, Part 3*, edited by M. Greene Robertson, 195–209. Pebble Beach, CA: Pre-Columbian Art Research and the Robert Louis Stephenson School.

Blomster, Jeffrey P. 2004. *Etlatongo: Social Complexity, Interaction, and Village Life in the Mixteca Alta of Oaxaca, Mexico*. Belmont, MA: Wadsworth / Thomson Learning.

Boos, Frank H. 1966. *Ceramic Sculptures of Ancient Oaxaca*. New York: A. S. Barnes.

Brzezinski, Jeffrey S. 2011. "Worldview, Ideology, and Ceramic Iconography: A Study of Late Terminal Formative Graywares from The Lower Río Verde Valley of Oaxaca, Mexico." Master's thesis, University of Central Florida.

Brzezinski, Jeffrey S. 2015. "Excavaciones en Cerro de la Virgen." In *Proyecto Río Verde, Informe final de la temporada 2013*, edited by Arthur A. Joyce and Sarah B. Barber, 288–509. Juárez, CDMX: Instituto Nacional de Antropología e Historia.

Brzezinski, Jeffrey S. 2019. "Terminal Formative Religion and Political Organization on the Pacific Coast of Oaxaca, Mexico: The Perspective from Cerro de la Virgen." PhD diss., University of Colorado, Boulder.

Brzezinski, Jeffrey S., Arthur A. Joyce, and Sarah B. Barber. 2017. "Constituting Animacy and Community in a Terminal Formative Bundled Offering from the Coast of Oaxaca, Mexico." *Cambridge Archaeological Journal* 27 (3): 511–31.

Brzezinski, Jeffrey S., Arthur A. Joyce, and Carlo J. Lucido. 2012. "Excavaciones de la Operación A." In *El Proyecto Río Verde: Informe técnico de la temporada de 2012*, edited by Sarah B. Barber and Arthur A. Joyce, 13–156. Mexico City: Instituto Nacional de Antropología e Historia.

Caso, Alfonso, and Ignacio Bernal. 1952. *Urnas de Oaxaca*. Mexico City: Instituto Nacional de Antropología e Historia.

Caso, Alfonso, Ignacio Bernal, and Jorge R. Acosta. 1967. *La cerámica de Monte Albán*. Mexico City: Instituto Nacional de Antropología e Historia.

Chase, Arlen F., and Diane Z Chase. 1996. "More than Kin and King: Centralized Political Organization among the Late Classic Maya." *Current Anthropology* 37 (5): 803–10.

Coe, Michael, and Richard A. Diehl. 1980. *In the Land of the Olmec*. Vol. 1. Austin: University of Texas Press.

Covarrubias, Miguel. 1946. *El arte olmeca o de la venta*. Mexico, DF: Cuadernos Americanos.

Cruz, Victor de la. 2007. *El pensamiento de los binnigula'sa': Cosmovisión, religión y calendario con especial referencia a los binnizá*. Centro de Investigaciones y Estudios Superiores en Antropología Social, Consejo Nacional para la Cultura y las Artes, el Instituto Nacional de Antropología e Historia y el Gobierno del estado de Oaxaca, Mexico City.

Elson, Christina M, and R Jason Sherman. 2007. "Crema Ware and Elite Power at Monte Albán: Ceramtic Production and Iconography in the Oaxaca Valley, Mexico." *Journal of Field Archaeology* 32 (3): 265–82.

Estrada-Belli, Francisco. 2011. *The First Maya Civilization: Ritual and Power before the Classic Period*. New York: Routledge.

Faulseit, Ronald K. 2011. "Collapse and Reorganization at Dainzú-Macuilxóchitl, Oaxaca, México." New Orleans, LA: Tulane University Press.

Faulseit, R. K. 2012. "State Collapse and Household Resilience in the Oaxaca Valley of Mexico." *Latin American Antiquity* 23 (4): 401–25.

Feinman, Gary M. 1985. "Changes in the Organization of Ceramic Production in Pre-Hispanic Oaxaca, Mexico." In *Decoding Prehistoric Ceramics*, edited by Ben A. Nelson, 195–223. Carbondale: Southern Illinois University Press.

Feinman, Gary M. 1999. "Rethinking Our Assumptions: Economic Specialization at the Household Scale in Ancient Ejutla, Oaxaca, Mexico." In *Pottery and People: A Dynamic Interaction*, edited by James M. Skibo and Gary M. Feinman, 81–98. Salt Lake City: University of Utah Press.

Feinman, Gary M., Sherman Banker, Reid F. Cooper, Glen B. Cook, and Linda M. Nicholas. 1989. "A Technological Perspective on Changes in the Ancient Oaxacan Grayware Ceramic Tradition: Preliminary Results." *Journal of Field Archaeology* 16 (3): 331–44.

Feinman, Gary M., and Linda M. Nicholas. 2007. "Craft Production in Classic Period Oaxaca: Implications for Monte Albán's Political Economy." In *Craft Production in Complex Societies: Multicraft and Producer Perspectives*, edited by Izumi Shimada, 97–121. Salt Lake City: University of Utah Press.

Feinman, Gary M., Linda M. Nicholas, and Helen R. Haines. 2002. "Houses on a Hill: Classic Period Life at El Palmillo, Oaxaca, Mexico." *American Archaeology* 13 (3): 251–77.

Flannery, Kent V., and Joyce Marcus. 1994. *Early Formative pottery of the Valley of Oaxaca*. Ann Arbor: University of Michigan Museum.

Forde, Jamie E. 2016. "The Polychrome Ceramics of Tututepec (Yucu Dzaa), Oaxaca, Mexico: Iconography and Ideology." *Ancient Mesoamerica* 27:389–404.

Freidel, David A., Linda Schele, and Joy Parker. 1993. *Maya Cosmos: Three Thousand Years on the Shaman's Path*. New York: William Morrow.

Grove, David C. 1987. "Comments on the Site and its Organization." In *Ancient Chalcatzingo*, edited by David C Grove, 420–33. Austin: University of Texas Press.

Grove, David C. 2000. "Faces of the Earth at Chalcatzingo, Mexico: Serpents, Caves, and Mountains in Middle Formative Period Iconography." In *Olmec Art and Archaeology in Mesoamerica*, edited by John E. Clark and Mary E. Pye, 277–95. Washington, DC: National Gallery of Art.

Guernsey, Julia. 2006. *Ritual in Power and Stone*. Austin: University of Texas Press.

Hamann, Byron. 2002. "The Social Life of Pre-sunrise Things." *Current Anthropology* 43 (2): 351–82.

Hedgepeth Balkin, Jessica D., Arthur A. Joyce, and Raymond G. Mueller. 2017. "Settlement beyond the Alluvial Plains: Recent Findings from the 2016 Rio Verde Settlement Project (RVSP), Coastal Oaxaca, Mexico." Paper presented at the 82nd Annual Meeting of the Society for American Archaeology, Vancouver, BC.

Hendon, Julia. 2000. "Having and Holding: Storage, Memory, Knowledge, and Social Relations." *American Anthropologist* 102 (1): 42–53.

Hepp, Guy David, and Arthur A. Joyce. 2013. "From Flesh to Clay: Formative Period Ceramic Figurines from Oaxaca's Lower Río Verde Valley." In *Polity and Ecology in Formative Period Coastal Oaxaca*, edited by Arthur A. Joyce, 256–99. Boulder: University Press of Colorado.

Hermann Lejarazu, Manuel A. 2009. "La serpiente de fuego o yahui en la Mixteca prehispánica: Iconografía y significado." In *Analisis del Museo de America XVII*, 64–77.

Hernández Sánchez, Gilda. 2008. "Vasijas prehispánicas tipo códice de centro y sur de México: Una mirada a rituales y cosmovisión antiguos a través de su iconografía." *Cuadernos del Sur* 26:7–23.

Hodder, Ian. 1989. "This Is Not an Article about Material Culture as Text." *Journal of Anthropological Archaeology* 8 (3): 250–69.

Houston, Stephen, and Karl Taube. 2000. "An Archaeology of the Senses: Perception and Cultural Expression in Ancient Mesoamerica." *Cambridge Archaeological Journal* 10 (2): 261–94.

Jansen, Maarten, and Gabina Aurora Pérez Jiménez. 2007. *Encounter with the Plumed Serpent: Drama and Power in the Heart of Mesoamerica*. Boulder: University Press of Colorado.

Joyce, Arthur A. 1991. "Formative Period Occupation in the Lower Río Verde Valley, Oaxaca, Mexico: Interregional Interaction and Social Change." PhD diss., Rutgers University, New Brunswick.

Joyce, Arthur A. 1993. "Interregional Interaction and Social Development on the Oaxaca Coast." *Ancient Mesoamerica* 4:67–84.

Joyce, Arthur A. 2000. "The Founding of Monte Albán: Sacred Propositions and Social Practices." In *Agency in Archaeology*, edited by Marcia-Anne Dobres and John Robb, 71–91. London: Routledge.

Joyce, Arthur A. 2003. "Imperialism in Pre-Aztec Mesoamerica: Monte Albán, Teotihuacan, and the Lower Río Verde Valley." *Ancient Mesoamerican Warfare*. Walnut Creek, CA: AltaMira.

Joyce, Arthur A. 2010. *Mixtecs, Zapotecs, and Chatinos: Ancient Peoples of Southern Mexico*. Malden, MA: Wiley-Blackwell.

Joyce, Arthur A., and Sarah B. Barber. 2011. "Excavating the Acropolis at Río Viejo, Oaxaca, Mexico." *Mexicon* 33:15–20.

Joyce, Arthur A. and Sarah B. Barber. 2015a. "Ensoulment, Entrapment, and Political Centralization: A Comparative Study of Religion and Politics in Later Formative Oaxaca." *Current Anthropology* 56 (6): 819–47.

Joyce, Arthur A. and Sarah B. Barber. 2015b. *El Proyecto Río Verde, informe final de la temporada de 2013*. Oaxaca: Instituto Nacional de Antropología e Historia.

Joyce, Arthur A., Sarah B. Barber, Jeffrey S. Brzezinski, Carlo J. Lucido, and Victor Salazar Chávez. 2016 "Negotiating Political Authority and Community in Terminal Formative Coastal Oaxaca." In *Political Strategies in Pre-Columbian Mesoamerica*, edited by Sarah Kurnick and Joanne Baron, 61–96. Boulder: University Press of Colorado.

Joyce, Arthur A., Laura Arnaud Bustamante, and Marc N. Levine. 2001. "Commoner Power: A Case Study from the Classic Period Collapse on the Oaxaca Coast." *Journal of Archaeological Method and Theory* 8 (4): 343–85.

Joyce, Arthur A., and Marc N. Levine, eds. 2009. *El Proyecto Río Verde 2000*. Final Report prepared for the Instituto Nacional de Antropología e Historia (INAH), Mexico DF.

Joyce, Arthur A., Marc N. Levine, and Sarah B. Barber. 2013. "Place-Making and Power in the Terminal Formative: Excavations on Río Viejo's Acropolis." In *Polity and Ecology in Formative Period Coastal Oaxaca*, edited by Arthur A. Joyce, 135–63. Boulder: University Press of Colorado.

Kubler, George. 1962. *The Art and Architecture of Ancient America*. Baltimore, MD: Penguin.

Levine, Marc N. 2011. "Negotiating Political Economy at Late Postclassic Tututepec (Yucu Dzaa), Oaxaca, Mexico." *American Anthropologist* 113 (1): 22–39.

Levine, Marc N. 2013. "Examining Ceramic Evidence for the Zapotec Imperialism Hypothesis in the Lower Río Verde Region of Oaxaca, Mexico." In *Polity and Ecology in Formative Period Coastal Oaxaca*, edited by Arthur A. Joyce, 227–63. Boulder: University Press of Colorado.

Levine, Marc N., Lane F. Fargher, Leslie G. Cecil, and Jamie E. Forde. 2016. "Polychrome Pottery Economics and Ritual Life in Postclassic Oaxaca, Mexico." *Latin American Antiquity* 26 (3): 319–40.

Lind, Michael D. 2012. "The Kingdom and Pilgrimage Center of Cholula." In *Children of the Plumed Serpent: The Legacy of Quetzalcoatl in Mexico*, edited by V. Fields, J. Pohl, and V. Lyall, 88–93. London: Scala Publishers.

Lipp, Frank J. 1991. *The Mixe of Oaxaca: Religion, Ritual and Healing*. Austin: University of Texas Press.

Lohse, Jon C. 2007. "Commoner Ritual, Commoner Ideology: (Sub)-Alternative Views of Social Complexity in Prehispanic Mesoamerica." In *Commoner Ritual and Ideology in Ancient Mesoamerica*, edited by Nancy Gonlin and Jon C. Lohse, 1–54. Boulder: University Press of Colorado.

López Austin, Alfredo, and Leonardo López Luján. 2009. *Monte sagrado—templo mayor: El cerro y la pirámide en la tradición religiosa mesoamericana*. Mexico City: Universidad Nacional Autónoma de México, Instituto de Investigaciones Antropológicas.

López Luján, Leonardo. 2005. *The Offerings of the Templo Mayor of Tenochtitlan*. Santa Fe: University of New Mexico Press.

Lucero, Lisa J. 2003. "The Emergence of Classic Maya Rulers." *Current Anthropology* 44 (4): 523–44.

Marcus, Joyce, and Kent V. Flannery. 1996. *Zapotec Civilization: How Urban Society Evolved in Mexico's Oaxaca Valley*. London: Thames and Hudson.

Markens, Robert. 2013. "El significado de la greca escalonada en la imaginaría prehispánica de Oaxaca: Una base del poder político." *Cuadernos del Sur* 18 (35): 67–81.

Markens, Robert. 2014. "Análisi sdel conjunto arquitectónico de las tumbas 1 y 2 de Zaachila." In *Zaachila y Su historia prehispánica: Memoria del 50° aniversario del descubrimiento de las tumbas, prehispánicas de Zaachila, 1962–2012*, edited by Ismael Vicente Cruz and Gonzalo Sánchez Santiago, 95–126. Oaxaca: Secretaría de las Culturas y Artes de Oaxaca y el Ayuntamiento de Villa de Zaachila, Oaxaca.

Markens, Robert, Marcus Winter, and Cira Martínez Lopez. 2008. "Ethnohistory, Oral History and Archaeology at Macuilxóchitl: Perspectives on the Postclassic period (800–1521 CE) in the Valley of Oaxaca." In *After Monte Alban: Transformation and Negotiation in Oaxaca, Mexico*, edited by Jeffrey P. Blomster, 193–215. Boulder: University Press of Colorado.

Martínez Lopez, Cira, and Robert Markens. 2004. "Análisis de la función política del Conjunto Plataforma Norte Lado Poniente de la Plaza Principal de Monte Albán." In *Memoria de la Tercera Mesa Redonda de Monte Albán*, edited by Nelly Robles Garcia, 75–99. Mexico City: Conaculta INAH.

Masson, Marilyn A. 2001. "El sobrenatural Cocijo y poder de linaje en la antigua sociedad zapoteca." *Mesoamerica* 41:1–30.

McAnany, Patricia A. 1995. *Living with the Ancestors: Kinship and Kingship in Ancient Maya Society*. Austin: University of Texas Press.

Monaghan, John. 1990. "Sacrifice, Death, and the Origins of Agriculture in the Codex Vienna." *American Antiquity* 55 (3): 559–69.

Monaghan, John. 1995. *The Covenants with Earth and Rain: Exchange, Sacrifice, and Revelation in Mixtec Sociality*. Norman: University of Oklahoma Press.

Monaghan, John, ed. 2000. "Theology and History in the Study of Mesoamerican Religions." In *Supplement to the Handbook of Middle American Indians*, 24–49. Vol. 6. Austin: University of Texas Press.

Orr, Heather S. 1994. "The Viboron Frieze and Sacred Geography at Monte Alban." Paper presented at the 93rd Annual Meeting of the American Anthropological Association, Atlanta, GA.

Orr, Heather S. 1997. "Power Games in the Late Formative Valley of Oaxaca: The Ballplayer Sculptures at Dainzu." PhD diss., University of Texas, Austin.

Orr, Heather S. 2001. "Procession Rituals and Shrine Sites: The Politics of Sacred Space in the Late Formative Valley of Oaxaca." In *Landscape and Power in Ancient Mesoamerica*, edited by Rex Koontz, Kathryn Resse-Taylor, and Annabeth Headrick, 55–67. Oxford: Westview Press.

Oudijk, Michel R. 2008. "The Postclassic Period in the Valley of Oaxaca." In *After Monte Albán: Transformation and Negotiation in Oaxaca, Mexico*, edited by Jeffrey P. Blomster, 95–118. Boulder: University Press of Colorado.

Palmer, David A. 2007. "A Study of Mesoamerican Religious Symbolism." *New Archaeology Review* (March):40–45.

Parsons, Elsie C. 1932. *Mitla: Town of the Souls and Other Zapoteco-Speaking Pueblos of Oaxaca, Mexico*. Chicago: University of Chicago Press.

Piña Chan, Roman. 1977. *Quetzalcóatl: Serpiente emplumada*. Mexico City: Fondo de Cultura Económica.

Preucel, Robert W. 2006. *Archaeological Semiotics*. Oxford: Blackwell.

Preucel, Robert W., and Alexander A. Bauer. 2001. "Archaeological Pragmatics." *Norwegian Archaeological Review* 34 (2): 85–96.

Redmond, Elsa M., and Charles S. Spencer. 2006. "From Raiding to Conquest: Warfare Strategies and Early State Development in Oaxaca, Mexico." In *The Archaeology of Warfare: Prehistories of Raiding and Conquest*, edited by Elizabeth N. Arkush and Mark W. Allen, 336–93. Gainesville: University Press of Florida.

Reilly, F. Kent, III. 1990. "Cosmos and Rulership: The Function of Olmec-Style Symbols in Formative Period Mesoamerica." *Visible Language* 24 (1): 12–37.

Reilly, F. Kent, III. 1996a. "The Lazy-S: A Formative Period Iconographic Loan to Maya Hieroglyphic Writing." In *Eight Palenque Round Table, 1993*, edited by Martha J. Macri and Jan McHargue, 413–44. San Fransisco: Pre-Columbian Art Research Institute.

Reilly, F. Kent, III. 1996b. "Art, Ritual, and Rulership in the Olmec World." In *The Olmec World: Ritual and Rulership*, edited by E. P. Benson, 27–45. Princeton, NJ: Princeton University Art Museum.

Robin, Cynthia. 2002. "Outside of Houses: The Practices of Everyday Life at Chan Noohol, Belize." *Journal of Social Archaeology* 2 (2): 245–68.

Rosenswig, Robert M. 2012. "Materialism, Mode of Production, and a Millennium of Change in Southern Mexico." *Journal of Archaeological Method and Theory* 19 (1): 1–48.

Russo, Alesandra. 2005. *El realismo circular: Tierras, espacios y paisajes de la cartografía novohispana, siglos XVI y XVII*. Mexico City: UNAM.

Schaafsma, Polly, and Karl A. Taube. 2006. "Bringing the Rain: An Ideology of Rain Making in the Pueblo Southwest and Mesoamerica." In *A Pre-Columbian World*, edited by Jeffrey Quilter and Mary Ellen Miller, 232–84. Washington, DC: Dumbarton Oaks.

Schele, Linda, and David Freidel. 1990. *A Forest of Kings: The Untold Story of the Ancient Maya*. New York: William Morrow.

Sellen, Adam T. 2002. "Storm-God Impersonators from Ancient Oaxaca." *Ancient Mesoamerica* 13 (1): 3–19.

Sellen, Adam T. 2007. *El cielo compartido: Deidades y ancestros en las vasijas efigies zapotecas*. Mérida: Universidad Nacional Autónoma de Mexico.

Sellen, Adam T. 2011. "Sowing the Blood with the Maize: Zapotec Effigy Vessels and Agricultural Ritual." *Ancient Mesoamerica* 22 (1): 71–90.

Shaplin, P. D. 1975. "An Introduction to the Stylistic Study of Oaxacan Urns." PhD diss., Wellesley College.

Signorini, Italo. 1997. "Rito y mito como instrumento de previsión y manipulación del clima entre los huaves de San Mateo del Mar (Oaxaca, México)." In *Antropología del clima en el mundo prehispánico*, edited by María Goloubinoff, Esther Katz, and Annamaría Lammel, 83–97. Quito: Abya-Yala.

Spencer, Charles S, and Elsa M Redmond. 2001. "Multilevel Selection and Political Evolution in the Valley of Oaxaca, 500–100 B.C." *Journal of Anthropological Archaeology* 20:195–229.

Spencer, Charles S., Elsa M. Redmond, and Christina M. Elson. 2008. "Ceramic Microtypology and the Territorial Expansion of the Early Monte Albán State." *Journal of Field Archaeology* 33 (3): 321–41.

Taube, Karl A. 1987. "A Representation of the Principal Bird Deity in the Paris Codex." In *Research Reports on Ancient Maya Writing* 6. Washington, DC: Center for Maya Research.

Taube, Karl A. 1996. "The Olmec Maize God: The Face of Corn in Formative Meso-america." *RES: Anthropology and Aesthetics* 29 (1): 39–81.

Taube, Karl A. 2000. "Lightning Celts and Corn Fetishes: The Formative Olmec and the Development of Maize Symbolism in Mesoamerica and the American Southwest." In *Olmec Art and Archaeology: Social Complexity in the Formative Period*, edited by John E. Clark and Mary Pye, 296–337. Washington, DC: National Gallery of Art.

Taube, Karl A. 2001. "The Breath of Life: The Symbolism of Wind in Mesoamerica and the American Southwest." In *The Road to Aztlan: Art from a Mythic Homeland*, edited by Virginia M. Fields and Victor Zamudio-Taylor, 102–23. Los Angeles: Los Angeles County Museum of Art.

Taube, Karl A. 2009. "El dios de la lluvia olmeca." *Arqueologia Mexicana* 16 (96): 26–29.

Thompson, J. Eric. 1970. *Maya History and Religion*. Norman: University of Oklahoma Press.

Urcid, Javier. 1994. "Un sistema de Nomenclatura para los Monolitos Grabados y los Materiales con Inscripciones de Monte Alban." In *Escritura Zapoteca prehispánica*, edited by Marcus Winter, 53–79. Oaxaca: Contribucion no. 4 del Proyecto Especial Monte Alban 1992–1994.

Urcid, Javier. 2002. "La faz oculta de una misteriosa mascara de piedra." In *Sociedad y patrimonio arqueológico en el valle de Oaxaca*, edited by Nelly M Robles Garcia, 212–48. Mexico City: Instituto Nacional de Antropología e Historia.

Urcid, Javier. 2005. "Zapotec Writing: Knowledge, Power, and Memory in Ancient Oaxaca." *Foundation for the Advancement of Mesoamerican Studies*. www.famsi.org/zapotec writing/.

Urcid, Javier. 2009. "Personajes enmascarados: Eel rayo, el trueno y la lluvia en Oaxaca." *Arqueología Mexicana* 16 (96): 30–34.

Urcid, Javier, and Marcus Winter. 2003. "Nuevas variantes glificas zapotecas." *Mexicon* 25 (5): 123–28.

Vogt, Evon Z. 1969. *Zinacantan: A Maya Community in the Highlands of Chiapas*. Cambridge, MA: Harvard University Press.

Workinger, Andrew. 2002. "Coastal/Highland Interaction in Prehispanic Oaxaca, Mexico: The Perspective from San Francisco de Arriba." PhD diss., Vanderbilt University.

Workinger, Andrew, and Arthur A. Joyce. 1999. "Excavaciones arqueológicas en Río Viejo." In *El Proyecto patrones de asentamiento del Río Verde*, edited by Arthur A. Joyce, 51–119. Final report submitted to the Consejo de Arquelogia, Instituto Nacional de Antropología e Historia, Mexico City.

Workinger, Andrew, and Arthur A. Joyce. 2009 "Reconsidering Warfare in Formative Period Oaxaca." In *Blood and Beauty: Organized Violence in the Art and Archaeology of Mesoamerica and Central America*, edited by Heather Orr and Rex Koontz, 3–37. Los Angeles: Costen Institute of Archaeology.

5

The Beginnings of Complexity in the Central Petén Lakes Area

PRUDENCE M. RICE AND KATHERINE E. SOUTH

INTRODUCTION

A notable physiographic feature of the central Department of El Petén, northern Guatemala, is a line or chain of eight lakes extending approximately 76 km east-west at ~17°–17.5° north latitude (figure 5.1). These bodies of water would have been attractive places for early sedentary human occupation. We can imagine that the living was easy, the watersheds teeming with terrestrial and aquatic protein sources—deer, peccary, agouti, turkey; fish, mollusks, turtles, waterfowl—along with forest and grassland products (food, timber, firewood, fibers), plus easy access to good soils for horticulture and abundant water, stone, and clay resources for construction and domestic uses in tools, containers, and so on.

Archaeological settlement surveys were carried out in multiple transects around all the lakes, beginning in 1973–74 with Lakes Yaxhá and Sacnab at the eastern end of the chain, as part of a larger historical ecology project into the impact of human occupation on a tropical lacustrine environment (Deevey et al. 1981; Rice 1976a; Rice and Rice 2016; Rice et al. 1985). When the project began, the lakes district was considered to be not only a hydro-geologico-physiographic

https://doi.org/10.5876/9781646422883.c005

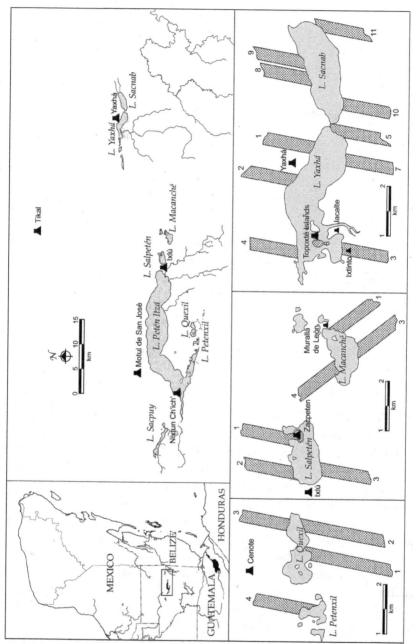

FIGURE 5.1: *The central Petén lakes area, showing Rice survey transects and sites mentioned in text.*

region but also a cultural (sub)region: an area defined by relatively homogeneous lacustrine topography plus relative socio-cultural (e.g., belief systems, material expressions, ethnolinguistics) homogeneity. That notion was immediately challenged, however, as studies of Late Postclassic and later (1300–1700 CE) pottery revealed marked geo-ethno-political divisions between east and west: Kowoj Maya controlling Yaxhá/Topoxté in the east and Itza Maya dominating Lake Petén Itzá in the west (Jones 1998; Rice and Rice 2009, 2018). Over the following decades, as fieldwork moved westward through the lake basins, we continued to observe differences between east and west in earlier periods, most recently in the Preclassic (South 2019). The Petén lakes area, then, is not technically a cultural region, as it exhibits east–west axes of variability in external interactions enduring nearly three thousand years.

Here, our aim is to examine the archaeological record of sites in the lake basins during "pre-Mamom" times (Terminal Early Preclassic/Formative; 1100–900 /800 BCE) and the Mamom Middle Preclassic/Formative period (900/800–500/400 BCE) to understand the development of societal complexity and the early roles of external affiliations. Our focus is on three categories of data: settlement, ceramics (pottery and figurines), and architecture (chiefly E Groups) as they address these issues. These data, particularly the pottery, suggest a gradual shift in identity focus, from the local to larger cultural groupings. In particular, they speak to the roles of accumulation and display of valued material goods as evidence of inchoate community social differentiation, or, phrased differently, as evidence of "social forms of identity, interaction, and organization . . . [in] the development of socio-political complexity" (Canuto 2016, 463).

THE CENTRAL PETÉN LAKES AND THE MIDDLE PRECLASSIC

The eight lakes in the central Petén chain are (from east to west) Sacnab, Yaxhá, Macanché, Salpetén, Petén Itzá, Quexil and Petenxil south of Lake Petén, and Sacpuy (figure 5.1). Topographically, the lakes are characterized by steep northern shores rising 100 m or more above the water levels and gently sloping southern shores extending about 1.5 to 3 km to haystack hills. They are closed basins with no external drainage and are surrounded by generally good soils. They differ, however, in areal size, depth, and water chemistry.

Around 2000 BCE, nearly worldwide climate changes occurred: the "4200 BP climate event," bringing increased aridity. In Mesoamerica, it is around this time that Proto-Yukatekan speakers are thought to have migrated into the lowlands from highland Guatemala (Campbell 2017; Kaufman 2017). Moreover, most indicators of human presence around the lakes begin about 2000 BCE: paleoecological (paleolimnological) evidence, such as pollen, reflects alterations to the surrounding forest, long interpreted as resulting from early slash-and-burn horticulture (see, e.g., Brenner 2018; Castellanos and Foias 2017). At present, no pre-1300

Early Preclassic or earlier Archaic/Preceramic archaeological sites—probably ephemeral macro- or micro-band encampments—or archaeologically retrieved evidence for early human activity (e.g., lithics) are known around the lakes.

Settlement

Because the central Petén lakes area lacks material evidence of small groups of mobile foragers/ hunters/gatherers/fisherfolk and shifting cultivators, it is unclear whether the earliest permanently settled villages were established by their more-or-less in situ descendants or by immigrants moving into the interior along riverine migratory routes (see, for example, Ball and Taschek 2003; Clark and Cheetham 2002; Puleston and Puleston 1971; Rice and Puleston 1981). The earliest evidence of settlement in the Petén lakes district, as throughout the lowlands, is difficult to recognize, largely because it is deeply buried below later construction and remodeling and incorporates scant artifacts. Sometimes it is seen in a layer of soil and rock to level uneven bedrock; sometimes the bedrock itself was scraped clean and leveled; at still other sites carved bedrock itself comprised the core of early civic ceremonial structures. Absence of evidence is not evidence of absence, of course, but it does make it difficult to understand the earliest stages of human occupation in the area. Data from later periods, Classic through Postclassic and into the present, reveal that the lakes area was a social and economic nexus, a crossroads for humans and goods moving both north-south over land and east-west by water.

In general, the earliest (Terminal Early and Middle Preclassic) sedentary occupations around the lakes are found primarily on relatively elevated points on the low southern shores but also on the steep northern escarpments. Early settlers also targeted the islands and peninsulas in the lakes, a favored location for later Postclassic occupation. As discussed below, deep test excavations into Postclassic structures have often revealed Middle Preclassic construction on bedrock.

Pottery

The early pottery of sites in the central Petén lakes zone displays traits of the better known ceramic spheres of Tikal and Uaxactún to the north, the Ceibal/Pasión area to the southwest, and areas to the east that include the Holmul River and the Belize Valley, especially Barton Ramie. This phenomenon of overlapping spheres prevails to varying degrees for all archaeological periods, from pre-Mamom through Postclassic and Spanish-Contact times. As for the period of interest here, pre-Mamom pottery in the central Petén lakes zone follows a similar pattern found throughout the lowlands: notable local variation on top of regional variation.

In general, the lakes' early pottery is most comparable typologically and formally to that of Tikal's Eb and Tzec Complexes (table 5.1; Culbert 1977, 1993; Culbert and Kosakowsky 2019). The lakes material has been organized into

TABLE 5.1. Early ceramic complexes in the central Petén lakes zone and related areas.

Period	Dates (BCE)	Belize Valley[a]	Tikal[b]	Yaxhá X	Macanché and Salpeten	Nixtun-Ch'ich'	Tayasal-Paxc[c]	Ceibal[d]
Late Middle	500/400–300/200	L. Jenney Creek	C. Tzec	Early Kuxtin	Chamaca	Late Nix	Chun-zalam	Escoba?
Middle	700–500/400	E. Jenney Creek	E. Tzec	Yancotil	Bocadilla (E & L)	Nix		Real 3
Early Middle	800–700	Cunil	Late Eb	Late Ah Pam	Late Amanece	Early Nix		Real 2
"Transitional"	900–800	?	?	?	?	Yum (mixed)	?	?
Term. Early 2	~1000–900	Cunil	Early Eb	Early Ah Pam	Early Amanece	Late Chich		Real 1
Term. Early 1	~1100–1000	Cunil				Early Chich		Xe
Late Early	~1300–1100?[b]	?				K'as		

Note: Shading indicates pre-Mamom complexes. Beginning and ending dates approximate.

[a] Cheetham et al. 2003, fig. 2.

[b] Rice 2019b, table 1; preliminary pre-Mamom dates from interpolation between radiometrically dated deposits.

[c] Chase 1983.

[d] Rice 2009, table 2.

separate ceramic "complexes" defined for each basin or basin pair. Concerning external ties and influences, Ah Pam pottery at Yaxhá-Sacnab is most similar to ceramics in Belize as well as Tikal; Amanece and Bocadilla at Macanché to Eb and Tzec and also that of Yaxhá-Sacnab; and pottery from sites in the large Lake Petén Itzá basin shares attributes with all the above, as well as the Pasión zone. Analysis of pottery from Nixtun-Ch'ich,' Tayasal, and Ixlú led to recognition of a distinguishable pre-Mamom complex (see Rice 2019b; South 2019).

Many ceramic groups and types are widespread and are present in the communities around multiple lakes. Nonetheless, Middle Preclassic and earlier pottery exhibits a great deal of variability in slips, decoration, and pastes. Slips are primarily red, black, and cream, but also brown and gray; they may be dull and streaky. Red slips are most diverse, varying from dull to waxy and from dark brownish to clear red. Cream-colored slips are generally grayish or tan in the early facets of the Middle Preclassic, becoming clear cream later. Decoration is primarily plastic, including incising (grooved or fine-line, pre- or post-slip) and some fluting and chamfering. Occasional resist decoration is noted. Dichromes were common except around western Lake Petén Itzá; at Yaxhá-Sacnab, red/cream dichromes were present in the Early Ah Pam complex; around Lakes

Macanché and Salpetén, dichromes included not only red/cream but also red/black and black/cream. Slipped wares have multiple pastes, including red-orange, tan with a dark core, dark gray brown, and soft yellowish (yellowish is also noted at Tikal in Eb: Culbert and Kosakowsky 2019, 16–17). Common inclusions (temper) are calcite, grog, and volcanic ash.

Forms are widely comparable. Slipped forms include tecomates, varied flare-sided plates with bolstered or everted rims, deep "flowerpots" (distinct from "cuspidors"), and drums. Unslipped wares are primarily jars of varied sizes and with varied mouth/neck forms.

Architecture and E Groups

It is in the lowest levels underlying monumental architecture around the Petén lakes that the earliest evidence of settlement can be found. Two architectural features are of note in early central Petén, as elsewhere in Mesoamerica: rare north-south axial layouts and common multistructure complexes known as E Groups.

North-south orientations are characteristic of early communities along the Gulf Coast and in Chiapas in what has been called the Middle Formative Chiapas (MFC) pattern. The MFC layout features a large pyramid in the north and an E Group in the south, demarcating a plaza; at the east side of the plaza is a large acropolis that may have been an elite compound (Clark and Hansen 2001, 4). In general, early north-south plans have been heavily overbuilt at lakes' sites, and sometime in the Middle Preclassic an east-west axis came to dominate. Nonetheless, vestiges of a north-south alignment and some MFC traits can be seen at Yaxhá, in the Macanché basin, and at Nixtun-Ch'ich'.

A more common and key characteristic of the early southern Maya Lowlands, including the lakes area, is the architectural assemblage known as an E Group (see Freidel et al. 2017). An E Group, named after a complex at Uaxactún, comprises a plaza with two facing structures: on the east, an elongate north-south platform with three buildings at the ends and center (distinct from later Triadic Groups), and in the west, a radial pyramid centered on the eastern platform. To an observer at the western pyramid, sunrise points on the solstices and equinoxes appeared to be marked by the three structures on the eastern platform (Blom 1924; Ricketson 1928).

Although these architectural arrangements exhibit some degree of standardization, they are also markedly variable, with at least two temporal and structural variants of the eastern platform known in Petén: the "Cenote style" and "Uaxactún style" (table 5.2; Chase 1983; Chase and Chase 2017). The Cenote variant usually has a large, central edifice offset to the east (back) from its north-south axis, with two smaller structures at the north and south ends of two extensions or wings. In the Uaxactún style, all three buildings are constructed

TABLE 5.2. E Groups and possible E Groups in the central Petén lake basins.

Lake Basin	Site	Type	Date[a]	Comment
Yaxhá-Sacnab	Yaxhá Plaza C	?		
	Yaxhá Plaza E	Uaxactún		
	Yaxhá Plaza F	Cenote		
	Ixtinto	Uaxactún		SW of the Topoxté Islands
	Yaxhá Hill	Uaxactún?		"Uapake"; S of isthmus
	Sacnab	Cenote		SE of lake; no W structure
	La Quemada Corozal	?	Late Precl.	Well south of the lake
Macanché	Cerro Ortiz	Cenote?	Middle Precl.?	Site has major M. Precl. constr.; MFC pattern
Petén Itzá	Tayasal	Uaxactún		2 superstrs. Postclassic?
	Tres Naciones	?		
	Chachakluum	?	Late Precl.?	Possibly earlier?
	N-C Sector A	?	Middle Precl.	
	N-C Sector Y	Uaxactún?	Middle Precl.	
	N-C Sector AA	?		
	T'up?	?		Not confirmed on ground
Quexil	Cenote	Cenote		
	Paxcamán	Cenote		
Sacpuy	Sacpuy 1	Cenote		Only E Group structures
	Ts'unun Witz	?	Late Precl.	Well south of the lake

Source: See Chase and Chase (2017, table 2.1), except as noted.

[a] Middle Preclassic dates of early construction usually determined by excavations (rare) and/or pottery among surface artifacts; Late Preclassic dates usually determined by surface artifacts, which lack Middle Preclassic pottery. Many early complexes were remodeled in the Late Preclassic or Early Classic.

on a single platform. Both typically have Middle Preclassic antecedents and exhibit some minor internal variability, but the Cenote style is primarily a Late Preclassic form, whereas the Uaxactún style dates to the Early Classic. Other variations exist, notably in the Belize Valley (Awe et al. 2017).

These monumental complexes had deep, widespread, and long-lived cultural significance: "As the earliest recognized form of public architecture in the Maya area, E Groups had to have been central to the social and political transformations that took place" as early as the Middle Preclassic and for subsequent centuries (Chase et al. 2017, 8).

MIDDLE PRECLASSIC OCCUPATION IN THE CENTRAL PETÉN LAKE BASINS

Here we briefly review select available archaeological data—on settlement, pottery, and E Group architecture—pertaining to Middle Preclassic occupation in the central Petén lake basins. The lakes differ slightly in their occupation histories. Settlement surveys have shown that all watersheds were occupied to some degree from Preclassic through Postclassic times (Rice and Rice 1990), but the density and intensity of those occupations varied from period to period. Only Lakes Yaxhá in the east and Petén Itzá in the west saw the rise of major Classic cities, as discussed below, while the others are perhaps better described as rural. We emphasize Yaxhá along with Nixtun-Ch'ich' in the west because we have more data from these two areas and because they illustrate the different extraregional contacts of lakes district residents. Estimates of Middle Preclassic occupations are probably underestimates, given the difficulty of encountering such early materials under two millennia or more of later construction.

Lakes Yaxhá and Sacnab

The twin basins of Lakes Yaxhá and Sacnab in northeastern Petén are the easternmost lakes in the chain, situated in elevated terrain about 50 m higher than the other lakes to the west. The largest site in their combined watershed, with more than five hundred structures, is Yaxhá on the high north shore, which was a secondary center under Tikal's dominion during the Late Classic period. The city's Preclassic pottery is related to Tikal's (and Uaxactún's) and also that of Barton Ramie, and its Classic architecture includes a twin-pyramid complex, best known from the nine such groups at Tikal. Yaxhá is one of the few sites in the lakes area that maintained its ancient name and had its own Emblem Glyph (Justeson 1975; Stuart 1985), read *yax* (blue, green) plus *a*, *ah*, or *ha* (water). In the Postclassic period, occupation and political weight shifted to the Topoxté Islands in the southwestern Yaxhá basin, a critical node of the Kowoj polity (Rice and Rice 2009).

Settlement

Excavations indicate that the area that became the city of Yaxhá was first settled in the Middle Preclassic period, with early ritual architecture in the vicinity of the North Acropolis, Plaza F (an E Group), and bedrock leveling under the East Acropolis (Hermes 2001, 151; Źrałka 2005, 104). Settlement surveys were carried out in ten transects on the steep northern and gently sloping southern shores of the Yaxhá-Sacnab watershed (including on Canté Island). Of a total of 851 mounds, 196 (23%) were tested; only 21 (10.7%) of those yielded evidence of Middle Preclassic occupation and use (Rice 1976a). Although surveys on the elevated north shores identified more structures than on the south, the latter had a greater percentage of Middle Preclassic construction episodes.

Five "minor centers"—probably tertiary sites in the Yaxhá polity—were identified (see below). One, Uapake, is a small site atop Yaxhá Hill, an 80 m high eminence at the base of the isthmus between the two lakes (Rice 1976b; Rice 1979). Never excavated, it was bulldozed by the Petén development organization FYDEP in creating a "road" to the site from the Flores-Melchor highway. Testing, however, revealed pre-Mamom Ah Pam sherds over bedrock and under a floor; above, Yancotil pottery in the fills of three floors dated construction to the Mamom Middle Preclassic (Rice 1976b, 435–36). Small early communities also have been identified in the area southwest of Lake Yaxhá and the Topoxté Islands (Hermes et al. 1999, 111). There, more recent surveys (Morales n.d.) revealed considerable Middle and Late Preclassic occupation and a three-level site-size hierarchy among eleven sites, but it is unclear when this hierarchy emerged. Surprisingly, the "main" island of Topoxté yielded scant evidence of Middle Preclassic or earlier usage: Yancotil pottery associated with a lower floor in the Main Plaza. No pre-Mamom pottery was noted. Similarly, no Middle Preclassic construction or pottery was identified in the transect survey and testing at Canté Island.

The Yaxhá-Sacnab basins experienced sustained exponential growth from the Middle Preclassic through the Terminal Classic, unlike most of the other lakes in central Petén (Rice 1976a, fig. 46).

Pottery

At the time of the Yaxhá-Sacnab excavations and analyses, Middle Preclassic pottery of the Mamom sphere was called Early Preclassic, and it was thought to have developed out of the Xe-Real traditions in the Río Pasión-Usumacinta region (Rice 1976a, 138, 231, citing personal communication from Gordon Willey). The first analysis of pottery from Yaxhá and the Lake Yaxhá basin identified two early complexes, Ah Pam and Yancotil (table 5.1; Rice 1979). This early material is related to that of Tikal and Uaxactún, but also to that of Barton Ramie (Gifford 1976), through the presence of imported Jocote Orange-Brown and Savanna Orange types. Calam Buff and Cabcoh Striated bespeak relations with Tikal. According to a reassessment (Cheetham et al. 2003), the Ah Pam complex is temporally and typologically equivalent to Culbert's (1977, 1993) Early Eb at Tikal, which is pre-Mamom; Yancotil is equivalent to Late Eb and Early Tzec, or early Mamom.

Architecture and E Groups

The architecture of Yaxhá exhibits both north-south and east-west axes, but the former is most pronounced. This axis, about 1 km long, is formed by two causeways, the Blom Causeway leading north from site center to the Maler Group and the Lake Causeway leading south from the center down the steep escarpment to the lake shore (Hermes et al. 1999, 110). The latter likely followed a Middle Preclassic path from the center downhill to the lake (Hermes et al. 1999, iii). Dual E Groups occupy epicentral space at the proximal ends of the two causeways; a third lies in the southeast part of the center.

Outside of Yaxhá proper, four minor centers south of the lakes have E Groups (table 5.2). One is Uapake, where a test unit in the eastern structure indicated Ah Pam and Yancotil construction, with four well-plastered floors above bedrock underlying a Yancotil structure (Rice 1976a, 186, 189). No western pyramid is evident. The minor center of Sacnab southeast of Lake Sacnab also had an E Group (Rice 1976a, fig. 40). Its eastern platform is oriented slightly north of east. The E Group at Ixtinto Plaza F, south of the Topoxté Islands, may date to the Middle Preclassic on the basis of sherds (including pre-Mamom) recovered in a looter's trench through a small western building (not the main western pyramid). Farther south, an E Group at La Quemada Corozal, in the top tier of the area's settlement hierarchy (Acevedo et al. 1996), dated to the Late Preclassic, suggesting that the hierarchy might have emerged then.

Lake Macanché

Small Lake Macanché lies at the western edge of the elevated terrain of northeastern Petén, 23 km southwest of Lake Yaxhá and 2 km southeast of Lake Salpetén. The basin has no single, large center, such as Yaxhá, but it does have three smaller sites, two of which are primarily Postclassic: Macanché Island (Rice 1987) and Muralla de León, its wall possibly a Terminal Preclassic/Protoclassic construction (Bracken 2018; Rice and Rice 1981). The early site of interest here is Cerro Ortiz on the southeast shore of the lake.

Settlement

Three settlement survey transects were investigated around Lake Macanché, one on the northwestern shore and two on the southeast. As at Yaxhá-Sacnab, Middle Preclassic occupation was found primarily on the southern shore. A total of 378 structures/mounds were mapped around the lake, with 69 (18.2%) test-excavated: of these, 19 (27.5%) had Middle Preclassic occupation/construction (Rice and Rice 1990, tables 6.1, 6.2), revealing a larger relative population than around Yaxhá-Sacnab. Of the nineteen structures with Middle Preclassic occupation, ceramic dating indicated a slight increase in construction/occupation from early to late facets. Macanché Island yielded no evidence of occupation before the Late Classic period; perhaps during the Middle Preclassic period the island, with a natural elevation of only 7–8 m above the lake waters in 1979 (Rice 1987, fig. 22), was largely submerged.

Pottery

The early pottery of the Macanché basin and that of Salpetén, Quexil, and Petenxil as well, was sufficiently different from the Yaxhá pottery that two new

Middle Preclassic complexes were defined: Amanece, equivalent to Ah Pam, and Bocadilla, equivalent to Yancotil, both with early and late facets. These are not further discussed here.

Architecture and E Groups

Cerro Ortiz, which sits atop a 6 m hill, part natural and part artificial, has a distinctive north-south layout similar to that of the MFC (Rice and Rice n.d.) with an E Group in the center. One of three test units excavated into a low platform revealed 5.1 m of Preclassic fills and floors. Clayey fill with Terminal Early Preclassic sherds leveled bedrock, above which was the first Middle Preclassic construction, about 1.8 m high. Four Middle Preclassic remodelings raised it about 3 m to the last surfacing of the plaza. The uppermost fill of the low platform itself had a mix of Preclassic and Postclassic pottery.

The E Group, its structures unexcavated (because of permit conditions), was either unfinished or heavily modified by later construction and occupation. Probably built in the Cenote style, the eastern platform had an offset central structure and lacked evidence of two end structures. The western building, also unexcavated, did not appear to be radial: probable later renovations slightly elongated it north–south and it had only one stairway.

LAKE SALPETÉN

Tiny Lake Salpetén is separated from the eastern tip of the main body of Lake Petén Itzá by a low, narrow isthmus at the base of the steep northern escarpment of the lake beds' fault line. Two significant sites in the basin, Zacpetén and Ixlú, are best known for their Postclassic and Contact-period occupations, but each was occupied in the Middle Preclassic as well. Zacpetén, occupying a peninsula off the northeastern edge of the lake, has two Postclassic temple assemblages, Group A and Group C, both perched upon elevated terrain (Pugh 2001; Rice n.d.; Rice and Rice 2009). Ixlú, on the isthmus, was probably the community the Spaniards identified as Saclemacal, which controlled the Postclassic Itza's main eastern port of Lake Petén Itzá (Rice and Rice 2016).

Settlement

Lake Salpetén was lightly occupied in the Middle Preclassic period. A total of 163 structures/mounds were mapped in three transects around the lake (excluding Zacpetén), with 39 (23.9%) test-excavated: of these, only seven (17.9%) had Middle Preclassic occupation/construction (Rice and Rice 1990, tables 6.1, 6.2). Middle Preclassic occupation was found mostly on the northeast shore (Rice 1976b), probably reflecting the later-explored early importance of the Zacpetén Peninsula (Pugh 2001; Rice and Rice 2009). Occupation and construction there began in the Middle Preclassic period and is particularly seen under temple assemblage Group A. Test units taken to bedrock at Structure 605 revealed construction of a nearly 2 m-high platform, but the fill lacked diagnostic artifacts for dating (Pugh 2001, 251, fig. 7–26). A test unit under nearby Structure 606, however, encountered two superposed pits excavated through a floor/platform surfacing, and two orthogonal stone walls creating the southeast corner of a structure. The intrusive pit held a cached incised, black-slipped (Desprecio Incised), flowerpot-like jar and a large obsidian blade covered with Middle Preclassic fill (Rice et al. 1996). Just to the west of Structure 606 was a large depression (excavated as Operation 1000), possibly an early borrow pit but later a Postclassic mass grave (Duncan 2005, 2009). Contents included Middle Preclassic pottery: three caches involving a whole but broken red-slipped, fluted (Xexcay Fluted) cuspidor, a possible drum, and the platter-like base of a large red-and-black dichrome dish, its walls and rim missing. Elsewhere at Zacpetén, tests in temple assemblage Group C also revealed Middle Preclassic pottery and other artifacts above bedrock, but most of the early fills are mixed.

It is not known if the small site of Ixlú functioned in port management as early as the Preclassic period, but its isthmian location made it a convenient location for north (Tikal)-south and east-west trade movements, terrestrial and waterborne, from earliest times. Middle Preclassic pottery was recovered primarily from levels above bedrock in Plaza B (Rice and Rice 2016, 29–33).

Pottery and Figurines

Early pottery from Zacpetén and Ixlú was recovered primarily from levels above bedrock: under Group A temple-assemblage structures at Zacpetén and under Plaza B—a possible primary deposit of unusually well-made pottery on bedrock—at Ixlú. These materials have been identified as local variants of the Chich (Terminal Early Preclassic) and Nix (Middle Preclassic) complexes defined at the site of Nixtun-Ch'ich' in western Lake Petén Itzá (see below; Rice 2019b; South 2019). With respect to red-slipped wares, the local Nix variant at Zacpetén has generally more friable paste textures and flaky slips, while the Ixlú variant tends to have thinner walls with hard, compact pastes and well-preserved slips.

Hand-modeled (not mold-made) anthropomorphic and zoomorphic figurines and musical instruments (whistles, ocarinas) were recovered with other Middle Preclassic artifacts under Plaza B at Ixlú. Anthropomorphic figurines frequently accompany the growth of complexity in other culture areas, indicating greater concern with identities and roles and with how people present themselves and were perceived by others (Coward and Dunbar 2014, 387). Neutron activation analysis (NAA) of a sample of these objects suggested possible manufacturing origins, including some thought to be made at or around Ixlú and others imported from Nixtun-Ch'ich' (Rice 2019a, 176).

Architecture and E Groups

Rather surprisingly, no E Groups are known at Ixlú or Zacpetén. At the latter, temple assemblage Group A was built over a possible Late / Terminal Classic Plaza Plan 2, and earlier (Preclassic) construction at that locus might have been an E Group (Rice n.d.). However, that is pure speculation, and any such early architectural complexes at these two sites might have been covered by late construction.

Lakes Petenxil and Quexil

Lakes Petenxil (or Petenchel) and Quexil (Eckixil) are two very small bodies of water south of the hilly Tayasal Peninsula and east of the southern arm of Lake Petén Itzá (table 5.1). Today they are joined together, and also to Lake Petén, by canals of unknown date, at least one of which, with a right angle, is clearly human made (Rice 1996). No Preclassic occupation, either Middle or Late, was noted in test excavation of structures around Petenxil, although Lake Quexil was home to a relatively substantial Middle Preclassic population (14 of 35 tested structures, 40%; Rice and Rice 1990, tables 6.1, 6.2). No major sites lie in these small watersheds, although two in the area have E Groups. Cenote, the type site for the Cenote style, occupies elevated grassy terrain north of Lake Quexil. Its eastern structure has a Middle Preclassic core of carved bedrock (Chase 1983, 92). Farther east, the site of Paxcaman also has an E Group, but it has not been excavated.

Lake Petén Itzá

Lake Petén Itzá is the largest (and deepest) lake in the Maya Lowlands and the second largest lake in Guatemala (after Lake Izabal). Stretching 30 km east-west, it has two basins: the large, deep main basin joined in the west with a much smaller, shallower southern basin, the two separated by the Tayasal and Candelaria Peninsulas. It is not surprising that this large body—a permanent source of fresh water and a major transportation artery—was attractive for settlement from earliest times to the present day. Many Postclassic sites are known around the lake, the western end of which was the core of the Itza polity; sites include modern Flores Island (the Itza capital, known as Tayza or Nojpeten), Tayasal, and Nixtun-Ch'ich, home of a rebellious Chak'an Itza faction. The site now known as Motul de San José, on the northwest shore, was important as a Late Classic satellite of Tikal (Foias and Emery 2012), and it, too, had smaller, subsidiary centers to the south, such as the port of Trinidad de Nosotros and Buenavista San José.

Excavations at most of these sites recovered deep occupations beginning in the Preclassic period, many in the Middle Preclassic and some earlier. Discussion here focuses on Nixtun-Ch'ich' with its atypical gridded layout imposed in the Middle Preclassic (Obrist-Farner and Rice 2019; Pugh and Rice 2017; Rice and Pugh 2017).

Settlement

Many Classic and Postclassic sites around Lake Petén Itzá were first occupied in the Middle Preclassic period, especially on elevated locales such as the north shore (Motul de San José) or the islands (Flores) and peninsulas (Tayasal) in the lake. The south shores of both its main and southern basins are broad and low lying, the latter covered with heavy modern construction and occupation (e.g., Flores "international" airport; contiguous and growing Santa Elena and San Benito communities), which have either hidden or destroyed any evidence of early settlement.

Nixtun-Ch'ich' is proposed to center a "primate" settlement distribution and incipient archaic state (Pugh et al. 2019; Pugh et al. 2022; Rice and Pugh 2021). In the former, a capital overwhelmingly dominates regional sociopolitico-economic relations, minimizing the roles of second-tier centers. Secondary centers under Nixtun-Ch'ich' minimally include Tayasal, Sacpuy 1 (below), and T'up, a newly discovered, very small site. Middle Preclassic Nixtun-Ch'ich' appears to have sat atop a two-tiered administrative hierarchy and a three-tiered settlement hierarchy.

Pottery and Figurines

Variability in Middle Preclassic pottery recovered in excavations in different areas of Nixtun-Ch'ich' suggests that this large site, which covers 2.5 km² and extends over the Candelaria Peninsula, may have begun as several distinct small settlements or neighborhoods. Of interest here are differences in slipped pottery from various parts of the site.

Pre-Mamom Chich complex pottery includes short-necked jars and small, thin-walled serving bowls and dishes that are either black or cream in color, whether slipped or unslipped. Decoration is largely limited to pre-slip, circumferential-line incising and fluting. Slipped pottery generally has compact, fine-textured pastes with ash inclusions, whereas unslipped pottery tends to have coarser pastes with calcite inclusions. The Nix (Mamom) complex includes unslipped short-necked jars, slipped larger serving vessels, and incensarios. Incised and fluted decoration continues, and chamfering and modeling are introduced. Red (Juventud ceramic group) is the most frequent slip color, followed by black and cream.

In addition to the Chich and Nix complexes, an earlier complex (K'as) has been tentatively identified at Nixtun-Ch'ich' and given a Late Early Preclassic temporal designation by radiocarbon dates (Rice 2009, 2019b). K'as pottery was recovered in the lowest excavated levels of Mound ZZ1, on the tip of the peninsula. Characterized by mostly unslipped sherds that vary in composition and surface appearance (South 2019, 215–16), K'as pottery has also been identified in the civic ceremonial area of Nixtun-Ch'ich', though in small quantities.

Chich complex pottery recovered from different areas at Nixtun-Ch'ich' shows interesting similarities and differences. General features are comparable, but variations in slipped wares are noteworthy, especially in color: dark red and streaky orange-red slips were more abundant in the monumental mainland core compared to the peninsula, where colors were mainly black and cream. Pottery from the core also exhibited more morphological heterogeneity and surface elaboration, including composite forms, tecomates, grooved vessel rims, hooked vessel rims, surface modeling, and appliqué (Rice 2019b, 473; South 2019). Similarly, more form diversity is noted in Nix complex pottery from different parts of the city. Cuspidors and spouted vessels have been found in the civic-ceremonial area (Rice 2019b, 475), especially in a feasting deposit adjacent to the Sector Y E Group, but are rare or absent to the east on the peninsula.

Middle Preclassic pottery has also been recovered at the site of Tayasal, on the Tayasal Peninsula east of Nixtun-Ch'ich', but the frequency is far lower. Generally, pastes were more friable with larger inclusions and slips were poorly preserved.

Anthropomorphic and zoomorphic figurines and musical instruments were recovered in excavations throughout Nixtun-Ch'ich', especially at Mound ZZ1 and also in civic ceremonial and residential contexts on the mainland (Rice 2019a). These figurines were hand-modeled of various clay-temper combinations and display diverse facial features and ornamentation. One subset made of white/cream-firing clay is proposed to have been produced in the city (Rice 2019a, 93, 172–75, 210).

Architecture and E Groups

With respect to axial orientations, Nixtun-Ch'ich' has traces of an early (pre-Mamom) north-south axis in the form of broad Avenues G and H. As at Yaxhá, these corridors lead into the ceremonial core but are interrupted by the site's east-west central axis.

As seen in table 5.2, six—possibly seven—E Groups are known around the shores of Lake Petén Itzá, including three on the Tayasal Peninsula (at Tayasal itself and farther east at Cenote and Paxcaman) and three at Nixtun-Ch'ich'. The latter are all aligned on the central *axis urbis* and may have had "nested" sightlines not only to sunrise positions but also to peaks on the north shore, the Tayasal Peninsula, Flores, and the south shore of the lake. The tiny site of T'up, midway between Nixtun-Ch'ich' and Sacpuy 1, has suffered some recent destruction, but drone mapping suggests that an E Group lies at its center. The earliest construction of the two excavated E Groups at Nixtun-Ch'ich' took place coevally in "archaeological time." They may have constituted the public architecture of two distinct and influential social groups. Like two of the three groups at Yaxhá, they were constructed on the city's central axis in its monumental core. As discussed elsewhere (Rice and Pugh 2017), the Sector Y E Group and its deep *fosa* likely centered the entire city itself.

It is rather odd that E Groups are absent at Motul de San José, an important Late Classic satellite of Tikal on the north shore of the lake, and at its large satellite and port Trinidad de Nosotros, given these complexes' ubiquity at other lakes area sites, small and large. Perhaps it relates to the fact that Motul did not have a large Middle Preclassic occupation, or maybe an E Group there was overbuilt.

Lake Sacpuy

During the Late Postclassic and Contact periods, the Lake Sacpuy basin lay within the territory of the Chak'an faction of the Itzas; little is known of its Classic occupation. The site of Sacpuy 1 was one of several identified and mapped during a Guatemalan archaeological atlas project (Martínez and Laporte 2010). It is a very small site on the south shore of the lake at the northwestern end. Its E Group, which appears to be in the Cenote style, is the only major architectural complex; other low structures could be residential or administrative in function. The entire complex and especially the eastern platform are angled to the southeast, as is that of T'up. Sacpuy 1 and T'up, neither of which have been excavated, are proposed to be satellites of Nixtun-Ch'ich', approximately 13 km to the east. Neither site would have been directly visible from that city, however, given intervening low natural hills (Pugh et al. 2019).

DISCUSSION

We have explored here the beginnings of societal complexity in the lakes area of central Petén using data obtained through various field and lab projects, with a focus on settlement, pottery, and E Group architecture. Surveys and excavations over the last fifty years have given us an idea of the favored locations for earliest settlement: elevated areas on the southern lakeshores. Islands were popular in the western lakes but not in the east, although whether this was a conscious preference or a reflection of very high lake stages is unknown. Fieldwork has also given hints of population sizes: perhaps little more than four thousand people total in the watersheds of Lakes Yaxhá, Sacnab, Macanché, and Salpetén in the Middle Preclassic (Rice and Rice 1990, table 6.6; excluding Yaxhá center, Lakes Petén Itzá and Nixtun-Ch'ich', and Sacpuy). Archaeological population estimates are notoriously problematic, but if ours are anywhere near realistic for the lakes they suggest sizes and densities in each basin well above the suggested active social-network threshold of about 150 persons enjoying close relations with others (Coward and Dunbar 2014, 387–88). The "weak ties" formed in such larger groupings foster scale-up into broader social networks, with generally hierarchized or layered relationships. Pottery and E Groups provide evidence of this scale-up in the face of proliferating social distinctions.

Pottery

Pottery, including figurines, sheds light on the earliest roles of material goods as evidence of community social, political, and economic differentiation. In terms of external relations, pottery of the early pre-Mamom Terminal Early Preclassic complexes in the lakes area displays morphological, decorative, and typological similarities to those of complexes in the Belize Valley to the east (Jenney Creek and Cunil), at Tikal in the north (Eb), and the Pasión River area in the south (Real Xe). Early lakes area complexes, while sharing much in common with each other and with these external complexes, are nevertheless mutually distinguishable in features such as paste composition, vessel form, slip color, and decoration. These differences are apparent at the site level, but they also occur within sites, as seen at Nixtun-Ch'ich'.

Chemical compositional analysis by NAA of this early material provided insights into intersite relations within the lakes district. Chich complex pottery from Zacpetén, Ixlú, and Nixtun-Ch'ich' is visually similar, but chemical analysis indicates different paste compositions (South 2019, 241–43). Nix Mamom pottery samples from both Zacpetén and Ixlú are chemically similar but differ from samples at Nixtun-Ch'ich' and Tayasal (South 2019, 246). And compositional analysis identified a distinct chemical group for Tayasal sherds, indicating highly localized raw material sourcing during early pottery production (South 2019, 242).

Similarly, NAA of a sample of figurines from Ixlú and Nixtun-Ch'ich' revealed multiple manufacturing origins, most presumed to be locales around the western lakes (Rice 2019a). Two major chemical compositional groups ("macro-groups") were formed, one with a subgroup of white/cream clays that appears to represent production at Nixtun-Ch'ich' and the other with a smaller subgroup thought be Ixlú products. The presence of figurines and whistles of each subgroup (and others) at both sites suggests some degree of intersite circulation, perhaps at least partly in connection with activities in the sites' E Groups. Among these, the artifacts made of white clay, which was not used for pottery containers, may represent a form of "specialized" production—not "craft specialization" per se but rather use of a special clay to make special artifacts by special persons who had access to it. The anthropomorphic figurines, which may represent living persons, ancestors, or supernaturals, are thought to have played a role in calendrical developments in the area, further tying them to E Groups (Rice 2019a).

The variability in Chich pre-Mamom pottery suggests multiple small, local producing groups with strong local bonds expressing local identities, through shared choices about tempering, forms, and slip colors. Red slips were particularly variable, the flaws (streaky, flaky, uneven color range; also seen in cream slips) suggesting that early lakes' potters lacked good control of firing, especially oxidation. The small-scale, localized production of Chich pottery is particularly notable when compared to the greater similarity (and firing control) seen in later Mamom complexes. Although the overall areal similarity of Mamom is not as striking as that of Late Preclassic Chicanel pottery, the complexes do cohere into ceramic spheres.

Comparisons between Terminal Early Preclassic and Middle Preclassic pottery complexes suggest a changing social dynamic in the lakes area. One point concerns general vessel forms. In the Terminal Early Preclassic complexes, form variability was relatively low; unslipped vessels were largely short-necked jars and slipped vessels were small, thin-walled serving bowls, dishes, and tecomates. Surfaces are either unslipped or slipped black or cream with limited decoration. Middle Preclassic complexes, in contrast, include a wider range of forms (incensarios, effigy vessels, serving platters) and (presumably) functions. Slipped wares tended to be large, open serving bowls, dishes, and plates with everted rims; red slip colors became increasingly important and of higher quality, and greater use of decorative elements came to include fluting, chamfering, and appliqué. These features were observed throughout the lakes area and are similarly present in other pottery complexes from the Middle Preclassic period in the lowlands. Changes in size and form—and perhaps even color—suggest a shift in use: vessels were not used just for serving individuals but also for serving groups. Vessels had greater volume and provided larger openings to display and access the contents, supporting the notion that social gatherings involving the use of pottery had become larger, more communal events. On a ceramic-complex level, these characteristics underscore a broader change from diverse sets of local pottery norms to incorporation of more widespread attributes used throughout the area.

Such communal usage reveals that pottery was becoming a social valuable in this transformational environment. Excavated contexts have yielded little evidence of differential domestic access to serving vessels or other vessels with high labor investment, suggesting that pottery itself may not have been a prestige good at this time. Social contexts such as feasting events, commemorative rituals, and cache placement—especially in physical contexts of monumental architecture, such as E Groups—tied vessels to specific public behaviors, strengthening group solidarity and place-based identities, and elevating their value through use and association. Their physical features may have dictated function, at least at the beginning of their use-life. The high labor cost of producing unusual forms, thin walls, decoration, and fine slips, for example, may have been dedicated to vessels for communal display. One instance of this was the use of presumably non-local volcanic ash as a tempering agent in the paste recipes for slipped pottery in the Chich complex around Lake Petén Itzá. Rather than calling attention to individual/family rank and wealth, the investment in early pottery appeared to focus on elevating shared activities. We hasten to add, however, that excavated Middle Preclassic contexts around the lakes were, in general, neither domestic/residential nor large in spatial area. At Nixtun-Ch'ich', an early primate city of an emerging state, we have identified no elite "palaces" and conceivably nearly all residents might have been of relatively significant ranking.

Together, the features of the early pottery in the lakes area point to a gradual shift from the importance of local identity to increasingly broader culture-group cohesion. This material suggests disparate and very localized groupings of producers and users, groups that the more ambitious leaders in the area would likely have wanted to bring into their orbit and unify in support. E Groups and the ceremonies conducted within them seem to have provided such integration.

E Groups

E Group architecture provides further evidence of the beginnings of the social differentiation seen in the pottery, through an accompanying need to facilitate interactions and order by forging common identities. Monumental architecture and the corporate labor mobilized for its creation make important contributions to the social fabric, especially during times of profound social change such as the Terminal Early and Middle Preclassic. For example, monuments symbolize continuities, especially through ancestors and mortuary practice. As public places of social interaction, they contribute to place-based identity formation through shared participation in rituals uniting time and the ancestors.

Eighteen—possibly nineteen—E Groups can be found at sites in the central Petén lake basins (table 5.2), and they are widespread throughout Petén. Nonetheless, their specific functions are unknown and doubtless varied over time. The most common interpretations center on solar observational astronomy and calendar ritual, although other activities associated with trade, agriculture, and mortuary ceremony might have been involved (see papers in Freidel et al. 2017). Over time they may have become largely commemorative (Aveni and Hartung 1989; Chase and Chase 1995; Fialko 1988; Laporte 1996). In broadest terms, E Groups are considered examples of "cultural standardization . . . the earliest recognized form of public architecture in the Maya area . . . central to the social and political transformations" occurring after about 1000 BCE (Chase et al. 2017, 8). They represent "the coalescence of formal Maya communities that shared a unified belief system" (Chase and Chase 2017, 32). The earliest excavated E Group in Petén dates to 1000 BCE at Ceibal (Inomata et al. 2013), but it is not unlikely that others have similar dates. Construction of two E Groups at Nixtun-Ch'ich' date to the Yum (pre-Mamom-Mamom) Transition about that same time.

Over an enormous area of the southern lowlands, E Groups provided deep but poorly understood anchors to unify and center changing sociopolitical realities, belief systems, roles of ancestors, and perceptions of the cosmos. Their existence testifies to the importance of early paramounts' recruitment of cooperative labor to build identity-affirming monuments deeply embedded in the landscape. These acted as magnets "for the social interaction of surrounding sedentary and semi-nomadic populations of farmers and hunter-gatherers to coexist peacefully if not with mutual benefit . . . creating ties between people and landscape in more permanent ways than was previously possible" (Estrada-Belli 2017, 319).

CONCLUSION

We have contemplated the beginnings of societal complexity in the central Petén lakes area through the lenses of settlement, ceramics, and architecture as they inform us about the earliest stages of social differentiation, organization, and identity formation. Our overall concern is with the contextual circumstances in which complexity was developing: the need to integrate peoples with varying subsistence patterns and degrees of sedentary settlement, varying origins (local versus immigrant), Mayan versus non-Mayan (?) languages, disparate belief systems and cosmologies, and so forth. Our review incorporated only three lines of evidence but nonetheless paints a compelling picture about different scales of affiliation and identity. The Terminal Early and Middle Preclassic periods in the lakes area established the foundations for two millennia of subsequent civilizational developments and transformations.

The lakes lie not too distant from the headwaters of various river systems flowing north, east, and west, and the earliest settlers in the area could have followed them upstream into the interior of the Yucatán Peninsula. These connections established the earliest contours of village life in the lakes area. In addition, the lakes and the fault line in which they formed trend east-west, particularly large Lake Petén Itzá, serving as natural conduits for interaction. Thus, it is unsurprising that the most long-lived feature of the earliest settlement is the differentiation in external contacts between eastern and western extremes of the lakes chain. And consequently, the lakes hydrological region was not technically a cultural region in the strictest sense of the term.

This east-west axis of variability is strongly evident in locally made pre-Mamom and Middle Preclassic ceramics. The eastern lake basins interacted with the Belize Valley and imported its pottery, while the western lakes area and Nixtun-Ch'ich' evidence little such contact and pursued its own agendas, which included the production of modeled anthropomorphic and zoomorphic figurines. The prominence of black and white/cream pottery around Mound ZZ1 on the Candelaria Peninsula suggests possible Olmec inspiration. In other words, pottery vessels (and other artifact categories not discussed) provide material evidence of early differences in external relations, local identities, access to resources, markers of rank distinctions, and so on.

At the same time, early monumental architecture—site orientations and E Groups—exerted integrative forces to tamp down the accelerating diversification propelled by emerging inequality. One wonders if the lake basins' many Middle Preclassic E Groups, early monumental gathering places, played a role in this. In furthering the development of place-based identities, perhaps they had the unintended consequence of fostering some level of antipathy toward those not in one's immediate surroundings. The survival of so many of the distinctive E Group arrangements in this area for nearly three thousand years is testimony to their deep meaning—a persistent, memory-laden, and long-lasting glue holding together the threads of an increasingly diverse Maya society.

We know more about early occupation at the eastern and western extremes of the lakes area than about the most central of the central Petén lakes (Macanché and Salpetén, except for Postclassic Zacpetén). Limited excavations into early contexts in these watersheds preclude confident assessments of such interregional arrangements. There is a substantial distance—about a day's walk—between Lake Macanché and Lake Yaxhá that might have constrained regular interactions. The presence of an MFC layout at Cerro Ortiz and vestiges of north-south axial orientations are intriguing, suggesting ties to the south and west, perhaps through Ceibal. Perhaps the early Macanché area was a contested boundary between east and west even before the Late Preclassic construction of the defensive wall around Muralla de León.

The lakes continued to be attractive foci for settlement through the Classic period. Interestingly, the most powerful Classic cities developed outside the lacustrine region, particularly to the north (e.g., Tikal). Sites on the lake's shores, such as Yaxhá and Motul de San José, were secondary centers in Tikal's realm, perhaps serving as points of control for monitoring north-south and east-west waterborne and terrestrial trade, interaction, and resource access through the lake system. Canal systems and ports, such as at Ixlú, developed to handle this trade. Pottery continued to be a valued good in households and rituals throughout this time, including the widely celebrated polychromes of the Late Classic period, but these differed in background colors: orange in the west and cream in the east. Populations in the lakes zone persisted through the Classic "collapse" and especially into the Postclassic period, when much of Petén was largely depopulated, but the east-west differences perdured. By the Late Postclassic and Contact periods, the Itza occupants of Nixtun-Ch'ich' and the Kowojs of the Lake Yaxhá basin identified as distinct ethno-politico-linguistic groups and were at war. Geography, then, was a major prime mover of events in the lakes district, from earliest Preclassic times.

Acknowledgments. We are grateful to the various funding sources that allowed the Rices to pursue archaeological research in the lakes area. These include several NSF grants: the initial grant (GB-32150) to Ed Deevey to investigate in the Yaxhá-Sacnab basins in the 1970s; subsequent funding (BNS-7813736) to Prudence and Don Rice for the 1979–81 field seasons at four other lakes, and DBS-9222373 and SBR-9515443 to the Rices and Grant Jones for Postclassic research in the 1990s (which led to recovery of Middle Preclassic material at the bottom of deep test pits); and BCS-1239622 for South's dissertation studies of the pottery. Excavations at Nixtun-Ch'ich' were initiated through NEH grant RZ-50520-06. Prudence Rice more recently worked with pottery from Nixtun-Ch'ich' excavated under Tim Pugh's grants from the NSF (BCS 1219646 and 1734036), Wenner-Gren Foundation (#9284), and City University of New York, but she was not supported by those funds. We thank the Guatemalan Instituto de Antropología e Historia for kindly permitting these excavations and related artifact studies.

REFERENCES

Acevedo, R., Bernard Hermes, and Zoila Calderón. 1996. "Ixtinto: Rescate arqueológico." In *IX Simposio de Investigaciones Arqueológicas en Guatemala, 1995*, edited by Juan Pedro Laporte and Héctor Escobedo, 207–22. Guatemala City: Museo Nacional de Arqueología e Etnología.

Aveni, Anthony F., and Horst Hartung. 1989. "Uaxactun, Guatemala, Group E, and Similar Assemblages: An Archaeoastronomical Reconsideration." In *World Archaeoastronomy*, edited by Anthony F. Aveni, 441–61. Cambridge, UK: Cambridge University Press.

Awe, Jaime J., Julie A. Hoggarth, and James J. Aimers. 2017. "Of Apples and Oranges: The Case of E Groups and Eastern Triadic Architectural Assemblages in the Belize River Valley." In *Maya E Groups: Calendars, Astronomy, and Urbanism in the Early Lowlands*, edited by David A. Freidel, Arlen F. Chase, Anne S. Dowd, and Jerry Murdock, 412–49. Gainesville: University Press of Florida.

Ball, Joseph W., and Jennifer T. Taschek. 2003. "Reconsidering the Belize Valley Preclassic: A Case for Multiethnic Interactions in the Development of a Regional Culture Tradition." *Ancient Mesoamerica* 14 (2):179–217.

Blom, Franz. 1924. "Report on the preliminary work at Uaxactún, Guatemala." *Carnegie Institution of Washington Yearbook* 23:217–19.

Bracken, Justin. 2018. "Preclassic Fortified Spaces: Within and beyond the Ramparts at Muralla de León." Paper presented at the 83rd Annual Meeting of the Society for American Archaeology, Washington, DC.

Brenner, Mark. 2018. "The Lake Petén Itzá Watershed: Modern and Historical Ecology." In *Historical and Archaeological Perspectives on the Itzas of Petén, Guatemala*, edited by Prudence M. Rice and Don S. Rice, 40–53. Boulder: University Press of Colorado.

Campbell, Lyle. 2017. "Mayan History and Comparison." In *The Mayan Languages*, edited by Judith Aissen, Nora C. England, and Roberto Zavala Maldonado, 43–61. New York: Routledge.

Canuto, Marcello A. 2016. "Middle Preclassic Maya Society: Tilting at Windmills or Giants of Civilization?" In *The Origin of Maya States*, edited by Loa P. Traxler and Robert J. Sharer, 461–506, Philadelphia: Museum of Anthropology, University of Pennsylvania.

Castellanos, Jeanette E., and Antonia E. Foias. 2017. "The Earliest Maya Farmers of Peten: New Evidence from Buenavista-San José, Central Peten Lakes Region, Guatemala." *Journal of Anthropology* 2017:145.

Chase, Arlen F. 1983. "A Contextual Consideration of the Tayasal-Paxcaman Zone, El Peten, Guatemala." PhD diss., University of Pennsylvania.

Chase, Arlen F., and Diane Z. Chase. 1995. "External Impetus, Internal Synthesis, and Standardization: E Group Assemblages and the Crystallization of Classic Maya Society in the Southern Lowlands." *Acta Mesoamericana* 8:87–101.

Chase, Arlen F., and Diane Z. Chase. 2017. "E Groups and the Rise of Complexity in the Southeastern Maya Lowlands." In *Maya E Groups: Calendars, Astronomy, and Urbanism in the Early Lowlands*, edited by David A. Freidel, Arlen F. Chase, Anne S. Dowd, and Jerry Murdock, 32–71. Gainesville: University Press of Florida.

Chase, Arlen F., Anne S. Dowd, and David A. Freidel. 2017. "The Distribution and Significance of E Groups: A Historical Background and Introduction." In *Maya E Groups: Calendars, Astronomy, and Urbanism in the Early Lowlands*, edited by David A. Freidel, Arlen F. Chase, Anne S. Dowd, and Jerry Murdock, 3–30. Gainesville: University Press of Florida.

Cheetham, David, Donald W. Forsyth, and John E. Clark. 2003. "La cerámica pre-Mamom de la cuenca del río Belice y del Centro de Petén: Las correspondencias y sus implicaciones." In *XVI Simposio de Investigaciones Arqueológicas en Guatemala, 2002*, edited by Juan Pedro Laporte, Bárbara Arroyo, Héctor Escobedo, and Héctor Mejía, 609–28. Guatemala City: Museo Nacional de Arqueología y Etnología.

Clark, John E., and David Cheetham. 2002. "Mesoamerica's Tribal Foundations." In *The Archaeology of Tribal Societies*, edited by William A. Parkinson, 278–339. Ann Arbor: International Monographs in Prehistory.

Clark, John E., and Richard Hansen. 2001. "The Architecture of Early Kingship: Comparative Perspectives on the Origins of the Maya Royal Court." In *Royal Courts of the Ancient Maya: 2. Data and Case Studies*, edited by Takeshi Inomata and Stephen D. Houston, 1–45. Boulder: Westview.

Culbert, T. Patrick. 1977. "Early Maya Development at Tikal, Guatemala." In *The Origins of Maya Civilization*, edited by Richard E. W. Adams, 27–43. Albuquerque, NM: School of American Research.

Culbert, T. Patrick. 1993. *The Ceramics of Tikal: Vessels from the Burials, Caches, and Problematical Deposits*. Tikal Report 25, Part A. Philadelphia: University of Pennsylvania University Museum.

Culbert, T. Patrick, and Laura J. Kosakowsky. 2019. *The Ceramics of Tikal*. Tikal Report 25B. Philadelphia: University of Pennsylvania University Museum.

Deevey, Edward S., Jr., Don S. Rice, Prudence M. Rice, Hague H. Vaughan, Mark Brenner, and M. Sid Flannery. 1981. "Mayan Urbanism: Impact on a Tropical Karst Environment." *Science* 206 (4416): 298–306.

Duncan, William N. 2005. "The Bioarchaeology of Ritual Violence in Postclassic El Petén, Guatemala (AD 950–1524)." PhD diss., Southern Illinois University.

Duncan, William N. 2009. "The Bioarchaeology of Ritual Violence at Zacpetén." In *The Kowoj: Identity, Migration, and Geopolitics in Late Postclassic Petén, Guatemala*, edited by Prudence M. Rice and Don S. Rice, 340–67. Boulder: University Press of Colorado.

Estrada-Belli, Francisco. 2017. "The History, Function, and Meaning of Preclassic E Groups in the Cival Region." In *Maya E Groups: Calendars, Astronomy, and Urbanism in the Early Lowlands*, edited by David A. Freidel, Arlen F. Chase, Anne S. Dowd, and Jerry Murdock, 293–327. Gainesville: University Press of Florida.

Fialko, Vilma. 1988. "Mundo Perdido, Tikal: Un ejemplo de complejos de conmemoración astronómica." *Mayab* 4:13–21.

Foias, Antonia E., and Kitty F. Emery, eds. 2012. *Motul de San José: Politics, History, and Economy in a Classic Maya Polity*. Gainesville: University Press of Florida.

Freidel, David A., Arlen F. Chase, Anne S. Dowd, and Jerry Murdock, eds. 2017. *Early Maya E-Groups, Solar Calendars, and the Role of Astronomy in the Rise of Lowland Maya Urbanism*. Gainesville: University of Florida Press.

Gifford, James B. 1976. *Prehistoric Pottery Analysis and the Ceramics of Barton Ramie in the Belize Valley*. Memoirs, vol. 18. Cambridge, MA: Peabody Museum of Archaeology and Ethnology, Harvard University.

Hermes, Bernard. 2001. "La secuencia de ocupación prehispánica en el área de la laguna Yaxha, Petén: Una síntesis." *XIV Simposio de Investigaciones Arqueológicas en Guatemala, 2000*, edited by Juan Pedro Laporte, A. C. Suasnávar, and Barbara Arroyo, 151–77 (digital version). Guatemala City: Museo Nacional de Arqueología y Etnología.

Hermes, Bernard, Paulino I. Morales, and Sebastián Möllers. 1999. "Investigación arqueológica en Yaxha, Petén: La calzada del lago y la vía 5." In *XII Simposio de Investigaciones Arqueológicas en Guatemala, 1998*, edited by Juan Pedro Laporte and Héctor Escobedo, 110–38. Guatemala City: Museo Nacional de Arqueología y Etnología.

Inomata, Takeshi, Daniela Triadan, Kazuo Aoyama, Victor Castillo, and Hitoshi Yonenobu. 2013. "Early Ceremonial Constructions at Ceibal, Guatemala, and the Origins of Lowland Maya Civilization." *Science* 340: 467–71.

Jones, Grant D. 1998. *The Conquest of the Last Maya Kingdom*. Stanford, CA: Stanford University Press.

Justeson, John S. 1975. "The Identification of the Emblem Glyph of Yaxha, El Peten." In *Studies in Ancient Mesoamerica*, edited by John A. Graham, 123–29. Vol. 2. Contribution 27. Berkeley: Archaeological Research Facility, University of California.

Kaufman, Terence S. 2017. "Aspects of the Lexicon of Proto-Mayan and its Earliest Descendants." In *The Mayan Languages*, edited by Judith Aissen, Nora C. England, and Roberto Zavala Maldonado, 62–111. New York: Routledge.

Laporte, Juan Pedro. 1996. "La cuenca del Río Mopán-Belice: Una sub-región cultural de las tierras bajas Maya central." In *IX Simposio de Investigaciones Arqueológicas en*

Guatemala, 1995, edited by Juan Pedro Laporte and Héctor Escobedo, 253–79. Guatemala City: Museo Nacional de Arqueología y Etnología and Asociación Tikal.

Martínez, Gerson O., and Juan Pedro Laporte. 2010. "Laguna Sacpuy en el centro de Petén y su asentamiento arqueológico." In XXIII Simposio de Investigaciones Arqueológicas en Guatemala, 2009, edited by Bárbara Arroyo, Adriana Linares, and Lorena Paiz, 331–457. Guatemala City: Museo Nacional de Arqueología y Etnología.

Morales, Paulino I. n.d. "Recent Notes on Archaeological Salvage Research at Sites Near Communities to the Southwest of the Yaxha-Nakum-Naranjo National Park." Foundation for the Advancement of Mesoamerican Studies. www.famsi.org/reports /03101/09paulino/09paulino.pdf.

Obrist-Farner, Jonathan, and Prudence M. Rice. 2019. "Nixtun-Ch'ich' and its Environmental Impact: Sedimentological and Archaeological Correlates in a Core from Lake Petén Itzá in the Maya Lowlands, Guatemala." Journal of Archaeological Science: Reports 26: 101868.

Pugh, Timothy W. 2001. "Architecture, Ritual, and Social Identity at Late Postclassic Zacpetén, Petén, Guatemala." PhD diss., Southern Illinois University.

Pugh, Timothy W., Evelyn M. Chan Nieto, and Gabriela W. Zygadło. 2019. "Faceless Hierarchy at Nixtun-Ch'ich', Peten, Guatemala." Ancient Mesoamerica 31 (2): 248–60.

Pugh, Timothy W., and Prudence M. Rice. 2017. "Early Urban Planning, Spatial Strategies, and the Maya Gridded City of Nixtun-Ch'ich', Petén, Guatemala." Current Anthropology 58 (5): 576–603.

Pugh, Timothy W., Prudence M. Rice, Evelyn M. Chan Nieto, and Jemima Georges. 2022. Complexity, Cooperation, and Public Goods: Quality of Place at Nixtun-Ch'ich', Petén, Guatemala. Special issue on Comparative Governance in Frontiers in Political Science 4 (March). https://doi.org/10.3389/fpos.2022.805888.

Puleston, Dennis E., and Olga S. Puleston. 1971. "An Ecological Approach to the Origins of Maya Civilization." Archaeology 24:330–37.

Rice, Don S. 1976a. "The Historical Ecology of Lakes Yaxhá and Sacnab, El Petén, Guatemala." PhD diss., Pennsylvania State University.

Rice, Don S. 1976b. "Middle Preclassic Maya Settlement in the Central Maya Lowlands." Journal of Field Archaeology 3 (4): 425–45.

Rice, Don S. 1996. "Hydraulic Engineering in Central Peten, Guatemala: Ports and Inter-lacustrine Canals." In Arqueología Mesoamericana: Homenaje a William T. Sanders, edited by Alba Guadalupe Mastache, Jeffrey R. Parsons, Robert S. Santley, and Mari Carmen Serra Puche, 109–22. Vol. 2. Mexico City: INAH.

Rice, Don S., and Dennis E. Puleston. 1981. "Ancient Maya Settlement Patterns in the Petén, Guatemala." In Lowland Maya Settlement Patterns, edited by Wendy Ashmore, 121–56. Albuquerque: University of New Mexico Press.

Rice, Don S., and Prudence M. Rice. 1981. "Muralla de León: A Lowland Maya Fortification." Journal of Field Archaeology 8:271–88.

Rice, Don S., and Prudence M. Rice. 1990. "Population Size and Population Change in the Central Peten Lakes Region, Guatemala." In *Precolumbian Population History in the Maya Lowlands*, edited by T. Patrick Culbert and Don S. Rice, 123–48. Albuquerque: University of New Mexico Press.

Rice, Don S., and Prudence M. Rice. 2016. "Forty Years in Petén, Guatemala: A Hagiographic Prosopography." In *Human Adaptation in Ancient Mesoamerica*, edited by Nancy Gonlin and Kirk D. French, 295–335. Boulder: University Press of Colorado.

Rice, Don S., Prudence M. Rice, and Edward S. Deevey Jr. 1985. "Paradise Lost: Classic Maya Impact on a Lacustrine Environment." In *Prehistoric Lowland Maya Environment and Subsistence Economy*, edited by Mary D. Pohl, 91–105. Papers, no. 77. Cambridge, MA: Peabody Museum of Archaeology and Ethnology, Harvard University.

Rice, Don S., Prudence M. Rice, Grant D. Jones, Romulo Sánchez Polo, et al. 1996. "La segunda temporada de campo del Proyecto Maya Colonial: Nuevas evidencias." In *X Simposio de Arqueología de Guatemala, 1995*, edited by Juan Pedro Laporte and Héctor Escobedo, 499–512. Guatemala City: Museo Nacional de Arqueología e Etnología.

Rice, Prudence M. 1979. "Ceramic and Non-ceramic Artifacts of Lakes Yaxha-Sacnab, El Peten, Guatemala. Part I: The Ceramics, Section A: Introduction and the Middle Preclassic ceramics of Yaxha-Sacnab, Guatemala." *Ceramica de Cultura Maya* 10:1–36. Philadelphia: Temple University.

Rice, Prudence M. 1987. *Macanché Island, El Petén, Guatemala: Excavations, Pottery, and Artifacts*. Gainesville: University Presses of Florida.

Rice, Prudence M. 2009. "Mound ZZ1, Nixtun-Ch'ich', Petén, Guatemala: Rescue Operations at a Long-Lived Structure in the Maya Lowlands." *Journal of Field Archaeology* 34 (4): 403–22.

Rice, Prudence M. 2019a. *Anthropomorphizing the Cosmos: Middle Preclassic Lowland Maya Figurines, Ritual, and Time*. Louisville: University Press of Colorado.

Rice, Prudence M. 2019b. "Early Pottery and Construction at Nixtun-Ch'ich', Petén, Guatemala: Preliminary Observations." *Latin American Antiquity* 30 (3): 471–89.

Rice, Prudence M. n.d. "Another Look at Zacpetén's Temple Assemblages." Unpublished manuscript, last modified September 5, 2021. Microsoft Word file.

Rice, Prudence M., and Timothy W. Pugh. 2017. "Water, Centering, and the Beginning of Time at Middle Preclassic Nixtun-Ch'ich', Petén, Guatemala." *Journal of Anthropological Archaeology* 48 (5): 1–16.

Rice, Prudence M., and Timothy W. Pugh. 2021. "Middle Preclassic Nixtun-Ch'ich': A lowland Maya primate / ritual city." *Journal of Anthropological Archaeology* 63: 101308.

Rice, Prudence M., Timothy W. Pugh, and Evelyn Chan Nieto. 2019. "Early Construction of a Maya Sacred Landscape: The Sector Y 'E-Group' of Nixtun-Ch'ich' (Petén, Guatemala)." *Journal of Field Archaeology* 44 (8): 550–64.

Rice, Prudence M., and Don S. Rice, eds. 2009. *The Kowoj: Identity, Migration, and Geopolitics in Late Postclassic Petén, Guatemala*. Boulder: University Press of Colorado.

Rice, Prudence M., and Don S. Rice. 2016. *Ixlú: A Contested Maya Entrepôt in Petén, Guatemala / Ixlú: Un disputado entrepôt en Petén, Guatemala*. Memoirs in Latin American Archaeology, No. 23. Pittsburgh: Center for Comparative Archaeology, University of Pittsburgh.

Rice, Prudence M., and Don S. Rice. 2018. *Historical and Archaeological Perspectives on the Itzas of Petén, Guatemala*. Boulder: University Press of Colorado.

Rice, Prudence M., and Don S. Rice. n.d. "Cerro Ortiz: A Small Preclassic Site in the Lake Macanché Basin, Petén, Guatemala." Unpublished manuscript, last modified August 7, 2021. Microsoft Word file.

Ricketson, Oliver G., Jr. 1928. "Astronomical Observatories in the Maya Area." *Geographical Review* 18:215–25.

South, Katherine E. 2019. "Value and Depositional History of Early Maya Pottery in the Petén Lakes Region of Guatemala." PhD diss., Southern Illinois University.

Stuart, David. 1985. "The Yaxha Emblem Glyph as *Yax-ha.*" *Research Reports on Ancient Maya Writing* 1. Washington, DC: Center for Maya Research.

Źrałka, Jaroslaw. 2005. "Terminal Classic Occupation in the Maya Sites Located in the Area of Triángulo Park and the Problem of Their Collapse." PhD diss., Jagiellonian University, Kraków.

6

Shifting Ceramic Styles in the Formative Period Basin of Mexico

WESLEY D. STONER AND DEBORAH L. NICHOLS

INTRODUCTION

Mesoamerica developed in a crucible of intensive cultural and economic inter-actions that experienced major directional shifts every few centuries over the Formative period (1400–100 cal BCE). We focus here on how local communities of practice monitored the reproduction of traditional ceramic systems against potential changes resulting from either generational modifications or outside influences. In particular, we seek to understand the changing local processes that shifted from early communities that were relatively open to sharing a pan-Mesoamerican cultural style of ceramics to later communities that increasingly defined their material culture to contrast that of their neighbors.

For the Basin of Mexico case study, we search for links between changes in ceramic style and the shifting cultural, social, and economic interactions that developed from the Early through Late Formative. We focus on four main vari-ables over this 1,300-year time frame: (1) the mechanisms of interaction that exposed basin groups to foreign symbols and ideas; (2) the strategies of local communities and leaders that disposed them to either adopt or reject foreign

https://doi.org/10.5876/9781646422883.c006

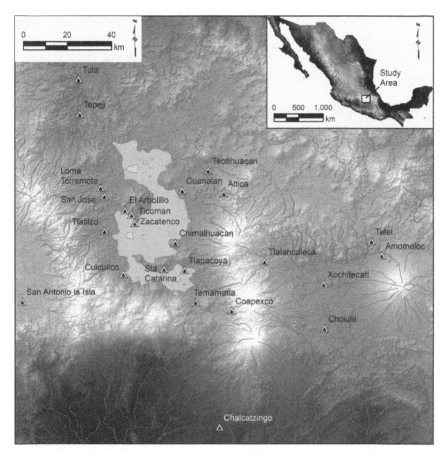

FIGURE 6.1. *Important sites and sites mentioned in the text.*

symbols; (3) the comparative pace of change of overt decorative expressions on pottery versus the more technical (unseen) attributes; and (4) the geographic areas over which ceramic styles were shared across Mesoamerica. We ultimately employ these variables to understand how regional communities of practice modified their pottery styles due to changing sociopolitical and economic processes.

In the following sections, we establish the theoretical and methodological bases to extract the desired information from the changing appearance of serving bowls in the Basin of Mexico (figure 6.1). We then present the data for changing ceramic style associations from the Early Formative through the Late Formative. We cannot discuss all ceramic types, but each phase presents dominant style associations that allude to, or reject, broader Mesoamerican trends. We find that the Basin of Mexico participated in many major cultural shifts as expressed specifically on serving bowls. The general pattern shifted from broadly shared style horizons to increasingly regionalized ceramic style expressions over time. This was partly due to a decreasing geographic range of pottery trade through the Formative period (Stoner and Nichols 2019b). We additionally argue that this pattern directly resulted from increasingly insular strategies for integrating regional settlement hierarchies and defining group solidarity among corporate groups, which consequently diminished the earlier importance of long-distance prestige networks (Blanton and Fargher 2016; Blanton, Fargher, and Heredia Espinoza 2005; Nichols and Stoner 2019).

CERAMICS AND THE GEOGRAPHY OF STYLE

Ceramics are plastic media of expression capable of depicting very complicated sets of culture-specific symbols and technology. Serving wares, the focus of this chapter, were exhibited to invited guests at feasts and rituals. Some aspects of the identity of the people who produced and consumed pottery can be gleaned from their decorative and technological styles. We are careful here to not equate pots with ethnicity, but potters both actively promote certain styles as an outward expression of their claimed identity and passively infuse the materials they produce with elements of their habitus (e.g., Dietler and Herbich 1998).

An experienced potter can easily replicate the overt pottery styles not of their own, and the ancient world has produced many examples of the rapid spread of decorative canons across broad geographic expanses. Archaeologists have long referred to broad geographic zones that share common artistic expressions as "style horizons" (Willey 1991). The reasons these "international styles" developed include shared cosmologies, ritual function, symbolism, prestige, adoption of better technologies, or maintenance of open social networks. The geographic extent of styles zones gives archaeologists a way to investigate the scale at which social and economic interactions developed into communities of practice.

Less easy to copy is the technological production sequence for ceramics—selection of raw materials, mixing of a paste, forming techniques, surface finishing techniques, firing process and facilities, post-firing surface treatment, decorative techniques, and others (e.g., Roux 2017; Sillar and Tite 2000). Technological aspects of the production sequence are less visible to the common observer but often take more mechanical skill and training to replicate successfully (Gosselain 2000). They are learned from the previous generation over many years if not decades of observation, hands-on instruction, and apprenticeships (Crown 2014).

The contrast between rapid esthetic change and the relative stability of more mechanistic steps of pottery production can be discerned through a multimethod approach that compares decorative style, technology, composition, and morphology over time. Copying of another culture's pottery esthetic based on casual observation of the finished pot does not foster an equal level of knowledge about the technological aspects of production. Other social learning opportunities, such as direct apprenticeships with external potting communities (through temporary or permanent migration), can facilitate more complete adoption of the entire production sequence and range of styles. Local material availability strongly influences composition, but selection of materials, mixing a paste, or choice of pigment materials may vary. Furthermore, composition gives archaeologists a way to differentiate imports from local imitations of foreign-style wares.

We argue that for cultural transmission of potting knowledge to develop into a style horizon, two conditions must be met. First, interactions over long distances must have been relatively intensive and direct. A single trade pot imported from the southern Gulf Lowlands or elsewhere was not sufficient to explain the thorough adoption of the Olmec-style elements, technology, and vessel forms in Central Mexico during the Early Formative. It must have taken either years of intensive pottery trade, the movement of potters between regions, or both to yield the level of stylistic similarity observed in regions across Mesoamerica during the Early and Middle Formative. While aDNA and isotope databases for Formative Mesoamerica have not yet significantly developed to address the role of migration in spreading ceramic styles, a potential parallel has recently come to light showing how the migration of neolithic farming populations contributed to the expansion of corded ware pottery across Eurasia (Kristiansen 2017).

Second, for style horizons to take hold, the receiving community needed to be relatively open to foreign cultural inputs and people. Pottery is one of many signaling materials used to broadcast and maintain group membership and contrast ingroups with outgroups (Barth 1969; Neff 2014; Stark 1998; Wobst 1977). We argue that the receptiveness of communities in the Basin of Mexico to adopting foreign pottery styles into their own ceramic industries changed from open to closed over time.

Stark (2017) suggests that the Early and Middle Formative periods were marked by intensive interactions among relatively open communities that brought a diversity of peoples together for the first time. This argument assumes a stable base population that mixed with immigrants rather than population replacement, such as that which might have taken place in neolithic southern England alongside the appearance of the first ceramics (Brace et al. 2019). The earliest sedentary villages were not large enough to be self-sustaining demographically, economically, or socially. Building local populations through external networks and immigration precipitated a number of changes in early villages, such as increasing the labor pool for monumental constructions, intensifying food production systems, and public ritual that provided the foundation for increasingly differentiated social systems (e.g., Rosenswig 2016). These factors contributed to the relatively rapid growth of the first villages into cities (Sanders et al. 1979).

Some individuals used imports to lay claim to a world beyond the reach of the average person. Control of esoteric knowledge, such as religious iconography depicted on pottery, and goods, such as obsidian and greenstone, also set those individuals apart from the general populace. Stark (2017) points out that groups in those networks likely did not understand each other's language, and commonly held symbols on ceramic pots might have facilitated nonverbal communication. These processes contributed to early status distinctions that ultimately, over centuries, culminated into social stratification and the more centralized religious and economic institutions controlled by the region's earliest cities.

Neff (2014) adds an important perspective for interpreting the pace of pottery style changes. Many early trade pots were laboriously decorated and even more laboriously transported over hundreds of kilometers, which Neff sees as a form of costly signaling. Once local potters began to make copies that were indistinguishable from the imports, however, the high cost of procuring them over long distances was no longer merited. Neff argues that the rapid appearance and disappearance of Olmec-style pottery at places outside the Olmec heartland was precisely because local reproductions undercut costly signaling. The receptiveness of the local community of potters to copying and elaborating upon these designs shows that social boundaries were relatively open and fluid early in the time frame examined here.

Contrasting the principle of community openness is a process of galvanization that led groups to maintain local ceramic traditions against outside influences. Several ethnographic cases, for example, document situations where potters who married into a community were pressured to relearn parts of the production sequence to conform to local customs (DeBoer 1990; Herbich and Dietrich 2008) or discouraged from modifying traditional forms (Reina and Hill 1974). Communities of practice monitor, both actively and passively, variation within the ceramic production system, and lasting change comes only through a complex negotiation that can be understood as the tensions between agency and structure (Giddens 1979) or the selective forces that produce directional change (Eerkens and Lipo 2007). By reinforcing the reproduction of traditional styles, the community reaffirms its internal social and kin relationships and simultaneously contrasts itself against its neighbors. This process results in the definition of ingroups and outgroups across a landscape that is reflected in the Mesoamerican case by the constriction of ceramic style zones over time.

By the late Middle to Late Formative in Mesoamerica, settlement systems became more regionally focused on developing and maintaining hierarchical political structures around emerging central places that hosted a variety of economic, religious, and administrative functions (e.g., Sanders et al. 1979). Long-distance trade never ceased, but exchange specifically of pottery became less tied to issues of prestige and external network building and more to material needs in an increasingly commercialized economic system over time. The early markets that accompanied these emerging polities typically were based on established social relationships that were intraregional in scope (Blanton and Fargher 2016, 83). Pottery imports, when present, source to more restricted geographic zones over time (Stoner and Nichols 2019b).

We suggest that these more regionalized pottery style zones were influenced by the gravitational forces that early cities had on social, religious, and economic networks, forming a pattern of urban/rural interaction. Monumental architecture at Cuicuilco, Teotihuacan, and a few other centers defined the activities of a clearly defined ruling class. Temples and ballcourts, like the Zacatenco phase ballcourt at Temamatla, became the centers of ritual life (Ramírez et al. 2000). By the late Middle Formative, the governments of Cuicuilco and Teotihuacan became introverted, focusing on integrating their own hinterlands and developing hydraulic works for agriculture that were later maintained mostly by localized kin and corporate groups (Nichols 2015, 414). Early markets, while difficult to identify with existing data, likely developed in these cities by the Ticomán phase as the region generally fit the conditions in which markets typically develop in other premodern states (Blanton and Fargher 2010, 213). While these central places were building corporate solidarity within the emerging subregional polities, the landscape between them became more competitive (Drennan and Peterson 2012; Spencer and Redmond 2004). In general, the Late Formative Basin of Mexico saw the development of regionalized polities focused on cities that reshaped patterns of interaction into orbits surrounding them (Blanton et al. 2005). Because social interactions gradually became focused on these central places, the communities of practice that negotiated ceramic styles were shaped accordingly. Additionally, the sharing of common material styles within polities helped to reaffirm group membership and build trust that common pool resources and public goods developed by corporate groups benefited only the participating members (Blanton 2015).

SHIFTING CERAMIC STYLES IN THE FORMATIVE BASIN OF MEXICO

We define the general ceramic traditions of each major phase but focus on changes and constants specifically in the appearance of serving bowls between phase transitions. Where possible, we draw upon our chemical and petrographic database for a large sample of Formative pottery spanning the Ayotla through Ticomán phases in the Basin of Mexico (Stoner and Nichols 2019b). The degree to which style associations were linked to the actual import (or not) of trade pots permits an evaluation of the mechanisms by which ceramic styles spread across Mesoamerica.

Ayotla Phase (1400–1150 cal BCE)

Few Ayotla phase sites have been identified in the Basin of Mexico, and those were concentrated entirely in the southern half of the region (Tolstoy et al. 1977). The southern basin boasted a slightly warmer climate than in the north, and the abundant freshwater resources of the basin's lake attracted populations that still relied heavily on collected food (Sanders et al. 1979). Data from Tlapacoya/Zohapilco demonstrate that residents depended heavily on lacustrine resources (Niederberger 2000).

Interpersonal social differentiation had begun by the Ayotla phase and its contemporaries in regions across Mesoamerica. The cemetery at Tlatilco presents a pattern of graves that had both rich offerings and those that had none (Tolstoy 1989). Tolstoy (1989) remarked based on grave offerings, sex, and burial orientations that the burial pattern there might represent two intermarrying moieties. Joyce (1999) offers that the burials were positioned in clusters likely representing households in a village with ephemeral residential structures that were not detected in excavations (García Moll et al. 1991). At Coapexco, households of different sizes were identified, which may reflect family size, importance, or both (Tolstoy 1989). Finally, Niederberger (2000) suggests that a simple settlement hierarchy had developed by this time, focused on Tlatilco and Tlapacoya, that served ritual functions for surrounding hamlets.

The Ayotla phase marked an increase in the import of exotic goods and materials over the preceding Nevada phase. In addition to ceramics (discussed below), imports included obsidian (both Otumba obsidian from the Teotihuacan Valley and Ucareo obsidian from West Mexico), iron ore mirrors, greenstone, and marine shells (Boksenbaum et al, 1987; García Moll et al. 1991; Niederberger 2000; Tolstoy 1989). These objects occurred mostly in burial contexts and likely marked the individual's achieved status. The Olmec and West Mexican style ceramics found there do not strictly correlate with status as inferred from the total number of grave goods. Ceramics at the time were therefore not just status symbols but also marked other aspects of claimed social affiliations, not only with external contacts but also to reinforce group membership within settlements.

The Ayotla phase Basin of Mexico took part in Mesoamerica's first true style horizon (Grove 1993; Pool 2007; Rosenswig 2010). During this time, Olmec carved symbols depicting abstract religious themes and deities spread across regions mainly on dark-colored burnished bowls and vases (figure 6.2). Rosenswig (2016) refers to this as an archipelago of complexity because Olmec cultural expressions appeared in relatively few disparate locations where societies began showing signs of complexity. Rosenswig (2016; see also Clark 1997) sees long-distance import as an important aspect of social differentiation. Few individuals could muster the resources to procure exotic ceramics (and other goods). Doing so separated them from the general populace.

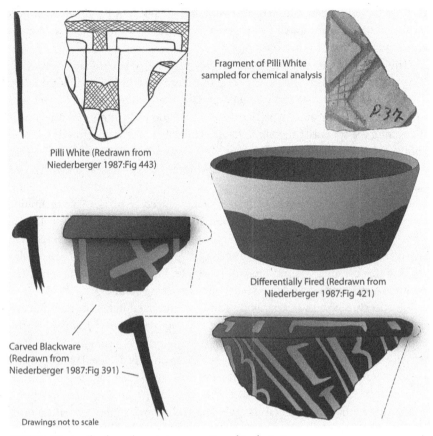

Fragment of Pilli White
sampled for chemical analysis

Pilli White (Redrawn from
Niederberger 1987:Fig 443)

Differentially Fired (Redrawn from
Niederberger 1987:Fig 421)

Carved Blackware
(Redrawn from
Niederberger 1987:Fig 391)

Drawings not to scale

FIGURE 6.2. *Ayotla phase ceramic types mentioned in the text.*

The primordial elements of Olmec cultural style developed earliest at San Lorenzo and the surrounding region of the southern Gulf Lowlands (Coe and Diehl 1980; Pool 2007; Rodríguez and Ortiz 1997). The style as applied to pottery includes distinctive carving and grooving and a suite of motifs that depicted religious themes (see Blomster 2017). Olmec-style elements on carved polished black pottery, as well as several other material styles, appeared suddenly during the Basin of Mexico's Ayotla phase and greatly contrast prior Nevada phase pottery styles, indicating that outside influences were partly responsible. Work conducted principally at Tlapacoya/Zohapilco, Tlatilco, and Coapexco recovered polished black pottery with carved Olmec motifs and Pilli-style figurines (Niederberger 1976, 2000; Paradis 2017, Tolstoy 1989). Compositional analyses have demonstrated that pottery trade was one mechanism that spread the style (Blomster et al. 2005; Stoner and Nichols 2019b). The overwhelming majority of pots and figurines of the Olmec style were locally produced, however, suggesting that trade wares served as templates for local replication. More importantly, local potters were receptive to exogenous cultural styles and quickly incorporated them into their repertoires.

Emulation of trade pots alone does not explain the great familiarity with Gulf Lowlands pottery technology and style that Basin of Mexico potters exhibited. This is perhaps best seen through differentially fired white-rimmed black wares (see figure 6.2), a ceramic type that receives far too little attention in terms of measuring the spread of the Olmec style. The effect of a light-colored rim band contrasting the black body of serving bowls was achieved through differential oxidation during firing or by partially burying the vessels with the rim exposed during open-air cooling. The parts exposed to air oxidized and turned a lighter color, while other parts deprived of oxygen reduced to black. This technique developed in stages in the region around San Lorenzo, with the first formal white-rimmed black wares appearing during the Chicharras phase, earlier than any other region of Mesoamerica (Rodríguez and Ortiz 1997). The process for making this ceramic type was relatively simple, but it was not something that multiple communities developed independently of each other.

We observed when working with Tolstoy's excavated materials that differentially fired pottery prominently appeared at Coapexco, a site abandoned by the end of the Ayotla phase (Tolstoy et al. 1977). At Tlapacoya, the same type, called Valle Borde Negativo by Niederberger (1976), also quickly declined in proportion shortly after the end of the Ayotla phase, the same time that carved Olmec-style motifs and figurines dramatically decreased in frequency. The adoption of the differentially fired ceramic style and technology indicates that (1) interaction was not limited to carved religious iconography, and (2) groups in the Basin of Mexico were claiming extraregional social connections that cannot be solely understood through a model of prestige interaction. While we agree with Rosenswig (2016) that early interactions involved prestige trade, for the majority of the Ayotla phase, this Olmec-style suite of materials was not solely associated with elites (Joyce 1999; Tolstoy 1989).

The ceramic style associations exhibited by groups in the Basin of Mexico extended to the west as well (Grove 2007, 2010; Ochoa 2005; Plunket and Uruñuela 2012). A completely distinct set of materials, dubbed the Tlatilco culture because it is best known from work conducted at that site, displays association with the contemporary Capacha Complex on Pacific Coast and Opeño in Michoacán (Oliveros Morales 2005). This includes distinctive decorative techniques, stirrup bottles, multichambered bottles, and a variety of figurines including Types D (slanted eyes formed by filleting into an elongated shaped with a stab in the middle representing the pupil, realistic mouth and teeth) and K (frog-like appearance with large oval-shaped filleted eyes, typically no pupil, mouth formed typically by two punctations), which are all common in Morelos and at Tlatilco (Niederberger

1976; Ochoa 2005; Vaillant 1930). The style likely spread from Morelos, where it is more prevalent, through a direct path north that was later closed by eruptions of the Xitle volcano (Grove 2007). The existence of this path of interaction may also explain why Tlapacoya and Coapexco in the southeast Basin of Mexico do *not* strongly exhibit West Mexican influences on their pottery styles. Beyond ceramics, a high percentage of the Basin of Mexico's obsidian assemblage was made up of West Mexican sources (Boksenbaum et al. 1987; Johnson and Hirth 2019).

Manantial Phase (1150–900 cal BCE) + the Tetelpan Transition (900–800 cal BCE)

We combine the Manantial and Tetelpan phases together here for brevity. Niederberger (2000) used the Tetelpan phase to indicate a "deculturation," specifically referring to the disappearance of Olmec influences. We see Niederberger's Tetelpan phase as a transition that exhibits ceramic elements of both the earlier Manantial and later Zacatenco styles. Part of our thesis is that external influences on potting technology largely declined by the Manantial phase. The ceramics we discuss for that phase represent a localized inheritance of ceramic technology. All decorative motifs, vessel forms, slipping techniques, and other technologies existed in some form during the prior Ayotla phase and were simply recombined in novel ways during the Manantial phase. Tetelpan phase ceramics likewise experienced minor alterations to Manantial vessel forms that seems to have been part of localized, generational transmission of potting knowledge without much influence from the outside.

Beginning during the Manantial Phase, settlement number and complexity increased in the Basin of Mexico. Settled villages appeared in the northern half of the Basin for the first time (Stoner and Nichols 2019a; Tolstoy et al. 1977). Basin populations began relying more heavily on cultivated crops, including maize (Niederberger 1976, 266). Altica in the eastern Teotihuacan Valley provides important data because its entire Formative period occupation was almost exclusively dated to the Manantial and Tetelpan phases, with very minor overlap with earlier and later phases (Stoner and Nichols 2019a). Our excavations there reveal an early population largely dependent on plants, but one that was struggling to adapt to this relatively new economy. Grinding slabs at the site present some of the earliest formal *metates* found in the region, though they did not yet possess tripod supports like later ones. The four burials excavated at the site returned carbon isotope values consistent with reference populations dependent on C_4 plants, like maize (Storey et al. 2019). Macrobotanical and microbotanical remnants of maize turned up in soil samples and as phytoliths washed from grinding tools (McClung et al. 2019). Maize was only part of a diverse subsistence strategy (including imported root crops from the lowlands), but the increased reliance on this crop during the Manantial phase foregrounds later subsistence practices.

Interregional exchanges intensified moving into the Manantial and Tetelpan phases, but exotic materials in the Basin of Mexico typically no longer displayed an explicitly Olmec style. Greenstone import continued through the subsequent Zacatenco phase, but unlike in other regions, almost none of it was carved with Olmec-style iconography. Obsidian exchange networks rerouted to emphasize consumption of the more proximate Otumba obsidian, while West Mexican and other Central Mexican sources declined greatly in proportion (Boksenbaum et al. 1987; Charlton 1984). Sites in the Basin of Mexico and Morelos became important exporters of Otumba obsidian, which reached lands as far away as the Gulf Lowlands, Oaxaca, and coastal Guerrero (see Stoner et al. 2015).

The overt style of pottery abruptly changed from the Ayotla phase, but much of the production technology and many of the motifs remained constant (figure 6.3). Carved Olmec-style decoration on pottery, Olmec-style Pilli figurines, and differentially fired ceramics disappeared or dramatically declined in proportion at the beginning of the Manantial phase. White-slipped dishes with post-slip incisions depicting double-line-break motifs along the rim and "pseudograter" (Cyphers 1987) motifs on the interior of flat bases (also on non-slipped variants) became the dominant serving wares. The double-line-break motif originated in the Basin of Mexico during the Ayotla phase (possibly by the end of the Nevada phase [Niederberger 1976, 162]), which was likely earlier than any other region (cf. Rodríguez and Ortiz 1997, 77–78). It first appeared as a series of "gum brackets" lined up end to end along the top of everted rims of Volcán Pulido and early Tortuga Pulido bowls (Niederberger 1976, 167, 170) (see figure 6.2). The white slipping technique also appeared first during the Ayotla phase on the type Pilli Blanco, which exhibited fine, trans-slip engraving and zones where the white slip was scraped away to reveal the underlying paste color (see figure 6.2). These two ceramic attributes did not appear in together on the same pots until the Manantial phase.

The combination of double-line-breaks and the white slip on the Manantial phase type Cesto Blanco clearly was a localized process of ceramic inheritance, as both of these traits appeared on separate wares during the previous Ayotla phase. This development took place in the Basin of Mexico at least one hundred years earlier than any other region but later spread to blanket much of Mesoamerica. The style therefore likely originated within the Basin of Mexico and then spread outward, though probably in a more decentralized manner than the spread of earlier carved black wares.

The hypothesis that trade vessels produced in the Basin of Mexico were exchanged to other regions of Mesoamerica to help spread the double-line-break white-ware horizon needs testing. Potential Central Mexican imports have been noted in the Tehuacán Valley (MacNeish et al. 1970) and Oaxaca (Flannery and Marcus 1994). We sampled some of the potential trade wares that MacNeish identified for neutron activation analysis and petrography (analysis forthcoming). While

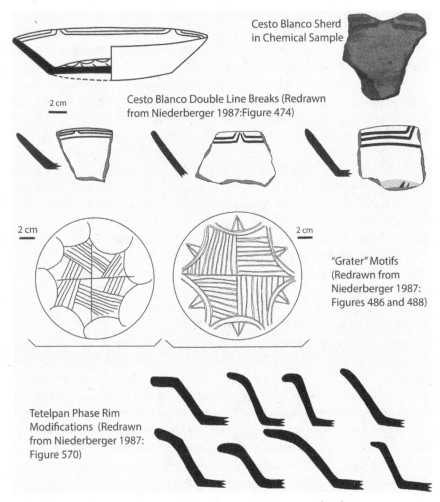

Cesto Blanco Sherd in Chemical Sample

Cesto Blanco Double Line Breaks (Redrawn from Niederberger 1987:Figure 474)

2 cm

2 cm

2 cm

"Grater" Motifs (Redrawn from Niederberger 1987: Figures 486 and 488)

Tetelpan Phase Rim Modifications (Redrawn from Niederberger 1987: Figure 570)

FIGURE 6.3. *Manantial and Tetelpan phase ceramic types mentioned in the text.*

the diversity of chemical composition among the Tehuacán ceramics implies that some were imported, none match any of our reference data for Central Mexico.

For the late Manantial and Tetelpan phases, we detected a large number of white ware bowls that were exchanged *into* the Basin of Mexico. These imports were found particularly at Altica in the Teotihuacan Valley, but also in smaller percentages at nine other sites in Central Mexico (Stoner and Nichols 2019b). We posit that these bowls were imported during the Tetelpan transition because some of them present vessel wall and rim modifications not typically seen among Manantial ceramics. These include curved vessel walls, rim tabs, and everted lips (see figure 6.3). We have tentatively sourced those imports to the metamorphic region of southwestern Puebla (Stoner and Nichols 2019b), and suggest that these form modifications, which became prevalent during the Zacatenco phase, might have been appropriated from imports beginning as early as the late Manantial or Tetelpan phase.

By the end of this time frame, the Basin of Mexico and neighboring Morelos to the south had begun to diverge in their ceramic styles. Morelos developed a prominent orange ware tradition, shared in common with lowland regions of the Gulf and Pacific coasts. The Basin of Mexico, by contrast, never developed a significant orange ware tradition during the Formative. For these two closely situated regions to diverge in their ceramic traditions marks the beginning of a regionalization process that intensified over time. Examples of orange Lacquer Ware, Niederberger's (1976) Chilapa Naranja, made their way into the Basin of Mexico, but our recent study shows that over half of this rare ceramic type was imported from Morelos or elsewhere (see also Cyphers 1987; Ochoa 2005, 555). Another type, Peralta Orange (Cyphers 1987), was developed in Morelos with style references to the Gulf Coast, but the type only reached the extreme southern portion of the basin at the site of Temamatla (Ramírez et al. 2000).

Zacatenco Phase (800–[500]400 cal BCE)

During the Zacatenco phase, all quadrants of the Basin of Mexico were occupied by at least a few settled villages (Tolstoy et al. 1977). The region's economy was similar to that for the Manantial phase, but those same trends intensified into the Zacatenco phase. The first irrigation canals appeared, demonstrating an intensification of agriculturally based subsistence economies and larger cooperative social organizations (Nichols 1987, 2015). Public monumental architecture strengthened a pattern of center-hinterland interactions. At the site of Temamatla in the southern basin, the region's earliest known ballcourt was constructed with stone-faced platforms nearby that might have represented elite residences (Serra Puche and Ramírez Sánchez 2001). The first stage of construction for the massive circular platform at Cuicuilco also had begun (Heizer and Bennyhoff 1958; Ramírez 2012). These activities mark the emergence of an institutionalized class of religious leaders that contrasts the individualized status of elites who built earlier externalized networks.

In terms of ceramic style, the Zacatenco phase can, at a minimum, be separated into early and late subphases (McBride1974; Niederberger 1976; cf. Ochoa 2005; Vaillant 1930). The first half of Zacatenco experienced continuation of previous ceramic technological traditions with some subtle variations in overt style (figure 6.4). White slipping and post-slip incision of double-line-breaks and pseudograter motifs continued in a fashion similar to the preceding phase, but early Zacatenco serving wares presented a greater variety of vessel forms. Bowls displayed mainly curved bases and either convex or composite silhouette walls

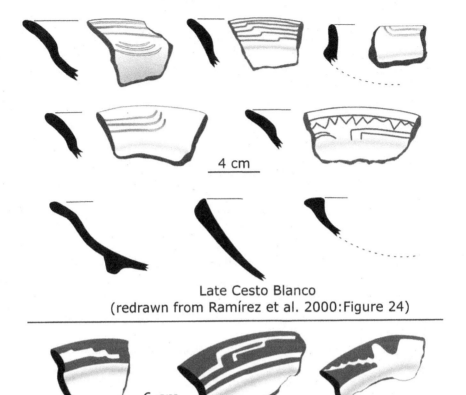

Late Cesto Blanco
(redrawn from Ramírez et al. 2000:Figure 24)

Zacatenco Red-on-White
(redrawn from Ramírez et al. 2000:Figure 41)

FIGURE 6.4. *Zacatenco phase ceramic types mentioned in the text.*

(see figure 6.4). The flat bases that dominated serving wares during Ayotla and Manantial phases largely disappeared by the Zacatenco phase. Zacatenco serving bowls also displayed more widely everted rims often with modifications, like tabs or double tabs where the break in the double-line incision would appear.

As mentioned above, our chemical sourcing sample contained several examples of bowls with rim tabs that we tentatively source to southwestern Puebla. Niederberger (1976; Lámina LXVI) depicts several of these samples under the type name Anahuac Blanco. The import of a small percentage of these wares from the metamorphic regions of Puebla is potentially significant to understand how, and from where, these changes originated. Such rim modifications were fairly common at the time across Mesoamerica, and the imports we identify suggest that trade among neighboring regions was a method for its spread. The presence of a small number of these imports at Altica suggests that their importation occurred no later than the early Zacatenco phase because the site was not occupied during late Zacatenco times.

Besides the white ware tradition, carinated bowls became a popular vessel form for plain monochrome serving wares. This was among the earliest type of restricted orifice bowls that emerged in the basin (except the small *tecomates* during the Early Formative), and they continued in popularity into the Ticomán phase (Müller 1990; Niederberger 1976). Carinated bowls were common at Altica in the Teotihuacan Valley, so we are confident that this vessel form enters the cultural sequence by the Tetelpan or early Zacatenco phases.

The late Zacatenco subphase experienced increased popularity of red-painted decoration over a white slip on composite silhouette bowls with widely everted rims (see figure 6.4). The transition in popularity from incision to red-on-white painted decoration was not discrete, but sites dating to the earliest years of Zacatenco possessed an overwhelming majority of incision compared to red-on-white painted decoration and sites dating to the latest years reverse that proportion. Red-on-white (or cream [McBride 1974] also lumped into "Polychrome" or "Trichrome" types [Müller 1990]) occurred across much of Central Mexico by the end of the Middle Formative, and it continued in small percentages into the Late Formative. By comparison, it was rare or absent in other regions of Mesoamerica at this time, demonstrating a continued constriction of style zones.

Red paint over white slip was not new for the Basin of Mexico, early examples go back to the Ayotla phase. Zacatenco white slips are indistinguishable from those dating to previous phases. Later painted motifs were very different, though, including frames, bars, step-frets, dots, diamonds, and naturalistic depictions that foreshadow Late Formative decorative changes.

Ticomán Phase ([500]400–100 cal BCE)

Major sociopolitical changes took place during the Ticomán phase. Cuicuilco arose as the region's first proto-urban settlement and dramatically refocused the Basin of Mexico's economy inward (Blanton et al. 2005; Carballo 2017, 76–79). Teotihuacan also emerged as a center in the northeast Basin of Mexico. These two cities became the seats of power for the region's first regional polities (Charlton and Nichols 1997; Sanders et al. 1979). Near the end of the Ticomán phase, Cuicuilco had integrated much of the western Basin of Mexico into a multitiered settlement hierarchy. The city itself contained a population of about twenty thousand people, and Teotihuacan grew to a similar size by the end of the Ticomán phase into the Terminal Formative period. Each of these emerging cities was at the center of a four-tiered settlement hierarchy by about 100 cal BCE (Sanders et al. 1979, 102).

At Cuicuilco and other sites throughout Central Mexico, the institutionalization of social classes and religion noted for the Zacatenco phase had become more apparent through ceremonial and residential architecture. In the Cuicuilco A sector, the massive circular pyramid was completed during this phase, which at 20 m height and 80 m diameter was the largest structure in the Basin of Mexico. To the west in the Cuicuilco B sector, several mounds and structures were identified (Müller 1990). Most of the structures were residences, but one elongated platform with several structures on top might have served as a temple complex with another (Mound 2) possibly representing a palace (Müller 1990, 277–80; Spencer and Redmond 2004, 191). Similar patterns of elite architecture have been noted during the Ticomán phase at Terremote-Tlaltenco and Temamatla in the southern basin (Serra and Lazcano 2009) and possibly at Loma Torremote (Santley 1993) and San José Cuauhtitlan (McBride 1974, 20–22) in the northwest basin, suggesting that many sites in the region hosted differentiated social classes. This process certainly has antecedents during the Zacatenco phase, but the pattern became more pervasive and more easily identified through substantial architectural variation during the Ticomán Phase.

The Chupícuaro influence on the Basin of Mexico during this phase has been recognized for decades (Porter 1956). Note that here we refer to the influence on common Ticomán phase serving bowls and not the suspected Chupícuaro imports typically found as grave offerings. This connection is, in part, demonstrated by the great prevalence of red-on-buff/cream ceramics executed on composite silhouette forms with short walls, curved bases, and large tripod supports that took globular, mammiform, or anthropomorphic leg forms (figure 6.5). These were not the first supports to appear on serving bowls, but earlier supports tended to be very small nubs and were relatively uncommon. "Slant eye" and "choker" style figurines (variants of Vaillant's [1930] Type H) also appeared alongside vessels of the Chupícuaro style.

Beginning about 500–400 cal BCE, these ceramic traditions appeared rapidly across the Basin of Mexico and slightly later in Puebla/Tlaxcala. The dramatic change to the ceramic repertoire and its rapid timing suggested to many that this shift was due to immigration of people bringing their materials and knowledge with them, but the source and direction of movement has been debated (Darras and Faugère 2007, 56–58). The style's distribution forms an arc from the Acámbaro Valley of Guanajuato up the Río Lerma and splitting to the southeast into the Tula region then into the Basin of Mexico. The western half of the basin contained some of the strongest expressions of the Chupícuaro-influenced ceramic styles, found principally at Cuicuilco, Ticomán, and San José Cuauhtitlan (McBride 1974; Müller 1990; Vaillant 1930), but it is also present in the eastern basin at sites like Cuanalan (e.g., Sanders et al. 1975). The appearance of this style in the Basin of Mexico represents an opportunity for future sourcing

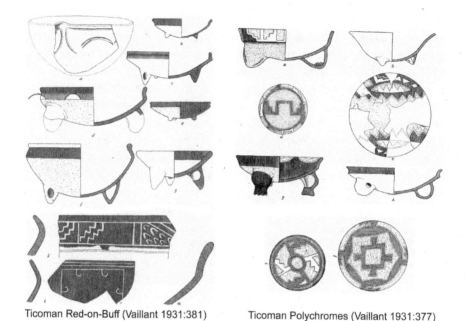

Ticoman Red-on-Buff (Vaillant 1931:381)   Ticoman Polychromes (Vaillant 1931:377)

FIGURE 6.5. *Ticomán phase ceramic types mentioned in the text.*

studies, but we note here that most elements of this style have no precedent in the Zacatenco phase.

The mechanisms by which this ceramic style arrived in the Basin of Mexico are unclear. Cuicuilco no doubt had an influence on the surrounding regions, but the nature of that influence is uncertain. Cuicuilco drew much of its obsidian from Michoacán (Plunket and Uruñuela 2012, 29–30), but those sources were not present at the Acámbaro Valley sites. Researchers have proposed the direction of influence as both from the Acámbaro Valley to the Basin of Mexico and the reverse. Darras and Faugère (2007) urge caution with these interpretations and contextualize the issue within their more recent work in Guanajuato. Settlements in the Acámbaro Valley and Cuicuilco both possess similar ceramics and circular structures during the first half of the Late Formative. Plunket and Uruñuela (2012) suggest that the cinnabar found in Guanajuato became important for the Late Formative ceramic traditions in the Basin of Mexico as deep reds and polychrome decoration became more popular. The desire to procure this pigment, which is found at Cuicuilco, might have fostered intensive interactions and similarities in painted decorative motifs.

We sampled a small number of Ticomán phase specimens from the site of San José Cuauhtitlan ($n = 37$) (McBride 1974) in the northwestern Basin of Mexico for compositional analysis. Others from Tepeji del Río ($n = 16$) and a salvage excavation in the historic center of Tula ($n = 33$) (Luis Gamboa, personal communication 2014) contained specimens that stylistically resemble late Zacatenco or early Ticomán ceramics. The majority from all three sites form a rather homogenous chemical cluster that serves as the basis to define a northwest basin chemical reference group. A minority of that sample displays divergent compositions. Two from Tepeji del Río display compositions closer to our Toluca Valley reference data. One from San José and six from the historic center of Tula returned higher transition metal concentrations than is typical for the region, which may represent import from the southeastern basin, but the data are too ambiguous to be certain.

Also from San José Cuauhtitlan we sampled Ticomán phase white wares, mostly thin-walled amphora of the type Blanco Granular. Müller (1990) identifies Blanco Granular as an import from either the Middle Balsas in Guerrero or Morelos. We lack Blanco Granular reference data from those regions, but we can confirm that those we sampled from San José Cuauhtitlan were produced outside the Basin of Mexico. These non-local white wares also stand apart from the local white-slipped ceramic tradition in surface color, form, paste texture and color, and vessel wall thickness. Preliminary x-ray fluorescence of the Blanco Granular slips indicates a calcium-based composition, while the same technique applied to locally produced specimens reveals a silicon-based composition, likely diatomaceous lake sediments. Unlike the integration of foreign pottery styles that took place during the earlier phases discussed here, there was no effort to integrate the styles of these imports into local ceramic assemblages. Importantly, none of the common Red-on-Buff ceramics in our sample were clearly produced outside the Basin of Mexico.

DISCUSSION AND CONCLUSION

Pottery trade was clearly one mechanism by which ceramic styles spread across Formative Mesoamerica (Stoner and Nichols 2019b). Pottery imports were identified during every phase discussed here except the Late Zacatenco phase, but our sample for that phase is not statistically robust. Trade pots during the Ayotla and Manantial/Tetelpan phases likely served as templates for local imitation of styles developed outside the Basin of Mexico. The reverse flow of goods from the basin to surrounding regions may also have been a mechanism for the spread of white wares with double-line-breaks during the early Manantial phase, but more compositional testing is necessary. By the end of the Tetelpan phase, however, other types of ceramics were being traded into the Basin of Mexico *without* localized adoption. We see this through the import of orange Lacquer Ware and possibly Peralta Orange from Morelos. These ceramic traditions developed in Morelos and among lowland groups on the Gulf and Pacific coasts. Basin potters were certainly aware of them, and traded to obtain them, but their own ceramic traditions had solidified enough that a style boundary formed at its border with Morelos. Later, during the Ticomán phase, Blanco Granular also was imported but not copied into basin ceramic assemblages. We found no evidence that the rapid appropriation of Chupícuaro-inspired ceramic traits in local pottery assemblages arrived via ceramic trade, though we note that our sample for that time frame is relatively small and focuses on serving bowls common to the local tradition.

For the Ayotla phase, there is little doubt that import of symbol-laden materials contributed to the rapid adoption of the Olmec style, but we observe that imports made up only about 3 percent of all Olmec-style carved vessels from Tlapacoya (Blomster et al. 2005), and our own identified imports for the phase were almost exclusively restricted to the type Xochiltepec White, a fine-paste kaolin ware that rarely displayed Olmec carved motifs. The rapid adoption of both the Olmec-style esthetic, paste colors, vessel forms, surface treatments, carving techniques, and the differential-firing technique suggests deeper knowledge and more thorough familiarity with the tradition than could have been learned through emulation of trade pots alone. Some direct mechanism of social learning, such as temporary or permanent migration, must have accompanied pottery trade. The only other phase that might represent significant immigration of people from other places in Mesoamerica was during the Ticomán phase, but we have no direct evidence of pottery import or migration from the Acámbaro Valley, Guanajuato. While the Ucareo obsidian at Cuicuilco demonstrates that an exchange relationship existed with West Mexico, Darras and Faugère (2007) note that sites in the Acámbaro Valley did not utilize the Ucareo source.

From the early Manantial through early Zacatenco phases, ceramic traditions within the Basin of Mexico were relatively stable, an observation that might also extend to the regional population. We can understand the emergence of Manantial white wares as an endogenous process resulting from the gradual modification of previous Ayotla phase styles and technologies over generations. Given the early development of white wares with double-line-breaks in the Basin of Mexico, we suspect that the region projected some influence outward on the pottery trends of surrounding regions, which all began to display this nearly ubiquitous ceramic tradition during the Middle Formative. This was likely not direct migration or long-distance trade, but serial interactions across each region where the ceramic style appeared. By the end of the Tetelpan phase, ceramic imports from neighboring Puebla might have influenced vessel lip and wall shapes in the Basin of Mexico, but these morphological changes were relatively minor and would have been applied to a relatively constant local pottery production sequence. Early Zacatenco pottery was likewise oriented toward reproduction of previous generations' pottery with some additional slow-paced changes to vessel form and decoration.

Finally, Willey (1991) identified this alternating trend between horizontal integration and regional diversification as an important process in the rise of civilizations but admitted to not having a good enough grasp on the cycles to explain why at the time. We present one case study here that features the expansion and contraction of ceramic style zones as tied to social, political, and economic interactions that alternated between external network alliance building and internal development of regional polities and marketing patterns centered on early cities. Local groups, in an effort to sustain the processes of social differentiation in the earliest settled villages, sought connections with external groups through both trade and migration. The basin's participation in Early and Middle Formative style horizons from the Ayotla through Tetelpan phases reflects this mostly externally focused strategy, though the direction of influence on ceramic styles changes over time. The emphasis shifted by the late Middle Formative (late Zacatenco phase in the Basin of Mexico) to increasingly centralized patterns of interaction inwardly focused on consolidating regional settlements into polities under the authority of institutionalized elites residing within emerging cities, the centralized flow of goods and materials within the region, and investment in public goods such as communal ritual structures, irrigated agricultural systems, and likely early market exchange patterns focused on emerging central places (Nichols and Stoner 2019). This shift caused local communities of practice to maintain more regionalized systems of ceramic production and style that contrasted those developed in neighboring regions, forming style boundaries that often transitioned abruptly across space. Such a boundary began to form between the Basin of Mexico and Morelos by the late Middle Formative as expressed through ceramic style contrasts including, but not limited to, the substantial orange ware tradition developed in Morelos that was never widely adopted in the Basin of Mexico.

This shift, as seen through ceramic styles over the Formative period, from external network building that signaled broadly defined group membership to more restricted style zones constrained to the areas covered by emerging polities, may have merit for studying collective action in the development of Late Formative polities across Mesoamerica. Barth (1969) treated ethnicity as a signaling system with the purpose establishing intergroup boundaries and verifying intragroup membership (see also Wobst 1977). Blanton (2015) extends that concept to collective action in which the signals shared by a group help to build trust in local cooperative arrangements by overriding fears that their efforts may not be undertaken in the common interest. The adoption of symbols that represent group membership, and which contrast symbols of the Other, serve to define corporate identities and institutions that transcend kinship and permit the scaling up of cooperative endeavors. It reaffirms that public goods and common pool resources are to be accessible only by the ingroup and not available to individuals outside the collective. Part of gaining that trust is a symbolic system that defines and constantly reaffirms membership within the group.

Many variables influence the style of a group's pottery, but the data presented here demonstrate that shrinking interaction networks (social and economic) are not the only factors of importance. Long-distance interaction did not cease, and we have demonstrated two commonly imported wares, Lacquer Ware and Blanco Granular, later in the sequence presented here that the community of potters within the Basin of Mexico never adopted into their basic ceramic repertoires. We urge that reproduction of traditional ceramic styles, as opposed to appropriation of styles external to the group, was one small part of the signaling system that defined emerging corporate polities by the late Middle Formative. The Late Formative Chupícuaro influence on ceramic styles in the Basin of Mexico confounds this notion and may represent another inflection point that signals a shift in the process toward using external symbols to build local group identities, but we note that the geographic range of Chupícuaro is much smaller than any of the style horizons that occurred earlier. Teotihuacan went through a similar process in the Early Classic as it drew upon certain Gulf Coast ceramic traditions, like lustrous wares and volute motifs, and incorporated them into their own symbolic system (Daneels 2008).

Acknowledgments. We thank Jennifer Carballo, Robert Cobean, Luis Gamboa, Richard Lesure, James Neely, Patricia Plunket, Mari Carmen Serra Puche, Yoko Sugiura, Paul Tolstoy, and Gabriela Uruñuela for permission to analyze samples of ceramics they collected that we use here to identify trade patterns. Funding for the projects that generated data in conjunction with the Altica Project was provided by the National Geographic Society, the National Science Foundation NSF No. 1424132-Nichols (Dartmouth), NSF Nos. 1451425 and 424184-Stoner (Arkansas), the Claire Garber Goodman Fund-Dartmouth, Rockefeller Center for the Social Sciences Urban Studies Grant-Dartmouth, Dickey Center for International Understanding-Dartmouth, and the Neukom Center for Computational Sciences-Dartmouth.

REFERENCES

Barth, Fredrik. 1969. "Pathan Identity and Its Maintenance." In *Ethnic Groups and Boundaries: The Social Organization of Culture Difference*, edited by Fredrik Barth, 117–34. Long Grove, IL: Waveland. First published 1969.

Blanton, Richard E. 2015. "Theories of Ethnicity and the Dynamics of Ethnic Change in Multiethnic Societies." *Proceedings of the National Academy of Sciences* 112 (30): 9176–81.

Blanton, Richard E., and Lane Fargher. 2010. "Evaluating Causal Factors in Market Development in Premodern States: A Comparative Study, with Critical Comments on the History of Ideas about Markets." In *Archaeological Approaches to Market*

Exchange in Ancient Societies, edited by Christopher Garraty and Barbara L. Stark, 207–26. Boulder: University Press of Colorado.

Blanton, Richard E., and Lane Fargher. 2016. *How Humans Cooperate: Confronting the Challenges of Collective Action*. Boulder: University Press of Colorado.

Blanton, Richard E., Lane Fargher, and Verenice Y. Heredia Espinoza. 2005. "The Mesoamerican World of Goods and its Transformations." In *Settlement, Subsistence, and Social Complexity: Essays Honoring the Legacy of Jeffrey R. Parsons*, edited by Richard E. Blanton, 260–94. Los Angeles: Cotsen Institute of Archaeology, UCLA.

Blanton, Richard E., Gary M. Feinman, Stephen A. Kowalewski, and Peter N. Peregrine. 1996. "A Dual-Processual Theory for the Evolution of Mesoamerican Civilization." *Current Anthropology* 37 (1): 1–14.

Blomster, Jeffrey P., and David Cheetham. 2017. *The Early Olmec and Mesoamerica: The Material Record*. Cambridge, UK: Cambridge University Press.

Blomster, Jeffrey P., Hector Neff, and Michael D. Glascock. 2005. "Olmec Pottery Production and Export in Ancient Mexico Determined through Elemental Analysis." *Science* 307:1068–72.

Boksenbaum, Martin William, Paul Tolstoy, Garman Harbottle, Jerome Kimberlin, and Mary D. Neivens. 1987. "Obsidian Industries and Cultural Evolution in the Basin of Mexico before 500 B.C." *Journal of Field Archaeology* 14 (1): 66–75.

Brace, Selina, Yoan Diekmann, Thomas J. Booth, Lucy van Dorp, Zuzana Faltyskova, Nadin Rohland, Swapan Mallick, et al. 2019. "Ancient Genomes Indicate Population Replacement in Early Neolithic Britain." *Nature: Ecology & Evolution* 3:765–71.

Carballo, David M., and Gary M. Feinman. 2016. "Cooperation, Collective Action, and the Archaeology of Large-Scale Societies." *Evolutionary Anthropology* 26: 88–96.

Charlton, Thomas H. 1984. "Production and Exchange: Variables in the Evolution of a Civilization." In *Trade and Exchange in Early Mesoamerica*, edited by Kenn Hirth, 17–42. Albuquerque: University of New Mexico Press.

Charlton, Thomas H., and Deborah L. Nichols. 1997. "Diachronic Studies of City-States: Permutations on a Theme, Central Mexico from 1600 BC to AD 1600." In *The Archaeology of City-States: Cross-Cultural Approaches*, edited by Deborah L. Nichols and Thomas H. Charlton, 169–207. Washington, DC: Smithsonian Institution Press.

Cheetham, David, and David M. Coe. 2017. "Ceramic Vessel Form Similarities between San Lorenzo, Veracruz, and Canton Corralito, Chiapas." In *The Early Olmec and Mesoamerica: The Material Record*, edited by Jeffrey P. Blomster and David Cheetham, 223–63. Cambridge, UK: Cambridge University Press.

Clark, John. E. 1997. "The Arts of Government in Early Mesoamerica." *Annual Review of Anthropology* 26:211–34.

Coe, Michael, and Richard A. Diehl. 1980. *In the Land of the Olmec*. Vol. 1. Austin: University of Texas Press.

Crown, Patricia L. 2014. "The Archaeology of Crafts Learning: Becoming a Potter in the Puebloan Southwest." *Annual Review of Anthropology* 39 (2): 335–43.

Cyphers, Ann. 1987. "Ceramics." In *Ancient Chalcatzingo*, edited by David Grove, 200–51. Austin: University of Texas Press.

Daneels, Annick. 2008. "Teotihuacan y el Golfo: Reflexiones en torno a la evidencia." In *Arte y arqueología en Teotihuacan: Nuevos trabajos*, 58–74. Barcelona: Universidad Autónoma de Barcelona.

Darras, Véronique, and Brigitte Faugère. 2007. "Chupícuaro, entre el occidente y el altiplano central: Un balance de los conocimientos y las nuevas aportaciones." In *Dinámicas culturales entre el Occidente, el Centro-Norte y la Cuenca de México del Preclásico al Epiclásico*, edited by Brigitte Faugère, 51–84. Michoacán: CEMCA—Colegio de Michoacán.

DeBoer, Warren R. 1990. "Interaction, Imitation, and Communication as Expressed in Style: The Ucayali Experience." In *The Uses of Style in Archaeology*, edited by Margaret Conkey and Christine Hastorf, 82–104. Cambridge, UK: Cambridge University Press.

Dietler, Michael, and Ingrid Herbich. 1998. "Habitus, Techniques, Style: An Integrated Approach to the Social Understanding of Material Culture and Boundaries." In *The Archaeology of Social Boundaries*, edited by Miriam T. Stark, 232–63. Washington DC: Smithsonian Institution Press.

Eerkens, Jelmer W., and Carl P. Lipo. 2007. "Cultural Transmission Theory and The Archaeological Record: Providing Context to Understanding Variation and Temporal Changes in Material Culture." *Journal of Archaeological Research* 15 (3): 239–74.

Flannery, Kent V., and Joyce Marcus. 1994. *Early Formative Pottery of the Valley of Oaxaca*. Ann Arbor: University of Michigan Museum.

García Moll, Roberto, Daniel Juarez Cossio, Carmen Pijoan Aguade, María Elena Salas Cuesta, and Marcela Salas Cuesta. 1991. *Catálogo de entierros de San Luis Tlatilco, México: Temporada IV*. México, DF: Instituto de Antropología e Historia.

Giddens, Anthony. 1979. *Central Problems in Social Theory: Action, Structure, and Contradiction in Social Analysis*. Berkeley: University of California Press.

Gosselain, Olivier P. 2000. "Materializing Identities: An African Perspective." *Journal of Archaeological Method and Theory* 7 (3): 187–217.

Grove, David C. 1993. "'Olmec' Horizons in Formative Period Mesoamerica: Diffusion or Social Evolution?" In *Latin American Horizons*, edited by D. S. Rice, 83–111. Washington, DC: Dumbarton Oaks.

Heizer, Robert F., and Jack Bennyhoff. 1958. "Archaeological Investigations at Cuicuilco, Valley of Mexico." *Science* 127 (3292): 232–33.

Herbich, I., and Michael Dietler. 2008. "The Long Arm of the Mother-in-Law: Learning, Postmarital Resocialization of Women, and Material Culture Style." In *Cultural Transmission and Material Culture: Breaking Down Boundaries*, edited by Miriam T. Stark, Brenda J. Bowser, and Lee Horne, 223–44. Tucson: University of Arizona Press.

Johnson, Nadia, and Kenneth G. Hirth. 2019. "Altica, Coapexco, and the Role of Middlemen in Formative Obsidian Exchange." *Ancient Mesoamerica* 30:295–310.

Joyce, Rosemary A. 1999. "Social Dimensions of Pre-Classic Burials." In *Social Patterns in Pre-Classic Mesoamerica*, edited by David C. Grove and Rosemary A. Joyce, 15–47. Washington, DC: Dumbarton Oaks.

Kristiansen, K., M. Allentoft, K. Frei, R. Iversen, N. Johannsen, G. Kroonen, and E. Willerslev. 2017. "Re-theorising Mobility and the Formation of Culture and Language among the Corded Ware Culture in Europe." *Antiquity* 91 (356):334–47.

MacNeish, Richard S., Frederick A. Peterson, and Kent V. Flannery. 1970. *The Prehistory of the Tehuacán Valley*. Vol 3, *Ceramics*. Austin: University of Texas Press.

McBride, Harold. 1974. "Formative Ceramics and the Prehistoric Settlement Patterns in the Cuauhtitlan Region, Mexico." PhD diss., University of California, Los Angeles.

McClung de Tapia, Emily, Guillermo Acosta Ochoa, Diana Martínez-Yrizar, Carrmen Cristina Adriano-Morán, Jorge Cruz-Palma, and Berenice Chaparro-Rueda. 2019. "Early–Middle Formative Period Subsistence in the Teotihuacan Valley, Mexico: Pre-Hispanic Plant Remains from Altica." *Ancient Mesoamerica* 30:339–54.

Müller, Florencia. 1990. La cerámica de Cuicuilco B: Un rescate arqueológico. México, DF: INAH.

Neff, Hector. 2014. "Pots as Signals: Explaining the Enigma of Long-Distance Ceramic Exchange." In *Craft and Science: International Perspectives on Archaeological Ceramics*, edited by M. Martinón-Torres, 1–11. Doha: Bloomsbury Qatar Foundation.

Nichols, Deborah L. 1987. "Risk and Agricultural Intensification during the Formative Period in the Northern Basin of Mexico." *American Anthropologist* 89 (3): 596–616.

Nichols, Deborah L. 2015. "Intensive Agriculture and Early Complex Societies of the Basin of Mexico: The Formative Period." *Ancient Mesoamerica* 26:407–21.

Nichols, Deborah L., and Wesley D. Stoner. 2019. "Before Teotihuacan: Altica, Exchange, Interactions, and the Origins of Complex Society in the Northeast Basin of Mexico." *Ancient Mesoamerica* 30 (2): 369–82.

Niederberger, Christine. 1976. *Zohapilco: Cinco milenios de ocupación humana en un sitio lacustre de la cuenca de Mexico*. Mexico DF: Instituto Nacional de Antropología e Historia.

Niederberger, Christine. 2000. "Ranked Societies, Iconographic Complexity, and Economic Wealth in the Basin of Mexico toward 1200 B.C." In *Olmec Art and Archaeology in Mesoamerica*, edited by John Clark and Mary Pye, 169–92. New Haven, CT: Yale University Press.

Ochoa Castillo, Patricia. 2005. "La cerámica del formativo en la cuenca de México." In *La producción alfarera en el México antiguo I*, edited by Beatriz Leonor Merino Carrión and Ángel García Cook, 523–74. México, DF: Instituto Nacional de Antropología e Historia.

Oliveros Morales, José Arturo. 2005. "La cerámica del occidente de México durante el Formativo." In *La producción alfarera en el México antiguo I*, edited by Beatriz Leonor

Merino Carrión and Ángel García Cook, 651–86. México, DF: Instituto Nacional de Antropología e Historia.

Paradis, Louise. 2017. "Early Horizon Materials in the Greater Basin of Mexico and Guerrero." In *The Early Olmec and Mesoamerica: The Material Record*, edited by Jeffrey P. Blomster and David Cheetham, 119–47. Cambridge, UK: Cambridge University Press.

Plunket, Patricia, and Gabriela Uruñuela. 2012. "Where East Meets West: The Formative in Mexico's Central Highlands." *Journal of Archaeological Research* 20:1–51.

Pool, Christopher A. 2007. *Olmec Archaeology and Early Mesoamerica*. Cambridge, UK: Cambridge University Press.

Porter Weaver, Muriel. 1956. "Excavations at Chupícuaro, Guanajuato, México." *Transactions of the American Philosophical Society* 46:515–637.

Ramírez, Felipe, Lorena Gámez, and Fernán González. 2000. *Cerámica de Temamatla*. México, DF: Universidad Nacional Autónoma de México, Instituto de Investigaciones Antropológicas.

Ramírez Sánchez, Felipe. 2012. "La erupción Xitle y el fin de Cuicuilco." *Revista de Arqueología Americana* 30 (Cambios climáticos en la antegüedad): 61–89.

Reina, Ruben E., and Robert M. Hill. 1974. *The Traditional Pottery of Guatemala*. Austin: University of Texas Press.

Rodríguez, María del Carmen, and Ponciano Ortíz Ceballos. 1997. "Olmec Ritual and Sacred Geography at Manatí." In *Olmec to Aztec: Settlement Patterns in the Ancient Gulf Lowlands*, edited by Barbara L. Stark and Philip J. Arnold, 68–95. Tucson: University of Arizona Press.

Rosenswig, Robert M. 2010. *The Beginnings of Mesoamerican Civilization: Inter-regional Interaction and the Olmec*. Cambridge, UK: Cambridge University Press.

Rosenswig, Robert M. 2016. "3.2. Olmec Globalization: A Mesoamerican Archipelago of Complexity." In *Handbook of Archaeology and Globalization*, edited by Tamar Hodos, 177–93. New York: Routledge.

Roux, Valentine 2017. "Ceramic Manufacture: The Chaîne Opératoire Approach." In *The Oxford Handbook of Archaeological Ceramic Analysis*, edited by Alice Hunt, 101–13. New York: Oxford University Press.

Sanders, William T., Jeffrey Parsons, and Robert S. Santley. 1979. *The Basin of Mexico: Ecological Processes in the Evolution of Civilization*. New York: Academic Press.

Sanders, William T., Michael West, Charles Fletcher, and Joseph Marino, 1975. *The Teotihuacan Valley Project*. Vol. 2, *The Formative Period Occupation of the Valley* (2 parts), Occasional Papers in Anthropology, No. 10. Pennsylvania State University, University Park.

Santley, Robert S. 1993. "Late Formative Period Society at Loma Torremote: A Consideration of the Redistribution vs. the Great Provider Models as a Basis for the Emergence of Complexity in the Basin of Mexico." In *Prehispanic Domestic Units in Western Mesoamerica*, edited by Robert S. Santley and Kenneth G. Hirth, 67–86. Boca Raton, FL: CRC Press.

Serra Puche, Mari Carmen, and Juan Carlos Lazcano Arce. 2009. "Arqueología en el sur de la cuenca de México. Diagnóstico y futuro. In memoriam W. T. Sanders." *Cuicuilco* 47: 19–38.

Serra Puche, Mari Carmen, and Felipe Ramírez Sánchez. 2001. "Temamatla: Un Sitio del Horizonte Formativo en el Sureste de la Cuenca de México." *Expresión Antropológica* 12.

Sillar, B. 2000. "The Challenge of [Technological Choices] for Materials Science Approaches in Archaeology." *Archaeometry* 42:2–20.

Spencer, Charles R., and Elsa M. Redmond. 2004. "Primary State Formation in Mesoamerica." *Annual Review of Anthropology* 33:173–99.

Stark, Barbara, L. 2017. "Figuring Out the Early Olmec Era." In *The Early Olmec and Mesoamerica: The Material Record*, edited by Jeffrey P. Blomster and David Cheetham, 288–312. New York: Cambridge University Press.

Stark, Miriam T. 1998. *The Archaeology of Social Boundaries*. Washington, DC: Smithsonian Institution Press.

Stoner, Wesley D., and Deborah L. Nichols. 2019a. "The Altica Project: Reframing the Formative Basin of Mexico." *Ancient Mesoamerica* 30 (2): 247–65.

Stoner, Wesley D., and Deborah L. Nichols. 2019b. "Pottery Trade and the Formation of Early and Middle Formative Style Horizons as Seen from Central Mexico." *Ancient Mesoamerica* 30 (2): 311–37.

Stoner, Wesley D., Deborah L. Nichols, Bridgett A. Alex, and Destiny L. Crider. 2015. "The Emergence of Early-Middle Formative Exchange Patterns in Mesoamerica: A View from Altica in the Teotihuacan Valley." *Journal of Anthropological Archaeology* 39:19–35.

Storey, Rebecca, Gina M. Buckley, and Douglas J. Kennett. 2019. "A Glimpse of the People of Altica: Osteological and Isotopic/Radiocarbon Analysis." *Ancient Mesoamerica* 30:355–68.

Tolstoy, Paul. 1989. "Coapexco and Tlatilco: Sites with Olmec Materials in the Basin of Mexico." In *Regional Perspectives on the Olmec*, edited by Richard A. Diehl, 85–121. Cambridge, UK: Cambridge University Press.

Tolstoy, Paul, Suzanne Fish, Martin Boksenbaum, Kathryn Blair Vaughn, and Carol Smith. 1977. "Early Sedentary Communities of the Basin of Mexico." *Journal of Field Archaeology* 4:91–106.

Vaillant, George. 1930. *Excavations at Zacatenco*. New York: American Museum of Natural History.

Vaillant, George. 1931. *Excavations at Ticoman*. New York: American Museum of Natural History.

Willey, Gordon R. 1991. "Horizonal Integration and Regional Diversity: An Alternating Process in the Rise of Civilizations." *American Antiquity* 56 (2): 197–215.

Wobst, H. Martin. 1977. "Stylistic Behavior and Information Exchange." Anthropological Papers No. 61, 317–42. Ann Arbor: Museum of Anthropology, Michigan University.

7

Urban Organization and Origins of Complexity in the Puuc Region of Northern Yucatán

MICHAEL P. SMYTH

INTRODUCTION

Stratified society in the Puuc Hills during the Terminal Classic "florescence" has long been attributed to northward migrations following collapse of Southern Lowland Maya civilization (Willey and Shimkin 1973). Recent research, however, renders the migration model implausible because of numerous Preclassic (~800 BCE–300 CE) archaeological sites in the Puuc that demonstrate a much longer and local developmental sequence (Andrews et al. 2018; Smyth et al. 2020). These findings raise the critical question of when complex societies and archaic states first arose. To this end, Xcoch, a large Preclassic site strategically located in the central Santa Elena Valley exhibits massive monumental architecture in the megalithic style and community patterns distributed across an extensive settlement landscape. The Preclassic at Xcoch supports a model of early urban organization for a primary central place heading a settlement hierarchy long before the rise of regional centers like Uxmal in the Terminal Classic (ca. 850–900 CE).

Investigations at Xcoch and its deep-water cave below the urban core have documented occupation in the Middle Preclassic (MP) with the primacy of

https://doi.org/10.5876/9781646422883.c007

monumental architecture by volume in the Late Preclassic (LP), suggesting large-scale labor mobilization under an administrative elite in an evolving complex society. Massive hydraulic features at the central monumental zone show attributes of large-scale water collection, storage, and dispersal engineered in response to the region's water-poor, seasonal rainfall that posed acute problems for large sedentary farming-based populations. Urban planning of hydraulic features included *aguadas* (human-made or -altered water reservoirs), immense catchment surfaces, drainage canals, and specialized water tanks before *chultuns* (underground cisterns) became widely used for water storage. A hiatus in social development at the end of the Preclassic was followed by reoccupation in the Early Classic (EP) (~500 CE), when the Maya restored water works and constructed buildings with stone vaulted roofs for the first time. The site reached its height around 850 CE just prior to general abandonment, although frequent returns to the cave (including John Stephens in 1841) underscore the deep-time memory and cultural significance of the place.

This chapter presents archaeological data at Xcoch including community patterns, strategic architectural contexts, hydraulic features, and related material remains as proxy measures of increasing complexity and development of social stratification. A model of urban organization is proposed based on behavioral reconstruction of architecture and settlement incorporating the pattern and presence of megalithic-style construction—large pillow-shaped boulders set in dry masonry with abundant chinking stones—visible on high platforms and pyramid structures that correlate with Preclassic society at Xcoch, the Puuc Hills, and across the northern Maya Lowlands (Taube 1995; Mathews 2003; Mathews and Maldonado 2006). Regional settlement patterns are also examined to show that Preclassic Xcoch was a primate center for the Santa Elena Valley and greater Puuc region. The environmental context of drought cycles impacted early agriculture and water storage playing a critical role in a Terminal Preclassic hiatus (ca. 200 CE). Ultimately, Uxmal would emerge as a Terminal Classic regional state producing some of Mesoamerica's architectural masterpieces before undergoing decline and abandonment (Kowalski and Dunning 1999; Smyth et al. 2017). However, the data presented here imply that the Puuc state emerged earlier and was more complex than generally recognized by traditional Maya archaeology.

PUUC STATE FORMATION

The emergence of Maya states in the north, a body politic of stratified class-based society with hierarchically organized leadership, is a compelling research question. The traditional migration model holds that the north was sparsely populated when collapse forced people in the south to migrate north bringing with them state-level organization (Willey and Shimkin 1973). This model, however, is inconsistent with significant Preclassic occupations in the Puuc region

TABLE 7.1. Time periods and chronologies related to ceramics and architectural styles and their characteristics from the Puuc region and the site of Xcoch.

Period	Middle-Late Preclassic	Early Classic	Late Classic	Terminal Classic
Chronology	800 BCE–300 CE	300–600 CE	600–800 CE	800–1000 CE
Ceramics	Mamom-Tihosuco	Cochuah	Motul	Cehpech
Architecture	Megalithic	Proto-Puuc	Early Puuc	Classic Puuc
Characteristics	pillow-shaped boulders with abundant chinking stones; rough to medium faced stones	medium to well-cut-faced stones; slab vault stones	medium to well-cut-faced stones; concrete hearting; triangular-shaped vault stones; columns	well-cut-faced stones; boot-shaped vault stones; decoration with colonettes, mosaics, etc.

and across Northern Yucatán. While most scholars concur that some northern societies with social stratification and elite leadership (i.e., political states) were in place by the Classic period, little investigation has focused on the Preclassic origins of complexity and *how* societies were complex. At Xcoch, for instance, when did an administrative elite divorced from direct food production and traditional social rules emerge? How did they regulate local and regional communities? Did they gain materially by instituting policies to tax, collect tribute, and demand labor? The perspective here is that the evolution of complexity was predominately a local cultural process characterized along multiple dimensions of variation (socio-political-economic-religious) and the degree of complexity reflected, in part, by the character and organization of diverse architectural features so typical of Puuc archaeological sites (table 7.1). Urban organization, therefore, refers to the scale and volume of megalithic monumental architecture, spatial extent of residential structures reflecting population size and distribution, and magnitude of central reservoirs and water-control systems. These key settlement features employed as surrogate measures can provide insights into dimensions of variation and degree of social complexity.

A hallmark of urban organization in the northern Maya Lowlands is monumental architecture (Andrews 1975, 1985; Kowalski and Dunning 1999; Andrews and Robles 2004; Anderson 2011; Peniche 2012). Although relatively simple societies sometimes undertake large-scale building projects without centralized control or ascribed leadership, volume and scale of monumental construction and the inferred complexity of labor coordination and resource management arguably require a central authority or managerial elite. Precisely when and how this first comes about at Xcoch is not altogether clear. The available evidence for initial monumental construction dates to around 600 BCE, with the initial stages of the Grand Platform, the earliest phases of the Great Pyramid, as

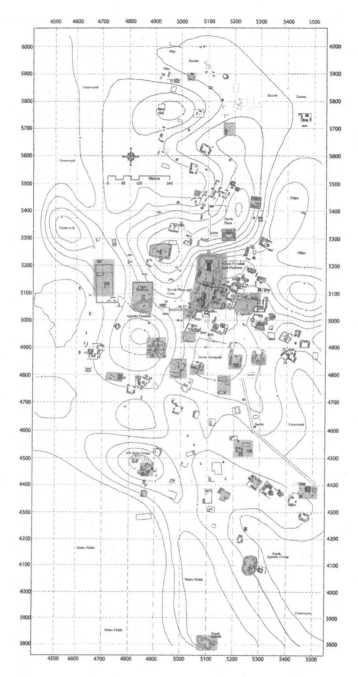

FIGURE 7.1. *Grid map of Xcoch showing metric coordinates on borders and highlighted settlement groups, megalithic architecture, and water features, including* aguadas *and reservoirs dated to the Preclassic period. The locations of excavation units are numbered throughout.*

well as the Xcoch Plaza's initial Cave Pyramid and associated E Group complex (figure 7.1). The limited spatial extent of MP monumental and residential architecture across the site landscape implies that a stratified political system was *not* yet in place, with leadership positions confined to internally ranked kin-based groups (lineages), implying some form of hierarchy or chiefdom-like authority closely tied to early farming and critical resources like water. The lack of early status architecture outside the central zone suggests a low population size and an absence of the stratified leadership exercised over non-kin necessary to support an extractive political economy. The political situation appears to change in the LP, as reflected by a building boom across the site that implies population expansion and greater political centralization. Status architecture such as large pyramid groups appear outside the site center for the first time. At central Xcoch, large-scale hydraulic works are constructed or expanded, and the water cave and Gondola Aguada were physically connected by a stone causeway, implying elite control along with the creation of a specialized architectural complex restricted access to the cave's permanent water source (below).

Urban Organization

Early state development and incipient urbanism at Puuc centers should be closely related (Smyth and Dore 1994). At Xcoch, the individual household was the most basic residential unit. The household cluster or neighborhood (local community) was a corporate territorial entity composed of many interacting households whose community activities provided a cooperative network of shared goods, services, and labor. Social differences, authority, and labor organization were traditionally structured by kinship ties, often lineages made up of related family groups.

Formalized interactions between communities, however, can be a sign of increasing sociopolitical complexity, especially when occurring outside kinship structure across a burgeoning urban center. Such interactions involve intercommunity relations coordinated and controlled by a central authority or elite class by circumventing kinship systems of social organization and egalitarianism to form new social and political institutions. Divine kingship is perhaps the most well-known leadership system of state polity formation among the Classic Maya, but other systems of corporate political centralization were certainly possible in the Preclassic (i.e., priestly leaders, ruling counsels, confederacies, etc.) as status systems evolved over more egalitarian-based social structures. If local communities underwent hierarchical ranking in order of social distance from a dominant polity, then certain communities may have become stratified and socially advantaged. Such an early polity may have resembled ranked Postclassic Maya communities territorially organized composed of kin-based lineages, or *ch'ibalo'ob* (or also the Aztec *capulli*) whose members lived, worked, held land, fought, and paid tribute as a group. As a result, the outcome of hierarchy leading to stratification is an overarching social and political order of administrative elite divorced from direct food production and traditional social rules who come to regulate local communities and gain materially by instituting policies to tax, collect tribute, and demand labor. Sanctioned by political and ceremonial ideology and sometimes outright coercion, elites develop an agenda separate from that of the rest of the society and seek to link communities together to perform activities that maintain the social order. One such self-interest policy would include coordinating major public construction projects, often monuments benefiting the elites themselves.

Community activities associated with status architecture should reflect distinctions between commoners and elites, especially under conditions of societal transition from kinship to stratified groups. Low-level commoner activities, such as agriculture and craft production, take place within and between households and promote corporate survival and reproduction of social units. High-level elite interactions across communities, conversely, entail politico-economic activities that support, maintain, and reproduce an elite social class associated with an ideology vested in monumental architecture that often serves as formal meeting grounds between the elite and the rest of society. Evidence for such a complex social process is arguably manifest in the LP via the diversity and scale of settlement features, especially widespread monumental megalithic architecture at Xcoch.

Social process is inferred by numerous megalithic-style high platforms and particularly pyramids (thirty-three identified to date), more than at any other known Puuc site, many dated to the Preclassic by stratigraphic excavations via ceramic types, architectural stratigraphy, and radiocarbon assays (below). A notable feature of the Preclassic in the Puuc was an emphasis on reservoir construction, such as the enormous Xpotoit *aguada* found at Yaxhom and the huge Gondola *aguada* at Xcoch, among others (Dunning et al. 2014b; Ringle et al. 2011; Smyth et al. 2011; Smyth et al. 2020). Excavations across Xcoch also show clear evidence for a hiatus in occupation and a pause in social development at the end of the Preclassic, when many site areas were abandoned and not reoccupied until the EC. One factor in Preclassic decline relates to climatic data from northern Yucatán, Belize, and the Caribbean Basin (e.g., Hodell et al. 2001; Haug et al. 2003; Medina-Elizalde 2015; Moyes et al. 2009; Webster et al. 2007). The second century CE was a period of cyclical drought that coincided with abandonment of many lowland Maya urban centers both north and south. (Dunning et al. 2014a).

Significant evidence for an early state at Xcoch includes a possible palace-type complex associated with the megalithic Great Pyramid, presumably a residence of high-status leadership in the LP (figures 7.1 and 7.2). In addition, three major *aguadas* at Xcoch, two in the central zone and one on southern periphery, were constructed and/or expanded at this time, suggesting a scale of administrative control

GREAT PYRAMID AND GRAND PLATFORM

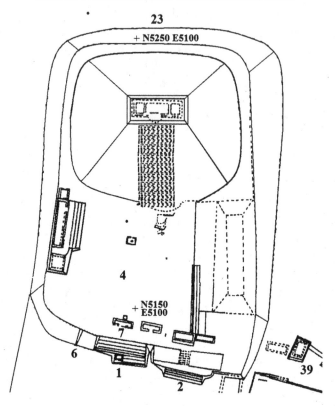

FIGURE 7.2. *Plan map of the Great Pyramid and Grand Platform showing the locations of numbered excavation units, the Megalithic Staircases (bottom), and the long megalithic structure for a potential Late Preclassic palace complex (east side).*

identified with state-level organization. Also, population size is estimated to have numbered in the thousands based on the volume and extent of LP monumental and residential architecture, not including megalithic structures recently identified outside the mapped settlement limits. These provisional data indicate a large resident population capable of supporting an elite class, who in turn organized local communities into a state-level polity by the first centuries CE if not earlier.

BEHAVIORAL RECONSTRUCTION

Survey and excavation data focused on reconstructing Preclassic occupation at Xcoch provide in-depth context and association information on material patterns and presence necessary to infer increased political centralization, economic intensification, and social stratification. Although the site reached its maximum size

TABLE 7.2. Preclassic and Early Classic radiocarbon dates from Xcoch, Yucatán. All dates were calculated using the accelerator mass spectrometer (AMS) technique from the National Ocean Accelerator Mass Spectrometry Facility (NOSAMS) and the Calib Radiocarbon Calibration Program.

Field Specimen	Lab# NOSAMS	Conventional ^{14}C Age BP	Uncalibrated Calendar Date	Calibrated ^{14}C Date (2σ)	Context
20013	78754	1460±25	490 CE	560–646 CE	S Aguada, Pozo I (200 cm)
20045	78756	2520±30	570 BCE	792–716, 695–539 BCE	Grand Platform, Op. 4, Lev. 6—Piso V
20046	78757	2550±30	600 BCE	800–743, 689–663, 647–549 BCE	Grand Platform, Op. 4, Lev. 7—Piso VI
20059	78758	2560±25	610 BCE	802–749, 687–666, 641–591, 578–567 BCE	Xcoch Plaza, Op. 5, Lev. 11—Piso X
20072	78760	2570±25	620 BCE	806–751, 686–667, 634–623, 614–594 BCE	Grand Platform, Niche Bldg, Op. 7, Lev. 3—Piso II
20082	78764	2490±30	540 BCE	776–508, 458–454, 438–419 BCE	Grupo Residencial, Op. 8, Lev. 9—Piso VIII
20124	84303	1750±45	200 CE	139–160, 165–196, 209–398 CE	Aguada Gondola, Pozo I (230cm), Lev. 5
20126	84304	2040±25	90 BCE	159–135 BCE, 114 BCE–24 CE	Aguada Gondola, Pozo I (310cm)
20162	84306	4010±30	2060 BCE	3356–1748 BCE	Chikin Mul, Op. 26, Lev. 3
20193	84309	2520±30	570 BCE	792–716, 695–539 BCE	East Pyramid Plaza, Op. 35, Lev. 8, Piso V (below)
20198	84310	2590±30	640 BCE	809–763, 680–673 BCE	West Sacbé, Op. 36, Lev. 4, Piso III (below)
20251	104688	2250±30	300 BCE	392–348, 317–207 BCE	S Terrace Pozo I 85 cm b.s.

and complexity by the LC, the largest architectural constructions by volume are LP, when the site grew significantly during a major phase of construction that included numerous platforms and pyramid structures, huge water storage features, and their sociopolitical correlates. At this time, the site's large resident population was concentrated not only in and around the site center but also at surrounding settlement zones sufficient to support a hereditary elite class. As the largest known Preclassic urban center in the Puuc, Xcoch headed a multitiered settlement hierarchy, which suggests that its rulers wielded political influence and/or control far beyond the site's settlement limits and deep into a regional hinterland.

Site Survey

Xcoch's deep-water cave is situated beneath an enormous Central Acropolis highlighted by the Great Pyramid and Grand Platform together reaching over 42 m in height and constructed mostly in the Preclassic (figure 7.1). Xcoch settlement spans more than 3 km², extending 1 km north and 1.5 km south outside the central zone, including a tall Preclassic pyramid and hilltop plaza (Op. 61) just north of the south *aguada*. Other significant settlement features about 1 km east and 0.5 km west include huge megalithic platforms topped with pyramids.

Following major LP occupation and EC reoccupation, Xcoch reached its zenith by 850 CE, a time when the site spanned at least 8 km² with an estimated agricultural sustaining zone of 30 km², making it the largest known Terminal Classic center in the Santa Elena Valley before Uxmal, both clear examples of state-level societies at this time (Smyth et al. 2017b). However, the finding of numerous megalithic surface structures and MP substructures dated by abundant Preclassic ceramic diagnostics and radiocarbon assays across 1.5 km², about half of the estimated site area in the LP, confirms a significant period of growth including expansion of status architecture consistent with a developing social stratification. In addition, new data now show that Xcoch centered a Preclassic regional settlement hierarchy, indicating political influence, control, or both over a wide hinterland. Noted for the Xcoch cave and the only permanent water source in the Santa Elena Valley, undoubtedly a significant centralizing factor, outlier settlements about a day's walk, together with their own outliers, village hamlets, and special purpose sites, formed a nested, multitiered central-place network (Smyth et al. 2020; figure 7.3).

ARCHITECTURAL MAPPING AND STRATIGRAPHIC EXCAVATION: URBAN CORE AND PERIPHERIES

Urban organization requiring labor mobilization and an administrative elite is inferred by the scale of monumental and residential architecture, hydraulic features, and their spatial contexts. Urban planning and managed labor are clearly evident at the massive, multilevel Central Acropolis in the megalithic style with at least ten architectural groups spanning ten hectares, one of the largest integrated constructions in the Puuc region (figures 7.1 and 7.2). This

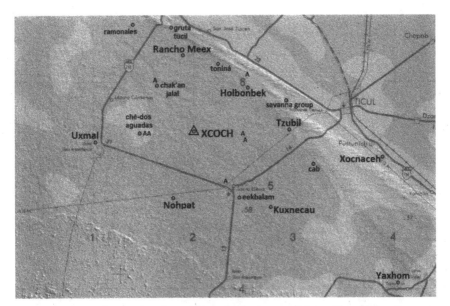

FIGURE 7.3. *Map of regional settlement hierarchy for the central Santa Elena Valley, Puuc Ridge, and modern towns highlighting Xcoch and surrounding Preclassic outliers, including hamlets and special-purpose sites near rural* aguadas *(shown at points A on the map).*

enormous acropolis conforms to the Middle Formative Chiapas urban pattern: high platforms and largest pyramid to the north, E Group complexes often to the south, platforms to the west, and elite residential precincts in the east (Clark and Hansen 2001, 3–12). For example, the Great Pyramid-Grand Platform are north, the Xcoch Plaza south, and the Cave Pyramid adjoins a long platform with three foundations facing an east pyramid that is suggestive of the E Group variant found at Dzibilchaltun. Extensive platforms and leveled plaza spaces define an Eastern Elite District, while high megalithic platforms west border major hydraulic features. This mature urban pattern at Xcoch chiefly emerges in the LP, with only renovations, expansions, and certain modifications attributable to later time periods.

Formal planning in the LP is revealed by the West Sacbé linking the water sources of the Gondola Aguada and Xcoch Cave. While most *chultuns* ($n = 108$) outside the urban core were probably in use during the Classic period, three depression features or tank-like reservoirs altered to hold water and three urban *aguadas*, two excavated in the central core and one on the southern site periphery, were fully functional in the Preclassic (figure 7.1). At least eight other *aguadas* and many smaller reservoirs have been identified at Xcoch and its rural hinterland. If the established Preclassic construction dates for urban *aguadas* also hold for rural *aguadas*, including special purpose sites, the harvesting of rainfall for irrigation and central management of agriculture across the Puuc watershed must have begun at an early date.

Stratigraphic excavations at megalithic contexts demonstrate the evolution of architectural construction at Xcoch. These data clearly show a medium-style variant of megalithic stonework associated with the earliest Preclassic architecture. This stonework was evident in the lowest levels of many units where medium-cut facing stones of pink limestone were associated with rich MP ceramic diagnostics and radiocarbon assays (table 7.2). Moreover, medium-style megalithic stonework is indistinguishable from the deepest excavated levels of Xocnaceh, a site with an enormous MP platform 20 km east of Xcoch (Gallareta and Ringle 2004; Bey 2006). LP megalithic style at Xcoch, however, is more finished on most dimensions yet still pillow-shaped, often employing alternative sources and colors (usually white) of limestone. Overall, LP megalithic stonework is more advanced and formalized and was the preferred dry masonry for all status-related architecture, especially on large-scale construction under elite control.

Ceramics from excavations provided relative dates at architectural and settlement contexts from *Cehpech* (750–950 CE), *Motul* (600–750 CE), and *Cochuah* (300–600 CE) complexes. Diagnostic EC Chac Polychrome water jars were found both inside and outside the Xcoch cave. Of special interest were large hemispherical vessels with cylindrical monopod supports and long narrow necks identified as Yotholin Patterned Burnished found in the Xcoch cave and at outside contexts with medium-style stones. Among the earliest ceramics in Yucatán, perhaps associated with the first farmers in the region, Yotholin is reported from caves, cenotes, and sites near Mani, Sacalum, Loltún, Tzucacab, and Xocnaceh (Brainerd 1958; Folan 1968; Smyth et al. 2020; cf. Andrews 1990; Smyth and Ortegón 2008). Significant quantities of MP (Mamom) and LP (Tihosuco) ceramics (~800 BCE–300 CE) were recovered at early megalithic contexts in sealed stucco floors and architectural stratigraphy. Tihosuco complex ceramics were also consistently found on the surface as well as in intermediate stratigraphic contexts.

In sum, large-scale construction at Xcoch in the LP indicate a settlement of first-rank in size and important central place administered by elite leadership who wielded influence, control, or both over critical resources like water, agriculture, and most importantly, the people residing on the landscape. Furthermore, megalithic surface architecture denoting LP occupation is followed by a Terminal Preclassic hiatus evident in stratigraphic excavations across the site and EC reoccupation when stone-roof buildings make their first appearance (Smyth et al. 2014; Smyth et al. 2011); similar patterns of architecture and occupation are emerging in the Santa Elena Valley and across the greater Puuc region (Smyth et al. 2020).

FIGURE 7.4. *Photo of the north face of the Great Pyramid during clearing showing the megalithic stonework nearly reaching to the summit.*

Urban Core

The Grand Platform

A massive megalithic platform supporting the Great Pyramid on the north side towers over the monumental core of the Central Acropolis. Clearly visible throughout the region (figures 7.2, 7.4, and 7.6), this monument is a tangible symbol of the power and status of Xcoch's Preclassic rulers. The megalithic Great Pyramid is crowned by a comparatively small LC building platform e by a southern staircase (table 7.1), where an old looters trench exposed at least three subsequent construction phases (including staircases) for earlier summit temples integrated into megalithic stonework; the last phase corresponds to an Early Puuc-style four-room building now mostly fallen. Below east on the Grand Platform is a badly ruined long building resting on a high platform extension connected to the Great Pyramid base by a megalithic staircase, stepped portico, and two adjacent outbuildings. This feature cluster forms a potential Preclassic palace complex and abode of high-status leadership. A wide megalithic staircase for the Great Platform gives formal access to the palace complex passing an unusual open-walled building with megalithic jambs and niches but no stone roof (below). An adjacent vaulted building in the Proto-Puuc style is likely part of the EC reoccupation and new political regime, while an Early Puuc building on the platform's west side appears to be contemporaneous with the final phase of construction at the Great Pyramid summit. An underlying megalithic platform and stairway suggest Preclassic substructures on the west side of the 1 ha. Grand Platform surface.

Three excavation units (Ops. 4, 6, and 7) sampled the Grand Platform, providing critical data on construction sequence and early hydraulic works. The largest and deepest was Op. 4, a 4 m × 4 m unit near the platform center reaching nearly 4 m below surface with five intact stucco floors (II–VI) dated to the Preclassic. Representing the LP construction phase, Floors 2–4 were hard stucco layers covering a heavy matrix of sascab (lime marl) and small stones interpreted as hydraulic surfaces sloping to the southwest diverting rainwater toward the Gondola Aguada (Smyth et al. 2017b). LP Sierra red ceramics were directly associated. Floor 5 showed a change of drainage direction toward the south-southeast and ceramics were replaced by MP diagnostics including Chunhinta black, Guitara incised, Joventud red, and Dzudzukil cream-to-buff. Floor 6 appeared beneath a thick matrix of medium-style stones and boulder ballast supporting a floor surface sloping toward the northeast. Cultural material below Floor 6 showed MP exotic materials included marine shell, black coral, greenstone-serpentine, bone, a partial Chunhinta black plate, and two wood charcoal radiocarbon dates of 570 ± 25 BCE and 600 ± 30 BCE (802–549 BCE, 2σ calibrated; table 7.2). Excavation terminated at 395 cm due to safety concerns, another 4 m of platform fill is estimated, with medium-style stones near the bottom, a pattern consistent with buried MP contexts across the site.

The Late-Terminal Preclassic was a time of demographic expansion and increasing social complexity at Xcoch that coincided with cycles of severe drought. The need to harvest and manage greater volumes of rainwater is evident in an unusual hydraulic feature discovered in Op. 6 near the southwest corner of the Grand Platform clearly connected to the drainage surface in Op. 4. A 1 m × 6 m trench exposed a stucco canal with concave steps-tiers linked to an expansive collection system of stone-lined-stucco surfaced channels, a boulder check dam, and a sluice way for rainwater to the Gondola Aguada, some 250 m southwest, also bordered by a huge cobblestone (ch'ich) catchment platform on the north side. Excavations at the Gondola Aguada produced multiple floor surfaces, stone features, LP ceramics, and radiocarbon assays; the original floor was not encountered, however (Dunning et al. 2014b; Smyth et al. 2017a). This enormous hydraulic system was part of the central monumental zone designed by rulers to effect control over a vital and seasonally scarce resource in the Puuc, water.

Op. 7 sampled the Niches Building at the top of the Megalithic Staircase on the Grand Platform, apparently a gateway to the LP palace complex. This unusual megalithic building shows no vaulted roof, large corner stones, heavy stone niches, and huge jambs forming a wide central entrance (figure 7.2). Floor 1, a stucco surface for an altar platform, was constructed above the original stone

FIGURE 7.5. *Photo looking northwest of a stratigraphic profile cut (Op. 7) showing the Niches Building entry and lower Late and Middle Preclassic platform floors and façade behind the west extension of the Megalithic Staircase. The lowest level of medium-style megalithic stonework below Floor 2 is radiocarbon dated to 620 BCE.*

foundation suggesting a later reuse of the building space. Floor 2, associated with a small columnar altar centered between jambs and niches, also appears to postdate the original building. This context yielded LP, EC, and LC wares though the latter two appear intrusive suggesting an LP date for the building. In support were pure LP diagnostics just below the floor, associated with a surface for the south façade of the Grand Platform, composed of white limestone megalithic boulders, now partially collapsed. Buried at the bottom of the unit within stone fill and a matrix of saturated sascab or pulverized stucco (figure 7.5) was an earlier south façade of pink limestone masonry. Pink limestone (also from Ops. 4 and 6) is known from two quarries along the Puuc ridge outside the towns of Muna and Ticul (figure 7.3), both within the Preclassic settlement orbit of Xcoch. All ceramics in this context were MP Dzudzuquil, associated with serpentine-greenstone, black coral, and a charcoal-based ^{14}C date of 620 ± 25 BCE, indicating a well-established trade in exotic goods at this time.

These data demonstrate an interior south façade of the Grand Platform with MP stonework and stucco surfacing contemporary with the lowest levels of Op. 4 that was subsequently covered with ballast and extended with white limestone megalithic masonry forming a monumental staircase in the LP. Ops. 1 and 2 sampled two stucco floors at the foot of the Megalithic Staircase dated with EC and LP ceramics, respectively, and providing the first evidence for a Terminal Preclassic hiatus at the site subsequently documented across urban Xcoch (Smyth et al. 2010, 2011). Interestingly, this context lies directly above the subterranean north passage of the Xcoch cave, which leads to the Great Pyramid, where an obsidian prismatic blade was apparently left as an offering (Weaver et al. 2015).

The Xcoch Plaza

At the epicenter of the Central Acropolis and early Xcoch community is a long plaza (100 m N-S × 50 m E-W) abutting the south end of the Great Platform. This architectural cluster contains significant status architecture including early pyramids and an E Group complex often identified with early kingship and emerging social stratification. Formerly an MP paved surface opposite the cave entrance, numerous later additions and architectural modifications created a significant monumental space. Three sizable pyramids on the plaza's east, south, and west sides include a megalithic pyramid above the Xcoch cave itself and its labyrinthine subterranean passages. Although badly fallen, the cave pyramid may have been a radial structure, but only portions of the eastern megalithic stairway are visible today; the other sides were covered, perhaps intentionally, with stone boulders (figure 7.6). The visible superstructure is a foundation for a low-walled, un-vaulted building with four entries showing well-faced block masonry dated to the EC by Dos Arroyos Polychrome sherds; below are boulder cornerstones for an earlier megalithic structure. Three megalithic buildings are found on a long platform at the foot of pyramid. Across the plaza is a similar platform supporting stone foundations aligned north-south adjacent to the East Pyramid. This architectural arrangement forms a long, narrow gallery for a potential Preclassic E Group complex characterized by an east-facing pyramid flanked by a long-terraced platform with three super-structures arranged along a north-south linear axis. E Groups in the Maya world are believed to relate to astronomical alignments (solar cycles) but likely involved other factors, including rituals for agriculture, cyclical time, and *katun* (twenty years) ending periods (Aimers and Rice 2006). While E Groups in the Northern Lowlands are rare (see Ringle 2011 for a possible Preclassic E-group at Yaxhom), they are argued to be emblematic of elite status and early Maya kingship (Clark and Hansen 2001).

Two excavation units (Ops. 3 and 5) in the Xcoch Plaza provide contextual evidence that the Cave and East Pyramids and their outbuildings were LP constructions. Op. 3 centered on the Cave Pyramid staircase near a cylindrical altar exposed the stone pavement (Floor 1) in Ops. 1 and 2 with stucco floors (2–5) below laid on compact layers of sascab with few ceramics. Beneath Floor 5, a tan sascab and thick layer of stones produced significant quantities of Late Preclassic Sierra Red ceramics. Floors 3–5 correspond to the Cave Pyramid complex and

FIGURE 7.6. *Photo looking west toward the Cave Pyramid showing the Preclassic megalithic stonework of a staged eastern staircase and boulder stones covering the structure.*

E Group, when the entire Xcoch Plaza was paved. Floor 6, an eastward sloping stucco surface above thick layer of ballast upon bedrock, dates to the MP.

Op. 5 probed the plaza floor near a megalithic altar aligned with the East Pyramid staircase. In level 1, a stone pavement again (Floor 1) appeared above stucco Floor 2. Floor 3, a gray-white layer, and Floor 4, a tan layer, suggest lime marl from two different quarries and possible chronological marker for a Terminal Preclassic hiatus also seen in Op. 3. There were few ceramics, and none were dateable while the lower stucco Floors 5–8 were completely devoid of pottery but contextually positioned in LP levels. However, a thick layer of construction ballast between Floors 9 and 10 yielded MP wares in quantity. Beneath Floors 10 and 11, animal bone and wood charcoal were recovered within leveled bedrock and a stone alignment along the north wall indicates a MP substructure when the plaza was relatively small and informal (610 ± 25 BCE; table 7.2).

Eastern Elite District

A formal corridor connects the Xcoch Plaza to the Eastern Elite District, a major monumental zone and potential abode of high-status residents created by an enormous labor investment planned and coordinated by a managerial-hereditary elite in the Preclassic. Multiple feature clusters, four pyramids (at least two of the largest are Preclassic), and megalithic buildings on high platforms are among numerous Proto-Puuc, Early Puuc, and Classic mosaic vaulted structures (table 7.1). Massive ballast in-filling and thick layers of lime stucco were required to level the karsted lunar landscape east of the Central Acropolis to create plaza surfaces across the entire district (below). In addition, high platforms supporting un-vaulted megalithic buildings flank the north end of the LP East Aguada showing early planning and hydraulic engineering designed to channel and capture huge amounts of rainwater (Dunning et al. 2014; figure 7.1).

Seven test pits at the Eastern Elite District including one in the East Aguada revealed a floor surface with Sierra red ceramics (Dunning et al. 2014b), confirming major Preclassic construction and evidence for elite residence and related activities. Op. 8 investigated the Residential Group and on-platform conical altar (Smyth et al. 2014). Below Floor 4, human bones (no burials), basalt, black serpentine, and abundant black stone nodules were identified as hydrocarbon-rich limestone (Bogdan Onac, personal communication 2010). Fragments of ground and polished iron ore (specular hematite) were also recovered, showing different stages of production suggesting debris from a mirror workshop. The presence of such prestige goods is argued to be an indicator of high-status groups subject to sumptuary rules in the Valley of Oaxaca during the Formative (Marcus and Flannery 1996). It is possible that local hydrocarbon-rich limestone was used in mirror manufacture and/or as a substitute for iron ore. Luxury items like iron ore were certainly difficult to obtain from distant places like San José Mogote in Oaxaca, where iron-ore mirrors were manufactured in the Early and Middle Formative periods (Pires-Ferreira 1976). Floors 4 and 5 were not sealed, but more black nodules were recovered with exotic materials such as marine shell, fish scales, and one obsidian blade, in addition to wood charcoal and Early Classic and LP ceramics. Floors 6–8, however, were intact, producing clear MP diagnostics; the lowest floor associated with wall alignments for a simple substructure with at least two rooms dated to 540 ± 30 BCE (table 7.2). Greenstone-serpentine and a large body sherd from a thin-walled cylinder vessel (Almeja Gray?) suggest offerings from a pre-Mamom residential context. Op. 9 just off-platform south by the Xcoch Plaza corridor recovered quantities of Late Preclassic ceramics (Floors 6 and 7) while Floors 8 and 9 produced MP diagnostics with stone alignments for a substructure on leveled bedrock.

At the Eastern Elite District, Ops. 35, 38, and 39 confirmed the timing and scale of plaza construction sampling multiple surface levels spread over more than 2 ha. Two units, Op. 35 and 38, placed west of two megalithic pyramids, uncovered well-preserved stucco floors and thick layers of stone ballast, confirming that this area was raised and leveled in Preclassic times. Ceramics date the upper floor to the EC reoccupation, but all intermediate floors, most plaza fill, and the largest un-vaulted buildings and pyramids appear to be LP based on architectural stratigraphy and associated ceramics. In Op. 35, a context below the lowest floor near bedrock provided a possible founding date for this area at around 570 ± 30 BCE (table 7.2). Data from the Eastern Elite District, importantly, support the presence of a large hereditary elite class at Xcoch in the LP.

Grotto Group Settlement

The Central Acropolis is approached on the south by a wide megalithic staircase and cluster of Classic period vaulted range structures permitting elite control of the Xcoch Cave. Restricted access associated with socially stratified groups likely began in the LP as indicated by cluster megalithic buildings between the staircase and the cave. Just above the cave entrance, the earliest settlement remains in the MP came from the lowest levels of Ops. 18 and 19, associated with a wall alignment for a substructure and slab boulders placed in upright positions. Farther south, a large megalithic foundation (Op. 21) revealed pavement stones of the same lime marl found in the cave and ceramics of the LP (Floor 2) and MP (Floors 3–5).

Further evidence of spatial segregation and social differentiation was found in Ops. 33, 34, and 41, testing the structures along the south edge of the chasm for the Xcoch Cave, undoubtedly a ritual-charged ceremonial space forming a terminus for the West Sacbé. These units produced a wide variety of Preclassic to Postclassic artifacts most notably water jars and incense burners such as EC Chac Polychrome and later Chichén Itzá and Mayapán diagnostics underscoring the supra-regional importance of the water cave after site abandonment.

Op. 41, a 12 m long trench extending from the cave entrance up to the edge of the chasm, revealed in cross-section the original descending nine-step staircase that, surprisingly, shows many of its original treads and risers *in situ* and still usable as an entry into the cave (figure 7.7). Clearing further showed a descending U-shaped megalithic staircase integrated into three sides of the chasm presumably in the LP, when the cave complex was connected by a causeway to the Gondola Aguada (below). This amphitheater-like space was clearly organized for rituals witnessed by visiting spectators and/or religious pilgrims. Restricted access and elite control are implied by surrounding buildings such as the Cave Pyramid, Xcoch Plaza, and various other structures to the south. The descending steps of the megalithic staircase produced thousands of ceramics and other artifacts dated from Preclassic to Postclassic times (even modern debris) demonstrating that the water cave continued to be an important place of visitation long after the fall of the Xcoch polity.

Fifty meters west of the cave, Ops. 36 and 37 sampled the causeway constructed in the LP, a time of increasing social complexity at the site. This causeway lies atop three successive stucco floors, the lowest with MP sherds as well as marine shell, greenstone-serpentine flakes, and wood charcoal dated to 640 BCE (table 7.2) confirming a paved area near the cave since formal occupation. Importantly, the land between the causeway, cave, and Gondola Aguada was largely vacant in

FIGURE 7.7. *Photo looking west of the descending megalithic staircase in the chasm leading to the Xcoch Cave entrance. Op. 43 was a 12 m trench that sampled contexts from the cave entrance up to the first descending staircase step.*

the Preclassic, except for water canals connecting the acropolis to the Gondola Aguada, suggesting a forest preserve or royal garden (~10 ha) at the heart of the central monumental core. This urban "green zone" would remain largely uninhabited throughout the occupation history of Xcoch.

Clearly, the Xcoch Cave, its permanent water source, and the causeway linked to the Gondola Aguada were of paramount importance to early rulers for expressing political authority and arguably reflect the emergence of a state religion in the LP. This statement is supported by evidence that much of the site's major central monumental architecture was completed by the Late Preclassic and constructed directly above the cave's labyrinthine subterranean passages and permanent water pool. The cave and its unique water source were undoubtedly sacrosanct and socially restricted by the site's early rulers.

Urban Peripheries

The North Plaza and West Sector

An extension of the Central Acropolis shows various surface levels and feature clusters indicative of a transitional zone between the urban core and densely inhabited residential areas. Some areas were occupied by relatively high-status residents in the Preclassic, based on the presence of monumental architecture

FIGURE 7.8. *Photo of two Late Preclassic vessels (a Sierra red plate and a Ciego composite vase) found at the pyramid platform near N5500 E5200.*

such as pyramids, high platforms, and large hydraulic features (figure 7.1). One noteworthy settlement group yielded Preclassic surface pottery at a high megalithic platform with stone buildings near a deep depression and open-air water reservoir. At the center of the plaza, a quadrangle of buildings atop a 5 m tall megalithic platform suggests early elite residence.

Three megalithic pyramid platforms were identified. One of note is accessed by a west stairway-ramp leading to a foundation with two LP serving vessels: a Sierra red plate and a Ciego composite vase (figure 7.8). The latter vessel is finely decorated with diagonally incised zones running in opposite directions suggesting a specialized container for elite beverages like chocolate. The bottom of a test unit (Op. 46) also exposed a well-preserved stucco floor and substructure associated with MP ceramics.

The "Old Pyramid Group" is an early residential zone centered by an archaic pyramid with no clear summit building flanked by multiple house foundations. Test excavations (Op. 42) produced no recognizable floor surface, but Preclassic ceramics were associated with an unusual foundation of upright boulders like Op. 19. A depression to the south produced abundant Preclassic diagnostics in a stratified midden capped by a poorly preserved floor of clay, sascab, and gravel, indicating a garbage dump converted to a small water reservoir about the time of Preclassic drought. A higher floor of plaster and gravel indicates renewal in the EC likely during site reoccupation (Dunning et al. 2014b; Smyth et al. 2017a).

The Chikin Mul Group focused on a 5 m tall megalithic platform west of the Great Pyramid bordering the vacant green zone mentioned above. A deep excavation (Op. 26) near the platform center dates initial construction to the MP with significant enlargement and occupation in the LP. Deeply buried within stone ballast was a cached metate along with MP ceramics. Below the platform on leveled soil above bedrock, a lithic flake and wood charcoal sample was dated to 2060 BCE ± 30 (uncorrected; see table 7.2). These data suggest a large megalithic platform contemporary with Grand Platform superimposed on a preceramic (?) activity surface of the late Archaic-Initial Formative.

Op. 43 sampled the western Chac-Na Group near a partially standing Proto-Puuc building on a massive multi-level platform with numerous megalithic buildings. Below a thick stucco floor, LP ceramic diagnostics imply an early date of construction for platform infrastructure and un-vaulted buildings. Importantly, this monumental west group and three large *aguadas* recently identified in the vicinity suggest that the Xcoch polity and its water managers extended economic control well beyond the site center (Smyth et al. 2020).

Southern District

South of the central monumental core are feature clusters that show significant residential occupation with monumental architecture in the Preclassic. On the south side of the green zone near the Xcoch Grotto is the Candelero Group, a 4 m high basal platform (figure 7.1) named from an enigmatic single-chambered rectangular vessel (receptacle for domestic ritual). Ironically, this platform contains numerous house foundations surrounding an archaic pyramidal platform where excavations (Ops. 47–51) documented a substantial LP occupation. Off-platform are two deep open-air depressions (but no *chultuns*), likely functioning as early water storage reservoirs.

Near modern beehives, the Apiary Group is flanked by a megalithic pyramid (~8 m tall) on a long, high platform above a *sascabera* (lime-marl quarry) connected to a deep, impassable cave system where LP wares (Sierra red) were recovered. Additionally, canal-like features, either natural, artificial, or both, connected to the platform lead toward a confirmed *aguada* on the site's western border, though the date of these potential hydraulic features is not known.

The Southwest Witz Group, situated atop an expansive hill, overlooks the current agricultural parcels of Santa Elena, some of the most productive farmland in the region. This monumental feature cluster shows a central plaza and south pyramid apparently constructed in Preclassic times (figure 7.1). On the west base of the pyramid, an undated upright slab apparently in situ displays an abstract bas-relief depicting luxuriant vegetation or abundant maize. Op. 53 exposed two lower platform levels and boulders beneath an eroded stucco floor suggesting a Preclassic context. Testing of the plaza floor on the north side near a

FIGURE 7.9. *South Aguada Group photo of Op. 61 showing a Middle Preclassic residential (?) structure and five superimposed floor surfaces visible in the wall profiles. All ceramics below Floor 1 were Preclassic, and the upper stucco floors were associated with the surface pyramid and plaza dated to the LP.*

megalithic foundation yielded abundant ceramics, confirming a Preclassic plaza and substructure (Ops. 52–55). On a westside plaza, a north-facing building with megalithic niches, jambs, and wide entrance is almost a twin of the LP Niches Building (Op. 7) on the Grand Platform. These data illustrate a major settlement complex for LP rulers in control of large labor forces that significantly reshaped the natural landscape far from the site core.

To the east are feature clusters in different architectural styles ascending a long hilly ridge adjacent to *zacate* grass, high forest, and modern agricultural fields. Found at the terminus of the site's Southeast Causeway, this settlement zone also shows significant status occupation in the Preclassic outside the central monumental core (Smyth et al. 2017b; table 7.1). On the ridge summit, two megalithic pyramids in an elite plaza appear to be LP constructions. This group has no *chultuns* but shows boulder alignments behind the largest pyramid connected to two deep depressions suggesting an integrated drainage system for rainwater capture.

Near the South Aguada is a monumental hilltop group dominated by a 12 m tall LP pyramid on a high megalithic platform. A wide staircase ascends a plaza of amorphous platforms and alignments, while a ramp on the east leads to residential groups in current farm fields. A test excavation (Op. 61) off the pyramid's south side (below the staircase) revealed four intact stucco floors with pure MP and LP diagnostics and a packed sascab surface for an early substructure composed of aligned and faced stones articulating with an oval boulder foundation (figure 7.9). These important data show a substantial Preclassic settlement group over 1 km from Xcoch's central monumental core in a rich agricultural zone potentially irrigated with water from the South Aguada (Dunning et al. 2014b). Irrigation farming using harvested rainfall in the LP further supports the case for a central authority and early polity at Xcoch holding sway over a far greater political territory than the settlement limits of the urban center.

REGIONAL SETTLEMENT HIERARCHY

Xcoch in the Preclassic was the largest known population center in the Santa Elena Valley, strategically positioned at the epicenter of a regional site hierarchy. Growing evidence for early settlements across the Puuc region includes Paso de Macho and Huntichmul (Gallareta and Ringle 2004), Kiuic (Andrews and Bey 2011, Andrews et al. 2018, Bey 2006), Xocnaceh (Gallereta and May 2007), and Yaxhom (Ringle et al. 2011), among others (figure 7.3). About a day's walk roundtrip from Xcoch (10 km radius) are settlements with Preclassic characteristics like megalithic architecture, hydraulic features, and Preclassic ceramics. These sites are organized hierarchically in apparent rank order based on distance from Xcoch, site size, and scale of monumental architecture, allowing estimates of relative political importance and dependency on a primate center (Smyth et al. 2020).

The most important secondary sites surrounding Xcoch are associated with *aguadas*, including Uxmal's megalithic North Group, situated almost due west, and an outlier known as Ché-Dos Aguadas midway between the two sites. Nohpat to the southwest exhibits a massive basal platform with a large pyramid at the north end constructed of megalithic stonework; Nohpat may have been a larger site than Uxmal in the Preclassic (Nick Dunning personal communication 2017). The site of Kuxnecau southeast of Xcoch also displays a huge megalithic acropolis and large east pyramid flanked by high platforms, suggesting a triadic group arrangement. East of Xcoch are high mounds abutting the Puuc ridge, known locally as Tzubil, where excavations by the Centro Regional de Yucatán (INAH) in 1990 produced abundant MP and LP diagnostics (Boucher 1990; Boucher and Palomo 2005; Dunning 1992). Northeast of Xcoch near Mexican Highway 184 is the little-known site of Holbonbek (Dunning 1992, 201; Garza Tarazona de Gonzalez and Kurjack 1980, site 31), noted for a large pyramid and acropolis with megalithic stonework. Another major center north of Xcoch near Highway 261 is Rancho Meex. Hanns Prem and Nicholas Dunning (1993) and Michael Smyth (2018 and 2019) reported an acropolis with a large north pyramid and massive east platform of megalithic stonework indicating a substantial Preclassic occupation. Rancho Meex is also surrounded by early outliers such as Ramonales and Gruta Tucil, where megalithic architecture and Preclassic ceramics have been identified (Smyth et al. 2020).

Numerous other outliers, hamlets, and apparent special purpose sites have also come to light including Eekbalam near the town of Santa Elena (site 224 in Dunning 1992, 265–66). Between Tzubil and Xocnaceh, the site of Cab (or Tzehta'bay) contains an 8 m tall megalithic pyramid at the north end of a large platform. Near Tzubil are Preclassic hamlets, including the Savanna Group situated inside the Puuc ridge where mounded features, an *aguada*, and several pool-sized *sartenejas* (solution holes) suggest an early pioneering farming community. To the north and west are outlier communities also with *aguadas* tied to Holbonbek, Rancho Meex, Uxmal, and Xcoch itself. Previous research at Xcoch's South Aguada, dated to as early as the Preclassic, showed attached canals likely for irrigation (Dunning et al. 2014b).

Two rural *aguadas* east of Xcoch largely devoid of settlement appear to be special purpose sites significant for understanding centralized political organization. One east *aguada* called Akal Si'ina'an Iik'k (scorpion wind) shows extensive earthworks and linear features as part of a sophisticated hydraulic system engineered for the harvesting and distribution of rainwater undoubtedly to irrigate adjacent farmland. These data imply large-scale intensification by a managerial elite exerting control over a distant watershed and agricultural landscape. How large was the political territory controlled by the Preclassic Maya rulers at Xcoch? A precise determination is currently not possible, but a rough estimate might include some 400–500 km² calculating the square of linear distance between the two farthest outlier centers (figure 7.3). However, the role of Xcoch as a Preclassic primate center in a central place network will require more information on hinterland settlements, including the political and temporal relationships among outliers. The high degree of complexity implicit in a regionally organized politico-economy in the Preclassic, importantly, suggests that the Xcoch polity and neighboring settlement hierarchies like one at the eastern Santa Elena Valley (Yaxhom-Loltun-Xocnacah) were at a comparable level of social development as the Mirador Basin.

DISCUSSION AND CONCLUSION

The LP at Xcoch saw the rise of an urban center with monumental and residential architecture in the megalithic-style distributed over some 3 km², suggesting political institutions associated with early state-level organization. The primacy of architectural volume often identified with socially stratified societies is manifest at Xcoch in the Preclassic and demonstrable by settlement and population size that far exceeded any site in the central Santa Elena Valley. Furthermore, the scale of diverse water-control features, including huge urban and rural reservoirs for harvesting rainfall and sustaining irrigation agriculture, required coordinated labor, central planning, and water management under the direction of a ruling class of hereditary elites. Xcoch's large resident population and water resources in the LP provided leaders transformative opportunity to restructure social relations by linking local communities and outlier settlements into a functioning urban entity, effectively bypassing and, in some cases, replacing traditional kinship structures of egalitarianism and hierarchical ranking. Sanctioned by ideology and perhaps outright coercion in a drought-prone region—which under normal conditions is rainless part of the year—the Xcoch Cave, its permanent water source, and large urban water reservoirs obviously played significant roles in the rise of social stratification. The politics of water, both ritually and practically, provided elites control over a critical resource and coercive power for developing an exclusive agenda apart from the rest of the society that served to compel communities to perform activities to maintain the social hierarchy. Such self-interest policies would have contributed to an extractive political economy involving coordinating major construction projects, performing major religious ceremonies, and implementing systems of taxation and tribute that included the right to demand local labor.

Identifying the type of stratified leadership at LP Xcoch is currently limited by a lack of evidence for writing, complex iconography, or high-status mortuary remains (rare in the Puuc for any period) that are so frequently associated with the institution of kingship at early Maya centers elsewhere. A possible relevant example of writing and iconography is found at Loltun Cave near Yaxhom, which involves various carved monuments including a huge bas-relief carved into the rock face above the Nahkab entrance depicting a Maya personage in royal regalia with associated glyphs dated to October 29, 100 CE (8.3.0.0.0 3 Ahaw 3 Xul) or LP (Grube and Schele 1996). Xcoch, unfortunately, has not undergone large-scale intervention of monumental architecture where evidence of early Maya kingship might be recovered. But it is also reasonable to consider alternate forms of stratified authority that emphasize the office held rather than the officeholder. Leadership at Teotihuacan, for example, was not commemorated in public imagery, suggesting that political power was not solely vested in individuals or single ruling families but was more formally exercised via group-based institutions (Cowgill 1997). Further possibilities include some form of shared authority (*multepal*) or confederacy-type government like that described by Spanish chroniclers for the former urban centers of Chichén Itzá and Mayapan (Cobos 2011; Pollock et al. 1962).

For the LP in northern Guatemala, Freidel (2018) argues that the mega-center of El Mirador evolved as a special place in the Maya Lowlands, becoming more complex than any other contemporary sociopolitical entity. As the first place in the Maya Lowlands with shamanistic-based kingship, he claims, this system was supported by large-scale intensification of agricultural production and an economic distribution system sanctioned by a highly developed maize mythology that progressively spread across the southern Maya Lowlands. Could a comparable model of state development apply to LP Xcoch in the northern Maya Lowlands? Water, which was certainly a critical resource in the Puuc hills, required large-scale control and management. The scarcity of water and religious significance of a deep-water cave are factors that cannot be underestimated in emerging complexity and social stratification.

A regional settlement hierarchy headed by Xcoch and composed of a diversity of sites identified by megalithic architecture, hydraulic features, and Preclassic ceramics formed a central polity that shaped complex interaction networks benefiting some places over others. Within Xcoch's settlement orbit, the second-rank centers of Uxmal, Nohpat, Tzubil, and others spaced within a 10 km radius or day's walk were places of greater importance, being larger sites with substantial monumental architecture. Tied to a primate center, these secondary sites were, in turn, surrounded by their own outliers that included tertiary settlements, agricultural hamlets, and special-purpose sites forming a rank-order hierarchy in the Santa Elena Valley; multitiered central-place networks are characteristic of complex societies with early state-level organization (Flannery 1976, 162–73; Marcus 1973). Although regional settlement data of the Xcoch hinterland are incomplete, the preliminary results suggest a hexagonal-shaped central-place model, but interpreting the rules or principles influencing settlement behavior and the nature of patron-client relationships must await future research (Smyth et al. 2020).

In 1841, John Stephens (1963) recognized Xcoch as an enigmatic urban center with a deep-water cave and gigantic pyramid. Little did he know that the site was even larger and more complex than he could have imagined and that it would now be counted at the top of a growing list of major Puuc sites dated to the Preclassic. Clearly, the traditional migration model of southern Maya decline and Terminal Classic florescence cannot be reconciled with evidence for a much longer and local development for the Puuc region and northern Maya Lowlands (Anderson 2011; Andrews et al. 2018; Andrews and Robles 2004; Brown and Bey 2018). The Preclassic Maya in the north were clearly on a parallel cultural-evolutionary trajectory with their southern lowland counterparts. Multiple paths to complexity leave little doubt that the early Maya state evolved in many places, at different times, and under diverse cultural-environmental conditions, a conclusion abundantly supported by the research at Xcoch.

Acknowledgments. This paper benefited from the critical comments of Lisa DeLance, Gary Feinman, and anonymous reviewers, but any deficiencies are solely the responsibility of the author. The research was funded by grants from the National Science Foundation (#0940183, #113206), the National Geographic Society (#7989-06), and Waitt Institute for Discovery (W62-09). Reconnaissance survey was made possible by contributions to the Foundation for Americas Research, Inc., including Dr. James and Desiree Hurtak of the Foundation for Future Science, California. We are greatly indebted to Anna M. Kerttula, director of the Arctic Social Sciences Program, John Echave, former senior editor of photography for National Geographic Magazine, and Fabio Amador of the NGS-Waitt Program. This project worked with the permission of Mexico's Instituto Nacional de Antropología e Historia and the Centro INAH Yucatán and the municipalities and ejidos of Santa Elena and Ticul. I wish to acknowledge the expertise of Nicholas Dunning, who shared his knowledge and data regarding a regional hierarchy surrounding Xcoch. Eric Weaver and his caver team performed the mapping and explorations of the Xcoch Cave in 2009–11. David Ortegón Zapata conducted the ceramic analysis for the project. I also thank Ezra Zubrow, Dustin Keeler, Daniel Griswald, Jeffrey Schieder, and Karen Crissy of the State University of New York at Buffalo (UB) for their services administering the NSF grants and to Dustin Keeler, Gregory J. Korosec, Rebecca Miller, Laurel Triscari, and Caitlin Curtis of the Department of Anthropology at UB, who provided fieldwork assistance in November 2011. Radiocarbon dating was conducted by the National Ocean Sciences Accelerator Mass Spectrometry Facility, agreement number OCE-0753487. I am also grateful to Daniel Griffin, Pilar Suárez Smyth, Sean-Michael Suárez Smyth, Sebastián Suárez Smyth, Jacob Shedd, Harry and Dorothy Goepel, Beth Cortright, Tammy Otten, Chasity Stinton, Melisa Bishop, Nikki Woodward, Humberto Bonilla Mian, Manuel Bonilla Camal, Marisol Dzul Tuyub, Karina Dzul Tuyub, and the local Maya workers of Santa Elena for their dedicated service. And finally, my deep gratitude goes to the people of Santa Elena and Muna, who kindly shared their friendship, patience, and good humor that provided an enriched experience for all the gringo archaeologists.

REFERENCES

Aimers, James, and Prudence Rice. 2006. "Astronomy, Ritual, and the Interpretation of Maya 'E-Group' Architectural Assemblages." *Ancient Mesoamerica* 17:79–96.

Anderson, David S. 2011. "Xtobo, Yucatán, México, and the Emergent Preclassic of the Northern Maya Lowlands." *Ancient Mesoamerica* 22:301–22.

Andrews, Anthony P., and Fernando Robles Castellanos. 2004. "An Archaeological Survey of Northwest Yucatan, Mexico." *Mexicon* 25:7–14.

Andrews, George. 1975. *Maya Cities: Placemaking and Urbanization*. Norman: University of Oklahoma Press.

Andrews, George. 1985. "Chenes-Puuc Architecture: Chronology and Cultural Interaction." In *Arquitectura y Arqueología: Metodologias en la cronologia de Yucatan*, CEMCA Etudes Mesoamerlcaines Serle 2, No. 8, 11–40. Mexico DF: Centre'd Etudes Mexicaines et Centrameicaines, Embajada Francia en Mexico.

Andrews, E. Wyllys, V. 1990. "The Early Ceramic History of the Lowland Maya." In *Vision and Revision in Maya Studies*, edited by Flora S. Clancy and Peter D. Harrison, 1–19. Albuquerque: University of New Mexico Press.

Andrews, E. Wyllys, V, and George J. Bey III. 2011. "Early Ceramics in the Northern Lowlands: New Interpretations from Komchen and Kiuic, Yucatan." Paper presented at the 8th Annual Maya Symposium and Workshop, "The Rise of Maya Civilization," New Orleans.

Andrews, E. Wyllys, V, George J. Bey III, and Christopher Gunn. 2018. "The Earliest Ceramics of the Northern Maya Lowlands." In *Pathways to Complexity: A View from the Maya Lowlands*, edited by M. Kathryn Brown and George J. Bey III, 49–86. Gainesville: University Press of Florida.

Bey, George J., III. 2006. "Changing Archaeological Perspectives on the Northern Maya Lowlands." In *Lifeways in the Northern Maya Lowlands: New Approaches to Archaeology in the Yucatán Peninsula*, edited by Jennifer P. Mathews and Bethany A. Morrison, 13–37. Tucson: University of Arizona Press.

Boucher, Sylviane, and Yoly Palomo. 2005. "Cerámica del Preclásico Medio y Tardío en depósitos sellados del sitio de Tzubil, Yucatán." *Temas Antropológicos* 27:153–88.

Brainerd, George W. 1958. *The Archaeological Ceramics of Yucatan*. Anthropological Records, Vol. 19. Berkeley: University of California.

Brown, M. Katheryn, and George J. Bey III. 2018. "Conclusion: Charting the Pathways to Complexity in the Maya Lowlands." In *Pathways to Complexity: A View from the Maya Lowlands*, edited by M. Katheryn Brown and George J. Bey III, 387–414. Gainesville: University Press of Florida.

Ceballos Gallareta, Teresa, and Fernando Robles Castellanos. 2012. "Las etapas más tempranas de la alfarería Maya en al noroeste de la península de Yucatán." *Ancient Mesoamerica* 23:403–19.

Clark, John E., and Richard Hansen. 2001. "The Architecture of Early Kingship: Comparative Perspectives on the Origins of the Maya Royal Court." In *Royal Courts of the Ancient Maya: 2. Data and Case Studies*, edited by Takeshi Inomata and Stephen D. Houston, 1–45. Boulder, CO: Westview.

Cobos, Rafael. 2011. "Multepal or Centralized Kingship? New Evidence of Governmental Organization at Chichen Itza." In *Twin Tollans: Chichen Itza, Tula, and the Toltecs*, edited by Jeff Karl Kowalski and Cynthia Kristan-Graham, 49–271. Washington, DC: Dumbarton Oaks.

Cowgill, George, L. 1997. "State and Society at Teotihuacan." *Annual Review of Anthropology* 26:129–61.

Dunning, Nicholas P. 1992. *Lords of the Hills: Ancient Maya Settlement in the Puuc Region, Yucatán, Mexico*. Monographs in World Prehistory No. 15. Madison, WI: Prehistory Press.

Dunning, Nicholas P. 1993. Datos preliminares sobre el sitio arqueológico del Rancho Mex, Yucatán. Report submitted to Centro Regional de Yucatán, Instituto Nacional de Antropología e Historia, Mérida, Yucatan, Mexico.

Dunning, Nicholas P., Timothy Beach, Liwy Grasiozo Sierra, John G. Jones, David L. Lentz, Sheryl Luzzadder-Beach, Vernon L. Scarborough, and Michael P. Smyth. 2013. "A Tale of Two Collapses: Environmental Variability and Cultural Disruption in the Maya Lowlands." *Diálogo Andino* 41:171–83.

Dunning, Nicholas P., David Wahl, Timothy Beach, John G. Jones, Sheryl Luzzadder-Beach, and Carmen McCormick. 2014a. "Environmental Instability and Human Response in the Late Preclassic East-Central Yucatán Peninsula." In *The Great Maya Droughts in Cultural Context*, edited by Gyles Ianonne, 107–26. Boulder: University Press of Colorado.

Dunning Nicholas P., Eric Weaver, Michael P. Smyth, and David Ortegón Zapata. 2014b. "Xcoch: Home of Ancient Maya Rain Gods and Water Managers." In *The Archaeology of Yucatán: New Directions and Data*, edited by Travis Stanton, 65–80. Oxford: Archaeopress.

Flannery, Kent V. 1976. "The Evolution of Complex Settlement Systems." In *The Early Mesoamerican Village*, edited by K. V. Flannery, 162–73. New York: Academic Press,

Folan, William J. 1968. "Un botellón monipodio del centro de Yucatán, México." *Estudios de Cultura Maya* 8:68–75.

Freidel, David. 2018. "Maya and the Idea of Empire." In *Pathways to Complexity: A View from the Maya Lowlands*, edited by M. Katheryn Brown and George J. Bey III, 363–86. Gainesville: University Press of Florida.

Gallareta Negrón, Tomás, and Rosana May Chi, eds. 2007. "Proyecto arqueológico Xocnaceh: Tercera temporada de campo (2005–2006)." Informe Técnico al Consejo Nacional de Antropología e Historia, México.

Gallareta Negrón, Tomás, and William Ringle. 2004. "The Earliest Occupation of the Puuc Region, Yucatán, Mexico: New Perspectives from Xocnaceh and Paso de Macho." Paper presented at the 103rd Annual Meeting of the American Anthropological Association, Atlanta, GA.

Garza Tarazona de González, Silvia, and Edward B. Kurjack. 1980. *Atlas arqueológico del estado de Yucatán.* México, DF: Instituto Nacional de Antropología e Historia.

Grube, Nikolai, and Linda Schele. 1996. "New Observations on the Loltun Relief." *Mexicon* 18:11–14.

Haug, Gerald H., Detlef Gunther, Larry C. Peterson, Daniel M. Sigman, Konrad A. Hughen, and Beat Aeschlimann. 2003. "Climate and the Collapse of Maya Civilization." *Science* 299: 1731–35.

Hodell, David A., Jason H. Curtis, Mark Brenner, and Thomas P. Guilderson. 2001. "Solar Forcing of Drought Frequency in the Maya Lowlands." *Science* 292:1367–70.

Kowalski, Jeffrey K., and Nicholas P. Dunning. 1999. "The Architecture of Uxmal: The Symbolics of Statemaking at Puuc Maya Regional Capital." In *Mesoamerican Architecture as a Cultural Symbol*, edited by J. K. Kowlski, 274–97. London: Oxford University Press.

Marcus, Joyce. 1973. "Territorial Organization of the Lowland Maya." *Science* 180:911–16.

Marcus, Joyce, and Kent V. Flannery. 1996. *Zapotec Civilization: How Urban Society Evolved in Mexico's Oaxaca Valley*. London: Thames and Hudson.

Mathews, Jennifer P. 2003. "Megalithic Architecture at the Site of Victoria, Quintana Roo." *Mexicon* 25:74–77.

Mathews, Jennifer P., and Ruben Maldonado Cardenas. 2006. "Late Formative and Early Classic Interaction Spheres Reflected in the Megalithic Style." In *Lifeways in the Northern Maya Lowlands: New Approaches to Archaeology in the Yucatan Peninsula*, edited by J. Mathews and B. Morrison, 95–118. Tucson: University of Arizona Press.

Medina-Elizalde, Martin, Stephen J. Burns, Josué Polanco-Martínez, Timothy Beach, Fernanda Lases-Hernandez, Chuan C. Shen, and Hoa C. Wang. 2015. "High-Resolution Speleothem Record of Precipitation from the Yucatán Peninsula Spanning the Maya Preclassic Period." *Global and Planetary Change* 138:93–102. https://doi.org/10.1016/j.gloplacha.2015.10.003.

Moyes, Holly, Jaime J. Awe, George A. Brook, and James W. Webster. 2009. "The Ancient Maya Drought Cult: Late Classic Cave Use in Belize." *Latin American Antiquity* 20:175–206.

Peniche May, Nancy. 2012. "The Architecture of Power and Sociopolitical Complexity in Northwestern Yucatan during the Preclassic Period." In *The Ancient Maya of Mexico: Reinterpreting the Past of the Northern Maya Lowlands*, edited by G. E. Braswell, 65–87. Sheffield: Equinox Publishing.

Pires-Ferreira, Jane W. 1976. "Shell and Iron-Ore Mirror Exchange in Formative Mesoamerica, with Comments on Other Commodities." In *The Early Mesoamerican Village*, edited by K. V. Flannery, 311–28. New York: Academic Press.

Pollock, Harry E. D., Ralph L. Roys, Tatiana Proskouriakoff, and A. Ledyard Smith. 1962. *Mayapan, Yucatan, Mexico*. Carnegie Institution of Washington, Publication 619. Washington, DC: Carnegie Institution.

Ringle, William M. 2011. *The Yaxhom Valley Survey: Pioneers of the Puuc Hills, Yucatan*. Report prepared for the National Geographic Society in fulfillment of Research Award 8913-11. Davidson College, Davidson, NC.

Ringle, William M., and E. Wyllys Andrews, V. 1988. "Formative Residences at Komchen, Yucatán, Mexico." In *Household and Community in the Mesoamerican Past*, edited by Richard R. Wilk and Wendy Ashmore, 171–97. Albuquerque: University of New Mexico Press.

Smyth, Michael P., and Christopher D. Dore. 1994. "Maya Urbanism at Sayil, Yucatán." *National Geographic Research and Exploration* 10:38–55.

Smyth, Michael P., Nicholas P. Dunning, Christopher Carr, and David Ortegón Zapata. 2020. "Preclassic Settlement Hierarchy and First Farmers: A Preliminary Reconnaissance of the Puuc Hills." *Mexicon* 42:38–55.

Smyth, Michael P., Nicholas P. Dunning, Eric M. Weaver, Philip van Beynen, and David Ortegón Zapata. 2017a. "An Enigmatic Maya Center: Climate Change, Settlement Systems, and Water Adaptations at Xcoch, Puuc Region, Yucatán." In *Recent*

Investigations in the Puuc Region of Yucatan, edited by Mehgan Rubenstein, 3–24. Oxford: Archaeopress.

Smyth, Michael P., Nicholas P. Dunning, Eric M. Weaver, Philip van Beynen, and David Ortegón Zapata. 2017b. "The Perfect Storm: Climate Change and Ancient Maya Response in the Puuc Hills Region of Yucatan." *Antiquity* 91: 490–509.

Smyth, Michael P., and David Ortegón Zapata. 2008. "A Preclassic Center in the Puuc Region: A Report on Xcoch, Yucatán, Mexico." *Mexicon* 30:63–68.

Smyth, Michael P., David Ortegón Zapata, Nicholas P. Dunning, and Eric M. Weaver. 2014. "Settlement Dynamics, Climate Change, and Human Response at Xcoch in the Puuc Region of Yucatán, Mexico." In *The Archaeology of Yucatán: New Directions and Data*, edited by T. Stanton, 45–64. Oxford: Archaeopress.

Smyth, Michael P., Ezra Zubrow, David Ortegón Zapata, Nicholas P. Dunning, Eric M. Weaver, Jane E. Slater, and Philip van Beynen. 2010. "Paleoclimatic Reconstruction and Archaeological Investigations at Xcoch and the Puuc Region of Yucatán, Mexico: Exploratory Research into Arctic Climate Change and Maya Culture Processes." Report to the National Science Foundation. www.farinco.org.

Smyth, Michael P., Ezra Zubrow, David Ortegón Zapata, Nicholas P. Dunning, Eric M. Weaver, Jane E. Slater, and Philip van Beynen. 2011. "Paleoclimatic Reconstruction and Archaeological Investigations at Xcoch and the Puuc Region of Yucatán, Mexico: Exploratory Research into Arctic Climate Change and Maya Culture Processes." Report to the National Science Foundation (www.farinco.org).

Stanton, Travis W., and Tómas Gallareta Negrón. 2002. "Proyecto Xocnaceh: 1ª temporada de campo marzo-julio 2002." Technical report submitted to the Consejo de Arqueología del Instituto Nacional de Antropología e Historia, México, DF.

Stephens, John Lloyd. 1963. *Incidents of Travel in Yucatán*. Vol. 2. New York. Dover Publications.

Taube, Karl, A. 1995. "The Monumental Architecture of the Yalahau Region and Megalithic Style of the Northern Maya Lowlands." In *The View from Yalahau: 1993 Archaeological Investigations of Northern Quintana Roo, Mexico*. Latin American Studies Program, Field Report Series, No. 2. Riverside: University of California Press,

Weaver, Eric M., Nicholas P. Dunning, and Michael P. Smyth. 2015. "Investigation of a Ritual Cave Site in the Puuc Region of Yucatan, Mexico: Actun Xcoch." *Journal of Cave and Karst Studies* 77:120–28.

Webster, James. W., George A. Brook, L. Bruce Railsback, Hai Cheng, R. Lawrence Edwards, Clark Alexander, and Philip P. Reeder. 2007. "Stalagmite Evidence from Belize Indicating Significant Drought at the Time of Preclassic Abandonment, the Maya Hiatus, and the Classic Maya Collapse." *Palaeogeography, Palaeoclimatology, Palaeoecology* 250:1–17.

Willey, Gordon V., and Demitri B. Shimkin. 1973. "The Maya Collapse: A Summary View." In *The Classic Maya Collapse*, edited by P. T. Culbert, 457–501. Albuquerque: University of New Mexico.

8

The Role of Monumental Architecture and Landscape Modification in the Development of Complexity at Early Xunantunich, Belize

ZOË J. RAWSKI AND M. KATHRYN BROWN

INTRODUCTION

The term *craft* often evokes an image of small-scale, portable objects such as figurines or ceramic vessels, beadwork, or woven cloth. Yet craftsmanship can apply to any scale of production, whether it be shell beads or monumental acropolei. In this chapter, we expand the idea of specialized production and crafting to incorporate a significantly larger scale—the construction of monumental architecture. Construction projects, which often include massive modifications to the natural landscape in order to prepare for building efforts, can best be understood as the aggregate product of a variety of individuals' (and possibly specialists') work (McCurdy 2016). Large-scale landscape modification occurs in the Maya Lowlands as early as the early Middle Preclassic period (1000–600 BCE), during which time sites such as Ceibal, Cival, and Blackman Eddy, to name a few, are established (Brown and Garber 2008; Estrada-Belli 2012; Inomata et al. 2013). Early Maya communities shaped their landscape through the leveling and preparation of the natural terrain, as well as through the construction of formal public architecture and spaces. The oldest and largest example of this documented to date can be

https://doi.org/10.5876/9781646422883.c008

found at the site of Aguada Fénix in Tabasco, Mexico, where an artificial plateau measuring 1,400 meters in length was recently documented (Inomata et al. 2020).

From an architectural project's initial inception and the preparation of the construction site to the last decorative stucco work, the erection of Preclassic centers involved a wide array of skilled labor. Yet the earliest examples of monumental centers do not provide us with clear evidence of hierarchical stratification (Estrada-Belli 2012). Cross-culturally, monumental structures have been documented among groups that might otherwise be described as egalitarian or non-hierarchical (Gibson 2004; Inomata et al. 2015). It has been suggested that some of the earliest centers in the Maya area were constructed by relatively mobile communities that would have come together for the construction of ceremonial architecture and to participate in the public rituals occurring there (Inomata et al. 2015). Certainly, there is evidence of this from sites outside of the Maya region, including the famous example of Göbekli Tepe in Anatolia (Dietrich et al. 2012; Schmidt 2000).

In the case of the Preclassic Maya Lowlands, it has been argued that the archaeological evidence largely supports "a consensus-based rather than a coercion-based mode of construction" for early ceremonial centers (McAnany 2010, 150). However, these two categories represent opposite ends of a spectrum that was undoubtedly far more diverse and complex. As Doyle observed, "Monumental works represent the manifestations of early institutions within frameworks of everyday power relations, at the intersection between cooperative and coercive social forces" (Doyle 2017, 26). While the construction of early monumental buildings would have served to center and integrate communities, social pressures may also have played a role in the participation of the builders.

Given the scale of these early works within relatively non-hierarchical societies, it is clear that the presence of monumental architecture should not be seen as a marker of hierarchical complexity in and of itself (Yoffee 2005). Rather, it likely played a major role in the development and maintenance of complexity and inequality, as spaces initially built communally and conceptualized for community use were gradually appropriated to legitimize an emergent elite (Brown 2003; Joyce 2004). Increasingly, it seems that the craft of monumental construction played a key role in place-making through spatial transformations and social transformations as well, as diverse communities were brought together and integrated (Inomata et al. 2015). Thus, it is productive to examine how communal building projects and public architecture may have shaped social difference. Questions of this nature may provide fruitful avenues of inquiry for future research into the development of complexity and inequality.

In this chapter, we explore this complex relationship between monumental construction efforts and the emergence of sociopolitical complexity and inequality at the site of Early Xunantunich, Belize. In so doing, we attempt to address deeper avenues of inquiry into the role of monumental construction in the production and reproduction of social roles and identities, including the crystallization of institutions such as divine kingship. Ongoing research at the site continues to explore models of sociopolitical complexity such as "corporate" and "network" political strategies, as well as non-hierarchical institutions such as heterarchies (Blanton et al. 1996; Brumfiel and Fox 2003; Crumley 1995). Complexity may also be understood as consisting of both inequality and heterogeneity, which allows us to understand complex social structures with heterogeneous social groupings independently of significant inequality, defined by differential access to material or social resources (McGuire 1983).

The activities and ritual performances taking place in monumental ceremonial spaces are of particular importance for studies of the ancient Maya, as the display of specialized ritual knowledge would have played a major role in the crafting of elite and non-elite identities. Given the size, elaboration, and specialized symbolic meanings of monumental architecture, monumental structures provide excellent loci for the studies of performance. The definition of performance varies widely in its uses throughout the anthropological literature (Inomata and Coben 2006). While some definitions may distinguish between rituals, in which the audience actively participates, and theater, which encompasses strictly prescribed acts in formalized locations, others emphasize a more inclusive concept of theatricality, focusing on the varying roles the audience can play, be it observer, evaluator, or some combination of the two (Inomata and Coben 2006). Similarly, performance can be seen as a mode of communication and social action that actively creates "meaning, identities, cognitive models, and social relations through the experience of doing and seeing" (Inomata and Coben 2006, 19). This definition reflects our understanding of ancient Maya ritual performance and allows us to explore the role of public rituals and ceremonies in the political realm of ancient Maya life.

The concept of the theater state, as originally discussed by Clifford Geertz (1980), has also been applied to the case of the ancient Maya with some success (Demarest 1992). The concept of the theater state specifically draws on literature related to Southeast Asian cultures, referred to by some as "galactic polities," which are loosely organized centers controlling a so-called galaxy of subordinate centers (Demarest 1992, 150). In galactic polities, there is "an extreme dependence on the personal performance of the ruler in warfare, marriage alliances, and above all, ritual" (Demarest 1992, 150). Thus, these ritual performances would have been of paramount importance to the maintenance of divine kingship as an institution.

For the study of monumental architecture, it is useful to focus on spectacles, which are a type of performance determined by the monumental scale of the performance both spatially and temporally (Inomata and Coben 2006). Thus, the use of the term *spectacle* to describe performative events brings with it a direct emphasis on the physical aspects of an event, including the locus of the spectacle as well as the construction of the space itself. Considering this, we focus our chapter on both the craft of monumental architectural construction and the statecraft involved in ritual performance in order to examine the origins of complexity and inequality at Early Xunantunich.

We argue that the site's early Middle Preclassic occupation lacks distinct evidence of sociopolitical inequality, though clear patterns of complexity begin to emerge during the late Middle Preclassic period. The monumental structures of this time are predominantly associated with naturalistic or animistic rituals, which observed natural phenomena such as solar and celestial events. By the Late Preclassic, in contrast, these buildings were clearly associated with the emergent institution of divine kingship, and by the end of this period, the site's emphasis on the E Group complex is replaced, we argue, with a shift to the Triadic complex of Actuncan.

EARLY XUNANTUNICH

The Mopan Valley Preclassic Project (MVPP) has been investigating the site of Xunantunich since 2008. Over a decade of research has shown that Xunantunich is composed of two separate ceremonial centers, Classic Xunantunich and Early Xunantunich (Brown 2017; Brown et al. 2016) (figure 8.1). The site of Early Xunantunich provides a unique opportunity to explore early ceremonial building practices and the rise of complexity in depth, as this location, which was occupied by at least 1000 BCE, was abandoned at the end of the Late Preclassic period and only partially reoccupied during the Classic period (Brown et al. 2011, 2016). Thus, the early ceremonial center's Preclassic architecture was not built over in later times and is more easily assessable for wide-scale investigation, allowing a more comprehensive picture of the form and function of early architecture.

Building on initial survey and explorative work conducted by the Xunantunich Archaeological Project (XAP) during the 1990s (Robin et al. 1994), MVPP has found that the site of Early Xunantunich consists of three plazas bounded by formal monumental architecture (Brown 2017; Brown et al. 2017). The ceremonial core includes an early E Group assemblage located at the heart of the site and a slightly later E Group to the west. The early ceremonial center also exhibited two monumental flat-topped platforms that form the northern and eastern boundaries of the site. Intensive investigations of the later E Group complex and plaza and the northern platform have provided a wealth of data related to early ritual activity and the site's history. MVPP's investigations at Classic Xunantunich, located 800 m to the west, have also uncovered buried Preclassic architecture and features that indicate that Early Xunantunich may have been larger than previously thought (Brown et al. 2016). Additionally, Preclassic hilltop shrines located to the east and

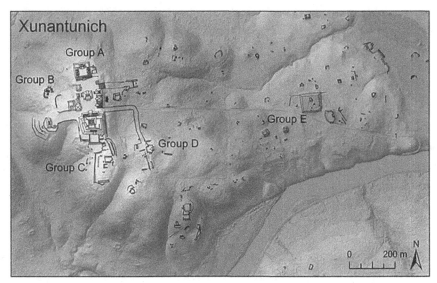

FIGURE 8.1. *Map showing location of Early Xunantunich in Belize.*

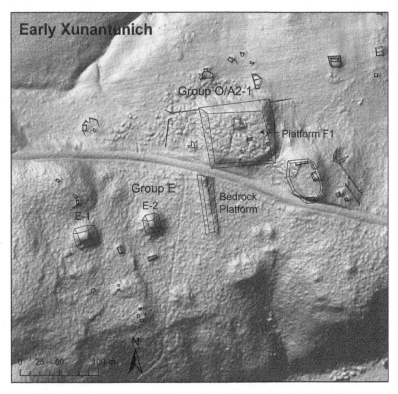

FIGURE 8.2. *Lidar and malerized features map of Early Xunantunich.*

west of Early Xunantunich indicate that Early Xunantunich was the center of a broader ritual circuit (Brown and Yaeger 2020; Lytle 2020).

In this chapter, we present Early Xunantunich as a case study for the exploration of landscape modification and monumental construction as a form of specialized production, both in the sense of physical construction efforts and in the process of statecraft, with a particular emphasis on ritual performance. We trace the rise and fall of Early Xunantunich through time and how the early inhabitants crafted, consecrated, redesigned, and eventually abandoned this Preclassic ritual center in the Mopan Valley of Belize. The data presented in this chapter focuses primarily on two locations at Early Xunantunich, the E Group complex and the northern platform, Structure F1.

THE E GROUP COMPLEX

Early Xunantunich was first occupied by 1000 BCE, when the early inhabitants modified bedrock and leveled the prehistoric soil on a ridge overlooking the Mopan River (Brown 2017). This first landscape modification was associated with the erection of an early E Group complex, similar to the first landscape modifications seen at the sites of Cival and Ceibal (Estrada-Belli 2011, 2012; Inomata et al. 2013). With this initial leveling and shaping of the natural terrace, it appears that the inhabitants carved a linear structure out of soft limestone bedrock (Brown et al. 2018). This long, linear bedrock feature served as the eastern structure of the earliest E Group at the site and was paired with Structure E-2 to the west (figure 8.3). To date, only limited excavations have been conducted on the eastern bedrock structure, but preliminary ceramic analysis suggests that it was first constructed during the early Middle Preclassic period. The bedrock feature appears to have been approximately 1–2 m tall with a single terrace step providing access to the flattened summit.

Structure E-2 is located to the west of the bedrock platform and has been intensively studied since 2008. Structure E-2 appears to have functioned as the western pyramid in the earliest E Group complex and was reoriented to face west sometime during the Middle Preclassic. With this reorientation of the E Group, Structure E-2 was rebuilt on a platform to form the eastern architectural assemblage of a new E Group complex (Brown et al. 2018). To date, excavations at Structure E-2 have focused mostly on the western face of the structure and have uncovered at least three construction phases, with several modification and possible sub-phases also present (Brown 2017; Brown et al. 2011). The westernmost building at Early Xunantunich, Structure E-1, was constructed as the western pyramid of the E Group complex. The plaza between Structure E-1 and Structure E-2 slopes downward from west to east (Brown 2017) (see figure 8.4).

The earliest phase encountered to date (Structure E-2–3rd) appears to be a three-tiered building oriented to the east and rising to approximately 4–4.5 m tall.

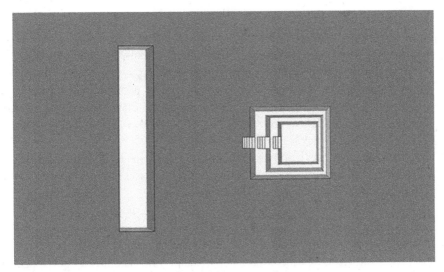

FIGURE 8.3. *Structure E-2–2nd with bedrock structure to the east.*

The upper tier of the platform was dismantled in antiquity. Excavations did not encounter a staircase leading to the summit of this phase on the western face, suggesting that the structure was oriented to the east. This supports the notion that this phase of the Structure E-2 was associated with the bedrock platform discussed above. Excavations during the 2018 season confirmed this hypothesis, uncovering a central staircase on the eastern face of the structure. The ceramics

FIGURE 8.4. *Structure E-2 with western pyramid and ramped plaza surface.*

from the fill within Structure E-2–3rd are pre-Mamom and therefore suggest that this phase dates to the early Middle Preclassic (1000–700 BCE).

Structure E-2–3rd, although modest in size by Classic period standards, represents a large building program for this early date in the Maya Lowlands. The three-tiered platform was built on a thick layer of white marl placed directly on a sticky, black paleosol, presumably the original soil layer overlying bedrock. The paleosol was leveled by the early community prior to this initial construction. Coupled with the modified bedrock structure, this construction event represents a significant modification of the natural landscape to prepare for a major construction event. Although the exact volume of this leveling program is as of yet unknown, it is clear that labor investment in this process was extensive.

The core of this building was constructed with dry-laid rubble. Cobble construction fill is the most typical type of architectural fill used in the Maya Lowlands and clearly has a long history of use. This dry-laid cobble fill was used as a core for the earliest construction phase, and wet-laid marl was used as a foundation below and behind the stone walls of the terraces. Wet-laid marl of this type solidifies and provides a solid foundation for building, making shifting less common. Marl, however, is an expensive building material as it must be mined from bedrock outcrops. Therefore, the use of a cobble fill within the core of the building makes sense. At the nearby site of Blackman Eddy, similar construction and materials were used and cobble fill was found within the core of the earliest platforms (Brown 2003).

The elaborate construction of Structure E-2–3rd very likely represents evidence for the beginning of skilled architectural specialists and/or craftsmen. By balancing both the relative cost of construction materials and their respective qualities as building materials, these emerging Preclassic specialists were able to create a monumental structure that stood for millennia. Although this was the structure's earliest phase, it is clear that this building was not the result of trial and error. Rather, it was the work of individuals who had already developed some expertise in the practice. Thus, crafts such as masonry, architecture, and engineering clearly date well back into the Middle Preclassic period.

Our excavations were able to reveal more about the penultimate phase (Structure E-2–2nd), which dates to approximately 600 BCE. This phase had a central staircase on the western side, suggesting that it faced west. We believe that this phase represents a reorientation of the E Group at this time and that Structure E-1 was built to serve as the western pyramid. Although the upper portions of the Structure E-2–2nd had been badly damaged by stone robbing in antiquity, the lower tier and basal steps of the central staircase remained intact, allowing us to understand its form. This phase was a two-tiered pyramid placed on a low platform that had wings extending to the north and south (Brown 2017; Brown et al. 2013) (figure 8.4). Structure E-2–2nd completely covered the earlier phase and was constructed predominately of pure white marl. The liberal use of white marl during the Middle Preclassic may have a practical function as mentioned above, but it may also have had deep symbolic meaning to the ancient inhabitants, representing pure earth and mountains (Brown 2017).

The final construction phase of Structure E-2 (Structure E-2–1st) was poorly preserved, and similar to the penultimate phase, most of the architectural stones were robbed in antiquity causing the construction fill to collapse. Although the form was difficult to understand, we believe that this Late Preclassic phase was a western-facing two-tiered pyramid placed on a low platform.

Within the summit of this phase, we encountered a formally constructed burial chamber that was tomb-like in nature (Brown et al. 2013). The burial chamber, however, was not vaulted and was filled in with sediment and fill. A line of large stones and an incised slate slab marked the burial location. An image of a personage in profile was incised on the slate slab, possibly a portrait of the individual buried within the chamber. Unfortunately, the slate was in a poor state of preservation and little iconographic detail could be discerned.

The burial chamber had been reentered in antiquity, and the remains of the individual or individuals interred therein were removed (Brown 2017). We believe that the reentering was related to ancestor veneration and occurred at the time of abandonment or shortly after. The summit surface of Structure E-2–1st, although poorly preserved, did not cover the burial location, suggesting to us that the floor was never patched. It is significant, however, that an individual, possibly a Late Preclassic ruler, was afforded the status of being interred in the eastern pyramidal complex of the Early Xunantunich E Group. This was the only burial uncovered within Structure E-2.

Our investigations of the E Group complex also included extensive excavations within the plaza area between Structures E-1 and E-2. Our excavations revealed that the sloping plaza itself consisted of a large plaza platform structure just to the west of Structure E-2. This platform appears to have been tiered and had inset limestone paved ramps located to the north and south sides (figure 8.4). The ramps were fairly wide (over 6 m) and would have allowed foot traffic, presumably for ritual processions. It is important to note that there was no direct access from Structure E-1 to E-2 on centerline as the paved ramps were located to the side, giving the impression that a ritual circuit may have been part of the performance at this important sacred location.

Investigations of early E Groups elsewhere in the Maya Lowlands, such as Cival and Ceibal, have demonstrated that elaborate offerings were placed beneath the plaza floors to commemorate the founding of the E Group and other consecration events. Although we have encountered a numbered of ritually placed artifacts, no cache similar in nature to other early E Groups has ever been found at Early Xunantunich. Instead, excavations in front of structure E-2 yielded a number of small postholes. These postholes were concentrated on centerline in front of the basal step of Structure E-2–2nd. Most of these postholes were covered with a thin layer of white marl, suggesting that they were patched at some point in antiquity.

This evidence, coupled with the large number of postholes (over forty), suggests that some type of small wooden perishable structure was erected repeatedly in this location (Brown 2017) (figure 8.5). We have interpreted these data as the periodic placement and dismantling of a perishable wooden altar, or *mesa*, for specific ritual celebrations. These data strongly suggest that this space was used for public ritual activities that were frequently repeated. Coupled with the presence of multiple fire features in front of Structure E-2, this assemblage attests to the importance of this place to the ceremonial lives of the residents of Early Xunantunich (Brown 2017). Thus, these architectural assemblages played a major role in crafting the Early Xunantunich community, as people would have

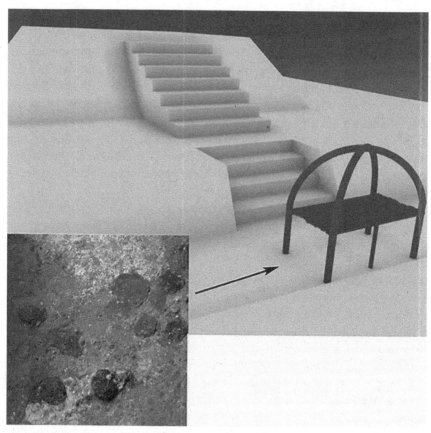

FIGURE 8.5. *Location of altar/mesa feature.*

gathered in this place to observe important ritual cycles. In so doing, the roles of participants and observers alike would have become increasingly central to community identity.

THE NORTHERN PLATFORM, STRUCTURE F1

While E Group complexes have been investigated in great detail and have yielded a wealth of data on Preclassic ritual and architecture (e.g., Freidel et al. 2017), monumental flat-topped platforms are still poorly understood in both their form and function. Although these structures have been documented across the Preclassic landscape and were clearly an important part of early ceremonial centers, few have been intensively investigated. Recent investigations at sites like Aguada Fénix are contributing significantly to this discussion (Inomata et al. 2020), however its relatively recent discovery underscores the likelihood that additional early monumental works are as of yet unknown. It is safe to assume that even more remain deeply buried beneath Classic Period acropolei, precluding their identification and investigation. Thus, the excavation of the northern platform, Structure F1, at Early Xunantunich provides an important contribution to our understanding of Preclassic monumental building activities.

Structure F1 of Group O/A2-1 was first documented by the Xunantunich Archaeological Project in the 1990s (Robin et al. 1994). Its massive size dwarfs the surrounding pyramids and other structures, and preliminary maps of the platform's latest form suggest that it measured over 60 m on each side and rose up to 13 m in height on its tallest side. The initial testing of this platform suggested a Middle Preclassic date and that the platform may have been constructed in a single phase, utilizing a natural bedrock outcrop as the foundation. Our work, however, has significantly revised the construction history of this platform.

According to the stratigraphy documented by XAP, the underlying natural geological deposits "form an undulating surface, the concave depressions in which are filled by consecutive layers of silt and sascab fill as part of the modification of this natural rise in the construction of platform F1" (Robin et al. 1994, 104). It is likely, then, that the earliest iteration of Structure F1 was created from modified bedrock. Later architectural phases also incorporated the natural bedrock outcrop, combining the natural and artificial in order to create their sacred landscape, as will be discussed in greater detail below (Rawski 2019, 2020).

Thus, even in the earliest stages of the platform's construction, the ancient Maya engaged in large-scale modification of the natural landscape to construct spaces for public and ceremonial purposes. Although monumental buildings are often hailed as evidence of major construction efforts, the leveling and clearing of the space for construction often requires just as much, if not more, labor investment. This is perhaps most saliently evidenced by the Middle Preclassic construction of the site of Cival, where the modification of the landscape resulted in a greater construction effort than all subsequent programs combined (Estrada-Belli 2012).

Structure F1 has been investigated by the Mopan Valley Preclassic Project since 2015 (Rawski 2020). These excavations, which have focused primarily on the structure's southern face, have provided an impressive dataset related to the construction and consecration of this enormous and important platform. Rather than a single construction event, Structure F1 appears to have had at least two major construction phases, both with minor additions and alterations.

As our investigation of this platform has focused on understanding the form of the platform and access ways that lead to the summit, we have not penetrated through the penultimate phase to date. Given the antiquity of the site's E Group, it is possible that earlier phases do indeed exist, but have not been uncovered. Due to the platform's lack of overlying later Classic period construction phases, excavations have prioritized more horizontal exposure of the southern face in order to gain critical knowledge regarding its architectural form that other

Preclassic platform investigations have been unable to collect. Few opportunities for such extensive horizontal exposure of Preclassic architecture exist, and much of the data we have from the Preclassic come from limited excavations of deeply buried architecture. One notable exception is Structure B1 at the nearby site of Blackman Eddy, where illegal bulldozing caused significant damage to the structure and the remaining portion of the mound was fully excavated through horizontal exposure (Brown 2003; Brown and Garber 2008).

The earliest construction phase documented by MVPP dates to the Middle Preclassic. Ceramics from within fill layers of this phase are dominated by the Jenney Creek complex and are predominated by Mars Orange and Jocote Orange-brown types (Rawski 2020). Wood charcoal from within the fill of structure's terraces and associated plaza floor yielded dates of 2475 ± 30 BP (771–431 BCE), 2565 ± 20 BP (804–598 BCE), and 2465 ± 20 BP (726–434 BCE) (PSUAMS-3444; charcoal; $\delta^{14}C = -265.1\%$; PSUAMS-3447; charcoal; $\delta^{14}C = -273.2\%$; PSUAMS-3440; charcoal; $\delta^{14}C = -264.3\%$). Plaster surfaces associated with this phase suggest at least one re-plastering event, indicating an extended use of the structure in this form. Carbon flecks were found across the plastered surfaces, suggesting ritual incense burning or other ritual burning activities may have occurred in these spaces.

Rather than the large cut limestone we typically see utilized in the construction of monumental buildings, Structure F1–2nd was constructed using small, pillow-like blocks, typically measuring only 15–20 cm wide by 10 cm tall (figure 8.6). For a structure of this size, the quantity of these small stones required to complete the building would have been enormous. Although highly unusual, this exact masonry style has also been documented for the staircase of the eastern structure of the Preclassic E Group at the nearby site of Actuncan (Simova and Mixter 2015). Furthermore, similar stone altar features at the summit of these staircases are found at both sites (Rawski 2020; Simova and Mixter 2015). These connections raise questions regarding the nature of the relationship between these two sites, as Actuncan rose to regional prominence around the same time that Early Xunantunich declined (Yaeger et al. 2016). Given the stylistic similarities between these two ceremonial structures, the two polities may be more connected than previously thought. It is also possible that Early Xunantunich and Actuncan were more connected than previously thought and may represent different ceremonial zones within a larger site. Either way, this specific architectural style is seemingly unique to the area, suggesting a possible regional tradition of masonry craftsmanship may have been taking place.

In some areas, the natural limestone bedrock was modified to accommodate the construction of this platform. In several areas, the bedrock was incorporated as the foundation of the platform, or, in the case of the platform's western side, possibly as the adjacent plaza surface. There, the bedrock appears to have been

FIGURE 8.6. *Small pillow stones from staircase of Structure F1–2nd.*

left exposed to serve as the surface on which the structure's basal terrace was built. Additionally, on the platform's southern face, architectural features were appended directly to bedrock outcrops, including cobble walls and a marl ramp (Rawski 2020). This deliberate juxtaposition of natural and artificial elements may have served to embed cosmological themes into the built environment. The symbolic associations between the building and the *witz*, or sacred mountain, would have helped sanctify both Structure F1–2nd and the ceremonial center more broadly.

Additional bedrock structures have been documented across Early Xunantunich, including the use of the modified bedrock structure in the site's early E Group complex discussed above (Brown 2017; Brown et al. 2018). The use and modification of bedrock for early ceremonial constructions is well documented across the Maya area, including sites such as Cival and Ceibal in the Petén (Estrada-Belli 2012; Inomata et al. 2013). It is probable that an earlier phase may be present beneath Structure F1–2nd that consists entirely of modified bedrock without the additional masonry structural elements seen in this phase. However, penetration of Structure F1–2nd has been limited, and no earlier phase has been documented to date.

Further similarities exist between the northern platform and other structures within the site of Early Xunantunich. Although the upper portion of the central staircase of Structure F1–2nd is inset, the lowest two steps are outset and terminate in a plastered ramp leading down to the plaza below. The presence of a ramp at the base of this structure is interesting, as it echoes the inset paved ramps discussed above, albeit smaller in scale.

Though the interpretations of the architectural evidence are preliminary, we believe that Structure F1's form was highly suggestive of public ritual performance. Seemingly devoid of a formal masonry superstructure, the platform's wide staircase was flanked by at least three terraces. We therefore suggest that the rituals taking place at this platform would have included an aspect of performance or spectacle, as these terraces and the platform surface itself would have provided stages or performance spaces overlooking the ceremonial plaza to the south. The large flat surface of the platform also provided an additional venue of visibility both from the ceremonial plaza and the hinterland communities beyond, including the nearby site of San Lorenzo, which has documented evidence of Middle Preclassic occupation (Brown et al. 2018; Ingalls 2020; Villarreal 2018).

Furthermore, fragmentary presence of stucco architectural decoration was encountered on these terraces, suggesting that these spaces may have been adorned with stucco deity masks. Thus, Structure F1 would have provided a religiously charged backdrop for performances. At the nearby site of Blackman Eddy, a Middle Preclassic platform was adorned with stucco masks (Brown 2003). During the Late Preclassic, elaborate stucco masks become more common and have been documented at sites such as Cerros, which is well known for its sequence of royal temples decorated with stucco depictions of the Maya cosmos which include important cosmological symbols (Freidel and Robertson 1986; Freidel et al. 1982). These masks, and more broadly the public ritual performances occurring at Cerros, have been linked to increasing complexity at the site (Reese-Taylor 1996). The new evidence from Structure F1 at Early Xunantunich, coupled with the data from Blackman Eddy, suggest that stucco architectural decoration of this form begins in the Middle Preclassic. Presumably, early public performances that sanctified emerging elites and rulers have their origins during this period as well.

As Estrada-Belli (2012) and others have noted, monumental structures may have emerged for communal purposes at their original inception, only later serving a generative role in the construction of power and inequality. If this is indeed the case at Early Xunantunich, the spectacles of construction and ritual taking place in these areas may have played some role in these developments. As theatrical performance and spectacle crafted and structured the identities of both performer and audience, bearers of specialized ritual knowledge would have become increasingly distinct from their audiences, amplifying their social difference.

As with all final phase architecture at Early Xunantunich, Structure F1–1st is very poorly preserved. Ceramic evidence suggests that this phase dates to the transitional period between the late Middle Preclassic and the beginning of the Late Preclassic, as the associated assemblage is a mix of both Jenney Creek and Barton Creek types, including some transitional Mamom-Chicanel types (Rawski 2020). Two wood charcoal radiocarbons samples from the fill of this phase further support this early Late Preclassic construction, yielding dates of 2200 ± 20 BP, or 360–200 BCE, and 2174 ± 20 BP, or 356–170 BCE (PSUAMS-3347; charcoal; $\delta^{14}C = -239.6\%$; and PSUAMS-3353; charcoal; $\delta^{14}C = -237.1\%$). The Structure F1–1st assemblage also contains increasing quantities of exotic goods including obsidian, marine shell, and unlike we see in the Middle Preclassic, greenstone.

The structure was left open to the elements, and the theft of nearly all facing stones by the site's Classic Period inhabitants resulted in a collapsed pile of cobble and boulder fill, with only the lowest two terraces distinguishable in their form. The basal terrace, constructed of cut limestone facing stones, allows us to gain a basic understanding of the structure's footprint. The second terrace, which no longer has facing stones in place, is visible due to the presence of a cobble core-facing wall. In total, excavations resulted in over twenty-one meters of exposed terrace wall on the platform's southern face, in addition to at least four meters E/W of an associated cobble staircase. These excavations took place dozens of meters apart; therefore, we can infer that the true length of this southern terrace face is much greater, likely in keeping with estimates of sixty meters or more (Rawski 2020).

In general, the form of Structure F1 between these two phases remains somewhat consistent. Each appears to be a terraced, flat-topped platform, with both ramps and staircases on its southern face. In the case of Structure F1–1st, the bedrock ramp documented was constructed to the west of the staircase rather than at its base. It is probable that this ramp is mirrored on the opposite side of the staircase, and it may be indicative of a ritual circuit which directed the movement of people up to and down from the platform.

Although much of the architectural data regarding the form of Structure F1–1st has been significantly damaged, what is very clear about this construction phase is the significant investment in expanding the structure's footprint on the landscape in a relatively short span of time. The fill of this structure consists of hard river cobbles and boulders, some of which measure over a meter in length, laid over the earlier structure at a depth of nearly a meter deep. Given the monumental footprint of the platform, the collective volume of this fill alone would have been as much as ten thousand cubic meters. This construction effort may be indicative of a competitive gesture on behalf of an emergent or even threatened elite, as the ability to marshal labor and resources would have been an impressive competitive display made visible at a great scale on the regional landscape (Rathje 2002). Competition with rival polities could be responsible for such a display, begging the question of whether the increased visibility was targeted toward anyone particular such as a neighboring polity, and if so, whom. This may have been important to the centralization of regional power in the Late Preclassic.

Indeed, the construction of this architectural phase occurred at a time when the nearby polity of Actuncan was beginning, making it as a possible contender for the neighboring rival (LeCount 2013; Simova et al. 2015). Alternatively, if Early Xunantunich and Actuncan were related during the Middle Preclassic, possibly representing different ceremonial places for related communities, then the massive construction effort we see at Structure F1 during the Late Preclassic may represent different lineages competing for power or even competition with other sites in the valley.

This abandonment by the end of the Late Preclassic coincides with an increase in construction of ceremonial architecture at Actuncan (Simova et al. 2018). While it is possible that this relationship was one of cycling political centers, we instead argue that it is more likely that the relationship provides evidence for contemporaneous, dispersed ritual nodes on the landscape that may be associated with the same population (Brown and Yaeger 2020; Rawski 2020). The contemporaneity and proximity of the two sites, in conjunction with their similar architectural styles and ritual features such as summit altars, suggests that it may be unproductive to think of the two as separate sites. Given the dispersed settlement patterns now documented in the Preclassic period, it seems that Preclassic centers are much more widely spread out than their Classic period successors (Reese-Taylor 2017). Thus, we should avoid preconceived notions of site boundaries based on Classic period data when examining the Preclassic landscape.

Consequently, it may prove productive to view Early Xunantunich and Actuncan as one larger, albeit dispersed site. Within this framework, we can better understand the changing emphasis on particular types of ceremonial architectural complexes and rituals that occurred during the Middle and Late Preclassic periods. It appears that during the Middle Preclassic the focus was on the E Group complexes and associated public rituals as well as the highly visible performances on Structure F1. During the Late Preclassic the triadic architectural complex at Actuncan was constructed and likely become the focus of rituals that celebrated the institution of kingship. These two nodes may be representative of separate founding lineages or perhaps dedicated to different deities or rituals. As one lineage waned in power or one ritual emphasis began to wane, the other node became the primary locus of ritual activity at the site. Similar processes have been documented at sites such as Tikal, where the Mundo Perdido complex falls into disuse, as well as at the site of San Bartolo, where the E Group complex is gradually abandoned as the focus of ritual activity shifts to Triadic groups across the lowlands (Laporte and Fialko 1993; Runggaldier 2009; Saturno et al. 2018). Across the lowlands in the Late Preclassic, the E Group complex is eschewed in favor of Triadic architecture, which has clear associations with royal power (Saturno et al. 2018).

FIGURE 8.7. *Greenstone effigies from the Structure F1 cache.*

Importantly, the ceremonial center at Actuncan does contain a Late Preclassic Triadic complex and a Late Preclassic carved stela, Stela 1 (McGovern 2004). The presence of a carved monument at the site has been interpreted as evidence of divine kingship (LeCount 2004; Simova et al. 2018). This stela, erected sometime between 400 BCE and 100 CE, depicts a dancing individual holding a feathered staff (Grube and McGovern 1995; McGovern 2004), further demonstrating the linkages between important individuals and ritual performance during the Preclassic. Although a Late Preclassic E Group was erected at Actuncan (Simova et al. 2018; Simova and Mixter 2015), multiple E Groups have been documented at other Preclassic sites such as Yaxnohcah (Reese-Taylor 2017).

Materials excavated from Structure F1 provide further evidence of increasing complexity and inequality at the end of the Late Preclassic, including direct ties between the platform and important sociopolitical institutions. Within the fill of Structure F1–1st, excavations uncovered two small bowls placed lip to lip. This Late Preclassic cache contained two small, greenstone effigies, often called bib-and-helmet pendants (figure 8.7). Similar effigies have been documented across the lowlands (Rawski 2020), perhaps most famously at the site of Cerros in northern Belize. There, David Freidel and colleagues uncovered a cache containing greenstone pendants of this style that they argue were likely royal diadem jewels worn on the headband of a Late Preclassic king (Freidel and Schele 1988). Freidel and Schele (1988) suggest that these types of jewels are kingly adornments that were intimately linked to the institution of *ajaw*.

The smaller of the two effigies closely resembles the greenstone diadem jewels discovered at Cerros. Furthermore, this effigy exhibits the same tripartite helmet that Freidel and Schele argue is diagnostic of early Jester God iconography (1988). The Jester God is closely associated with kingship throughout the Preclassic and Classic periods. The second effigy from the cache is stylistically distinct from the first, as it appears to have been created by an artist engaging heavily with the Middle Formative Ceremonial Complex (David Freidel, personal communication 2015). This style closely resembles the jade pectoral found in the same cache as the Jester God diadem jewels at Cerros (Freidel and Schele 1988). As this second effigy was heavily worn, it may represent an heirloom piece. However, it is also plausible that this diadem jewel may represent an artisan attempting to duplicate earlier artistic traditions.

This cache provides important evidence of the presence of kingship at Early Xunantunich, placing it within a wider regional pattern of sociopolitical complexification in the Late Preclassic. As caches such as this would likely have been interred in ritual spectacles, the placement of this cache further demonstrates the correlation between kingly performance at Early Xunantunich and this monumental northern platform. Through reconstruction over time, this place remained central to the maintenance of sociopolitical institutions that were becoming increasingly ideologically entrenched.

It is likely that whatever individual was associated with these diadem jewels was also associated with the platform's construction, either sponsoring its construction or as the subject of its reverence (most likely the former). These kingly symbols were found in association with the platform's latest architectural phase, F1–1st, suggesting that the institution of kingship was likely well-established at Early Xunantunich by the Late Preclassic period. It is also important to note that the formal burial chamber, discussed above (Brown et al. 2013; Brown 2017), was placed within the Late Preclassic phase, Structure E-2–1st. It is not likely a coincidence that kingly diadem jewels were placed as an offering to the northern platform during the same period as the first formal burial chamber was constructed within the eastern structure of the E Group.

Furthermore, the direct association of an individual with the construction of monumental ceremonial architecture links them directly the religious institutions of the time, a potent way to consolidate power (Aldenderfer 2010). By the Late Preclassic, religious institutions placed greater emphasis on exalted individuals than was seen during the Middle Preclassic period. This shift is evidenced at Early Xunantunich by the burial in Structure E-2, in addition to the Structure F1 cache (Brown 2017; Rawski 2020).

Though individuals are not typically interred within public architecture in the Middle Preclassic, patterns documented across the Maya Lowlands suggest that by the Late Preclassic, certain individuals received such special burial locations, including within ceremonial structures. Although caches and offerings consecrated early domestic architecture, during the Late Preclassic period we begin to see similar types of offerings, albeit more elaborate, placed beneath stairs and floors of ceremonial buildings as well (Brown 2003). The ritual placement of these offerings and caches in ceremonial buildings suggest direct affiliations with important individuals as seen in the Late Preclassic Structure F1 lip-to-lip cache with carved jade heads that likely represent kingly diadem jewels. Furthermore, the widespread presence across the lowlands in the Late Preclassic of greenstone diadem jewels similar to those documented in the cache demonstrates that the cache is part of a much larger Late Preclassic ritual economy and shared symbol system (Rawski 2020).

SUMMARY AND DISCUSSION

Research at Early Xunantunich is ongoing, and each field season yields exciting new data that help us to better understand the development of sociopolitical complexity and inequality at the site. It appears that the modification of the natural landscape and construction of monumental ceremonial centers may have played a major role in these processes.

The earliest inhabitants of Early Xunantunich initiated a large-scale building program that sculpted the natural landscape to fit their needs. This began with the leveling of the preceramic paleosol and the modification of natural bedrock outcrops that formed the foundation of the ceremonial center. This effort, monumental in its own right, literally laid the foundations of the construction program to come. The process would have had a nucleating effect on disparate community members, who may have been maintaining relatively mobile lifeways at the beginning of the Preclassic (Inomata et al. 2015). The simple act of formalizing a space for community members to gather would have promoted such gatherings, which likely served a combination of religious, social, political, and economic purposes.

Once these early large-scale modifications were complete, Early Xunantunich built up, constructing an E Group complex and likely other ritual structures, including an early phase of the monumental northern platform. The widespread presence of the E Group complex across the Maya Lowlands during this time suggests that integrative, communal ritual celebrating cycles of time and other natural events took precedence in ceremonial centers (Freidel et al. 2017). Thus, veneration of the natural world was likely more important than the veneration of individuals in the Middle Preclassic period, a common pattern seen in early societies (Buikstra and Charles 1999; Durkheim 1912).

These construction efforts would have required the specialized skills of myriad individuals, from masons and architects to stucco artisans and other construction specialists. At Structure E-2, the earliest phases demonstrate a clear mastery of the construction materials, suggesting that these construction practices were already deeply ingrained in the community by the Middle Preclassic. Later, in the late Middle Preclassic, the earliest documented phase of Structure F1 was constructed using a unique local masonry technique documented only in the Mopan Valley. This unique architectural style suggests that the builders of Early Xunantunich were simultaneously bringing together and integrating their own community while differentiating themselves from other polities in the region.

Throughout the Middle and Late Preclassic, these buildings were repaired, rebuilt, and elaborated upon. In some cases, such as at Structure F1, there is a clear effort to significantly increase the visual impact of the ceremonial center on the regional landscape. Again, this would provide a symbol of community to those who were a part of the Early Xunantunich polity.

To date, evidence of divine kingship and clear crystallized sociopolitical hierarchies is lacking for the Middle Preclassic of Early Xunantunich's history, as it is across the lowlands. Middle Preclassic ceremonial buildings typically lack burials or caches. However, there is documented evidence of strategically placed burials within E Group plazas, including at Early Xunantunich, Chan, and Las Ruinas de Arenal, suggesting some emerging social distinctions at this time (Brown et al. 2018). Certainly, the presence of marine shell, decorated pottery, obsidian, and other long-distance exchange goods suggests that Early Xunantunich was already part of an increasingly complex regional network. Additional comparisons of Middle Preclassic households to the site's ceremonial center would contribute greatly to this discussion, but with the data available, it appears that a hierarchical social system was only in the beginning stages of formation.

Rather, these institutions appear to emerge toward the end of Early Xunantunich's fluorescence in the Late Preclassic, as the presence of possible kingly jewels and the internment of an elite individual in a public building are associated with the later phases of these structures. The probable connection between an elite individual (or individuals) and the Late Preclassic monumental architectural program at the site suggests that the dominant sociopolitical institutions of the era utilized architecture to legitimize their emergent role in the community. Be it through the sponsoring of the construction effort itself, the performance of important rituals within the ceremonial center, or likely both, the connection between early emergent rulership and monumentality is clear.

The eventual abandonment of the center may be indicative of political cycling. However, if Actuncan is indeed a ritual node of the same community as Early Xunantunich, this shift may instead reflect changing ritual practices that supported and legitimized the institution of kingship (Brown and Yaeger 2020; Rawski 2020; Saturno et al. 2018). Religious institutions in the Late Preclassic shift from the Middle Preclassic, placing greater emphasis on exalted individuals. Eventually, the E Group complex is eschewed in favor of Triadic architecture, which has clear associations with royal power (Saturno et al. 2018). The veneration of individuals is often evidenced by elaborate mortuary traditions, and by the Classic period, ties to ancestral cults helped rulers to achieve and maintain social status, as evidenced by the presence of royal tombs and burials in many pyramidal temples (McAnany 1995, 2010). We argue that the elite burial within Structure E-2 is an early example of this increasingly elaborate tradition, by which ancestors and deities become an important additional focus of ritual activity.

These patterns demonstrate that monumental architectural programs and the development of complexity are intricately linked. By investigating this relationship and exploring how landscape modification, monumental architecture, and changing forms of ritual performance would have crafted communities and social roles and identities, we can begin to shed light on early social and political developments that paved the way for institutions such as divine kingship.

REFERENCES

Aldenderfer, Mark. 2010. "Gimme That Old Time Religion: Rethinking the Role of Religion in the Emergence of Social Inequality." In *Pathways to Power*, edited by T. Douglas Price and Gary M. Feinman, 77–94. New York: Springer.

Blanton, Richard E., Gary M. Feinman, Stephen A. Kowalewski, and Peter N. Peregrine. 1996. "A Dual-Processual Theory for the Evolution of Mesoamerican Civilization." *Current Anthropology* 37 (1): 1–14.

Brown, M. Kathryn. 2003. "Emerging Complexity in the Maya Lowlands: A View from Blackman Eddy, Belize." PhD diss., Southern Methodist University, Dallas.

Brown, M. Kathryn. 2017. "E Groups and Ancestors: The Sunrise of Complexity at Xunantunich, Belize." In *Maya E Groups: Calendars, Astronomy, and Urbanism in the Early Lowlands*, edited by David A. Freidel and Arlen F. Chase, 386–411. Gainesville: University Press of Florida.

Brown, M. Kathryn, Jaime J. Awe, and James F. Garber. 2018. "The Role of Ideology, Religion, and Ritual in the Foundation of Social Complexity in the Belize River Valley." In *Pathways to Complexity: A View from the Maya Lowlands*, edited by M. Kathryn Brown and George J. Bey III, 87–116. Gainesville: University Press of Florida.

Brown, M. Kathryn, Jennifer Cochran, Leah McCurdy, and David Mixter. 2011. "Pre-ceramic to Postclassic: A Brief Synthesis of the Occupation History of Group E, Xunantunich." In *Research Reports in Belizean Archaeology* 8:209–19. Belmopan: Belize Institute of Archaeology.

Brown, M. Kathryn, and James F. Garber. 2008. "Establishing and Re-using Sacred Space: A Diachronic Perspective from Blackman Eddy, Belize." In *Ruins of the Past: The Use and Perception of Abandoned Structures in the Maya Lowlands*, edited by Travis W. Stanton and Aline Magnoni, 147–70. Boulder: University Press of Colorado.

Brown, M. Kathryn, Whitney Lytle, Zoë Rawski, Victoria Ingalls, and Alessandra Vil-larreal. 2017. "Understanding the Preclassic Ritual Landscape in the Mopan Valley: A View from Early Xunantunich." In *Research Reports in Belizean Archaeology*, edited by John Morris, Melissa Badillo, Sylvia Batty, and George Thompson, 53–64. Vol. 14. Bel-mopan: Belize Institute of Archaeology.

Brown, M. Kathryn, Leah McCurdy, Whitney Lytle, and Thomas Chapman. 2013. "Recent Investigations of the Mopan Valley Preclassic Project at Xunantunich, Belize." In *Research Reports in Belizean Archaeology* 10:137–46.

Brown, M. Kathryn, and Jason Yaeger. 2020. "Monumental Landscapes, Changing Ideologies, and Political Histories in the Mopan Valley." In *Approaches to Monumental Landscapes of the Ancient Maya*, edited by Brett A. Houk, Bárbara Arroyo, and Terry G. Powis, 290–312. Gainesville: University Press of Florida.

Brown, M. Kathryn, Jason Yaeger, and Bernadette Cap. 2016. "A Tale of Two Cities: LiDAR Survey and New Discoveries at Xunantunich." *Research Reports in Belizean Archaeology* 13:51–60.

Brumfiel, Elizabeth M., and John W. Fox, eds. 2003. *Factional Competition and Political Development in the New World*. Cambridge, UK: Cambridge University Press.

Buikstra, Jane E., and Douglas K. Charles. 1999. "Centering the Ancestors: Cemeteries, Mounds, and Sacred Landscapes of the North American Midcontinent." In *Archaeolo-gies of Landscape: Contemporary Perspectives*, edited by Wendy Ashmore and Arthur Bernard Knapp, 201–28. Malden, MA: Blackwell.

Crumley, Carole L. 1995. "Heterarchy and the Analysis of Complex Societies." *Archaeo-logical Papers of the American Anthropological Association* 6 (1): 1–5.

Demarest, Arthur. 1992. "Ideology in Ancient Maya Cultural Evolution: The Dynam-ics of Galactic Polities." In *Ideology and Pre-Columbian Civilizations*, edited by Arthur Andrew Demarest and Geoffrey W. Conrad, 135–58. Santa Fe, NM: School of Ameri-can Research.

Dietrich, Oliver, Manfred Heun, Jens Notroff, Klaus Schmidt, and Martin Zarnkow. 2012. "The Role of Cult and Feasting in the Emergence of Neolithic Communities. New Evidence from Göbekli Tepe, South-Eastern Turkey." *Antiquity* 86 (333): 674–95.

Doyle, James A. 2017. *Architecture and the Origins of Preclassic Maya Politics*. Cambridge, UK: Cambridge University Press.

Durkheim, Émile. 1912. *The Elementary Forms of Religious Life*. Translated by Carol Cosman and Mark Sydney Cladis. Oxford: Oxford University Press.

Estrada-Belli, Francisco. 2011. *The First Maya Civilization: Ritual and Power before the Classic Period*. New York: Routledge.

Estrada-Belli, Francisco. 2012. "Early Civilization in the Maya Lowlands, Monumentality, and Place Making: A View from the Holmul Region." In *Early New World Monumentality*, edited by Robert M. Rosenswig and Richard L. Burger, 198–230. Gainesville: University Press of Florida.

Freidel, David A., Arlen F. Chase, Anne S. Dowd, and Jerry Murdock, eds. 2017. *Early Maya E-Groups, Solar Calendars, and the Role of Astronomy in the Rise of Lowland Maya Urbanism*. Gainesville: University of Florida Press.

Freidel, David A., and Robin A. Robertson, eds. 1986. *Archaeology at Cerros, Belize, Central America*. Dallas, TX: Southern Methodist University Press.

Freidel, David, Robin Robertson, and Maynard B. Cliff. 1982. "The Maya City of Cerros." *Archaeology* 35 (4): 12–21.

Freidel, David A., and Linda Schele. 1988. "Kingship in the Late Preclassic Maya Lowlands: The Instruments and Places of Ritual Power." *American Anthropologist* 90 (3): 547–67.

Geertz, Clifford. 1980. *Negara: The Theatre State in Nineteenth-Century Bali*. Princeton, NJ: Princeton University Press.

Gibson, Jon L. 2004. "The Power of Beneficent Obligation in the First Mound Building Societies." In *Signs of Power: The Rise of Cultural Complexity in the Southeast*, edited by Jon L. Gibson and Philip J. Carr, 254–69. Tuscaloosa: University of Alabama Press.

Grube, Nikolai, and James McGovern. 1995. "A Preclassic Stela from Actuncan, Cayo District, Belize." Paper presented at the 60th Annual Meeting of the Society for American Archaeology, Minneapolis, MN.

Inomata, Takeshi, and Lawrence S. Coben, eds. 2006. *Archaeology of Performance: Theaters of Power, Community, and Politics*. Lanham, MD: Altamira Press.

Inomata, Takeshi, Jessica MacLellan, Daniela Triadan, Jessica Munson, Melissa Burham, Kazuo Aoyama, Hiroo Nasu, Flory Pinzón, and Hitoshi Yonenobu. 2015. "The Development of Sedentary Communities in the Maya Lowlands: Co-existing Mobile Groups and Public Ceremonies at Ceibal, Guatemala." *PNAS* 112 (14): 4268–73.

Inomata, Takeshi, Daniela Triadan, Kazuo Aoyama, Victor Castillo, and Hitoshi Yonenobu. 2013. "Early Ceremonial Constructions at Ceibal, Guatemala, and the Origins of Lowland Maya Civilization." *Science* 340:467–71.

Inomata, Takeshi, Daniela Triadan, Verónica A. Vázquez López, Juan Carlos Fernandez-Diaz, Takayuki Omori, María Belén Méndez Bauer, Melina García Hernández, et al. 2020. "Monumental Architecture at Aguada Fénix and the Rise of Maya Civilization." *Nature* 582:530–33.

Joyce, Rosemary A. 2004. "Unintended Consequences? Monumentality as a Novel Experience in Formative Mesoamerica." *Journal of Archaeological Method and Theory* 11 (1): 5–29.

LeCount, Lisa. 2013. *The Actuncan Archaeological Project: Report of the Fifth Field Season in 2012*. Belmopan: Belize Institute of Archaeology.

LeCount, Lisa. 2004. "Looking for a Needle in a Haystack: The Early Classic Period at Actuncan, Cayo District." In *Research Reports in Belizean Archaeology* 1:27–36. Belmopan: Belize Institute of Archaeology.

McAnany, Patricia A. 1995. *Living with the Ancestors: Kinship and Kingship in Ancient Maya Society*. Austin: University of Texas Press.

McAnany, Patricia A. 2010. *Ancestral Maya economies in archaeological perspective*. Cambridge, UK: Cambridge University Press.

McCurdy, Leah. 2016. "Building Xunantunich: Public Building in an Ancient Maya Community." PhD diss., University of Texas, San Antonio.

McGovern, James O. 2004. "Monumental Ceremonial Architecture and Political Autonomy at the Ancient Maya City of Actuncan, Belize." PhD diss. University of California, Los Angeles.

McGuire, Randall H. 1983. "Breaking Down Cultural Complexity: Inequality and Heterogeneity." *Advances in Archaeological Method and Theory* 6:91–142.

Rathje, William L. 2002. "The Nouveau Elite Potlatch: One Scenario for the Monumental Rise of Early Civilizations." In *Ancient Maya Political Economies*, edited by Marilyn A. Masson and David A. Freidel, 31–40. Lanham, MD: Altamira Press.

Rawski, Zoe J. 2019. "Naturalizing Authority: Sociopolitical Inequality and the Construction of Monumental Architecture at Early Xunantunich, Belize." Paper presented at the 84th Annual Meeting of the Society for American Archaeology, Albuquerque, NM.

Rawski, Zoe J. 2020. "Constructing Power in the Preclassic: Monumental Architecture and Sociopolitical Inequality at Early Xunantunich, Belize." PhD diss., University of Texas, San Antonio.

Reese-Taylor, Kathryn. 1996. "Narratives of Power: Late Formative Public Architecture and Civic Center Design at Cerros, Belize." PhD diss., University of Texas, Austin.

Reese-Taylor, Kathryn. 2017. "Founding Landscapes in the Central Karstic Uplands." In *E Groups, Solar Calendars, and the Role of Astronomy in the Rise of Lowland Urbanism*, edited by David A. Freidel, Arlen F. Chase, Anne S. Dowd, and Jerry Murdock, 480–514. Gainesville: University Press of Florida.

Robin, Cynthia, L. Theodore Neff, Jennifer J. Ehret, John Walkey, and Clarence H. Gifford. 1994. "Early Monumental Construction at Xunantunich: Preliminary Investigations of Group E and O/A2–1." In *Xunantunich Archaeological Project: 1994 Field Season*. University of California, Los Angeles.

Saturno, William, Franco D. Rossi, and Boris Beltrán. 2018. "Changing Stages: Royal Legitimacy and the Architectural Development of the Pinturas Complex at San Bartolo, Guatemala." In *Pathways to Complexity: A View from the Maya Lowlands*, edited by M. Kathryn Brown and George J. Bey III, 315–35. Gainesville: University Press of Florida.

Schmidt, Klaus. 2000. "Göbekli Tepe, Southeastern Turkey: A Preliminary Report on the 1995–1999 Excavations." *Paléorient* 26, no. 1 (2000): 45–54.

Simova, Borislava, and David W Mixter. 2015. "On-Going Excavations at Structure 26 in Actuncan's E-Group." In *Actuncan Archaeological Project: Report of the Eighth Season*, edited by Lisa J. LeCount and David W Mixter, 9–39. Report submitted to the Belize Institute of Archaeology, Belmopan.

Simova, Borislava, David W. Mixter, and Lisa J. LeCount. 2015. "The Social Lives of Structures: Ritual Resignification of the Cultural Landscapes at Actuncan, Belize." In *Research Reports in Belizean Archaeology* 12:193–204. Belmopan: Belize Institute of Archaeology.

Simova, Borislava, E. Christian Wells, David W. Mixter, and Lisa LeCount. 2018. "Exploring Changes in Activities in Maya E-Groups: Archaeological and Geochemical Analysis of E-Group Plaster Floors at Actuncan, Belize." *Research Reports in Belizean Archaeology* 15: 27–37. Belmopan: Belize Institute of Archaeology.

Villarreal, Alessandra. 2018. "Preclassic Maya Ceramic Production and Distribution: Preliminary Petrographic Analysis from the Mopan Valley, Belize." Paper presented at the 83rd Annual Meeting of the Society for American Archaeology, Washington, DC.

Yaeger, Jason. 2000. "Changing Patterns of Social Organization: The Late and Terminal Classic Communities at San Lorenzo, Cayo District, Belize." PhD diss., University of Pennsylvania.

Yaeger, Jason, M. Kathryn Brown, and Bernadette Cap. 2016. "Locating and Dating Sites Using Lidar Survey in a Mosaic Landscape in Western Belize." *Advances in Archaeological Practice* 4 (3): 339–56. doi:10.7183/2326-3768.4.3.339.

Yoffee, Norman. 2005. *Myths of the Archaic State: Evolution of the Earliest Cities, States, and Civilizations*. Cambridge, UK: Cambridge University Press.

9

The Complexity of Figurines

Ancestor Veneration at Cahal Pech, Cayo, Belize

LISA DELANCE AND JAIME J. AWE

WHY COMPLEXITY?

One of the long-standing concerns in archaeology is understanding the emergence and growth of complex, hierarchically organized social systems. In 2014, Kintigh and colleagues identified the emergence of social complexity as one of the major challenges for archaeological research (Kintigh et al. 2014). Nevertheless, there is relatively little agreement on what actually constitutes social complexity and how social complexity is reflected in artifactual patterns.

For Marcello Canuto (2016, 467), any theory on the rise of complexity (among the Maya) should explain how social practices developed in smaller communities and how those social practices contributed to the development of ideologies involving hereditary inequality and the divine rulership that came to characterize many of the Maya polities in the Classic period. Complexity is not solely a matter of economics; rather, it is the result of individuals (or entrepreneurs) who actively created conditions in which other members of society were indebted to others through systems of obligation, fealty, and competition. It is the interplay of these conditions that contributes to the rise of complexity. Essentially,

https://doi.org/10.5876/9781646422883.c009

complexity rests in the hands of individuals actively manipulating not only their physical environment but also their social environment. These individuals are active agents, "with competencies in highly specialized practices that are themselves learned and therefore to be regarded as products rather than as innate individual capabilities" (Canuto 2016, 467–68).

King (2016, 448–49) defines complex societies as constituted of "differentiated and interrelated parts, integrated into a socio-political unit governed by a hierarchy of authority such that different roles in a society are differentially valued and status is ascribed rather than achieved." Although King bases her discussion in the context of the ancient Maya, she makes two critical points that are vital to the understanding of complexity. First, the economic conditions in Mesoamerica were highly variable, thus making any economic considerations of complexity necessarily different in different regions. The roots of social differentiation are complicated and differ from place to place and region to region. This leads to a second critical point, namely that the archaeological evidence indicates that different "constellations of factors" were involved at different sites during different times. Simply put, because of the variability in environment, in available resources, and the human agentic factor, we see that "people made economic and other choices, and they made them repeatedly" (King 2016, 449).

Foias (2013) advocates a hierarchical form of leadership in complex societies from those who advocate for heterarchical relationships. Directly confronting the tensions between hierarchy and heterarchy, Foias (2013, 5) suggest that "the reality of the past is that systems were predominately neither hierarchical nor equal, the truth lies somewhere in between, depending on local circumstances and historical contingencies." Taking an agentive approach, Foias contends that material culture is in itself a series of discourses that are the products of the accumulation of decisions and actions of individuals within their communities. Complexity can be seen not simply in power structures but in the dynamic materials left behind by peoples. The challenge then is to interpret material culture not as "pale reflections of political, social, economic, and religious structures" but as dynamic and active material traces through which power and authority were used and mobilized in a variety of ways, forms, and for a variety of motives (Foias 2013).

David Carballo (2012) calls attention to the importance of the dynamics of collective action and cooperation in our conceptions of social complexity. Is social complexity the result of competition between individuals and groups, or is it the result of collective action of individual community members? It is notoriously difficult to understand motive in the archaeological record, because motive is not simply self-interest but is based on multiple and often overlapping interests (Carballo 2012, 110). Simply put, there are many different forms and scales of cooperation and overlapping interests. It is also important to note, however, that cooperation and competition play out differently depending on the size of the community (Carballo 2012, 114–15). This is not to advocate that a simple cost/benefit analysis be applied to archaeological data but rather to promote an understanding that human beings, even those within the same social group, may have different interests and motivations for pursuing a particular course of action, and those interests may connect or conflict with the interests of other group members. For Carballo, social complexity can be most directly seen when we examine the archaeological evidence in light of the negotiations that both individuals and groups made in order to achieve their goals.

Complexity as Process

Complexity is variably influenced by individual agents within the community, networks of interpersonal and intergroup relationships, and the ability and willingness of communities to recursively adapt and develop political, social, economic, ideological, and environmental conditions. In this sense, complexity is not a state to arrive at but a fluid process that is crafted by individuals and social groups in a variety of circumstances, in a variety of ways, and in a variety of environments.

What makes complexity particularly difficult to define as a concept is the fact that a social group may have any number of components interacting in a number of different ways to produce unique "flavors" of complexity. The variability in these flavors of complexity is sufficiently broad that there is no definitive list, nor can there be, of complex societies or specific features that all complex societies should have (Lesure and Blake 2002). As Hepp notes (this volume), social complexity should not be exclusively thought of as unequal hierarchical relationships reflecting either ascribed or inherited status, or both. Indeed, this calls attention to the concept of heterarchy, that is, that interpersonal and intergroup relationships were multidimensional, recursive, and subject to ongoing negotiation (Carballo et al. 2012; Crumley 1995, 2004).

Because complexity is a process, one that is crafted in unique ways based on a number of factors—including (but certainly not limited to) individual and group agency, the intersection of both hierarchical and heterarchical relationships, environmental constraints, and intra- and inter-group relationships—we may not find consistent features common to all complex societies. Social organization in Mesoamerica involved interpersonal relationships between individuals and between groups. While certain facets of complexity may never be visible to archaeologists (e.g., individual motivation), we can explore changes in the use and deposition of certain types of material culture to elucidate changes to the larger social order.

This chapter examines the use and deposition of ceramic figurines and their implications for exploring social change and the development of complexity at the ancient Maya polity of Cahal Pech, Belize. Ceramic figurines have been found in the earliest stratigraphic levels of Cahal Pech, recovered in multiple contexts from burials to construction fill to middens, through the end of the site's over two thousand years of occupation. Ceramic figurines at Cahal Pech are associated with the smallest, most meager house mounds and the largest temples and elaborate burials, but they appear in different frequencies through time and between contexts. Figurines, then, appear to be one of a very few classes of artifacts that were used by people from all walks of life, and as such, they make an excellent proxy for exploring issues of emergent/changing social complexity. In particular, we focus on the corpus of Preclassic period (1200/1100 BCE—300 CE) figurine fragments from the site in an attempt to ascertain changes in the use and deposition of figurines during a critical transition when social, political, and economic inequality were increasing across the Maya Lowlands. The evolution of complexity during the approximately 1,150 years of Preclassic occupation at Cahal Pech may be understood, in part, by exploring the changing uses, treatment, and deposition of figurines as a medium or tool of ancestral veneration and group identity within the community.

FIGURINES IN MESOAMERICA

Over the past century, archaeological excavations in the Maya Lowlands have yielded thousands ceramic figurines. The abundance of figurines at most lowlands sites provide us with clues as to how the ancient Maya conceptualized human, supernatural, and animal bodies while also providing avenues of investigation related to social status and inequality (Gillespie 2000; Grove and Gillespie 1984, 1992; Halperin 2009, 2014), political machinations (Brumfiel 1996), ritual ancestor worship (see below), and trade (Halperin 2007), among others.

Research on Mesoamerican figurine use generally considers figurines to be an implement of ancestor veneration rituals (Blomster 2009; Flannery and Marcus 2005; Hepp et al. 2014; Hepp and Joyce 2013; Joyce 2000, 2009; Marcus 1998). Recognizing and honoring ancestral connections was a significant component of ancient Maya social life (Ashmore 2015; Ensor 2013; Hendon et al, 2014; McAnany 2013; Novotny 2015). From household rituals (Marcus 1998) to elaborate burials (Novotny 2015), from public monuments (Miller 1999) to small scale iconography (Taube and Tabue 2009), the Maya left a wide variety of evidence elucidating the importance of ancestral links to a larger, cyclical Maya worldview. Given the importance of ancestral relationships to the proper functioning of everyday life, it is quite possible (even likely) that the Maya honored these connections in a multitude of ways, in both public and private spheres and in groups and individually. These connections could be manipulated by state actors (Halperin 2014; Peniche May 2016; Peniche May et al. 2018), kin groups (DeLance 2016; Peniche May 2016), and/or individuals (DeLance 2016; Marcus 1998) to further specific goals related to the survival and prosperity of communities. The connection between these small, portable, generally handheld artifacts (found in abundance at many sites) to ancestral practice illuminates the importance of consistent engagement with forebearers. The depth and level of social practices connecting ancestors to figurines is fairly broad and may have had variations on the regional, local, household, and individual levels.

Awe (1992) discusses the use of figurines at Cahal Pech as a medium for ancestor veneration and animation. The connection between figurines and ancestral connections is supported by multiple lines of evidence at Cahal Pech, including the repurposing of Middle Preclassic figurines for use in Classic period dedicatory caches (Awe 1992, 274–75), the use of Preclassic figurine fragments in Classic burials (Awe 1992, 334–38), and in conjunction with non-residential, publicly accessible structures (Awe 1992, 284–86). Most convincingly, the connections between figurine fragments and cyclical connections with the past at Cahal Pech may be understood by exploring a Terminal Classic (750–850 CE) structure at the site. Terminal Classic construction occurred only in the eastern portion of the site, in Plazas C and H, where final residents of Cahal Pech undertook a large construction project renovating all buildings bordering Plaza H (Douglas et al. 2015, 219). The stones used in this construction were taken from nearby administrative structures that had fallen into disrepair by the Terminal Classic. The reuse of construction material is common, however, what is uncommonly significant about the Terminal Classic Plaza H construction is that the Formative Period construction fill, including pot sherds and figurine fragments, was also transposed from the administrative buildings (DeLance 2016; Douglas et al. 2015). The builders of Plaza H, then, took not only stone building materials from earlier constructions; they took with them the construction fill containing Middle Preclassic figurine fragments. These figurine fragments were then interred within the Terminal Classic structure, further highlighting the links between figurine fragments and notions of multigenerational continuity.

While none of this is prima facie evidence of ancestor veneration alone, taken together, different lines of evidence at Cahal Pech seem to support the idea that figurines supported a multigenerational continuity within the community and suggest that figurines were, at least in part, related to the creation and maintenance of ancestral ties. This idea is commonly expressed among Mesoamerican archaeologists and has merit in ethnoarchaeological studies showing that even today, many Indigenous Maya still practice forms of ancestor veneration and utilize figural images, a phenomenon that lends additional weight to assertions of ancestor veneration in the ancient past (Molesky-Poz 2006; Smith 2002).

Joyce Marcus (1998, 2009) regards figurines as the domain of women's ritual connected to ancestor veneration in Formative Period Oaxaca. Marcus draws on comparisons of ethnographic evidence from China, Japan, and several West African communities that not only practice forms of ancestor worship, but also use figurines to do so, an assertion that strengthens the argument for figurine use for ancestor worship in the ancient Maya case. Figurines, in Marcus's assessment, were embodied spirits of ancestors that needed to be maintained at the household level to ensure proper maintenance and functioning.

Grove and Gillespie (1984), in their analysis of figurines from the site of Chalcatzingo (see also Cyphers-Guillén 1993), argue that figurines may represent portraits of rulers and thus were tied directly to ancestor cults. While this assertion has merit at Chalcatzingo, evidence for ruler portraiture on figurines is not consistent across Maya sites. For example, the vast majority of Formative Period figurines at Cahal Pech illustrate very similar features (an extensive overbite), but to date, none of the dozens of human remains recovered at the site have shown the presence of an overbite. While absence of evidence is not evidence of absence, it does require us to consider that figurines, at least at Cahal Pech, may not be a form of ruler portraiture.

Likewise, fertility fetish explanations have been suggested for some localized groups of Mesoamerican figurines (Grove and Gillespie 1984). Fertility-based arguments are difficult to make on a broad scale due to general Mesoamerican stylistic conventions against displaying detailed sexual characteristics directly on figurines. Within the Cahal Pech figurine corpus, primary sex characteristics are universally absent. Additionally, the assignation of secondary sex characteristics is ambiguous in many (although not all) cases. Absent evidence of biological sex on figurines, any fertility-based explanation for the presence of Preclassic figurines at Cahal Pech is speculation at best.

As the three brief examples discussed above demonstrate, archaeological research in Mesoamerica has established that figurines are associated with multiple contexts and, potentially, a vast array of ritual practice associated with ancestral veneration. Although fertility fetish and ruler portraiture explanations may be applicable to localized figurine traditions (Cyphers-Guillén 1993; Grove and Gillespie 1984), multiple lines of evidence indicate that the Preclassic figurines from Cahal Pech were likely associated with ancestral connections and multigenerational continuity. Figurines have been found to be associated with nearly every socioeconomic status group, from the most elite palaces and burials to the humblest house mounds (DeLance 2016). They were used in abundance, discarded, and in some cases reused multiple generations later. The citizens of Cahal Pech, then, were using figurines in ways that seem to honor those who came before, to recognize the cyclical nature of life, and in celebration of the continuity of past, present, and future.

CAHAL PECH

The hilltop that would eventually become the site core of Cahal Pech was initially settled in the Early Preclassic period circa 1200/1100 cal BCE and was continuously occupied until the Terminal Classic period (ca. 850 CE). The nearly

TABLE 9.1. Formative period chronology of Cahal Pech.

Year Range	Period	Ceramic Phase
1200/1100–900 BCE	Early Preclassic	Cunil Phase
900 BCE–300 BCE	Middle Preclassic	Kanluk Phase
300 BCE–3000 CE	Late Preclassic	Xakal Phase

two thousand years of continuous cultural history and development at the site allows archaeologists to explore diachronic political, social, and technological change. While this chapter focuses specifically on changing figurine use and deposition over the duration of the Preclassic, it is important to note that political, social, and technological change is evident at the Cahal Pech site core in a number of ways, including increasingly monumental and privatized architecture (Awe 1992), increasing differential status reflected in burials (Awe 1992), and increasing flow of goods throughout the Maya Lowlands (Horn 2015).

The earliest architectural evidence for occupation at Cahal Pech is found in the southeast portion of what became the site core (figure 9.1), where an apsidal structure, Str. B4-sub 13, supported a wattle and daub structure (Healy et al. 2004, 107). During the Early Preclassic, Structure B4 underwent five distinct construction episodes, 2σ calibrated (95.4% confidence) radiocarbon dating of materials recovered from construction fill showing the five episodes as taking place at various time spans between 1275 cal BCE and 795, associated with the Cunil ceramic phase (Ebert et al. 2017; Healy et al. 2004, 106). Evidence of Cunil phase occupation also occurs elsewhere in Plaza B, where Cheetham (1995, 20) located as many as four distinct residential units (Healy et al. 2004, 108). Awe (1992) noted that Cunil phase dwellings have been found on either slightly raised, tamped marl floors or on house platforms. Dwellings themselves were constructed of wattle and daub and had thatched roofs (Awe 1992; Horn 2015; Peniche May 2016). Excavations have also uncovered daub fragments from these earliest dwelling containing a red pigment, so it is probable that some of these early wattle and daub structures were painted (Awe 1992, 345–46).

Some Cunil phase structures were also associated with ritual caches which contained jadeite mosaic pieces, obsidian, marine shell, chert, and drilled pendants made of animal bone (Awe 1992; Healy et al. 2004, 121; Porter 2020). Although some ceramic figurines have been found associated with the Cunil phase at Cahal Pech, they are not as common at the site as they are in later Middle Preclassic contexts (Awe 1992, 346).

From the initial sedentary occupation of the site, the residents of Cahal Pech were likely engaged in long-distance trade. This is evidenced by the presence of obsidian from highland Guatemala and marine shell resources from the Caribbean present at very early stratigraphic levels (Awe 1992, 346–47; Ebert

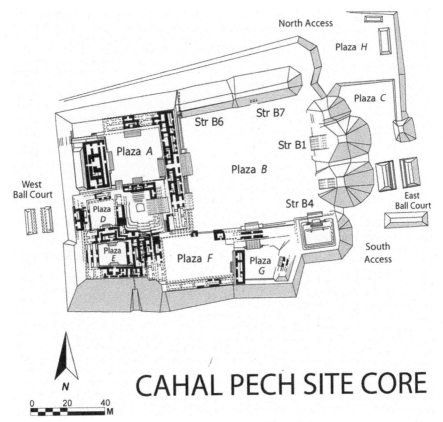

Plaza H

North Access

Plaza C

Str B7

Str B6

Str B1

Plaza A

Plaza B

West
Ball Court

Str B4

East
Ball Court

Plaza
D

Plaza
E

Plaza F

Plaza
G

South
Access

N

0   20   40
M

CAHAL PECH SITE CORE

FIGURE 9.1. *Map of the Cahal Pech site core. (Courtesy of Jaime J. Awe.)*

2017). The end of the Cunil phase is generally marked by the end of the residential occupation of Structure B4 and its initial renovation for use as a public building (Healy et al. 2004, 107).

The Middle Formative period in Mesoamerica is believed to be a time of increasing growth of social complexity throughout the Maya Lowlands, and Cahal Pech is certainly no exception. Several trends are evident in the archaeological record of the upper Belize River Valley broadly, and Cahal Pech in particular, including population increases (Awe 1992; Ford 1990; Ford and Fedick 1992), the construction of monumental architecture (Awe 1992; Estrada-Belli 2011; Hansen 1998; Inomata et al. 2015; Peniche May 2016), the development of visible social inequality (Awe 1992; Ebert 2017), along with increasing long-distance trade (Awe 1992; Hammond 1991; Hohmann 2002; Horn 2015). Not only do these trends first appear clearly in the archaeological record during the Middle Formative period, but they became widespread relatively quickly across the Maya Lowlands (Horn

2015). This is evident in new forms of pottery that emerged during this time. Beginning in the early Middle Formative, new pottery styles across the Maya Lowlands indicate both increasing interaction between communities, especially in the exchange of Mars Orange finewares between the Petén and the Belize Valley (Ebert et al. 2019).

In his research on Middle Formative spheres of interaction in the Belize River Valley, Horn suggests that these networks of interaction were a critical component to the development of social complexity, particularly as participation in these interaction spheres "drove the increasing social differentiation in the Middle Formative record" (Horn 2015, 73–74). Furthermore, Middle Formative communities in the Belize River Valley were, per Horn, "loosely organized networks of households or corporate groups that are interconnected by economic, kinship, political, and other special relationships" (Horn 2015, 88–89). Horn further cites variability of exotic goods found within different residential groups as indicative of unequal participation in these spheres of interaction with other communities and suggests that participation in interaction spheres involving trade played a significant role in the development of social stratification at Cahal Pech (Horn 2015, 134–35), such that "active manipulation of exchange relationship, and the goods, information, and status they provided may have allowed brokers in the Middle Formative small-world network to accrue substantial quantities of both material and social capital" (Horn 2015, 681; Powis and Cheetham 2007; Pye and Demarest 1991; Rice 1976; Sanders 1974).

At the beginning of the Middle Formative period at Cahal Pech, the residential units in the central precinct of the hilltop site were deliberately collapsed and plastered over to create the first Plaza B floor (Healy et al. 2004, 108), a building technique that quickly became standard during this time (Awe 1992, 350). Furthermore, this large open appears to have been transformed into a public space (Healy et al. 2004, 108–9) with full masonry buildings constructed in it (Awe 1992, 350; Peniche May 2016).

The Early Middle Formative period also saw the first major increase in the population of the site, and new residential structures were erected surrounding the site core (Awe 1992, 351) (figure 9.2). Along with this growth in population, there appears to have been significant increase in the presence of exotics such as obsidian and jade. In addition to increasing construction and extended trade networks, figurine production rose dramatically (Peniche May et al. 2018). Although figurines were recovered in Cunil phase levels, by far the most figurines found at Cahal Pech (Awe 1992, 553) were recovered from Middle Formative period levels. These figurines are nearly all in the same style and provide a diagnostic example of Formative period figurines from the Belize River Valley. Healy and colleagues (2004, 114) note that the figurine corpus from Cahal Pech was at that time "the largest collection of hand-modeled figurines from any Lowland

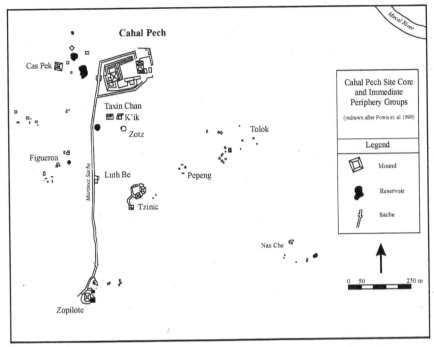

FIGURE 9.2. *Map of Cahal Pech site core and periphery settlements. (Courtesy of Claire Ebert.)*

Maya site." Since this publication, the collection of hand-modeled figurines from Cahal Pech has grown considerably, with the clear majority of figurines coming from Middle Formative Period contexts.

Awe (2013) notes that the first (and earliest known) burial at Cahal Pech was placed within one of the first masonry structures in Plaza B, and while the cranium and the body were placed in two separate burial crypts on which a square platform was constructed, they are believed to have belonged to the same person, an early leader of the Cahal Pech community (Awe 2013, 34). Compared to later, Classic period burials, this early Middle Formative burial "lacks several of the indicators for high-ranking elite Maya burials" (Awe 2013, 36), however, when compared to other Middle Formative period burials, the postmortem treatment of interment within a square structure with caches established at each of the corners indicates that the individual was of significant status (Green 2016; Santasilia 2013).

Of interest to this discussion is the fact that two Middle pre-Classic fragmented figurines were found associated with this burial and interred in the northwest and northeast corners of the newly constructed burial platform (Awe 2013, 36). This Early Middle Formative construction coincides with the Kanluk ceramic phase denoted by several new pottery types that show up in the Belize River Valley (Awe

1992, 351), and these diagnostic pottery types were found within the platform burial in Plaza B (Awe 2013). Significantly, many of the new pottery styles and designs that appear in the archaeological record of the Early Middle Formative period were decorated with pan-Mesoamerican symbolism that demonstrate interregional contact between different Maya groups while still retaining specific markers of community identification (Bartlett and McAnany 2000; Horn 2015).

Of the twenty-three individual sets of recovered skeletal remains dating to the Middle Formative period at Cahal Pech, most showed some level of skeletal pathology, including periodontal infection, minor trauma, and some examples of osteoarthritis, along with deliberate skeletal modification such as artificial modeling of crania and teeth (Green 2016). Although the pathologies may initially seem severe, they are, in fact, much less severe than the skeletal pathologies noted in Classic period remains. Healy and his colleagues (2004) suggest that this indicates some social stratification in the earlier times, as indicated by lack of nutritional resources for some individuals, but not a significant level of stratification to conclude a drastic difference in access to nutritional resources. Skeletal evidence combined with architectural and artefactual evidence such as the construction of periphery groups of varying wealth indicates that during the Middle Formative period, the processes of social, economic, and political stratification were well underway.

In conjunction with the rise of periphery groups during this time, we also see evidence that the site core of Cahal Pech was being continuously remodeled such that what in the Early Formative period had been residential structures in the center of the hilltop site became a large public plaza adjacent to public, administration-style buildings (Cheetham 1996; Healy et al. 2004; Horn 2015). The creation of formal public space during this time, coupled with the construction and expansion of monumental architecture in the site core, indicate that during this time, civic and ritual activities became more important (Horn 2015, 175).

The cultural, political, and economic developments of the Middle Formative period were crucial to the later developments in the Late Formative and Classic periods. Indeed, the archaeological record shows that the antecedents of the Classic period Maya splendor began to coalesce during the Middle Formative period such that by the beginning of the Classic period, the social, economic, and political characteristics that define the broader Maya cultural arena were firmly entrenched in eastern lowland Maya social groups.

During the Late Formative Period (350 BCE—250 CE), Cahal Pech established itself as one of the preeminent sites in the upper Belize River Valley (Awe 1992, 356). Settlements stretching to the confluence of the Macal and Mopan Rivers likely continued to control trade to and from the Petén lowlands and the Maya mountains, as communities in those areas were beginning to flourish. New industries and technologies developed, including the production of pyrite plaques, or mirrors, and obsidian sources shifted from El Chayal to San Martin Jilotopeque (Awe 1992, 356–57; Ebert 2017).

Construction episodes continued, and during this time, truly monumental architecture, including several pyramids and the palace complex, were constructed (Ebert et al. 2017). Awe (1992) notes that the increase in construction episodes signifies that the people at the top of the system had the ability to "mobilize large groups of people for the construction of public and special function structures" (Awe 1992, 357–58; Peniche May 2016), although the specific form that mobilization took (in the form of cooperation or coercion) is currently unknown. While monumental construction is not indicative of social stratification in and of itself, the presence of monumental architecture combined with the evidence of highly ornate and differential burials indicates the presence of persistent and significant social stratification by the Late Formative period. The system of social stratification that appears to have begun in the Early Middle Formative was deeply entrenched by this time and can be seen not only in the differences between domestic and public architecture but also in the deposition of artifacts signifying wealth and differential access to resources (Awe 1992, 360). In keeping with the Middle Formative burials, the grave goods in Late Formative burials lack the elaborate ornamentation that often accompanied grave goods found in later Classic period burials; however, the burial locations, inside the relatively newly constructed ritual structures, indicate that even before the Classic period, and likely even before the Late Formative, people were differentiated based on social status. Burial evidence at Cahal Pech (Green 2016) demonstrates that by the Late Preclassic period, individuals were being interred with differential levels of prestige goods, and architectural evidence (Peniche May 2016) shows the construction of large buildings that exclude the general public (i.e., palace and administrative buildings). Together, both lines of evidence demonstrate that by the Late Preclassic period at Cahal Pech, the community was stratified, with differential access to resources. Nascent signs of this stratification can be found in the early Middle Formative, and by the start of the Classic period, Cahal Pech had become a significant regional center of the Belize River Valley (Awe et al. 2013, 268; Horn 2015, 56).

FIGURINES AT CAHAL PECH

When Awe (1992) began his dissertation research, figurine fragments had been recovered in excavations at Cahal Pech and the site's periphery settlements since 1988. Subsequent excavations at Cahal Pech revealed that figurines were in use from the establishment of the community until the Terminal Classic period (see DeLance 2015; Peniche May et al. 2018). These figurines come in a variety of forms, including anthropomorphic (figure 9.3a–b), zoomorphic (figure 9.3c–d), and supernatural (figure 9.3e).

By far, most of the figurine fragments were found in construction fill used in public structures and plazas at the site core. A single fragment was recovered from a residential context at an early house mound (Garber et al. 2005), while nine fragments were associated with a midden (Cheetham 1996). A total of four figurine fragments were found within a ritual deposit that has been interpreted by Garber at al. (2005) to be a ritual cache near the center of Plaza B. While most Middle and Late Formative period figurine fragments appearing in construction fill were broken, the same is true of figurines found in the burials and ritual deposits and caches. If figurines were imbued with an animate spirit that was released upon breakage, leaving the figurine fragment an empty vessel appropriate for disposal as ritual garbage, we would not expect to find similarly broken fragments in highly meaningful contexts such as burials and ritual caches.

Burial B4–3 (figure 9.4), located within Structure B4 in the Cahal Pech site core, is a decidedly ritualized cache, featuring a cranium and mandible placed inside a round bowl with a second bowl inverted and placed on top. The bowl was then surrounded by fragmented ceramic figurines and placed on top of a series of long bones and an alligator carved out of a conch shell. Awe (2013) has connected the symbolism of the burial to the Maya view of the quadripartite universe. Considering this research, what is significant about both ritual deposits is that they are deeply meaningful and that they contained fragmented figurines. If the fragmented figurines were considered ritual trash, there likely would be no reason for their inclusion in either caches or burials, or both, rather, they would have been disposed of in a different manner. It may thus be concluded that, even when figurines are fragmented, they may have retained significant meaning for the ancient Maya of Cahal Pech.

Should the figurines simply have been broken at structurally weak points and discarded, it would be expected that the approximate six broken parts (two legs, two arms, one torso, and one head) would be found somewhat close together. This is not the case. In attempting to refit the figurine fragments, we found that none of the collected fragments, even fragments found within the same excavation unit and at the same level, fit together. Several figurine fragments show evidence of intentional breakage and defacement. Figure 9.5b shows a figurine that had deep crosshatched gouges carved on both sides, while figure 9.5a is broken vertically through the strongest area of the figurine. It would appear, then, that the figurine fragments were not only broken but also broken and scattered (Tsukamoto and Inomata 2014), further implying a level of significance to the distribution of figurine fragments used in construction fill. The fact that many figurines show signs of intentional breakage, defacement, and scattering encourages archaeologists to consider the possibility that the composition of construction fill was intentional.

A relatively small portion of figurine fragments were found in association with the first domestic construction phases at Cahal Pech dating to the Early Formative

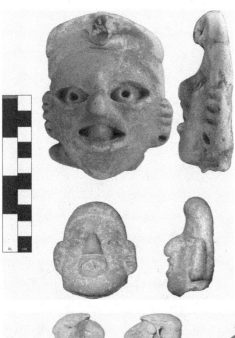

FIGURE 9.3. *(a–b) Formative period anthropomorphic figurines; (c) Formative period zoomorphic ocarina-bird head within a bird mouth; (d) Formative period zoomorphic dog figurine; (e) Formative period supernatural monkey figurine.*

A–B.

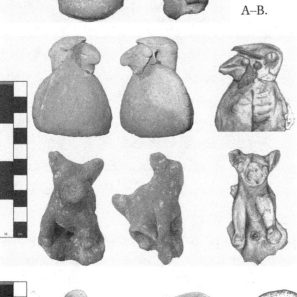

C–D.

E.

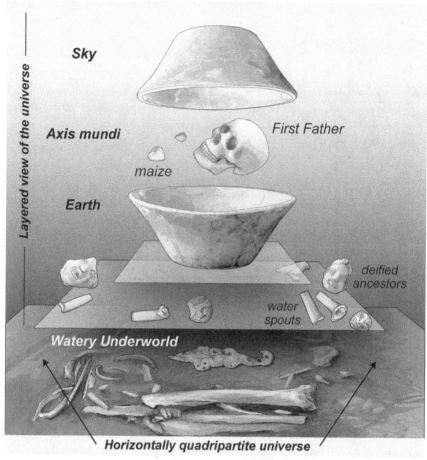

FIGURE 9.4. *Cahal Pech Burial B4-3. (Reconstruction courtesy of Jaime J. Awe.)*

period. When public and private spaces, as well as domestic and ritual spaces, were more explicitly defined during the Middle Formative, figurine fragments appear in large quantities in construction fill. Indeed, most of the figurine fragments recovered at Cahal Pech were found in Middle Formative construction fill, with the majority of fragments dating to the end of the Middle Formative (table 9.2). By the Late Formative period, the separation between public and private appeared to be fully entrenched, as are status differences demonstrated by differential residential structures and burials. The population continued to rise, and public construction took on a new fervor; however, fewer figurines appear in construction fill.

The abundance of figurine fragments in the archaeological record dating to the Middle Formative period, in particular the Early Middle Formative period, appears to coincide with the initial construction of public buildings and each of the periphery groups. During the Early Middle Formative period, the site core of Cahal Pech was significantly remodeled as the once small cluster of residential structures gave way to public buildings surrounding a large plaza (Cheetham 1994; Healy et al. 2004; Horn 2015). It is in the construction fill of these initial public buildings, connected with civic and ritual activities (Horn 2015, 175), that we find a large portion of figurine fragments dating to the Early Middle Formative. Perhaps even more significantly, by the Late Middle Formative period, public construction expanded at a rapid rate, with the construction of even more public buildings and extensive renovations of existing structures using construction fill in which we find the largest collection of ceramic figurines at the site.

By the Late Formative period, the elaborateness of burials at Cahal Pech rose, along with the differentiation between burials, indicating not only economic stratification but also social and perhaps political stratification (Awe 1992; Horn 2015). While it is likely that these types of stratification had their roots in the Middle Formative eriod, it is during the Late Formative period when these status differences become engrained in the Cahal Pech social order. During the Late Formative period, the first truly monumental architecture was constructed, including the four pyramids at the site and the initial palace complex,

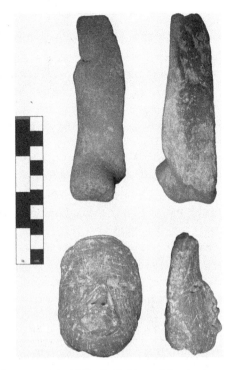

FIGURE 9.5. (a) Vertically bisected figurine torso; (b) Figurine head with crosshatched gouges.

TABLE 9.2. Cahal Pech Formative period figurine distribution.

Period	Quantity	Percentage of Assemblage
Early Formative	9	1.4
Early Middle Formative	205	31
Late Middle Formative	320	48.2
Middle Formative (undifferentiated)	28	4.2
Early Late Formative	71	10.7
Late Late Formative	23	3.5
Late Formative (undifferentiated)	7	1.0
Total	663	100

indicating links to what would become dynastic development. Furthermore, Awe (1992) notes that the increase in construction signifies that the people at the top of the system had the ability to "mobilize large groups of people for the construction of public and special function structures" (Awe 1992, 357–58).

This system of social stratification can be seen not only in the differences between domestic and public architecture but also in the deposition of artifacts signifying economic wealth and differential access to resources (Awe 1992, 360). By the time these status differences had become institutionalized in the Late Formative period, figurine use dropped significantly at the site, especially in comparison with earlier Middle Formative period use.

What the figurine fragment assemblage clearly indicates is that figurines were created and used since the beginning of the settlement of the small hilltop that would later become Cahal Pech. During the initial transition from community-based to public-based community structure, figurines were widely used in construction fill, a trend that continued during a period of increasing status differentiation. By the time status differences were fully entrenched, however, relatively few figurine fragments were found in construction fill.

INTERPRETATIONS

The figurine corpus at Cahal Pech tells a story of diachronic social and political change. Beginning with the initial settlement of the hilltop now known as Cahal Pech and ending with the post-abandonment reoccupation, the presence of figurine fragments over the course of nearly two thousand years illustrates the long process of complexity and the effect that increasing social complexity had on the use of figurines connected to ancestor veneration rituals.

We suggest that Cahal Pech was more hierarchically organized during the Late Formative period, in part, through the cooption and manipulation of community-based ancestral veneration rituals by an increasingly stratified political order. By the Late Formative period (300 BCE—250 CE), Cahal Pech was a large and thriving trade community utilizing its strategic location at the confluence of the Macal and Mopan Rivers to engage in long-distance trade with the now flourishing communities in the Petén Lowlands to the west and the Maya Mountains to the south. Significantly, while burials from the Middle Formative period tended to be comparatively very modest with few grave goods, Late Formative period burials were lined with specially cut limestone and contained elaborate offerings (Green 2016; Santasilia 2013), indicating that by this time, status differentiation had become entrenched in the social order of Cahal Pech, and true monumental construction began. Four distinct pyramids were constructed in the site core: the eastern Triadic Group along with the large palace pyramid and the highly restricted palace complex. Changes in mortuary practice, coupled with a dramatic increase in monumental construction, indicates that Late Formative period social relations at the site were marked by inequality. The inequality on which the system relied may have arisen in part from the manipulation of specific ancestor veneration practices in order to sanction elite power and authority as has been demonstrated in other parts of the world (Awe 1992; Gailey 1987; McAnany 2013).

The sharp increase in social differentiation correlated with a sharp decrease in the use and deposition of figurine fragments in construction fill hints at a possible relationship between the two. The evidence of a causative relationship between increasing social differentiation and the decrease in the presence of figurine fragments in construction fill does not allow us to definitively assert that this occurred. However, the evidence of a correlation between the two is sufficient to merit a discussion of the implications of this hypothetical relationship.

The early social structure of Cahal Pech would have likely been marked by multiple kin-based groups working cooperatively to maintain a small but growing trade-based community that utilized the Macal and Mopan Rivers to import goods from the Caribbean, modify them, and export them to sites farther inland and vice versa (Awe 1992). We know from the presence of figurines found at Early Formative levels that from the earliest settlement of the site, figurines were made and used. With the rapid population increase of the early Middle Formative and the initiation of the production of several large residential groups in addition to the first public buildings in the site core, we see figurine use sharply increase, as they are fragmented and deposited en masse in construction fill for buildings erected during this time.

By the Late Formative period, we see a sharp increase in status differentiation, as indicated by burial goods, the initial construction of restricted buildings, and the distribution of exotic goods, and an effective restructuring of the kin-based community identity that had likely characterized the Early and Middle Formative periods. Within a regional context, Bartlett and McAnany (2000) discuss the importance of community identity formation and solidification against a backdrop of increasing institutionalized inequality characteristic of the Late Formative. In particular, they claim that the development of unique pottery styles within a region may be the response of a community trying to maintain a unique identity and cohesiveness during a time when Maya sites were becoming larger, more stratified, and more diverse (Bartlett and McAnany 2000, 102–3), although this interpretation is not without its critics (Hegmon 1992, 1998; Hodder 1997). The use of specific community-oriented pottery styles within ritual contexts may be understood as "a medium for the expression of social identity . . . meant to symbolize community affiliation" (Hodder 1997, 114). For Bartlett and McAnany, the deposition of community-stylized pottery indicates that group cohesion and the expression of community identity in the face of increasing stratification was an important consideration in negotiating social status within a larger community (Bartlett and McAnany 2000, 117).

Corresponding to the rise of differentiation and inequality at Cahal Pech, we see a decline in the placement of figurines in construction fill. It is not a matter of fewer construction episodes; in fact, it appears that construction episodes increased greatly (Awe 1992; Healy et al. 2004) during the Late Formative period. What is significant is that figurine deposition in construction fill drastically declined during the same time that status differentiation was increasing and inequality was becoming prevalent. It is important to note that, although construction accelerated in the Late Formative period, the total number of figurines recovered from Late Formative period contexts is drastically smaller than those recovered from Middle Formative period contexts. Yaeger and Canuto (2000) suggest that public works projects, such as building construction, constitute a meaningful practice in the formation and maintenance of community identity, and it may be that the placement of these figurines within construction fill was a way of facilitating and fostering community identity.

By the start of the early Classic period at Cahal Pech the separation between public and private, and divisions of class became much more pronounced, as royal and administrative buildings were modified to be both larger and to restrict access even further than they had during the Late Formative period. Plaza B, the area that had originally been the location of the earliest residences and first masonry buildings, became a large public area, but it was bracketed on the north, west, and south sides by administrative buildings and on the east side by a Triadic Pyramid Group that was the site of several elite and highly elaborate burials.

Working from the standpoint that fragmented figurines are not simple trash but meaningful objects connected to ancestral veneration practices, we can begin to see an overall picture of kin groups purposely fragmenting and depositing their figurines within the base of new structures. We suggest that this act may have provided a sense of community and an ancestral continuity in the face of increasing inequality Eleanor Harrison-Buck (2004, 67) notes that in Formative period Mesoamerica, "a person's right to land was legitimized through personal offerings," and we further suggest that the Middle Formative deposition of potential heirloom figurine fragments in construction fill functioned as a sort of offering on behalf of the ancestral groups to the construction project and the community as a whole.

The figurine corpus at Cahal Pech tells a story. From the initial founding of the community, figurines were in use, likely as a tool of ancestral veneration rituals. As the population of the site grew and new construction, both public and private, developed, the placement of fragmented figurines within construction fill rose sharply. By the end of the Late Preclassic period, however, the use of fragmented figurines in construction fill declined sharply, even as construction episodes were increasing. Concurrent with the decline in figurine deposition is evidence (in the form of burials and architectural design) that Cahal Pech was becoming increasingly stratified. While we cannot determine per se that increasing stratification directly led to a decline in figurine use, the negative correlation suggests that ancestral veneration rituals using figurines were altered in the face of increasing complexity and stratification.

Acknowledgments. This research was made possible by funding from the UCR Center for Ideas and Society and the Belize Valley Archaeological Reconnaissance Project. We would like to thank Wendy Ashmore, Travis Stanton, Christine Gailey, Julie Hoggarth, and Claire Ebert for their support and thoughtful comments as this research progressed. I would also like to extend gratitude to the Belize National Institute of Culture and History and the citizens of Belize for welcoming and supporting archaeological research.

REFERENCES

Ashmore, Wendy. 2015. "Contingent Acts of Remembrance: Royal Ancestors of Classic Maya Copan and Quirigua." *Ancient Mesoamerica* 26:213–31.

Awe, Jaime J. 1992. "Dawn in the Land between the Rivers: Formative Occupation at Cahal Pech, Belize and Its Implications for Preclassic Development in the Maya Lowlands." PhD diss., University of London.

Awe, Jaime J. 2013. "Journey on the Cahal Pech Time Machine: An Archaeological Reconstruction of the Dynastic Sequence at a Belize Valley Maya Polity." *Research Reports in Belizean Archaeology* 10:33–50.

Awe, Jaime J., Julie A. Hoggarth, and Christophe Helmke. 2014. "Prehistoric Settlement Patterns in the Upper Belize River Valley and their Implications for Models of Low-Density Urbanism." *Acta MesoAmerica* 27:263–86.

Bartlett, Mary Lee, and Patricia A. McAnany. 2000. " 'Crafting Communities': The Materialization of Formative Maya Identities." In *The Archaeology of Communities: A New World Perspective*, edited by M. A. Canuto and J. Yaeger, 102–22. New York: Routledge.

Blomster, Jeffrey P. 2009. "Identity, Gender, and Power: Representational Juxtapositions in Early Formative Figurines from Oaxaca, Mexico." In *Mesoamerican Figurines: Small-Scale Indices of Large-Scale Social Phenomena*, edited by Christina T. Halperin, Katherine A. Faust, Rhonda Taube, and Aurore Giguet, 119–48. Gainesville: University Press of Florida.

Brumfiel, Elizabeth M. 1996. "Figurines and the Aztec State: Testing the Effectiveness of Ideological Domination." In *Gender and Archaeology*, edited by Rita P. Wright, 143–66. Philadelphia: University of Pennsylvania Press.

Canuto, Marcello A. 2016. "Middle Preclassic Maya Society: Tilting at Windmills or Giants of Civilization?" In *The Origin of Maya States*, edited by Loa P. Traxler and Robert J. Sharer, 461–506, Philadelphia: Museum of Anthropology, University of Pennsylvania.

Carballo, David M., ed. 2012. *Cooperation and Collective Action: Archaeological Perspectives*. Boulder: University Press of Colorado.

Cheetham, David. 1996. "Reconstruction of the Formative Period Site Core of Cahal Pech, Belize." In *Belize Valley Preclassic Maya Project: Report on the 1995 Field Season*, edited by Paul F. Healy and Jaime J. Awe, 1–33. Occasional Papers in Anthropology No. 12, Trent University Department of Anthropology, Peterborough, Ontario.

Cheetham, David. 2004. "The Role of 'Terminus Groups' in Lowland Maya Site Planning: An Example from Cahal Pech." In *The Ancient Maya of the Belize Valley: Half a Century of Archaeological Research*, edited by J. F. Garber, 125–48. Gainesville: University Press of Florida.

Cheetham, David T., Gerald Trainor, James Mower, Esther Pozzani, Suzanne Duggan, Anies Hassan and Prasun Amin. 1994. "On the Road Again: The Third Season of Excavations at the Zopilote Group, Cahal Pech, Belize." In *The Belize Valley Archaeological Reconnaissance Project: Progress Report of the 1994 Field Season*, edited by James M. Conlon and Jaime J. Awe, 1–10. Vol. 2. London: Institute of Archaeology.

Crumley, Carole L. 1995. "Heterarchy and the Analysis of Complex Societies." *Archaeological Papers of the American Anthropological Association* 6 (1): 1–5.

Crumley, Carole L. 2004. "Contextual Constraints on State Structure." In *Alternativity in Cultural History: Heterarchy and Homoarchy as Evolutionary Trajectories, Third International Conference Hierarchy and Power in the History of Civilizations*, edited by Dmitri M. Bondarenko and Alexandre A. Nemirovskiy, 3–22. Moscow: Center for Civilizational and Regional Studies of the RAS.

Cyphers Guillén, Ann. 1993. "Women, Rituals, and Social Dynamics at Ancient Chalcatzingo." *Latin American Antiquity* 4 (3): 209–24.

DeLance, Lisa. 2016. "Enchaining Kinship: Figurines and State Formation at Cahal Pech, Cayo, Belize." PhD diss., University of California, Riverside.

Douglas, John E., Linda J. Brown, and Jaime J. Awe. 2015. "The Final Occupation: The Terminal Classic Evidence from Plaza H, Cahal Pech, Belize." *Research Reports in Belizean Archaeology* 12:217–25.

Ebert, Claire E. 2017. "Preclassic Maya Social Complexity and Origins of Inequality at Cahal Pech, Belize." PhD diss., Pennsylvania State University.

Ebert, Claire E., Daniel Pierce, and Jaime. J. Awe. 2019. "Preclassic Ceramic Economy in Belize: Neutron Activation Analyses at Cahal Pech." *Antiquity* 93:1266–83.

Ensor, Bradley E. 2013. *Crafting Prehispanic Maya Kinship*. Tuscaloosa: University of Alabama Press.

Estrada-Belli, Francisco. 2011. *The First Maya Civilization: Ritual and Power before the Classic Period*. New York: Routledge.

Feinman, Gay M., and Joyce Marcus, eds. 1998. Introduction to *Archaic States*, 3–13. Santa Fe, NM: School of American Research.

Flannery, Kent V., and Joyce Marcus. 2005. *Excavations at San José Mogote 1: The Household Archaeology*. Memoir 40 of the Museum of Anthropology, University of Michigan, Ann Arbor.

Foias, Antonia E. 2013. *Ancient Maya Political Dynamics*. Gainesville: University Press of Florida.

Ford, Anabel. 1990. "Maya Settlement in the Belize River Area: Variations in Residence Patterns of the Central Maya Lowlands." In *Precolumbian Population History in the Maya Lowlands*, edited by T. P. Culbert and D. S. Rice, 167–81. Albuquerque: University of New Mexico Press.

Ford, Anabel, and Scott Fedick. 1992. "Maya Settlement Patterns in the Upper Belize River Area: Initial Results of the Belize River Archaeological Settlement Survey." *Journal of Field Archaeology* 19:35–49.

Gailey, Christine Ward. 1987. *Kinship to Kingship: Gender Hierarchy and State Formation in the Tongan Islands*. Austin: University of Texas Press.

Garber, James F., Jennifer L. Cochran, and Jaime J. Awe. 2005. "Excavations at Plaza B at Cahal Pech: The 2004 Field Season." In *The Belize Valley Archaeological Project: Results of the 2004 Field Season*, edited by James F. Garber, 4–41. San Marcos: Texas State University.

Gillespie, Susan D. 2000. "Beyond Kinship: An Introduction." In *Beyond Kinship: Social and Material Reproduction in House Societies*, edited by R. A. Joyce and S. D. Gillespie, 1–21. Philadelphia: University of Pennsylvania Press.

Green, Kristen A. 2016. "The Use of Stable Isotope Analysis on Burials at Cahal Pech, Belize, in Order to Identify Trends in Mortuary Practices over Time and Space." PhD diss., University of Montana.

Grove, David C., and Susan D. Gillespie. 1984. "Chalcatzingo's Portrait Figurines and the Cult of the Ruler." *Archaeology* (July / August): 27–33.

Grove, David C. and Susan D. Gillespie. 1992. "Archaeological Indicators of Formative Period Elites: A Perspective from Central Mexico." In *Mesoamerican Elites: An Archaeological Assessment*, edited by D. Z. Chase and A. F. Chase, 191–205. Norman: University of Oklahoma Press.

Halperin, Christina T. 2007. "Materiality, Bodies, and Practice: The Political Economy of Late Classic Maya Figurines from Motul de San Jose, Peten, Guatemala." PhD diss., University of California, Riverside.

Halperin, Christina T. 2009. "Figurines as Bearers of and Burdens in Late Classic Maya State Politics." In *Mesoamerican Figurines: Small Scale Indices of Large Scale Social Phenomena*, edited by C. T. Halperin, K. A. Faust, R. Taube, and A. Giguet, 378–403. Gainesville: University Press of Florida.

Halperin, Christina T. 2014. *State and Household: The Sociality of Maya Figurines*. Austin: University of Texas Press.

Hammond, Norman, ed. 1991. "Obsidian Trade." In *Cuello: An Early Maya Community in Belize*, 197–98. Cambridge, UK: Cambridge University Press.

Hansen, Richard D. 1998. "Continuity and Disjunction: The Pre-Classic Antecedents of Classic Maya Architecture." In *Function and Meaning in Classic Maya Architecture*, edited by S. D. Houston, 49–122. Washington, DC: Dumbarton Oaks.

Harrison-Buck, Eleanor. 2004. "Nourishing the Animus of Lived Space through Ritual Caching." In *K'axob: Ritual, Work, and Family in an Ancient Maya Village*, edited by P. A. McAnany, 65–85. Los Angeles: Cotsen Institute of Archaeology.

Harrison-Buck, Eleanor, ed. 2012. "Rituals of Death and Disempowerment among the Maya." In *Power and Identity in Archaeological Theory and Practice: Case Studies from Ancient Mesoamerica*, 103–15. Salt Lake City: University of Utah Press.

Healy, Paul F., David Cheetham, Terry G. Powis, and Jaime J. Awe. 2004. "Cahal Pech: The Middle Formative Period." In *The Ancient Maya of the Belize Valley: Half a Century of Archaeological Research*, edited by J. F. Garber, 103–24. Gainesville: University Press of Florida.

Hegmon, Michelle. 1992. "Archaeological Research on Style." *Annual Review of Anthropology* 21:517–36.

Hegmon, Michelle. 1998. "Technology, Style, and Social Practices: Archaeological Approaches." In *The Archaeology of Social Boundaries*, edited by Miriam T. Stark, 264–79. Washington, DC: Smithsonian Institution.

Hendon, Julia A., Rosemary A. Joyce, and Jeanne Lopiparo. 2015. *Material Relations: The Marriage Figurines of Prehispanic Honduras*. Boulder: University Press of Colorado.

Hepp, Guy David, Sarah B. Barber, and Arthur A. Joyce. 2014. "Communing with Nature, the Ancestors, and the Neighbors: Ancient Ceramic Musical Instruments from Coastal Oaxaca, Mexico." *World Archaeology* 46 (3): 380–99.

Hepp, Guy David, and Arthur A. Joyce. 2013. "From Flesh to Clay: Formative Period Ceramic Figurines from Oaxaca's Lower Río Verde Valley." In *Polity and Ecology in Formative Period Coastal Oaxaca*, edited by Arthur A. Joyce, 256–99. Boulder: University Press of Colorado.

Hodder, Ian. 1977. "The Distribution of Material Culture Items in the Baringo District, Western Kenya." *Man* 2:239–69.

Hohmann, Bobbi M. 2002. "Preclassic Maya Shell Ornament Production in the Belize Valley, Belize." PhD diss., University of New Mexico.

Horn, Sherman W., III. 2015. "The Web of Complexity: Socioeconomic Networks in the Middle Preclassic Belize Valley." PhD diss., Tulane University.

Inomata, Takeshi, Jessica MacLellan, Daniela Triadan, Jessica Munson, Melissa Burham, Kazuo Aoyama, Hiroo Nasu, Flory Pinzón, and Hitoshi Yonenobu. 2015. "The Development of Sedentary Communities in the Maya Lowlands: Co-existing Mobile Groups and Public Ceremonies at Ceibal, Guatemala." *PNAS* 112 (14): 4268–73.

Joyce, Arthur A. 2000. "The Founding of Monte Albán: Sacred Propositions and Social Practices." In *Agency in Archaeology*, edited by Marcia-Anne Dobres and John Robb, 71–91. London: Routledge Press.

Joyce, Arthur. A. 2009. "The Main Plaza of Monte Albán: A Life History of Place." In *The Archaeology of Meaningful Places*, edited by B. Bowser and N. Zedeno, 32–52. Salt Lake City: University of Utah Press.

King, Eleanor M. 2016. "Rethinking the Role of Early Economies in the Rise of Maya States: A View from the Lowlands." In *The Origin of Maya States*, edited by Loa P. Traxler and Robert J. Sharer, 417–60, Philadelphia: University of Pennsylvania Press.

Kintigh, Keith, Jeffrey H. Altschul, Mary C. Beaudry, Robert D. Drennan, Ann P. Kinzig, Timothy A. Kohler, W. Fredrick Limp, et al. 2014. "Grand Challenges for Archaeology." *PNAS* 111:879–80.

Lesure, Richard G., and Michael Blake. 2002. "Interpretive Challenges in the Study of Early Complexity: Economy, Ritual, and Architecture at Paso de la Amada, Mexico." *Journal of Anthropological Archaeology* 21 (1): 1–24.

Lucero, Lisa J. 2003. "The Emergence of Classic Maya Rulers." *Current Anthropology* 44 (4): 523–44.

Marcus, Joyce. 1998. *Women's Ritual in Formative Oaxaca: Figurine Making, Divination, Death and the Ancestors*. Ann Arbor: University of Michigan Press.

Marcus, Joyce. 2009. "Rethinking Figurines." In *Mesoamerican Figurines: Small-Scale Indices of Large-Scale Social Phenomena*, edited by C. T. Halperin, K. A. Faust, R. Taube, and A. Giguet, 25–50. Gainesville: University Press of Florida.

McAnany, Patricia A. 2013. *Living with the Ancestors: Kinship and Kingship in Ancient Maya Society*. rev. ed. Cambridge, UK: Cambridge University Press.

Miller, Mary Ellen. 1999. *Maya Art and Architecture*. New York: Thames and Hudson.

Molesky-Poz, Jean. 2006. *Contemporary Maya Spirituality: The Ancient Ways Are Not Lost*. Austin: University of Texas Press.

Novotny, Anna. 2015. "Creating Community: Ancient Maya Mortuary Practice at Mid-level Sites in the Belize River Valley, Belize." PhD diss., Arizona State University, Tucson.

Peniche May, Nancy. 2016. "Building Power: Political Dynamics at Cahal Pech, Belize during the Middle Preclassic." PhD diss., University of California, San Diego.

Porter, Mark L. B. 2020. "Caching Aggrandizers: Ritual Caching Practices, Competitive Generosity, and the Rise of Inequality in the Preclassic Maya Lowlands." Master's thesis, Northern Arizona University.

Powis, Terry G., and David Cheetham. 2007. "From House to Holy: Formative Development of Civic Ceremonial Architecture in the Maya Lowlands." *Research Reports in Belizean Archaeology* 4:177–86.

Pye, Mary E., and Arthur A. Demarest. 1991. "The Evolution of Complex Societies in Southeastern Mesoamerica: New Evidence from El Mesak, Guatemala." In *The Formation of Complex Society in Southeastern Mesoamerica*, edited by W. R. Fowler, 77–100. Boca Raton, FL: CRC Press.

Rice, Don S. 1976. "Middle Preclassic Maya Settlement in the Central Maya Lowlands." *Journal of Field Archaeology* 3 (4): 425–45.

Rice, Prudence M. 2015. "Middle Preclassic Interregional Interaction and the Maya Low-lands." *Journal of Archaeological Research* 23:1–47.

Sanders, William T. 1974. "Chiefdom to State: Political Evolution at Kaminaljuyu." In *Reconstructing Complex Societies: An Archaeological Colloquium*, edited by C. B. Moore. Supplement to the Bulletin of the American Schools of Oriental Research No. 20. American Schools of Oriental Research, Cambridge, MA.

Santasilia, Catharina E. 2013. "Investigations of a Late Classic Elite Burial at the Summit of Structure B1 at the Site of Cahal Pech, Belize." Master's thesis, University of Copenhagen.

Smith, Michael E. 2002. "Domestic Ritual at Aztec Provincial Sites in Morelos." In *Domestic Ritual in Ancient Mesoamerica*, edited by Patricia Plunket, 93–114. Monograph no. 46. Los Angeles: Cotsen Institute of Archaeology.

Stanton, Travis W., M. Kathryn Brown, and Jonathan B. Pagliaro. 2008. "Garbage of the Gods? Squatters, Refuse Disposal, and Termination Rituals among the Ancient Maya." *Latin American Antiquity* 19:227–47.

Taube, Karl and Rhonda Taube. 2009. "The Beautiful, the Bad, and the Ugly: Aesthetics and Morality in Maya Figurines." In *Mesoamerican Figurines: Small Scale Indices of Large-Scale Social Phenomena*, edited by Christina T. Halperin, Katherine A. Faust, Rhonda Taube, and Aurore Giguet, 236–60. Gainesville: University Press of Florida.

Tsukamoto, Kenichiro, and Takeshi Inomata, eds. 2014. *Mesoamerican Plazas: Arenas of Community and Power*. Tucson: University of Arizona Press.

Walker, Debra Selsor. 1998. "Maya Dedications of Authority." In *The Sowing and the Dawning: Termination, Dedication, and Transformation in the Archaeological and Ethnographic Record of Mesoamerica*, edited by Shirley Boteler Mock, 65–80. Albuquerque: University of New Mexico Press.

Yaeger, Jason, and Marcello A. Canuto. 2000. "Introducing an Archaeology of Communities." In *The Archaeology of Communities: A New World Perspective*, edited by M. A. Canuto and J. Yaeger, 1–15. New York: Routledge.

10

From Shell Beads to Symbolic Royal Bodies

A Diachronic Comparison of Body Ornamentation Production,
Consumption, and Social Complexity at Prehispanic Pacbitun, Belize

JON SPENARD, GEORGE J. MICHELETTI,
KAITLIN CROW, TERRY G. POWIS,
AND TERESA TREMBLAY WAGNER

INTRODUCTION

The Middle Preclassic (Formative) period (1000–300 BCE) in the Maya Lowlands was long believed to have been a time when nomadic hunter-gatherers slowly settled into egalitarian agricultural villages. Over the next seven hundred years, some of these small villages transformed into large urban centers, with socio-politically complex communities marking the transition into the Late Preclassic period (300 BCE–250 CE). That period also witnessed the origins of the "great achievements" of the Classic period (250–900 CE) society defined by divine king-ship, royal courts populated with sub-royal elites, hieroglyphic writing, cities, calendrics, mathematics, and high art, to name a few. Archaeological research in the southern Maya Lowlands over the past two decades has challenged this view. Those newer data indicate that the transition to sociopolitical complexity occurred much earlier than previously believed and even may have already begun before people settled into permanent dwellings (Estrada-Belli 2012; Hansen 2016; Inomata et al. 2015; Inomata et al. 2020; Powis 2005; Rice 2019). Among the more common markers of social complexity during that period are marine shell and

https://doi.org/10.5876/9781646422883.c010

greenstone beads, the raw materials for which were acquired via long-distance trade networks from the Caribbean Sea and highland Guatemala, respectively (Hansen 2016, 353; Hohmann 2002; Horn 2015; Powis et al. 2016).

Belize is one of the earliest known settled regions in the Maya Lowlands, and the Belize Valley is home to several of the earliest known villages, including Blackman Eddy and Cahal Pech, both with initial occupations dating to approximately 1100 BCE (Awe 1992; Garber et al. 2004; Healy, Cheetham, Powis, and Awe 2004; Lohse 2010; Sullivan et al. 2009). Some two hundred years later, the site of Pacbitun was settled on the southern rim of the Belize Valley. There it thrived nearly two thousand years, into the Early Postclassic period (900–1000 CE) (Powis et al. 2017; Powis et al. 2020). During the Middle Preclassic period, when Pacbitun was a small village with a population of approximately fifty people, marine shell bead production was a major economic activity, yet many, if not most, of the objects were traded away from the area (Healy et al. 2007; Hohmann 2002; Hohmann et al. 2018; Powis 2020; Spenard et al. 2013). Although the finished objects were exported, crafting them appears to have been a primary driver of nascent social complexity there. By social complexity we mean a hierarchical social structure with a formal government.

Pacbitun had grown into a small urban center with well-developed social stratification by the start of the Classic period. Community-level marine shell bead production had fallen out of practice by that time and with it, community identity tied to the practice. Yet a connection between crafted body ornaments and social complexity remained. Rather than markers of community identity though, crafted items made from a variety of materials were used as markers of social status (Helmke et al. 2006; Hohmann 2002; Powis et al. 2017; Spenard 2014; Spenard et al. 2013).

In this chapter, we discuss changes in body ornament production and use at Middle Preclassic period Pacbitun within a broader Mesoamerican framework to understand the relationship between emerging social complexity and crafting there. We then move to the Classic period at the site to investigate the social role of body ornaments after complexity was fully emerged. The chapter ends with a discussion of the use of crafted items as a form of symbolic royal self-sacrifice in an unsuccessful attempt to alleviate ritually the social and environmental stressors of the Terminal Classic period. That discussion allows us to appreciate how deeply embedded the relationship between crafted items and social complexity had become when the site was abandoned.

SITE DESCRIPTION

Pacbitun is a medium-sized prehispanic Maya settlement nestled at the base of the northern foothills of the Maya mountains, and on the southern rim of the Belize Valley (figure 10.1). Archaeologists divide the settlement into three areas;

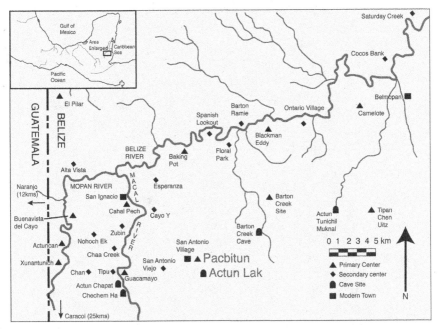

FIGURE 10.1. *Map of the Belize River Valley.*

the Epicenter, Core, and Periphery Zones (figure 10.2) (Healy et al. 2007, 17). The Epicenter contains the main religious and administrative structures; forty-one known masonry buildings surround three main plazas, and an additional two adjacent to the north side, all aligned east-west (figure 10.3) (Healy 1990, 250). An additional architectural group, dubbed the "North Group," is located to the northeast of Plaza A (Cheong 2013).

The Core Zone includes the Epicenter and extends outward from there, incorporating all architecture within a one-square kilometer buffer, including a terminus group (Healy et al. 2007). The Periphery Zone is the sustaining area for the site and consists of several hundred small house mounds spread over the landscape, as well as several smaller hilltop pyramidal structures, plaza groups, minor centers, agricultural terraces, springs, reservoirs, sinkholes, causeways, and workshops (Healy et al. 2007, 18; Skaggs et al. 2020; Spenard, Mai, and Mai 2012; Ward 2013; Weber 2011; Weber and Micheletti 2016; Weber and Powis 2014). The area of the Periphery Zone extends at least nine square kilometers beyond the Core Zone; yet settlement continues unbroken, although less dense, in all directions but south into the vicinity of other nearby major centers making hinterland sociopolitical affiliations difficult to identify (Healy 1990, 251; Spenard, Mai, and Mai 2012; Spenard, Reece, and Powis 2012). Lastly, caves, rock shelters, bedrock outcrops, sinkholes, and other such geologic landmarks, as well as

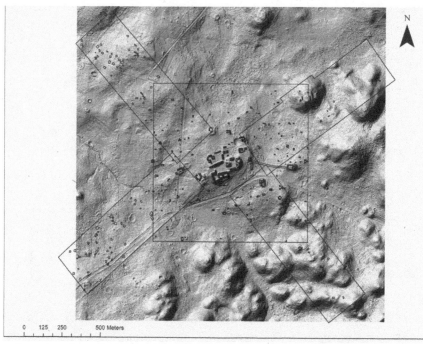

FIGURE 10.2. *Composite lidar and plan view map of Pacbitun and periphery. The polygons represent archaeological surveys. The Core Zone is the dense concentration of structures in the center of the map. The Core Zone is the area within the large square. The Periphery Zone is the area outside the large square. (Map by Sheldon Skaggs and Nicaela Cartagena after Healy et al. [2007, fig. 3].)*

springs and agricultural terraces, abound in the southern and eastern areas of the Periphery Zone (Spenard 2014).

Pacbitun was first settled in the Middle Preclassic period (Mai phase 900–300 BCE) as a small farming village with an estimated population of around fifty people (table 10.1). Yet earlier Cunil ceramics have been recovered in mixed deposits, suggesting that its founding may have been contemporaneous with Cahal Pech and Blackman Eddy (Awe 1992; Powis et al. 2017, 194; Powis et al. 2020, 25). In addition to farming, Pacbitun's early inhabitants also crafted marine shell beads that functioned as the site's other major economic pursuit throughout the Middle Preclassic period. The geographic footprint of the site and its population expanded steadily for the next two millennia, reaching their maximum during the latter half of the Late Classic period (late Coc phase 700–800 CE). Population reached between four thousand and seven thousand inhabitants, and archaeologically tested mounds were inhabited in all three settlement zones

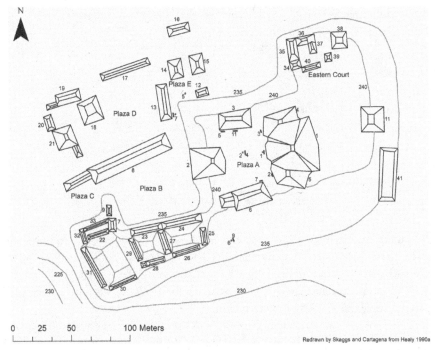

FIGURE 10.3. *Map of Pacbitun's Core Zone. (Map by Nicaela Cartagena and Sheldon Skaggs.)*

Redrawn by Skaggs and Cartagena from Healy 1990a

(Healy et al. 2007). As with many sites in the southern Maya Lowlands, Pacbitun experienced a great social and political upheaval during the Terminal Classic period (Tzib phase 800–900 CE) that was exacerbated by a series of multidecadal droughts, food shortages, weakening of divine kingship, and possibly warfare (Helmke and Awe 2012; Kennett et al. 2012; Powis et al. 2017; Spenard 2014; White et al. 1993). Despite a marked uptick in cave and landmark ritual at the onset of the Terminal Classic, by the end of the period, the population crashed, malnutrition was prevalent, and building activity had ceased in the Core Zone.

THEORETICAL OVERVIEW

Middle Preclassic Maya people used body ornaments commonly as markers of social status, indicating that the human body was a field of social display (Houston and Inomata 2009, 76). Considering that marine shell beads were common markers of social identity at that time, understanding their production and use gives insight into nascent social complexity. This aspect of our discussion is founded on the notion that craft production plays a vital role in the formation and maintenance of social identity (Costin 1998; Turner 1980). More specifically, costume, decoration, and modification of an individual's body symbolically

TABLE 10.1. Pacbitun chronology and ceramic sequence (after Powis et al. 2017).

Date range	Period name	Phase name
900–1000 CE	Early Postclassic	Canto phase
800–900 CE	Terminal Classic	Tzib phase
700–800 CE	Late Classic	Late Coc phase
550–700 CE	Early Late Classic	Early Coc phase
300–550 CE	Early Classic	Tzul phase
100 BC–300 CE	Terminal Preclassic	Ku phase
300–100 BCE	Late Preclassic	Puc phase
600–300 BCE	late Middle Preclassic	Late Mai phase
900–600 BCE	early Middle Preclassic	Early Mai Phase

communicates their social statuses and allegiances. Additionally, differences in craft specialization are strongly correlated with levels of political integration and social stratification in pre-industrial societies; thus, the study of body ornamentation and production are ideal vehicles for studying the emergence of social complexity (Cark and Parry 1990, 315).

Such signification via body decoration was prevalent throughout prehispanic Mesoamerica. For example, textiles and cloth were used to mark different social statuses, particularly those pertaining to economic and gender statuses (Anawalt 1981; Looper 2009, 227; Tremain 2017, 2020). Additionally, some prehispanic age groups in Mexico distinguished themselves using hair treatments such as shaving, parting in different ways, and wearing headdresses (Joyce 1998, 156). For Classic period Maya people, identity was located in an individual's head and face, and rulers were frequently depicted in art wearing headdresses bearing their names; the origins of this practice possibly dating back to the Early Preclassic period (Houston et al. 2006, 68). One of the hieroglyphs used for accession roughly translates as "to tie the headband" or "bind to kingship," suggesting that wearing a cloth headband signified that the wearer was a regent. Individuals also signaled their social status through cranial and dental modifications and through scarring and tattooing of the face (Sharer 1994, 479, 482; Tozzer 1941, 91).

A MESOAMERICAN PERSPECTIVE ON MIDDLE PRECLASSIC PERIOD SHELL BEAD PRODUCTION

Shell artifacts are a ubiquitous artifact class of Preclassic through Postclassic period archaeological deposits in the Maya Lowlands. Although shell ornaments have long been of interest to archaeologists, early studies of them have been limited to typological and taxonomic classifications (Kidder 1947; Willey 1972, 1978; Willey et al. 1965, 509). While these early studies have provided significant information on the raw materials used for production and the types of items created, only in the last three decades have archaeologists moved beyond such limited analytical techniques and begun addressing broader questions of cultural behavior such as the role of shell in Maya social, political, and economic activities (Buttles 2002; Dreiss 1994; Garber 1989; Hohmann 2002, 2014; Hohmann et al. 2018; Isaza 1997; Isaza and McAnany 1999; Moholy-Nagy 1987, 1994; Taschek 1994, 60–61). This chapter adds to that growing body of literature through an exploration of the relationship between their production and the origins of social complexity at Pacbitun.

A variety of shell artifacts were produced in prehispanic Mesoamerica, including ornamental and utilitarian items. Archaeologists have traditionally identified shell-working areas by the presence of large quantities of raw materials, artifacts in various stages of the production process, and / or various types of manufacturing technology (e.g., drills, blades, abraders / grinding stones) recovered. Although the raw materials, artifact type, and tool technology may differ somewhat from region to region, the basic shell-working toolkit remains the same in many prehistoric contexts.

While the presence of shell debris has suggested shell crafting at individual sites, few archaeologists have identified actual household workshops. Those restricted to the Formative (Preclassic) period include the villages of San Jose Mogote and Tierras Largas in the Valley of Oaxaca (Flannery and Winter 1976, 36–39; Pires-Ferreira 1976, 1978). Evidence from house floors and peripheral deposits indicates many residents were involved in shell-working activities during that early period. At San Jose Mogote, shell-working debris consisted of chert debitage and tools, shell detritus, and shell ornaments in various stages of production. Those deposits were typically concentrated in the corners of structures, but debris was also encountered in general excavations in the household clusters.

In the Maya area, shell ornaments have been recovered from Preclassic deposits at many lowland sites, including Altun Ha (Pendergast 1979), Blue Creek (Haines 1997), Cerros (Garber 1989), Chan Chich (Robichaux 1998), Colha (Buttles 2002; Dreiss 1994), Cuello (Hammond 1991), K'axob (Isaza 1997; Isaza and McAnany 1999) in Belize; Altar de Sacrificios (Willey 1972), Nakbe (Hansen 2016), Seibal (Willey 1978), Tikal (Moholy-Nagy 1987, 1994), and Uaxactún (Kidder 1947) in Guatemala; and Dzibilchaltun (Taschek 1994, 60–61) in Mexico. While the objects were found in a variety of depositional contexts at those sites, very few have good contextual data for comparative purposes.

In the Belize Valley, multiple sites have also produced shell ornaments, including Barton Ramie (Willey et al. 1965), Blackman Eddy (Cochran 2009), Cahal Pech (Awe 1992; Cheetham 1995, 1996; Ferguson et al. 1996; Healy, Cheetham, Powis, and Awe 2004; Powis 1996), Chan (Keller 2012), Dos Chombitos (Robin 2000), and Zubin (Ferguson 1995; Iannone 1996). The artifacts have been identified in a variety of depositional contexts, including burials, caches, construction fill, and middens dating to both the Middle and Late Preclassic periods. Like many of the other sites previously mentioned, few Belize Valley sites have good contextual data for comparison. Excavations at Cahal Pech over the past thirty years have provided strong evidence for shell working throughout the Middle Preclassic period (Awe 1992; Cheetham 1995; Horn 2015; Peniche May 2016). There, marine shell ornaments, marine shell detritus, and chert microdrills have been found in the central precinct (in front of Structures B4 and B5 in Plaza B) and in the periphery settlements of Tolok and Cas Pek. While shell-working materials have been found in those areas of Cahal Pech, there is little direct evidence of where the production activities took place. At Tolok, the material was recovered from a primary midden where the artifacts were deposited as refuse (Powis 1996; Powis et al. 1999). At Cas Pek, archaeologists recovered them entirely from construction fill (Lee 1996; Lee and Awe 1995).

PRECLASSIC PERIOD SHELL PRODUCTION AT PACBITUN

One of the best case studies for shell ornament production in the Maya Lowlands comes from Pacbitun, where substantial Preclassic period deposits producing a large number of Middle Preclassic period shell artifacts have been recovered (Hohmann 2002, 2014; Hohmann et al. 2018; Powis 2020). The Pacbitun assemblage represents the largest Preclassic collection in the Belize Valley, with 8,783 artifacts. It consists of 5,670 worked marine shell objects and 3,113 pieces of marine shell detritus (Hohmann et al. 2018, 126). The raw material for those beads was obtained through long-distance trade networks with the Caribbean Sea (Hohmann 2002, 2014; Hohmann et al. 2018; see also Powis 2020, 28, for a discussion on down-the-line trade with Belize River communities). In direct association with the shell artifacts were 390 chert microspalls and microdrills, dominating the formal stone tool assemblage at Pacbitun (Hohmann et al. 2018, 133) (figure 10.4). The artifacts were recovered from Plazas B, C, and D of the Epicenter Zone, and all date to the Middle Preclassic period.

In the following sections, we present a diachronic overview of shell bead crafting at Pacbitun during the Middle Preclassic period, revealing it to have been a major socioeconomic factor leading to social complexity in the early village. Specifically, we show how changes in the crafting process are associated with, or perhaps spurred on, transformations in site layout, design, and novel construction techniques and structures. Collectively, those transformations of the site suggest an emergent elite class whose political power stemmed in part from success in the shell bead crafting economy.

Pacbitun Community Organization: Shell Crafting and Living Spaces

All known Middle Preclassic period shell-working activity areas at Pacbitun are found in Plaza B, where three early Mai phase (900–600 BCE) platforms (Substructures B1, B4, and B16) and five late Mai phase (600–300 BCE) platforms

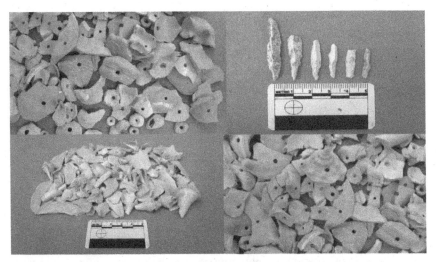

FIGURE 10.4. *Representative samples of shell beads, detritus, and chert microdrills from Plaza B excavations.*

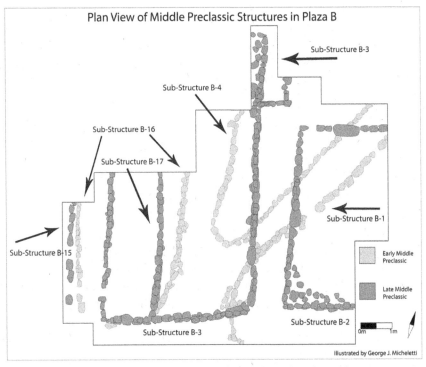

FIGURE 10.5. *Map of Middle Preclassic period structures beneath Pacbitun Plaza B.*

(Substructures B2, B3, B5, B11, B13) have been recorded (Hohmann 2002; Hohmann and Powis 1996, 1999; Hohmann et al. 1999; Hohmann et al. 2018; Micheletti et al. 2018; Powis 2020; Powis et al. 2009). The structures are arranged in a dense cluster and separated by one-meter-wide alleyways offering little privacy between neighbors (figure 10.5). While shell beads, shell detritus, and chert microdrills were associated with each of the platforms investigated, they were unevenly distributed. Some platforms contained significantly high concentrations of beads, detritus, and chert microdrills, while others contained domestic refuse and smaller concentrations of shell production materials, an indication that a small amount of production may have occurred within house structures with the majority of work being conducted on adjacent platforms seemingly dedicated to the craft.

The late Mai phase platforms (Substructures B2, B3, B5, B11, B13) were built directly over those from the earlier Mai phase (Substructures B1, B4, and B16); their shape and orientation sharply contrasting with their precursors (Hohmann and Powis 1999). All three early Mai phase platforms are apsidal in shape with two running in a northeast-southwest direction (Substructures B1 and B4) and the third oriented north-south (Substructure B16). Although the three early Mai platforms remain to be fully excavated, they are between 10–15 cm tall × 8 m long × 4.5 m wide. The late Mai platforms are twice the height of the earlier ones measuring 25–30 cm tall, are rectangular shaped, and are consistently oriented twenty degrees west of north. Only one of the late Mai platforms (Substructure B2) has been fully excavated and its dimensions measure 9 m east-west × 6 m north-south (Powis et al.2009).

The two best-studied platforms of the late Mai phase community beneath Plaza B are Substructure B3 and Substructure B2. Evidence of shell bead production on both include the presence of shell beads, shell detritus, and chert microdrills. However, the floor deposits of Substructure B3 differs drastically from those of Substructure B2 in that comparatively less shell material was found in the former, but some domestic refuse was present. Given their proximity, shared orientation, use of a tamped floor surface, and similarities in construction methods and materials, the two platforms may constitute a single household. Such patterning of platforms is consistent throughout the Middle Preclassic period in the Plaza B village, indicating that shell artifact production was likely conducted at the household level. Nevertheless, with their compact and nucleated character, the design of Pacbitun's early and late Mai phase communities appeared to have promoted social cohesion, suggesting that shell bead production provided a foundation for community identity (Spenard et al. 2013).

Sometime between 500 and 300 BCE, the late Mai phase community was buried by a thick midden (50–100 cm) with materials spanning the late Middle Preclassic through early Late Preclassic periods. The midden contained a variety of artifacts, including ceramics, lithics, animal bones, charcoal, and shell. Both shell beads and pieces of detritus were recorded, as were tens of thousands of *jute* river snail shells (Hohmann and Powis 1999, 6).

In sum, the Middle Preclassic community planning observed in Plaza B suggests a multigenerational, village-wide goal of economic success focused on marine shell bead production. The evidence is clear for shell-working activities at Pacbitun, but their use on site is far more limited in the Middle Preclassic. Of the thousands of shell beads found in primary contexts in and around sub-plaza platforms in Plaza B, only one deposit has been identified in a ritual context. Cache 1 consisted of fifty-one irregular-shaped marine shell beads stacked together in a posthole in Substructure B1 in the early Mai Plaza B community (Powis 2020, 28). The arrangement of the beads indicates that they were strung together as part of a necklace at the time they were deposited (Hohmann et al. 2018, 136). Given the volume of marine shell beads found in Plaza B, it is far more likely that shell artifacts were produced for consumption beyond the household and village level, suggesting that the product was probably destined for markets elsewhere in the Belize Valley. We note that these marine shell beads may have also been exported to large urban centers in the Petén such as Nakbe and El Mirador, where they are found in large quantities in elite and ritual contexts (Hansen 2016, 253). Although this latter connection has yet to be tested archaeologically, if true, it suggests integrated long-distance regional economic exchange networks were a key component of the emergence of social complexity in the Middle Preclassic period throughout the southern Maya Lowlands.

El Quemado

Investigations of the Middle Preclassic period in Plaza A have revealed substantially different patterns than in Plaza B. In Plaza A, an elaborate Middle Preclassic platform dubbed El Quemado (the burned one), or "Q," was constructed and later buried (figure 10.6). Unlike the other platforms in Plaza B, Q is monumental in size and ceremonial in nature. Constructed around 600 BCE, it is the only known such structure within the site core from that time (Micheletti and Powis 2015; Micheletti et al. 2016; Micheletti et al. 2017; Powis 2020; Powis et al. 2019; Powis et al. 2020). It is a rectangular-shaped, south-facing, stepped platform that measures 31.5 m × 20.5 m and is oriented sixteen degrees west of north. The only other architectural features associated with Q are small appendages to the east, west, and north sides of the structure. Much of the platform and all appendages remain coated with a thick, well-preserved layer of calcined plaster.

Despite Q's great state of preservation, it was burned and partially dismantled prior to its abandonment near the end of the late Middle Preclassic period, sometime between 400 and 300 BCE. Although the platform's calcined plaster surface may be the result of multiple burning events tied to fire rituals, the methodical

FIGURE 10.6. *Reconstruction of the El Quemado structure, Pacbitun Plaza A.*

nature of additional seemingly calculated modes of desecration, including symmetrically chopped architectural features, partial removal of plaster surface, masses of melted plaster thought to be masks, suggest a single termination event.

Likely simultaneous with the burial of Plaza B, sometime around 400–300 BCE, Q was swept meticulously clean of all artifacts and then covered purposefully under a series of marl and clay deposits. Once completely buried, Q was sealed beneath successive plaster floors of a reconditioned Plaza A. That new plaza space served as an artificial platform on which the subsequent ceremonial architecture of the Late Preclassic and Classic period was built (Micheletti 2020; Powis 2020; Powis et al. 2019). Despite the presence of variant attributes, the newly built ceremonial assemblage in Plaza A demonstrates Pacbitun's participation in a pan-Maya ideological shift during the Late/Terminal Preclassic periods manifest in the widespread construction of E Group complexes—a ceremonial assemblage tied to ritual and political authority and the institution of Maya kingship (Freidel et al. 2017). Those changes to the architectural layout of the site suggest that political authority, in addition to economic and status inequalities stemming from differential success in the marine shell bead crafting economy, would have served to further social divides and strengthened the power of the emergence of ruling elite. Thus, while Pacbitun's Epicenter would always function as a communal hub, Plaza A became increasingly restricted to elite activities.

Q is for Community and Complexity

El Quemado and the massive Plaza A construction project helps shed light on Pacbitun's Middle Preclassic community, the emergence of social complexity at the site, and the role marine shell bead production played in that transition. The inception of Q coincides with the significant reorganization of the Plaza B village in the late Mai phase. As the platforms of Plaza B became more complex in size and shape, the marine shell artifact refinement process also changes with the beads becoming increasingly standardized (smaller and more circular) over time (Hohmann 2002, 2014; Hohmann and Powis 1999; Hohmann et al. 2018). Current evidence indicates that the Middle Preclassic period craft specialists living in Plaza B only manufactured disk beads up to two cm in diameter (Hohmann 2002). Even though marine shell disk beads were recovered in Q, they were different than the small disk ones found in the Mai phase platforms in Plaza B. The ones associated with the platform were larger, measuring 4–7.5 cm in diameter. Either the large beads associated with Q were manufactured at a yet undefined workshop at the site, or they originated from a different location, perhaps imported from another settlement.

We propose that social complexity emerged during the early Middle Preclassic period at Pacbitun, in part through success in shell bead production. Social differentiation, which we understand to be a marker of social complexity, is evidenced by the presence of structures of large, finely cut limestone blocks dating to the late Mai phase near bedrock in Plaza A (Micheletti 2016; Powis 2020). The small, unshapely stones of the rough-and-ready constructions beneath Plaza B pale in comparison to those beneath Plaza A. It should be noted that the Plaza A structures, constructed on a natural hillock, were situated about 5 m above the Plaza B platforms (Powis 2020, 38). Because those more elaborate structures date to the late Mai phase, we propose that social inequality developed in part from the different socioeconomic roles linked to the early Mai phase shell bead production. While it is likely that some form of administration, divisions of labor, and/ or rights to resources existed during the early Mai phase, evidence of social differentiation has yet to be identified for the time period. Therefore, the elevation and elaboration of the Plaza A structures may represent the first solid evidence of Middle Preclassic social stratification potentially signaling a nascent elite class at Pacbitun. Furthermore, the context of the large disk shell beads—directly associated with both Q and the elaborate structures of Plaza A—alludes to their prestigious nature and/or ritual/ceremonial significance, providing additional support for an emerging elite class during the late Mai phase.

With the development of Pacbitun's shell bead crafting economic institution starting during the early Mai phase, the physical act of constructing Q during the late Mai phase seems to support the success of the site's craft production endeavors. That success is marked by the ability to command resources and labor for a project that would have greatly exceeded the requirements needed to construct practical architecture (Trigger 1990). Furthermore, the presence of the elaborate, elevated Plaza A structures suggests the success was distributed unevenly, potentially due in part to the development of hierarchically arranged socioeconomic roles tied to craft production. Those with elevated status and excess resources seem to be the most likely influencers and/or sponsors for organizing labor for a project as momentous as Q. Throughout the Maya Lowlands, the earliest monumental construction projects were "the beginning of a political and cultural process that integrated previously separated regional communities" (Estrada-Belli 2012, 221). Therefore, the presence of the ceremonial platform, El Quemado, implies the initiation of ritual centralization and a shared communal identity through ideology. Pacbitun's Middle Preclassic community, replete with specialized craft production, well-integrated long-distance trade networks, social divisions, and the commencement of a politico-religious institution, clearly experiences an early rise to complex society centuries before the construction of its E Group complex. It is also important to keep in mind that rather than being an overt attempt at demonstrating social difference, the construction of Q and the subsequent modifications to Plaza A may have unintentionally reinforced and further entrenched the burgeoning social distinctions that arose from shell bead production (Joyce 2004).

The subsequent reorganization of Plazas A and B at the beginning of the Late Preclassic period Puc phase (300–100 BCE), which included the burial of Q and the entirety of the Middle Preclassic village, coupled with a population boom in the Periphery Zone, indicates that these social divisions took hold quickly and that the site core became an elite place. Powis et al. (2017, 198) note that the mass population movement to the Periphery Zone is indicative of "an elite class capable of expressing control over the population, convincing or coercing them to abandon and bury their homes after generations, ultimately [for] making a space for the ensuing monumental [elite-focused] constructions." Simply put, these changes are markers of how a small, egalitarian community transformed into one with expanding social class distinctions. No longer was the Pacbitun community united by proximity and shared experiences centered on crafting shell beads. Instead, those with social and political power, stemming from their success in shell bead production, commandeered the site core and distinguished themselves as special and distinct from the rest of the community. In this way, the crafting of shell beads played a primary role in the emergence of social complexity at Preclassic period Pacbitun.

CLASSIC PERIOD (250–900 CE) CRAFTING AND COMPLEXITY AT PACBITUN

Pacbitun's Classic period (250–900 CE) witnessed a radical reconfiguration of the relationship between social complexity and crafting from the earlier Preclassic period. Whereas Middle Preclassic Pacbitun community identity was expressed through the shared production of marine shell ornaments, crafted goods became

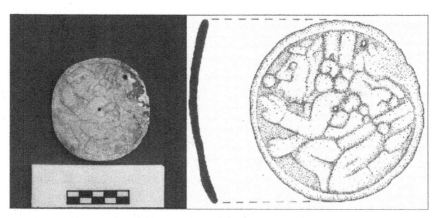

FIGURE 10.7. *Photograph and drawing of* Spondylus *sp. pendant from Tzul phase, crypt, Burial 1–6. The ornament is incised with a representation of a human figure, possibly a ball player, with a bead at the tip of the nose. (Photograph by Paul F. Healy; line drawing by Lori Wright.)*

vehicles for expressing individual social status at the site in the Classic period. Moreover, with one possible exception, our data are insufficient for identifying who the crafters were then. By the middle of the Early Classic period (250–500 CE), the nascent social complexity of the Preclassic period had become an institutionally stratified society, as most evident in the depiction carved into a stela of a ruler performing a ritual on the Long Count date of 9.2.10.0.0 (March 22, 485 CE) (Helmke et al. 2006). With monarchs come attendants, courtesans, and other sub-royal elite, as well as a sustaining population of commoners; in other words, formalized social complexity (Houston and Stuart 2001). Although far removed from Middle Preclassic craft production and nascent social complexity, the following discussion is ultimately concerned with tracing the relationship between crafted objects and Pacbitun's social and political complexity to the end of the polity's life. Doing so allows us to appreciate just how integral crafting and crafted items are to understanding social complexity at Pacbitun.

A significant difference exists between the Classic period shell assemblages from Pacbitun's Periphery Zone and elite Core Zone (Wagner 2009). Most shell artifacts from the Periphery Zone were remains of freshwater shells, whereas the Core Zone shell assemblage is dominated by marine shell ornaments. Social status appears to have been the major factor granting access to marine shell ornaments at Pacbitun in the Classic period (Wagner 2009). Both whole and modified shell specimens were recovered only from elite burials, such as two *Spondylus* sp. disk pendants, likely ear ornaments, (figure 10.7) recovered from the only known Early Classic period burial at Pacbitun (Healy et al. 2014). *Spondylus* shell is widely recognized as a prestige material for prehispanic Maya people (Stone and Zender 2011:167). Marine shell ornaments were absent in all low-ranking interments excavated suggesting the objects marked elevated status in Classic period Pacbitun.

One mound in the Periphery Zone had large quantities of marine shell detritus suggestive of a workshop. This finding suggests that lower-status individuals may have been involved with crafting marine shell ornaments, even if they were not permitted to wear their products.

This pattern of distribution and use is markedly distinct from that of the Middle Preclassic period where the ubiquity of detritus and shell beads indicates everyone in the community was producing them, but few used them as body ornaments. Thus, rather than markers of social cohesion in the Classic period, marine shell body ornaments came to be symbols of social difference and hierarchy, in other words, social complexity.

Royal Body Ornament Use in the Late Classic to Terminal Classic Periods (700–900 CE) at Actun Lak

Investigations at Actun Lak cave in Pacbitun's Periphery Zone has uncovered examples of other Late to Terminal Classic period Maya body decorations made from a variety of material classes that displayed social rank (figure 10.8). Crafted ornaments recovered from Actun Lak include ear spools and beads made from greenstone, limestone, and soda straw cave formations, ornaments comprising the royal regalia of Pacbitun rulers (figure 10.9). Our evidence suggests one of Pacbitun's final rulers drew on the symbolic connection between the ornaments and the royal identity tied to them to make a ritual sacrifice in an unsuccessful attempt to alleviate a major drought and budding social upheaval during the Terminal Classic period (Spenard 2014).

Actun Lak is a heavily modified cavern 43 m in length. Pertinent to this study are two coeval primary Late/Terminal Classic period cultural features in the cave. One is a large-scale modification of the hillside and entrance environs of the cave. The modifications include a set of rubble steps connecting the cavern to another below it. The steps led to an earthen platform at the entrance of Actun Lak that partially blocked its entrance. Beyond the platform and extending into the cave, the modification project includes the floor, artificially raised by several meters (Spenard 2014). The other primary cultural feature is a tabletop altar near the rear of the cavern made from broken and cut cave formations (figure 10.10). Everything surrounding the altar, including the cave walls and ceiling, is charred black from heavy burning, and the matrix on the floor is mostly crushed charcoal. Ceramics from the altar area stylistically date primarily to the Late Coc and Tzib phases (700–900 CE). A piece of burned wood was radiocarbon dated to cal 770–940 CE (Spenard 2014, 219).

Excavations also recovered 125 biconically drilled beads and bead fragments, fragments of two ear spools, and ten undefined worked pieces, all of greenstone.

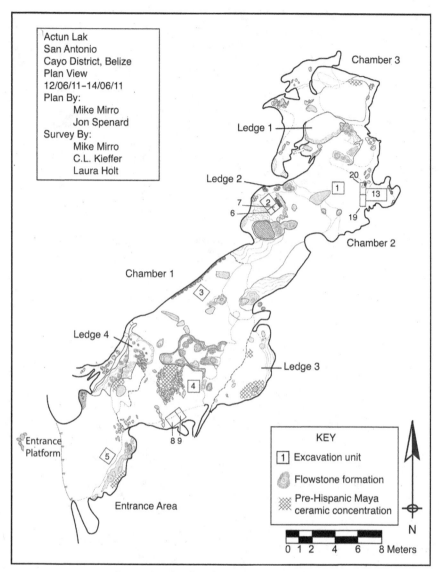

FIGURE 10.8. *Plan view sketch map of Actun Lak.*

Additionally, seven limestone beads and bead fragments and seven soda straw cave formation beads were collected. Our excavations sampled only approximately 30 percent of the floor at the altar's base, suggesting the quantity of artifacts there is much higher than were collected. Ornaments crafted from soda straw cave formations have heretofore gone largely unidentified in the archaeological record, likely due to the fragility of the minerals (Spenard et al. 2013). The

FIGURE 10.9. *Representative sample of the jade, limestone, and soda straw beads from the altar in Actun Lak. The soda straw beads are on the far right; they have been cut diagonally. The left side of each shows a heavily polished wear consistent with having been cut.*

FIGURE 10.10. *Speleothem altar, Actun Lak, chamber 2.*

pieces were identified based on the presence of smooth, angular parallel cuts on their ends.

Greenstone, commonly referred to as jadeite, or jade in the Maya area, was synonymous with Maya kingship (Taube 2005). Rulers appear on carved stelae ornamented with items such as belt celts, necklaces, ear spools, and crown-like head ornaments made from the material. Simply put, jade ornaments were among the primary embodiments of royal identity among the Classic period Maya. Moreover, Maya rulers depicted on monuments are costumed so heavily (quite literally) with the regalia of their statuses–quetzal feathered headdresses, jade ear spools, elaborate necklaces, bracelets and anklets, and more–that their physical bodies become subordinate to the ornamentation, while the physical weight of the objects manifested the perceived substantial burden of their responsibility (Halperin et al. 2018; Meskell and Joyce 2003, 23). In other words, the crafted objects were just as significant, if not more so, as the regent's physical body to the identity of that social station.

Although jade is often recovered archaeologically in both commoner and elite contexts, abundance is a distinct marker of high-status contexts (Spenard 2014, 427). Greenstone artifacts are relatively rare at Pacbitun. For example, the most elaborate royal burial discovered there, located in Structure 1, contained only three jade beads, while the North Group, an elite compound adjacent to Plaza A, contained only four objects of the material, two beads and two "Charlie Chaplin" figurines (Cheong 2013; Healy, Awe, and Helmuth 2004, 231). That over one hundred greenstone artifacts were recovered around the Actun Lak altar, the largest collection yet found at Pacbitun, points to royal ritual.

The question remains, if jade was so rare at Pacbitun, why did body ornaments made of it end up as part of an offering on an altar in the back of a cave in the site's periphery? The answer to that question lies in the recognition that Maya people believed that caves were the ultimate source of rain, and that one of the primary roles of prehispanic Maya kings was ritual communication with various sacred forces and deities on behalf of their polity, particularly those of fertility and rain (Demarest 1992; Inomata 2006a, 2006b; Taube 2001). Their performances involved much pageantry and showmanship, including ostentatious displays of wealth, conspicuous consumption, and the use of elaborate goods.

Pacbitun's Terminal Classic period was a tumultuous time. Population quintupled during late Coc phase, and isotopic evidence from burials at the site indicates malnutrition was common (Powis et al. 2017; White et al. 1993). Prior farming methods strained to feed the rapidly expanded population. Pacbitun farmers experimented with agricultural technologies, especially hillside terracing, to alleviate the problem, but seemingly to no avail (Healy et al. 2007, 33). Moreover, hieroglyphic texts from the site of Caracol in southern Belize may suggest a Pacbitun king was defeated at the start of the Late Coc phase (Helmke and Awe 2012, 70). Collectively, these lines of evidence point to a weakened regent whose power was waning and continued to do so as the basic biological needs of their subjects went unfulfilled. Then, two multidecadal droughts struck the Maya Lowlands between 800 and 900 CE, further undermining the foundation of royal authority (Kennett et al. 2012). Such was the social and political context within which the rituals and construction efforts were made at the altar in Actun Lak.

As communication with the supernatural forces on the behalf of the populace was the purview of the royal lineage (Demarest 1992), curing the drought was the responsibility of the ruler. Presumably, the severity of the drought required large-scale theatrical ritual performances, thus the hillside and Actun Lak's entrance were extensively modified, and an altar for extensive burning events was erected in the cave's interior. Important for our purposes is the stone body ornaments offered at the altar because those objects tell the end of the story of crafting and complexity at Pacbitun. The symbolic connection between the greenstone body ornaments and rulership was deep enough that the objects were used as a proxy for the royal body, a form of self-sacrifice. Emerging from the cave devoid of the objects that marked them of their royal status, the ruler would have demonstrated to all witnesses that they gave their all to ending the drought and making the world work correctly again. Ultimately, those actions were unsuccessful. By the end of the Terminal Classic period around 900 CE, Pacbitun's political system had failed, construction in the Core Zone ceased, and though some people remained in the region for another hundred or so years, all current evidence indicates that the Epicenter was abandoned at that time.

CONCLUSION

In this chapter, we have explored how social complexity arose beads at the pre-hispanic Maya site of Pacbitun, Belize, in part through the crafting of marine shell beads. Crafting the objects was a major economic activity in the early village. Although production occurred among households, the entire community appears to have participated. The shared activity would have fostered social cohesion at first, but it also paved the way for the emergence of social complexity later. In the latter half of the Middle Preclassic period, as production became more standardized, individuals and families experienced differential success with the marine shell bead economy. That economic success elevated the social and political power of some in the community over others. Those with elevated status moved to higher ground, where they exercised their new-found power to build better homes with better materials than used in the original settlement. Presumably that same group also commanded a large labor force to create a novel monumental ceremonial platform that was used to celebrate community rituals. Such changes were not restricted to Pacbitun. In fact, they have been documented throughout Belize and beyond, indicating that the Pacbitun experience was part of a larger, still poorly understood transition to social complexity throughout the Maya region.

In the subsequent Late Preclassic and Classic periods, as the nascent social hierarchy of the Middle Preclassic period became institutionalized, the collective community identity centered on marine shell bead production gave way to the use of crafted body ornaments as markers of individual status differentiation. Body ornaments became more elaborate and made from other prestige materials, including *Spondylus* shell in the Classic period. Yet shell was only one of several media from which elite body ornaments were crafted. Excavations in Actun Lak uncovered Terminal Classic period body ornaments from a royal costume, crafted from jade, limestone, and soda straw cave formations. In this case, the objects were used specifically for their status as markers of the royal body in an unsuccessful effort to ritually stave off a devastating drought, which helped foster Pacbitun's demise. In the end, the objects that once marked and reinforced community cohesion and egalitarian social structure, that is, body ornaments and their crafting when Pacbitun was first settled, came to symbolize hierarchical social organization to such a degree that their sacrifice was just as potent as a ruler giving their life at the end of that site's history.

REFERENCES

Anawalt, Patricia Rieff. 1981. *Indian Clothing before Cortés: Mesoamerican Costumes from the Codices*. Norman: University of Oklahoma Press.

Awe, Jaime J. 1992. "Dawn in the Land between the Rivers: Formative Occupation at Cahal Pech, Belize and Its Implications for Preclassic Development in the Maya Lowlands." PhD diss., University of London.

Buttles, Palma J. 2002. "Material and Meaning: A Contextual Examination of Select Portable Material Culture from Colha, Belize." PhD diss., University of Texas, Austin.

Cheetham, David T. 1995. "Excavations of Structure B-4, Cahal Pech, Belize." In *Belize Valley Preclassic Maya Project: Report of the 1995 Field Season*, edited by Paul F. Healy and Jaime J. Awe, 18–44. Occasional Papers in Anthropology No. 10, Trent University Department of Anthropology, Peterborough, Ontario.

Cheetham, David. 1996. "Reconstruction of the Formative Period Site Core of Cahal Pech, Belize." In *Belize Valley Preclassic Maya Project: Report on the 1995 Field Season*, edited by Paul F. Healy and Jaime J. Awe, 1–33. Occasional Papers in Anthropology No. 12, Trent University Department of Anthropology, Peterborough, Ontario.

Cheong, Kong. 2013. "Archaeological Investigation of the North Group at Pacbitun, Belize." Master's thesis, Trent University.

Clark, John E., and William Parry. 1990. Craft Specialization and Cultural Complexity. *Research in Economic Anthropology* 12:289–346.

Cochran, Jennifer. 2009. "A Diachronic Perspective of Marine Shell Use from B1 at Blackman Eddy, Belize." Master's thesis. University of Texas, Arlington.

Costin, Cathy Lynne. 1998. "Introduction: Craft and Social Identity." *Archeological Papers of the American Anthropological Association* 8:3–16.

Demarest, Arthur. 1992. "Ideology in Ancient Maya Cultural Evolution: The Dynamics of Galactic Polities." In *Ideology and Pre-Columbian Civilizations*, edited by Arthur Andrew Demarest and Geoffrey W. Conrad, 135–58. Santa Fe, NM: School of American Research.

Dreiss, Meredith L. 1994. "The Shell Artifacts of Colha: The 1983 Season." In *Continuing Archaeology at Colha, Belize*, edited by T. R. Hester, H. J. Shafer, and J. D. Eaton, 181–97. Studies in Archaeology 16. Texas Archeological Research Laboratory, University of Texas, Austin.

Estrada-Belli, Francisco. 2012. "Early Civilization in the Maya Lowlands, Monumentality, and Place Making: A View from the Holmul Region." In *Early New World Monumentality*, edited by Robert M. Rosenswig and Richard L. Burger, 198–230. Gainesville: University Press of Florida.

Ferguson, Jocelyn. 1995. "Jewels among the Thorns: An Examination of the Modified Shell Artifacts from Zubin, Cayo District, Belize." In *Belize Valley Archaeological Reconnaissance Project: Progress Report of the 1994 Field Season*, edited by Gyles Iannone and James M. Conlon, 152–71. London: Institute of Archaeology.

Ferguson, Jocelyn, Tina Christensen, and Sonya Schwake. 1996. "The Eastern Ballcourt, Cahal Pech, Belize: 1995 Excavations." In *Belize Valley Preclassic Maya Project: Report on the 1995 Field Season*, edited by Paul F. Healy and Jaime J. Awe, 34–58. Occasional Papers in Anthropology No. 12, Trent University Department of Anthropology, Peterborough, Ontario.

Flannery, Kent V., and Marcus C. Winter. 1976. "Analyzing Household Activities." In *The Early Mesoamerican Village*, edited by K. V. Flannery, 34–47. New York: Academic Press.

Garber, James F. 1989. *Archaeology at Cerros, Belize, Central America*. Vol. 2, *The Artifacts*. David A. Freidel, series editor. Dallas, TX: Southern Methodist University Press.

Garber, James F., M. Kathryn Brown, Jaime J. Awe, and Christopher J. Hartman. 2004. "Middle Formative Prehistory of the Central Belize Valley: An Examination of Architecture, Material Culture, and Sociopolitical Change at Blackman Eddy." In *The Ancient Maya of the Belize Valley: Half a Century of Archaeological Research*, edited by James F. Garber, 25–47. Gainesville: University Press of Florida.

Haines, Helen R. 1997. "Continuing Excavations of Preclassic Deposits at Structure 9." In *The Blue Creek Project: Working Papers from the 1996 Field Season*, edited by W. D. Driver, H. L. Clagett, and H. R. Haines, 19–24. Maya Research Program, St. Mary's University, San Antonio.

Halperin, Christina T., Zachary X. Hruby, and Mongelluzzo. 2018. "The Weight of Ritual: Classic Maya Jade Head Pendants in the Round." *Antiquity* 92 (363): 758–71.

Hammond, Norman, ed. 1991. "Ceramic, Bone, Shell, and Ground Stone Artifacts." In *Cuello: An Early Maya Community in Belize*, 176–91. Cambridge, UK: Cambridge University Press.

Hansen, Richard D. 2016. "Cultural and Environmental Components of the First Maya States: A Perspective from the Central and Southern Maya Lowlands." In *The Origins of Maya States*, edited by Loa P. Traxler and Robert J. Sharer, 329–416. Philadelphia: University of Pennsylvania Museum of Anthropology and Archaeology.

Healy, Paul F. 1990. "Excavations at Pacbitun, Belize: Preliminary Report on the 1986 and 1987 Investigations." *Journal of Field Archaeology* 17:247–62.

Healy, Paul F., Jaime J. Awe, and Hermann Helmuth. 2004. "Defining Royal Maya Burials: A Case from Pacbitun." In *The Ancient Maya of the Belize Valley: Half a Century of Archaeological Research*, edited by James F. Garber, 228–37. Gainesville: University Press of Florida.

Healy, Paul F., David Cheetham, Terry G. Powis, and Jaime J. Awe. 2004. "Cahal Pech: The Middle Formative Period." In *The Ancient Maya of the Belize Valley: Half a Century of Archaeological Research*, edited by J. F. Garber, 103–24. Gainesville: University Press of Florida.

Healy, Paul F., Kitty F. Emery, Teresa Wagner, Bobbi Hohmann, Polydora Baker, and Norbert Stanchly. 2014. "Maya Artifacts of Bone and Shell from Pacbitun." In *Zooarchaeology of the Ancient Maya Centre of Pacbitun (Belize)*, edited by Paul F. Healy and Kitty F. Emery, 97–151. Occasional Papers in Anthropology No. 16, Trent University Department of Anthropology, Peterborough, Ontario.

Healy, Paul F., Christophe Helmke, Jaime J. Awe, and Kay S. Sunahara. 2007. "Survey, Settlement, and Population History at the Ancient Maya Site of Pacbitun, Belize." *Journal of Field Archaeology* 32:17–39.

Helmke, Christophe G., and Jaime J. Awe. 2012. "Ancient Maya Territorial Organisation of Central Belize: Confluence of Archeological and Epigraphic Data." *Contributions in New World Archaeology* 4:59–90.

Helmke, Christophe G., Nikolai Grube, Jaime J. Awe, and Paul F. Healy. 2006. "A Reinterpretation of Stela 6, Pacbitun, Belize." *Mexicon* 28 (4): 70–75.

Hohmann, Bobbi M. 2002. "Preclassic Maya Shell Ornament Production in the Belize Valley, Belize." PhD diss., University of New Mexico.

Hohmann, Bobbi M. 2014. "Middle Preclassic Shell Working at Pacbitun." In *Zooarchaeology of the Ancient Maya Centre of Pacbitun (Belize)*, edited by Paul F. Healy and Kitty F. Emery, 56–78. Occasional Papers in Anthropology No. 12, Trent University Department of Anthropology, Peterborough, Ontario.

Hohmann, Bobbi M., and Terry G. Powis. 1996. "Excavations at Pacbitun, Belize: Archaeological Investigations of the Middle Preclassic Occupation in Plaza B." In *Belize Valley Preclassic Maya Project: Report of the 1995 Field Season*, edited by Paul F. Healy and Jaime J. Awe, 98–127. Occasional Papers in Anthropology No. 12, Trent University Department of Anthropology, Peterborough, Ontario.

Hohmann, Bobbi M., and Terry G. Powis. 1999. "The 1996 Excavations of Plaza B at Pacbitun, Belize." In *Belize Valley Preclassic Maya Project: Progress Report on the 1996 and*

1997 Field Seasons, edited by Paul F. Healy, 1–18. Occasional Papers in Anthropology No. 13. Trent University Department of Anthropology, Peterborough, Ontario.

Hohmann, Bobbi M., Terry G. Powis, and Carmen Arendt. 1999. "The 1997 Investigations at Pacbitun, Belize." In *Belize Valley Preclassic Maya Project: Report of the 1995 Field Season*, edited by Paul F. Healy, 19–30. Occasional Papers in Anthropology No. 13, Trent University Department of Anthropology, Peterborough, Ontario.

Hohmann, Bobbi M., Terry G. Powis, and Paul F. Healy. 2018. "Middle Preclassic Maya Shell Ornament Production: Implications for the Development of Complexity at Pacbitun, Belize." In *Pathways to Complexity: A View from the Maya Lowlands*, edited by M. Kathryn Brown and George Bey III, 117–46. Gainesville: University Press of Florida.

Horn, Sherman W., III. 2015. "The Web of Complexity: Socioeconomic Networks in the Middle Preclassic Belize Valley." PhD diss., Tulane University.

Houston, Stephen D., and Takeshi Inomata. 2009. *The Classic Maya*. Cambridge, UK: Cambridge University Press.

Houston, Stephen D., and David Stuart. 2001. "Peopling the Classic Maya Court." In *Royal Courts of the Ancient Maya*, edited by Takeshi Inomata and Stephen D. Houston, 54–83. Boulder, CO: Westview Press.

Houston, Stephen D., David Stuart, and Karl A. Taube. 2006. *The Memory of Bones: Body, Being, and Experience among the Classic Maya*. Austin: University of Texas Press.

Iannone, G. 1996. "Problems in the Study of Ancient Maya Settlement and Social Organization: Insights from the 'Minor Center' of Zubin, Cayo District, Belize." PhD diss., University of London.

Inomata, Takeshi. 2006a. "Plazas, Performers, and Spectators: Political Theaters of the Classic Maya." *Current Anthropology* 47 (5): 805–42.

Inomata, Takeshi. 2006b. "Politics and Theatricality in Mayan Society." In *The Archaeology of Performance: Theaters of Power, Community, and Politics*, edited by Takeshi Inomata and Lawrence S. Coben, 187–221. New York: AltaMira.

Inomata, Takeshi, Jessica MacLellan, Daniela Triadan, Jessica Munson, Melissa Burham, Kazuo Aoyama, Hiroo Nasu, Flory Pinzón, and Hitoshi Yonenobu. 2015. "The Development of Sedentary Communities in the Maya Lowlands: Co-existing Mobile Groups and Public Ceremonies at Ceibal, Guatemala." *PNAS* 112 (14): 4268–73.

Inomata, Takeshi, Daniela Triadan, Verónica A. Vázquez López, Juan Carlos Fernandez-Diaz, Takayuki Omori, María Belén Méndez Bauer, Melina García Hernández, et al. 2020. "Monumental Architecture at Aguada Fénix and the Rise of Maya Civilization." *Nature* 582:530–33.

Isaza Aizpurúa, Ilean Isel. 1997. "Shell Working and Social Differentiation at the Formative Maya Village of K'axob." Master's thesis, Boston University.

Isaza Aizpurúa, Ilean Isel, and Patricia A. McAnany. 1999. "Adornment and Identity: Shell Ornaments from Formative K'axob." *Ancient Mesoamerica* 10:117–27.

Joyce, Rosemary A. 1998. "Performing the Body in Pre-Hispanic Central America." *RES: Anthropology and Aesthetics* 33:147–65.

Joyce, Rosemary A. 2004. "Unintended Consequences? Monumentality as a Novel Experience in Formative Mesoamerica." *Journal of Archaeological Method and Theory* 11 (1): 5–29.

Keller, Angela H. 2012. "Creating Community with Shell." In *Chan: An Ancient Maya Farming Community*, edited by Cynthia Robin, 253–70. Gainesville: University Press of Florida.

Kidder, A. V. 1947. The *Artifacts of Uaxactun, Guatemala*. Carnegie Institution of Washington Publication 576, Washington, DC.

Kennett, Douglas J., Sebastian F. M. Breitenbach, Valorie V. Aquino, Yemane Asmerom, Jaime J. Awe, James U. L. Baldini, Patrick Bartlein, et al. 2012. "Development and Disintegration of Maya Political Systems in Response to Climate Change." *Science* 338 (6108): 788–91.

Lee, David F. 1996. "Nohoch Na (The Big House): The 1995 Excavations at the Cas Pek Group, Cahal Pech, Belize." In *Belize Valley Preclassic Maya Project: Report on the 1995 Field Season*, edited by Paul F. Healy and Jaime J. Awe, 77–97. Occasional Papers in Anthropology No. 12, Trent University Department of Anthropology, Peterborough, Ontario.

Lee, David F., and Jaime J. Awe. 1995. "Middle Preclassic Architecture, Burials, and Craft Specialization: Report on the 1994 Investigations at the Cas Pek Group, Cahal Pech, Belize." In *Belize Valley Preclassic Maya Project: Report on the 1994 Field Season*, edited by Paul F. Healy and Jaime J. Awe, 95–115. Occasional Papers in Anthropology No. 10, Trent University Department of Anthropology, Peterborough, Ontario.

Lohse, Jon C. 2010. "Archaic Origins of the Lowland Maya." *Latin American Antiquity* 21 (3): 312–52.

Looper, Matthew G. 2009. *To Be like Gods: Dance in Ancient Maya Civilization*. The Linda Schele Series in Maya and Pre-Columbian Studies. Austin: University of Texas Press.

Meskell, Lynn, and Rosemary A. Joyce. 2003. *Embodied Lives: Figuring Ancient Maya and Egyptian Experience*. New York: Routledge.

Micheletti, George J. 2016. Reinvestigating Sub-Structure A-2 in Plaza A at Pacbitun. In *Pacbitun Regional Archaeological Project (PRAP): Report on the 2015 Field Season*, edited by Terry G. Powis, 74–83. Report Submitted to the Institute of Archaeology, National Institute of History and Culture, Belmopan City, Belize.

Micheletti, George J., Kaitlin E. Crow, and Terry G. Powis. 2017. "Q and A: Exposing El Quemado's Architectural Configuration in Plaza A at Pacbitun, Belize." *Research Reports in Belizean Archaeology* 14:23–30.

Micheletti, George, Kaitlin Crow, and Terry G. Powis. 2018. "Expanding Sub-plaza Explorations of Middle Preclassic Architecture at the Site of Pacbitun, Belize." *Research Reports in Belizean Archaeology* 15:17–26.

Micheletti, George J., and Terry G. Powis. 2015. "Origins of the Block Party: Investigations of Preclassic Architecture over and under Plaza A at Pacbitun, Belize." *Research Reports in Belizean Archaeology* 12:205–15.

Micheletti, George J., Terry G. Powis, Sheldon Skaggs, and Norbert Stanchly. 2016. Early Maya Monumental Architecture in the Belize River Valley: Recent Archaeological Investigations of El Quemado at Pacbitun. *Research Reports in Belizean Archaeology* 13:43–50.

Moholy-Nagy, Hattula. 1987. "Formed Shell Beads from Tikal, Guatemala." In *Proceedings of the 1986 Shell Bead Conference: Selected Papers*, edited by C. F. Hayes III and L. Ceci, 139–56. Research Records 20. Rochester Museum and Science Center, Rochester, NY.

Moholy-Nagy, Hattula. 1994. "Tikal Material Culture: Artifacts and Social Structure at a Classic Lowland Maya City." PhD diss., University of Michigan.

Pendergast, David M. 1979. *Excavations at Altun Ha, Belize, 1964–1970*. Vol. 1. Toronto: Royal Ontario Museum Publications in Archaeology.

Peniche May, Nancy. 2016. "Building Power: Political Dynamics at Cahal Pech, Belize, during the Middle Preclassic." PhD diss., University of California, San Diego.

Pires-Ferreira, Jane W. 1976. "Shell and Iron-Ore Mirror Exchange in Formative Mesoamerica, with Comments on Other Commodities." In *The Early Mesoamerican Village*, edited by K. V. Flannery, 311–28. New York: Academic Press.

Pires-Ferreira, Jane W. 1978. "Shell Exchange Networks in Formative Mesoamerica." In *Cultural Continuity in Mesoamerica*, edited by D. L. Browman, 79–100. Paris: Mouton.

Powis, Terry G. 1996. "Excavations of Middle Preclassic Period Round Structures at the Tolok Group, Cahal Pech, Belize." Master's thesis, Trent University.

Powis, Terry G. 2005. "Formative Mesoamerican Cultures: An Introduction." In *New Perspectives on Formative Mesoamerican Cultures*, edited by Terry G. Powis, 1–14. British Archaeological Reports (BAR), International Series 1377, Oxford, England.

Powis, Terry G. 2020. "Middle Preclassic Community Organization at Pacbitun, Belize." In *An Archaeological Reconstruction of Ancient Maya Life at Pacbitun, Belize*, edited by Terry G. Powis, Sheldon Skaggs, and George J. Micheletti, 25–39. BAR International Series 2970, Archaeology of the Maya, Vol. 4. Oxford: BAR Publishing.

Powis, Terry G., Paul Healy, and Bobbi M. Hohmann. 2009. "An Investigation of Middle Preclassic Structures at Pacbitun, Belize." *Research Reports in Belizean Archaeology* 6:169–78.

Powis, Terry G., Sherman Horn III, Gyles Iannone, Paul F. Healy, James F. Garber, Jaime J. Awe, Sheldon Skaggs, and Linda A. Howie. 2016. "Middle Preclassic Period Maya Greenstone 'Triangulates': Forms, Contexts, and Geology of a Unique Mesoamerican Groundstone Artifact Type." *Journal of Archaeological Science: Reports* 10:59–73.

Powis, Terry G., George J. Micheletti, Kaitlin Crow, Sheldon Skaggs, Norbert Stanchly, Nicaela Cartagena, and Jeffrey A. Powis. 2019. "Early Maya Ceremonial Architecture at Pacbitun, Belize." *Latin American Antiquity* 30 (4): 836–42.

Powis, Terry G., George Micheletti, Jon Spenard, and Sheldon Skaggs. 2020. "A Discussion of Early Monumentality at Pacbitun, Belize." In *Approaches to Monumental Landscapes of the Ancient Maya*, edited by Brett Houk, Barbara Arroyo, and Terry G. Powis, 268–89. Gainesville: University of Florida Press.

Powis, Terry G., Sheldon Skaggs, and George Micheletti. 2020. "An Introduction to the Archaeology of Pacbitun, Belize." In *An Archaeological Reconstruction of Ancient Maya Life at Pacbitun, Belize*, edited by Terry G. Powis, Sheldon Skaggs, and George J. Micheletti, 1–8. BAR International Series 2970, Archaeology of the Maya, Vol. 4. Oxford: BAR Publishing.

Powis, Terry G., Jon Spenard, Sheldon Skaggs, George Micheletti, and Christophe G. Helmke. 2017. "An Ancient Maya City Living on the Edge: The Culture History of Pacbitun." *Research Reports in Belizean Archaeology* 14:191–212.

Powis, Terry G., Norbert Stanchly, Christine White, Paul F. Healy, Jaime J. Awe, and Fred Longstaffe. 1999. "A Reconstruction of Middle Preclassic Maya Subsistence Economy at Cahal Pech, Belize." *Antiquity* 73:1–13.

Rice, Prudence M. 2019. "Early Pottery and Construction at Nixtun-Ch'ich', Petén, Guatemala: Preliminary Observations." *Latin American Antiquity* 30 (3): 471–89.

Robichaux, Hugh R. 1998. "Excavations at the Upper Plaza." In *The 1997 Season of the Chan Chich Archaeological Project*, edited by Brett A. Houk, 31–52. Papers of the Chan Chich Archaeological Project No. 3. Center for Maya Studies, San Antonio, TX.

Robin, Cynthia. 2000. "Towards an Archaeology of Everyday Life: Maya Farmers of Chan Noohol and Dos Chombitos Cik'in, Belize." PhD diss, University of Pennsylvania.

Sharer, Robert J. 1994. *The Ancient Maya*. 5th ed. Stanford, CA: Stanford University Press.

Skaggs, Sheldon, George Micheletti, Mike Lawrence, Nicaela Cartagena, and Terry G. Powis. 2020. "Identification of an Ancient Maya Ground Stone Production Site in the Periphery of Pacbitun, Belize." In *An Archaeological Reconstruction of Ancient Maya Life at Pacbitun, Belize*, edited by Terry G. Powis, Sheldon Skaggs, and George J. Micheletti. BAR International Series 2970, Archaeology of the Maya, Vol. 4. Oxford: BAR Publishing.

Spenard, Jon. 2014. "Underground Identity, Memory, and Political Spaces: A Study of the Classic Period Maya Ceremonial Karstscape in the Pacbitun Region, Cayo District, Belize." PhD diss., University of California, Riverside.

Spenard, Jon, Javier Mai, and Oscar Mai. 2012. "They Lived Where?!: A Report on the 2011 Settlement Reconnaissance around Pacbitun, Cayo District, Belize." In *Pacbitun Regional Archaeological Project (PRAP): Report on the 2011 Field Season*, edited by Terry G. Powis, 125–43. Report submitted to the Institute of Archaeology National Institute of Culture and History, Belmopan, Belize.

Spenard, Jon, R., Bryan Reece, and Terry G. Powis. 2012. "Identifying Hinterland Borders: An Initial Report on the 2011 Archaeological Investigations at Sak Pol Pak, Cayo District, Belize." *Research Reports in Belizean Archaeology* 9:107–18.

Spenard, Jon, Teresa Wagner, and Terry G. Powis. 2013. "Of Shells, Soda Straws, Caves, and Kings: Crafting, Body Practices, and Identity Making among the Ancient Maya of Pacbitun, Belize." *Research Reports in Belizean Archaeology* 10:147–55.

Stone, Andrea J., and Marc Zender. 2011. *Reading Maya Art: A Hieroglyphic Guide to Ancient Maya Painting and Sculpture*. New York: Thames & Hudson.

Sullivan, Lauren, M. Kathryn Brown, and Jaime J. Awe. 2009. "Refining the Cunil Ceramic Complex at Cahal Pech, Belize." *Research Reports in Belizean Archaeology* 6:161–68.

Taschek, Jennifer T. 1994. *The Artifacts from Dziblchaltun, Yucatán, Mexico: Shell, Polished Stone, Bone, Wood, and Ceramics*. Middle American Research Institute Publication 50. Tulane University, New Orleans.

Taube, Karl A. 2001. "The Breath of Life: the Symbolism of Wind in Mesoamerica and the American Southwest." In *The Road to Aztlan: Art from a Mythic Homeland*, edited by Virginia M. Fields and Victor Zamudio-Taylor, 102–23. Los Angeles: Los Angeles County Museum of Art.

Taube, Karl A. 2005. "The Symbolism of Jade in Classic Maya Religion." *Ancient Mesoamerica* 16:23–50.

Tozzer, Alfred A. 1941. *Landa's relación de las cosas de Yucatán*. Papers of the Peabody Museum of American Archaeology and Ethnology, Vol. 18.

Tremain, Cara Grace. 2017. "A Study of Dress and Identity in the Late Classic Maya Court." PhD diss., University of Calgary.

Tremain, Cara Grace. 2020 "Translucent Textiles of the Ancient Maya: Insights from a Museum Collection." *Dress*. doi:10.1080/03612112.2020.1712124.

Turner, Terence. 1980. "The Social Skin." In *Not Work Alone: A Cross-Cultural View of Activities Superfluous to Survival*, edited by Jeremy Cherfas and Roger Lewin, 112–40. Beverly Hills, CA: Temple Smith.

Wagner, Teresa. 2009. "Ancient Lowland Maya Mollusk Exploitation at Pacbitun, Belize." Master's thesis, Trent University.

Ward, Drew. 2013. "Investigations of a Ground Stone Tool Workshop at Pacbitun, Belize." Master's thesis, Georgia State University.

Weber, Jennifer U. 2011. "Investigating the Ancient Maya Landscape: A Settlement Survey in the Periphery of Pacbitun." Master's thesis, Georgia State University.

Weber, Jennifer U., and George Micheletti. 2016. "Implementing Airborne LiDAR Data for Archaeological Analysis and Prospection at the Ancient Maya Site of Pacbitun, Belize." In *Pacbitun Regional Archaeological Project (PRAP): Report on the 2015 Field Season*, edited by Terry G. Powis, 36–40. Report submitted to the Institute of Archaeology National Institute of Culture and History, Belmopan, Belize.

Weber, Jennifer U., and Terry G. Powis. 2014. "Assessing Terrestrial Laser Scanning in Complex Environments: An Approach from the Ancient Maya Site of Pacbitun, Belize." *Advances in Archaeological Practice* 2 (2): 60–74.

White, Christine D., Paul F. Healy, and Henry P. Schwarcz. 1993. "Intensive Agriculture, Social Status, and Maya Diet at Pacbitun, Belize." *Journal of Anthropological Research* 49:347–75.

Willey, Gordon R. 1972. *The Artifacts of Altar de Sacrificios*. Papers of the Peabody Museum of Archaeology and Ethnology, Vol. 64. Harvard University, Cambridge, MA.

Willey, Gordon R. 1978. *Excavations at Seibal*. No. 1, *Artifacts*. Memoirs of the Peabody Museum, Vol. 14. Harvard University, Cambridge, MA.

Willey, Gordon R., William R. Bullard Jr., John B. Glass, and James C. Gifford. 1965. *Prehistoric Maya Settlements in the Belize Valley*. Papers of the Peabody Museum of Archaeology and Ethnology, Vol. 54. Harvard University, Cambridge, MA.

11

Why the Mesoamerican Formative Period Matters

Vantages on Human Aggregation and Cooperation

GARY M. FEINMAN

According to the United Nations Department of Economic and Social Affairs (UN DESA 2018), 54 percent of the world's population currently lives in urban areas, and that proportion is expected to increase to 66 percent by 2050. Yet from the long vantage of human history, cities are a comparatively recent phenomenon established only during the last eight thousand years (Smith 2007). The global spread and growth of urban metropoles is astounding as living in cities requires major socioeconomic adaptations, especially when juxtaposed to the open, fluid, face-to-face networks that characterized humanity's long career as mobile hunter-gatherers prior to the advent of more settled communities. Cities require interpersonal cooperation—behaviors that deliver benefits to other individuals or are advantageous to both actor and recipient—between unrelated individuals at scales not seen in any other species (e.g., Melis and Semmann 2010). Human aggregations and coalitions are larger and more diverse than those of other primates (e.g., Dunbar 2007; Tomasello 2014). How and in what contexts did these social arrangements arise, and might there be lessons from historical steps in these global processes that can serve us today?

https://doi.org/10.5876/9781646422883.c011

Mesoamerica is one of the world's settings where cities arose autochthonously, without stimuli from beyond the macroregion. Compared to other parts of the globe, the first urban centers in Mesoamerica were founded comparatively quickly following the advent of the area's earliest sedentary communities (Clark and Cheetham 2002). In more than a few regions of Mesoamerica, both of these key settlement transitions occurred during the Formative period, when the tempo of change was rapid (Lesure 2008, 115), often at a faster pace than in other global macroregions (Bandy 2008, tab. 1), and key innovations were spurred (Clark 2004; Joyce and Grove 1999). At that time, the nature of early towns and later cities that emerged in Mesoamerica were far from uniform in spatial layout, size, or modes of governance (e.g., Blanton 2012; Feinman and Carballo 2018; Pool 2012; M. Smith 2002). Likewise, region to region across Mesoamerica, the Formative era processes of change did not follow a unilineal temporal path. The Mesoamerican Formative period is important because it provides an opportunity to study comparative courses of human cooperation across an environmentally diverse macroregion. What changed at what pace, when, where, and why? In today's urbanized world, there are potentially valuable lessons in the distant past concerning human cooperation, innovation, and sustainability and the interplay between demographics, governance, and the built environment. Through archaeology's perspective on deep history, we have the opportunity to explore outcomes, which are nearly impossible to know or assess with contemporary cases (Smith 2010, 237–38).

As the papers in this collection illustrate amply, our empirical perspective on the Mesoamerican Formative period is richer than it was more than forty years ago when the period was initially introduced to the entire discipline of archaeology through what is recognized as a classic tome (Flannery 1976). Not only do archaeologists now have information on more regions of the prehispanic Mesoamerican world, but they also possess data from a larger number of ancient communities within most of these regions. Whether focused on funerary contexts, settlement patterns, houses, or artifact distributions, the sample sizes discussed in the papers tend to exceed what was available decades ago, and, following the skeptical graduate students caricatured in the *Early Mesoamerican Village* (Flannery 1976), key aspects of these data are presented quantitatively. Nevertheless, in their focus on Formative period histories of their specific areas, what is less evident in this volume's papers are discussions of the cross-regional and conceptual issues that the findings from the Mesoamerican Formative (here and elsewhere) allow us to probe.

New findings and conceptual perspectives require the reconsideration of certain core tenets and assumptions that have guided archaeological research on the Mesoamerican Formative for decades and even longer. To reframe the issue, I first adopt a macroscale perspective on the beginnings of the Mesoamerican

Formative era to reset key questions regarding shifts in scale and cooperation. A discussion of theoretical considerations and analytical dimensions follows, including reflections on the consequences of sedentism, as well as cooperation, leadership, demographic increase, innovation, and sustainability. By raising these broader intrinsically comparative, thematic foci, my intent is to take brief stock of what is known, outline plausible scenarios and hypotheses, and chart potentially productive directions for future investigations.

MACROSCALE VANTAGE ON EARLY MESOAMERICA

Although mobile peoples colonized the macroregion at least eight thousand years earlier (Acosta Ochoa 2012), it was only after the widespread advent of more sedentary settlements across the area (ca. 1900–1500 BCE) that Mesoamerica as a networked world came to be, loosely delineated by lessened degrees of connectivity with the arid regions to the north and the Chibchan-speaking areas to the south (Evans 2012). Mesoamerica was a socioeconomic entity, albeit highly diverse environmentally. Clearly, the domestication and farming of corn in Mesoamerica was (and is) a critical element of life in this world (Evans 2012). Yet corn was domesticated and dispersed millennia before the start of the Formative period (e.g., Flannery 1986), and as it spread rapidly and broadly, its role in subsistence was significant beyond Mesoamerica (Clark and Cheetham 2002; Piperno and Smith 2012; Rosenswig 2015).

Across Mesoamerica, by later in the Archaic period (ca. 4000–1900 BCE), maize was a key component of subsistence regimes, especially in certain lowland regions, but in general, it was not yet a predominant staple (Kennett 2012; Kennett et al. 2020; Piperno and Smith 2012; Rosenswig 2015). The plant, which through human selection increased in productivity and environmental adaptability over time, undoubtedly laid an economic foundation for the transition to the Formative period in Mesoamerica. But its mere consumption did not provoke an immediate shift to permanent settlements or marked demographic changes (Clark and Cheetham 2002; Lesure 2008); in most Mesoamerican regions, the presence of corn preceded the shift to more sedentary lifeways by several millennia. Yet in other areas, sedentary communities had diverse subsistence regimes with only limited reliance on maize (e.g., Inomata et al. 2015; Killion 2013).

Shortly after 2000 BCE, ceramics, semipermanent dwellings, and other indications of less mobility are evidenced across Mesoamerica (Clark and Cheetham 2002; Pool 2012). The dating of these archaeological indicators for sedentary ways of life are timed consistently, within a span of five hundred to eight hundred years, across the entire macroregion, in both highland and lowland environments (Clark and Cheetham 2002; Rosenswig 2015). Although economically underpinned by domesticates in many Mesoamerican regions, the transition to sedentism (and hence the onset of the Formative period) was not purely a subsistence-driven process, since neither the dietary reliance on cultigens nor farming practices by which they were produced was equivalent across regions (Clark and Cheetham 2002; Kennett 2012; Piperno and Smith 2012). Furthermore, if this was merely an outgrowth of local population-resource calculations, why was the timing so consistent across such highly diverse geographic settings? A central tenet, then, is that the Formative period, defined by a marked increase in the longevity of settlements, associated investments in proximate landscapes (Lesure 2008), and the construction of civic ceremonial features (Inomata et al. 2019, 2020) was principally a social process, and, to a degree, it must be examined through that lens to understand the significant changes that occurred during that era.

Among the dramatic shifts that took place were pronounced increases in socioeconomic differentiation, political complexity, and demographic growth and nucleation (DeLance chapter 1, this volume). In certain regions of Mesoamerica, specific shifts were timed with the earliest establishment of more permanent settlements (Pool 2012), but most commonly, dramatic transitions were manifest following a couple of centuries (Carballo 2016; Clark and Cheetham 2002, fig. 3; Feinman 1991). In general, the tempo of change was rapid. But as seen in this collection of papers, the local and regional paths of these shifts were not uniform, although overarching parallels are evident across Mesoamerica. Before discussing the specific ramifications of more sedentary Mesoamerican lifeways, I introduce and address theoretical frames, analytical dimensions, and key concepts.

FRAMING THE FORMATIVE PERIOD

My colleagues and I (Blanton et al. 1993) have outlined four key analytical dimensions—scale, complexity, integration (modes of connectivity), and boundedness—to examine long-term change in human social relations and institutions (sensu Holland-Lulewicz 2020). Scale refers to size, and here I employ it principally to discuss the size and density of human groupings. Complexity denotes the multiplicity of differentiated parts in a social network (Kowalewski 1990), functional differentiation. Complexity may be manifest along either horizontal or vertical dimensions. Horizontal complexity refers to specialization, different roles that do not directly involve distinctions in rank. Vertical complexity entails differences in rank and political power. It includes leadership roles and institutions (Kowalewski and Birch 2020; Kowalewski and Heredia Espinoza 2020), although these may take markedly different forms (e.g., Blanton and Fargher 2008; Blanton et al. 1996; Feinman 2013; Feinman and Carballo 2018). Integration or variable modes and means of connectivity reflect the nature of socioeconomic relations between participants in a network. It encompasses both the nature of material and information flows as well as degrees of interdependence. Boundedness refers to the relative openness or closure of social networks.

The transition to more sedentary patterns of life, which occurred across Mesoamerica within a short temporal duration associated with the onset of the Formative period (Clark 2004), set in motion dramatic changes along all four of these analytical dimensions. I conceptually explore the social mechanisms (sensu Hedström and Swedberg 1996) that undergird these shifts and that lead to suggested reconsiderations of certain theoretical tenets and lenses that archaeologists traditionally have employed. As Mesoamerican people settled down more permanently, they constructed new niches (sensu Smith 2012; Sterelny and Watkins 2015; Watkins 2017), in regard both to landscapes they exploited through burning, clearing, and planting and to the dwellings, ceremonial features, and settlements that they built and in which they resided (Inomata et al. 2020; Lesure 2008). The significant changes and the mechanisms and processes that were triggered at the advent of the Formative period can be conceptualized as a "social tipping point" (Cobb 2018; Pruitt et al. 2018), a time when new institutions were established (Kowalewski and Heredia Espinoza 2020, 496) that dynamically altered the courses of Mesoamerican socioeconomic life and the region's subsequent long-term history. Although the Formative period was an era of significant changes, its onset was not sparked by a brief event or a flashpoint in the sense that the transitions were immediate or coincidently timed; rather, key changes took place over centuries.

To underpin this social tipping point, it is necessary to review relevant aspects of Mesoamerica's long Archaic period and mobile hunting and gathering lifeways more generally (Blanton et al. 1993, 35–49). For mobile hunter-gatherers, networks of social relationships generally are dispersed, open, ephemeral, and changing with regularity as groups and individuals split apart and nucleate. But the most stable unit is small, made up of close kin (and those who are proximate) who have in-depth knowledge of each other (Apicella et al. 2012). These individual relations tend to be face-to-face, personal, and biographical (Coward and Gamble 2008). Yet hunting and gathering populations are not purely egalitarian, as inequities are often manifest along the lines of age, sex, and ability (Cashdan 1980; Flanagan 1989). Likewise, especially during aggregational episodes, leaders and specialists may arise, but their roles tend to be situational and ephemeral (Feinman 1995; Flannery 1972; Thompson and Birch 2018). Within Mesoamerica, during the Archaic period, spatial spheres of more intense interaction did emerge and were marked by stylistic differences in stone tool assemblages, but these interactional zones were extensive (Kennett 2012; MacNeish and Nelken-Terner 1983; Rosenswig 2015).

SCALE

Globally, there is ample evidence that the transition from mobile lifeways to more permanent settlements precipitated demographic growth (Bandy and Fox 2010; Bellwood and Oxenham 2008; Bocquet-Appel 2011), although the specific suite of causal factors may not be uniform. The data presented here on the size and/or number of settlements during the Formative period in regions of Mesoamerica conform with this wider, cross-cultural pattern (see also Feinman 1991). With more permanent settlements and tended fields that entailed householder labor and resource investments or sunk-costs (Janssen et al. 2003), departure from settled communities (fissioning) became a less viable option than in more mobile networks. In Mesoamerica (and other regions where sedentary communities were formed), population aggregations that both were larger and had greater longevity than typical for hunter-gatherer camps were established (Birch 2013).

Larger, denser settlements have marked and wide-ranging implications (Birch 2013; Smith 2019) for human social networks, their complexity, and integration. As community size increases arithmetically, the potential number of interpersonal interactions expands exponentially (Coward and Dunbar 2014; Johnson 1982). The abandonment of fission-fusion mobility in the shift to habitual co-residence in larger aggregations exacerbates social stresses, and these had to be met coincidently with economic adjustments and changes in resource procurement, storage, risk cycles, and travel times (Pool 2012). No longer could network size map directly onto resource availability (Coward and Dunbar 2014).

Michael Smith (2019, 37) sees "the concentration of formerly dispersed people into villages, towns, and cities—as one of the most consequential processes" in human history. He (Smith 2019) also rightly notes that although scholars across the social sciences view this process as a critical transition, there are disparities in framing, with some focused on scalar costs and others on the benefits. Arguments concerning scalar stresses have been widely discussed in the anthropological literature (Birch 2013; Feinman 2011, 2013; Fletcher 1995; Johnson 1982) and emphasize how greater densities and interaction foment shifts in organizational complexity. At the same time, researchers in economics and geography emphasize the positive effects of "energized crowding" (Kostof 1991, 37), where in larger and denser settlements, increases in face-to-face social interaction provoke technological innovation, accelerated transfers of knowledge, and economic growth (Bettencourt 2013; Ortman and Coffey 2017; Smith 2019). The properties of social networks are nonlinear, so as settlements grow in size they foment exponential changes in the use of space, comprehension of information, productivity, and labor divisions. These processes did not begin at the onset of cities but materialized when people aggregated in permanent co-resident communities; subsequently, they were scaled up as further nucleation occurred.

INTEGRATION/CONNECTIVITY

With co-residence in larger, denser settlements, not only the number but also the nature of social ties change. The burdens of sustaining and servicing social relationships strain time and energy budgets, increasing demand on memory and social cognition (Roberts 2010). The specific scope of human cognitive capabilities is individually variable, and there is debate over precise capacities (de Ruiter et al. 2011; Dunbar 2011; Hill and Dunbar 2003; Wellman 2007). But there is little disagreement over the fact that constraints do exist and that they range around no more than several hundred associations (Sutcliffe et al. 2012; Wellman 2012). Thus, once proximate social networks exceed that size, the nature of relations shift (Coward and Dunbar 2014) so that ties with close affiliates (multiplex, biographical) differ from those farther afield (categorical, role-based).

Similar differences in interpersonal ties were present in mobile networks as well, but there the option to fission could diminish stresses. Furthermore, the proportion of people linked through weak ties (generally non-biographical relations) (Granovetter 1973, 1983) would become much greater as settlements expanded. The size of networks and communities may grow, and still endure, only if individuals are able to cope not merely with increasingly large sets of social ties but also with a lesser familiarity with an expanded set of contacts. The ability to stabilize weak ties represents an important adjustment for human existence in larger social formations that offsets the cognitive, temporal, and energetic costs of processing greater quantities of social information and large sets of interpersonal relationships (Coward and Dunbar 2014). As the scale of population concentrations grows, interactions are mediated less by in-depth mutual knowledge and more by symbols linked to place and status, by social role (Coward 2016; Sterelny and Watkins 2015).

The integration of relational networks, some with weak ties and others with strong ties, allows communities to grow and expand rather than break apart. Shared practice, and the associated material culture, can help scaffold and affirm weak ties, just as drinking, feasting, and reciprocal exchanges may solidify less-intimate relations (Coward and Dunbar 2014; Nettle and Dunbar 1997). Cooperation is contingent and situational (Blanton and Fargher 2013; Carballo et al. 2014) and so is fostered through specific practices. In Early–Middle Formative period Mesoamerica, the creation of shared regional ceramic traditions (Brzezinski et al., this volume; Rice and South, this volume; Stanton et al., this volume; Stoner and Nichols, this volume), the implementation of suprahousehold feasts (Hepp, this volume), and the practice of small-scale economic specialization and local exchanges (Spenard et al, this volume) helped solidify weak ties and build communities (see also Pool 2012).

In small-scale aggregations, most aspects of daily activity occur in communal contexts that are broadly visible (Whitelaw 1991). With growth, social networks became dominated by individuals who were less intimately connected. Residential domiciles, built in more permanent settlements across Mesoamerica, provide a mechanism for privacy among those with strong ties, while increasing the opportunity for the householders to opt when, what, and how to present to less-intimate community co-residents what was private and what was shared more widely. As group size expands and a greater proportion and number of relations are weak, these ties also become more heterogeneous as the specific relations to others diversify. In consequence, people may have adopted an increasing array of identities and roles, which they signaled in more complex ways (Coser 1975; Granovetter 1983; Perry-Smith 2006), and the emergence of these identities and affiliations likely fostered the increasing creativity, innovation, and elaborate/diversified signaling (in ceramics, figurines, and other media) that we see during the Mesoamerican Formative period.

BOUNDEDNESS

Based on the papers in this collection and the Mesoamerican Formative period literature more broadly, certain long-standing tenets concerning early sedentary communities also should be opened for serious question and reconsideration. In a paper that succinctly set out what were traditional views (but still underlie much current thinking), Robert Carneiro (2002) proposed that early sedentary villages often have two key organizational features, economic self-sufficiency and political autonomy. The inference was that these processes led to small, locally distinct cultural units. But the transition from the Archaic to the Early Formative period was not marked by the cessation of mobile lifeways, stark declines in interregional interaction and exchange, or intensified regional boundedness.

For example, in some parts of the Maya Lowlands (ca. 1500–1250 BCE), investments in civic-ceremonial architecture preceded sedentary residence (Inomata et al. 2015, 2017, 2019, 2020). Across Mesoamerica, population movements contributed to frequent, rapid episodes of demographic growth and aggregation during the Formative period (e.g., Feinman 1991; Feinman and Nicholas 2013; Sanders 1972; C. Smith 2002). Intercommunity and interregional exchanges were important elements of broad-scale connectivity during the Formative period (e.g., Blanton et al. 1993; Carballo 2011; Ebert et al. 2015; Flannery and Marcus 1994; Golitko and Feinman 2015, fig. 4; Hirth et al. 2013; Lesure et al. 2013; Rosenswig 2010; Stark 2017). Based on the analysis of archaeological obsidian samples, sourced to their outcrops, we can see two basic networks or sub-graphs of exchange (Ebert et al. 2015; Golitko and Feinman 2015, fig. 4; Hirth et al. 2013) during the Early–Middle Formative period. One encompassed the Central and Southern Highlands and the Pacific Coast, northwest of the Isthmus of Tehuantepec, and the other included the Isthmus, the Maya region, and the Gulf Coast. The networks (sub-graphs) of obsidian exchange conform spatially (e.g., Golitko and Feinman 2015, fig. 4) to the two Early Formative "style provinces" that were defined years earlier based on ceramic distributions (Clark 1991: fig. 8; Flannery and Marcus 2000; Rosenswig 2011, fig. 11.1). The shared red-on-buff complex was associated with the highland regions, while the eastern, more lowland province was characterized by neckless jars with bichrome slips and fluting or cross-hatching.

These findings indicate that at the onset of sedentism in Mesoamerica, communities were part of networks that exchanged materials and information and that extended broadly, far beyond the bounds of physiographic regions (Stark 2017). Of course, certain transfers of goods and knowledge transcended these "style provinces," yet at lower interactional intensities (Flannery and Marcus 1994; Marcus 1989; Pool 2009, 2012). These empirical patterns are precisely the converse of what would be expected if villages were autonomous, self-sufficient, and culturally distinct at that time. With this transition, mobility, movement, and intra-settlement flux diminished, but they did not end. Furthermore, variation in burial practices and community plans (e.g., Carballo 2016; Carpenter 2019; Pugh et al. 2019) have been noted between contemporaneous settlements in specific regions. These patterns of variation in key domestic practices imply that there was not one static, homogeneous, culturally determined tradition for each region (Rice and South, this volume; Stoner and Nichols, this volume). Rather, the transition to sedentism, with associated shifts in demographic scale and densities, was an era of cultural innovation, experimentation, aggregation/disaggregation, and the creation/ dissemination of practices that were shared widely (e.g., Bandy 2010; Coward and Dunbar 2014; Watkins 2008), but not in uniform ways, nor was one region or site the "beacon" from which ideas and goods emerged with other populations receiving them (e.g., Flannery and Marcus 2000; Marcus 1989). The role of human agency in the construction of social affiliations and networks can no longer be minimized (Blanton 2015, 9176; Kalin and Sambanis 2018).

COMPLEXITY

As this book is focused on understanding complexity, I have left discussion of that analytical dimension to last. Above, I outlined some of the factors that may have spurred greater horizontal complexity with the transition to more sedentary lifeways. In larger, denser communities, a greater number of co-residents would have been known only peripherally, not biographically. Not only were there increased challenges of privacy and scalar stress, but there was a collective challenge/opportunity to integrate and cooperate with people who were outside the sphere of regular, intimate interaction (Coward and Dunbar 2014; Dunbar 2013). The potential disruptions of constant fissioning, distrust, and free-rider problems had to be managed and avoided, while collective action problems, such as defense, had to be faced. For example, in the Valley of Oaxaca at the head town of San José Mogote, a defensive palisade was built relatively early in the center's occupation (Flannery and Marcus 2005, 115–17).

New roles and categorical markers emerged at the outset of the Mesoamerican Formative era. For example, at San José Mogote, houses were arranged in residential wards, which were differentially associated with one of two sets of symbolically iconic motifs on ceramic vessels (Marcus 1989). Smaller hamlets in the region were principally characterized by only one of these symbol sets. The placement of these symbolically imbued artifacts in intra-community burial contexts also served to link people, living and dead, to specific places and through funerary rituals to tie those who survived both to place and to others in the social network to which the deceased belonged (e.g., Gillespie 2011; McAnany 2011). In small communities, death may provoke interpersonal fissioning as the affinal and agnatic ties linked through that individual are severed. Ancestor veneration (DeLance and Awe, this volume), as well as other funerary rituals and practices, provide ritual bases to alleviate the likelihood of such disruptions.

Across Mesoamerica at this time, economic interdependence between households was fostered through specializations and exchange. Personal adornments (Pires-Ferreira 1976; Spenard et al., this volume), elaborate ceramic serving wares, and new consumables (e.g., Henderson et al. 2007) led householders to procure, acquire, and/or produce goods that they then exchanged with their neighbors. A wide range of domestic production activities for exchange, not evidenced earlier, have been identified in Early–Middle Formative contexts, including bitumen (Wendt 2009), magnetite mirrors (Marcus 1989), pottery, and shell beads (Balkansky and Croissier 2009).

Social and economic axes of horizontal complexity can foster cooperation and collective action in communities and closely linked social networks that range up to two to three thousand people in size (although hierarchical structures can be present), but above that scale, supra-household leadership (vertical complexity) generally is found (e.g., Bernard and Killworth 1973, 1979; Feinman 1998, 2011, 2013; Kosse 1990; Lekson 1985). Of course, horizontal affiliations do not disappear and tend to be maintained through neighborhood organizations (e.g., Arnauld et al. 2012), dyadic exchanges, sodalities, and other socioeconomic interactive modes (e.g., Tuzin 2001). In many regions during the Mesoamerican Formative period, vertical complexity (differential power, leadership, and levels of decision making above domestic units) tended to develop shortly after (or even at the time of) the transition to sedentism. For example, in the Valley of Oaxaca, beginning in the earliest phase of village life, one valley community (San José Mogote) was larger than all others and had non-domestic architectural features not found at contemporaneous communities. These patterns were by no means unique to the Valley of Oaxaca (e.g., Clark and Cheetham 2002). Intra-regional settlement distinctions, although not great at first, were further exaggerated through time (e.g., Carballo 2016; Feinman 1991; Feinman and Nicholas 2013; Pool 2007). Nevertheless, during the Mesoamerican Formative, vertical complexity, leadership, and supra-household governance took a range of forms, and this variation is evident across both space and time.

FORMATIVE PERIOD GOVERNANCE

At the beginning of the Mesoamerican Formative, means and modes of supra-household governance were not uniform. For example, non-residential architecture (e.g., Adler and Wilshusen 1990; Bandy 2008; Peterson and Drennan 2012) provides one critical comparative vantage on the rituals and civic-ceremonial activities that appear associated with emergent leadership and broad-scale cooperation. For the first half of the Formative era, archaeologists have recorded small, non-domestic structures with lime-plastered floors at San José Mogote (Flannery and Marcus 2015), E Groups across the Maya Lowlands (Rawski and Brown, this volume; Stanton et al., this volume; Inomata 2017; Inomata et al. 2015), a ballcourt at Paso de la Amada in the Soconusco region of Pacific Coast Chiapas (Hill et al. 1998), circular platforms and a carved stone obelisk at Cuicuilco (Plunket and Uruñuela 2012), monumental carved stone heads and tabletop altars/thrones at San Lorenzo (Cyphers and Di Castro 2009), and rectangular plazas and platforms in various arrangements at many settlements (e.g., Carballo 2016; Clark 1997; Smyth, this volume).

Civic-ceremonial activities during the Early–Middle Formative period were enacted in distinctive ways with variation both in the constructed spaces where rituals were performed as well as the scale of the labor efforts deployed to construct non-residential structures and associated spaces. One key difference was the emphasis placed on specific individuals in positions of power in parts of the Mesoamerican lowlands (most notably at sites near the Gulf Coast) compared to the highlands. At sites such as San Lorenzo and La Venta, in the Gulf Lowlands, monumental sculptures were used to portray charismatic individuals, and these settlements also had palatial residences and elaborate mortuary contexts that are not found elsewhere at that time (Carballo 2016; Cyphers and Di Castro 2009; Pool 2007). Iconic symbols and supernatural imagery were evident more widely, but outside the Gulf Coast, depictions of actual people were rare; and when they were present, they more frequently represent mythic narratives than efforts to legitimize and display personal power (Carballo 2016, 17; Grove 1999; Grove and Gillespie 2009). Beyond the Gulf Coast centers, Formative ritual precincts tended to be more open and broadly accessible, residential architecture and funerary contexts were less starkly differentiated, and public art portraying individual personages was rare (Grove 2014, 182). Given the emphasis on public spaces and buildings, various architectural innovations, including adobes, stone masonry, and lime plaster, were evidenced first in these highland regions (Flannery and Marcus 2000, 30).

Across Formative Mesoamerica at the outset (or within a few centuries following sedentism), there are indications that more vertically complex institutions and relations arose as evidenced by the emergence of head towns with civic-ceremonial architecture (absent in smaller settlements), distinctions in residential architecture and burials, and differentiation in access to ritual spaces and goods (e.g., Carballo 2016; Clark and Cheetham 2002), but the nature of leadership varied in ways that parallel differences both in other global macroregions after the onset of sedentism (e.g., Renfrew 1974) and at larger scales during subsequent eras in prehispanic Mesoamerica (Feinman and Carballo 2018). At the aforementioned Gulf Coast centers, leadership focused on individuals, who were glorified, legitimized, and depicted larger than life in power-laden attire. Elsewhere, for the most part, individualizing rulership was not evidenced at that time and public spaces were prominent.

A key point here is that once head towns and leadership positions were established, the relevant axis of variation is not between completely bottom-up and top-down governance, but rather it is in the nature of relations between leaders and followers (Ahlquist and Levi 2011). Governance is always relational, and it may take a continuous range of forms, but above scales of several thousands, closely knit networks always have supra-household institutions. At one end of that continuum (Blanton and Fargher 2008, 2016; Carballo 2016; Carballo et al. 2014; Feinman 2018; Feinman and Carballo 2018) are more collective forms of rule, in which leaders are officeholders subject to checks, balances, and limits on their clout. Voice and wealth tend to be more equitably distributed. At the other pole of the axis are more autocratic, individualizing rulers, who are able to centralize power and wealth, rule through personality cults, and face few checks from the rest of the populace. This continuum of ruler-follower dynamics, and its associations with the uses of non-residential spaces, has been illustrated for Postclassic Highland Mesoamerican centers (Fargher et al. 2011, 2020).

Significantly, when the temporal perspective is expanded to the Formative period, it becomes evident that these different modes of governance are not entirely consistent within specific spatial or environmental realms or necessarily across time in a single location (Feinman 2018). David Carballo (2016) synthesized differences in governance and religious behaviors for the Central Highlands during this era, while Christopher Pool (2007, 2009, 2012) noted that not all Gulf Coast regions conformed to the patterns evidenced at San Lorenzo and La Venta. In the lowland Maya region later in the Formative, not all centers adopted modes of individualizing rule at the same time or tempo (Estrada-Belli 2011; Hansen 2017). Furthermore, at Tres Zapotes (Pool et al. 2010) on the Gulf Coast, leadership was initially more in parallel with the individualizing rule at contemporaneous La Venta, but subsequently, governance shifted to a more collective formation, in which specific rulers were not depicted ostentatiously and power was shared (Pool and Loughlin 2016; Wade 2017a). The Formative period Mesoamerican world was a shifting mosaic of many diverse polities that not only varied in their degree of vertical political complexity but also were not uniform in the relational ways they forged coalitions and implemented cooperation.

At the same time, these regional political units were linked in macroscalar networks in which innovations, ideas, people, and goods were regularly moved (e.g., Pool 2009; Rosenswig 2010, 2011).

TAKING STOCK: TENETS, MODELS, FRAMES, AND WAYS FORWARD

Although I can offer no definitive, overarching answers to account for temporal/spatial variability in complexity during the Mesoamerican Formative period, it does seem that the time is ripe to take stock and jettison a number of traditionally accepted models and presumed tenets. Early Mesoamerican villages were neither autonomous nor economically self-sufficient. In fact, for the most part, they were the opposite, as local/regional traditions were not uniform or static. The long-held tenet that cultural traditions were adopted, discrete, and set for the long term with sedentism and a curtailment of broader-scale networks requires recalibration. Mother-culture, beacon-like models that see material and information flows disseminated in just one direction, also clearly do not fit the data that we now have on hand. Archaeologists long have recognized that Formative Mesoamerica was never politically dominated or controlled by a sole center (Flannery 1968); likewise, flows and ideas did not emanate from one place in one direction.

Based on the marked differences, it now seems subject to question whether leaders during the Mesoamerican Formative arose solely as aggrandizers (e.g., Clark and Blake 1994; cf. Pugh et al. 2019; Rice 2021) who amassed power by concentrating and brokering material wealth or by imposing ideological constructs strictly from above. As with supra-regional networks of interaction, governance and institution building during this time was more apt to be a two-way than a one-way process. As outlined for coastal Oaxaca (Brzezinski, this volume), social contracts that constructed mutual expectations and obligations sometimes were established, so that edicts and clout did not always proceed exclusively from the top down. Likewise, it seems mistaken to outright assume that the cities that developed at the close of the Formative were all ruled by divine kings who wielded absolute power. That model may characterize many sectors of the Classic Maya domain (e.g., Freidel 2008), but it does not seem to fit the basis of governance at Teotihuacan (e.g., Carballo 2016; Cowgill 2017). Throughout the long span of prehispanic Mesoamerican history, highly individualized, autocratic, exclusionary forms of rule may have been no more prevalent than more collectively organized institutions and arrangements (Feinman 2018; Feinman and Carballo 2018; Wade 2017b).

In an earlier paper that preliminarily examined twenty-six cities, which spanned the prehispanic era in Mesoamerica, David Carballo and I (2018) found that there was a basic relationship between modes of governance and how political institutions were funded. In that comparison, we drew heavily on the cross-cultural findings from research on preindustrial cities by Richard Blanton and Lane Fargher (2008, 2016). In their investigation, which focused on the fiscal foundations of collective action, they found that when the control of key revenues can be monopolized or controlled directly by rulers or their agents (external), governance will tend toward a concentration of power with few expenditures on public goods or works, limited bureaucracy, and minimized voice for subalterns. Alternatively, when government depends on internal revenues, drawn from (and thus reliant on) the local populace, power tends to be more distributed, expenditures on public services more robust, and bureaucracies larger, both to collect taxes and to implement services (Blanton and Fargher 2008, 112–116; see also Levi 1988).

Clearly, this model cannot provide a complete roadmap to understand the diversity of Formative period social formations, since human institutions and cooperative arrangements are complicated, and history does matter. Yet it does present a conceptual and testable perspective to understand certain key aspects of variability in human cooperative institutions. And it links that relationship to the quantities and the means through which resources are acquired by governing authorities, as well as to the works and goods that are delivered. Although such variables as primary productivity, available technologies, and, particularly, population size and density factor into the kinds and amount of resources governing authorities could potentially accumulate, critical, too, were the specific ways in which (and from where) revenues were acquired.

A focus on fiscal financing does offer insight into those Formative (and Classic) period contexts in Mesoamerica, where power seems to have been concentrated in specific individuals. Both Gulf Coast centers, San Lorenzo and La Venta (Cyphers 1996; Pool 2007, 2009, 2012), as well as the emergent Maya head towns along the Usumacinta River and the corridors of Tikal and Calakmul (Gunn et al. 2014; Woodfill and Andrieu 2012) have been thought to have relied heavily on long-distance exchange, particularly in exotic, highly valued goods (e.g., Feinman 2017a). Trade corridors, such as river routes, are considered an external resource (Feinman 2017b; Feinman and Nicholas 2016) that offer ample opportunity to monopolize (Blanton and Fargher 2008, 112–16). Alternatively, most other Formative era centers were less dependent on the exchange of precious commodities, with a reliance on decentralized systems of agrarian and craft production (internal resources). At Tres Zapotes, a decline in extraregional exchange networks was timed with a shift toward more decentralized, less individualizing governance (Pool 2009, 2012; Pool and Loughlin 2016). Obviously, a fuller analysis and more in-depth empirical evaluation is requisite, but these preliminary observations yield a frame to guide us forward.

In sum, the Mesoamerican Formative does matter. Historically, it provides a vantage into the diverse ways that humans adjusted to living and cooperating in groups as their numbers and densities grew. It catalogues how people cooperated and built institutions to get things done (e.g., Holland-Lulewicz et al. 2020; Kowalewski 2013). The scales were much smaller millennia ago, but zoom forward in time, and many of the relational challenges and processes of accommodation are not unique; rather, they are scaled up (e.g., Coward and Gamble 2008; Smith 2019), fostered by new technologies and larger aggregations. For the present and future, understanding these processes, beginnings, and the long-term outcomes is important for evaluating which paths make sense to follow or to steer away from today. In the aforementioned comparison of Mesoamerican centers (Feinman and Carballo 2018), we found that more collectively organized head towns and cities were significantly more enduring in time, as compared to more autocratic formations. Likewise, the site of Tres Zapotes retained centrality centuries longer than its Gulf Coast contemporaries, perhaps because the settlement's occupants shifted to and forged more distributed power arrangements (Pool and Loughlin 2016). Do these patterns bear out more broadly in prehispanic Mesoamerica? Would these relationships between governance and sustainability hold up to more in-depth, even broader comparative, analyses? Are similar associations found elsewhere across time and in other global regions? These are questions that only future comparative analyses and investigations can resolve, but there is no question that the answers to those queries would be worth knowing. Concerted, problem-focused, empirically based studies of the Mesoamerican Formative era remain a key and essential step in the quest for this historical knowledge and perspective about human cooperative arrangements, their variability, and sustainability.

REFERENCES

Acosta Ochoa, Guillermo. 2012. "Ice Age Hunter-Gatherers and the Colonization of Mesoamerica." In *The Oxford Handbook of Mesoamerican Archaeology*, edited by Deborah L. Nichols and Christopher A. Pool, 129–40. Oxford: Oxford University Press.

Adler, Michael A., and Richard H. Wilshusen. 1990. "Large-Scale Integrative Facilities in Tribal Societies: Cross-Cultural and Southwestern U. S. Examples." *World Archaeology* 22:133–46.

Ahlquist, John S., and Margaret Levi. 2011. "Leadership: What It Means, What It Does, and What We Want to Know about It." *Annual Review of Political Science* 14:1–24.

Apicella, Coren L., Frank W. Marlowe, James H. Fowler, and Nicholas A. Christakis. 2012. "Social Networks and Cooperation in Hunter–Gatherers." *Nature* 481:497–501.

Arnauld, M. Charlotte, Linda R. Manzanilla, and Michael E. Smith, eds. 2012. *The Neighborhood as a Social and Spatial Unit in Mesoamerican Cities*. Tucson: University of Arizona Press.

Balkansky, Andrew K., and Michelle M. Croissier. 2009. "Multicrafting in Prehispanic Oaxaca." *Archeological Papers, American Anthropological Association* 19:58–74.

Bandy, Matthew S. 2008. "Global Patterns of Early Village Development." In *The Neolithic Demographic Transition and Its Consequences*, edited by Jean-Pierre Bocquet-Appel and Ofer Bar-Yosef, 333–57. Berlin: Springer.

Bandy, Matthew S. 2010. "Population Growth, Village Fissioning, and Alternative Early Village Trajectories." In *Becoming Villagers: Comparing Early Village Societies*, edited by Matthew S. Bandy and Jake R. Fox, 19–36. Tucson: University of Arizona Press.

Bandy, Matthew S., and Jake R. Fox. 2010. "Becoming Villagers: The Evolution of Early Village Societies." In *Becoming Villagers: Comparing Early Village Societies*, edited by Matthew S. Bandy and Jake R. Fox, 1–16. Tucson: University of Arizona Press.

Bellwood, Peter, and Marc Oxenham. 2008. "The Expansion of Farming Societies and the Role of the Neolithic Demographic Transition." In *The Neolithic Demographic Transition and Its Consequences*, edited by Jean-Pierre Bocquet-Appel and Ofer Bar-Yosef, 13–34. Berlin: Springer.

Bernard, H. Russell, and Peter D. Killworth. 1973. "On the Social Structure of an Ocean-Going Research Vessel and Other Important Things." *Social Science Research* 2:145–84.

Bernard, H. Russell, and Peter D. Killworth. 1979. "Why Are There No Social Physics?" *Journal of the Steward Anthropological Society* 11:33–58.

Bettencourt, Luis M. A. 2013. "The Origins of Scaling in Cities." *Science* 340:1438–41.

Birch, Jennifer. 2013. "Between Villages and Cities: Settlement Aggregation in Cross-Cultural Perspective." In *From Prehistoric Villages to Cities: Settlement Aggregation and Community Transformation*, edited by Jennifer Birch, 1–22. New York: Routledge.

Blanton, Richard E. 2012. "Cities and Urbanism in Prehispanic Mesoamerica." In *The Oxford Handbook of Mesoamerican Archaeology*, edited by Deborah L. Nichols and Christopher A. Pool, 708–25. Oxford: Oxford University Press.

Blanton, Richard E. 2015. "Theories of Ethnicity and the Dynamics of Ethnic Change in Multiethnic Societies." *Proceedings of the National Academy of Sciences* 112:9176–81.

Blanton, Richard, and Lane Fargher. 2008. *Collective Action in the Formation of Pre-modern States*. New York: Springer.

Blanton, Richard E., and Lane F. Fargher. 2013. "Reconsidering Darwinian Anthropology: With Suggestions for a Revised Agenda for Cooperation Research." In *Cooperation and Collective Action: Archaeological Perspectives*, edited by David M. Carballo, 93–127. Boulder: University Press of Colorado.

Blanton, Richard E., and Lane Fargher. 2016. *How Humans Cooperate: Confronting the Challenges of Collective Action*. Boulder: University Press of Colorado.

Blanton, Richard E., Gary M. Feinman, Stephen A. Kowalewski, and Peter N. Peregrine. 1996. "A Dual-Processual Theory for the Evolution of Mesoamerican Civilization." *Current Anthropology* 37:1–14.

Blanton, Richard E., Stephen A. Kowalewski, Gary M. Feinman, and Laura M. Finsten. 1993. *Ancient Mesoamerica: A Comparison of Change in Three Regions*. Cambridge, UK: Cambridge University Press.

Bocquet-Appel, Jean-Pierre. 2011. "When the World's Population Took Off: The Springboard of the Neolithic Demographic Transition." *Science* 333:560–61.

Carballo, David M. 2011. "Advances in the Household Archaeology of Highland Mesoamerica." *Journal of Archaeological Research* 19:133–89.

Carballo, David M. 2016. *Urbanization and Religion in Ancient Central Mexico*. Oxford: Oxford University Press.

Carballo, David M., Paul Roscoe, and Gary M. Feinman. 2014. "Cooperation and Collective Action in the Cultural Evolution of Complex Societies." *Journal of Archaeological Method and Theory* 21:98–133.

Carneiro, Robert L. 2002. "The Tribal Village and Its Culture: An Evolutionary Stage in the History of Human Society." In *The Archaeology of Tribal Societies*, edited by William A. Parkinson, 34–52. Archaeological Series 15. Ann Arbor, MI: International Monographs in Prehistory.

Carpenter, Lacey B. 2019. "Households and Political Transformation: Daily Life during State Formation at Tilcajete, Oaxaca, Mexico." PhD diss., University of Michigan.

Cashdan, Elizabeth. 1980. "Egalitarianism among Hunters and Gatherers." *American Anthropologist* 82:116–20.

Clark, John E. 1991. "The Beginnings of Mesoamerica: Apologia for the Soconusco Early Formative." In *The Formation of Complex Society in Southeastern Mesoamerica*, edited by William R. Fowler Jr., 13–26. Boca Raton, FL: CRC Press.

Clark, John. E. 1997. "The Arts of Government in Early Mesoamerica." *Annual Review of Anthropology* 26:211–34.

Clark, John E. 2004. "The Birth of Mesoamerican Metaphysics: Sedentism, Engagement, and Moral Superiority. In *Rethinking Materiality: The Engagement of Mind with the Material World*," edited by Elizabeth DeMarrais, Chris Gosden, and Colin Renfrew, 205–24. Cambridge, UK: McDonald Institute for Archaeological Research, University of Cambridge.

Clark, John E., and Michael Blake. 1994. "The Power of Prestige: Competitive Generosity and the Emergence of Rank Society in Lowland Mesoamerica." In *Factional Competition and Political Development in the New World*, edited by Elizabeth M. Brumfiel and John W. Fox, 17–30. Cambridge, UK: Cambridge University Press.

Clark, John E., and David Cheetham. 2002. "Mesoamerica's Tribal Foundations." In *The Archaeology of Tribal Societies*, edited by William A. Parkinson, 278–339. Ann Arbor, MI: International Monographs in Prehistory.

Cobb, Charles R. 2018. "It Took a Childe to Raze the Village." In *The Archaeology of Villages in Eastern North America*, edited by Jennifer Birch and Victor D. Thompson, 192–204. Gainesville: University Press of Florida.

Coser, Rose Laub. 1975. "The Complexity of Roles as a Seedbed of Individual Autonomy." In *The Idea of Social Structure: Papers in Honor of Robert K. Merton*, edited by Louis A. Coser, 237–62. New York: Harcourt Brace Jovanovich.

Coward, Fiona. 2016. "Scaling Up: Material Culture as Scaffold for the Social Brain." *Quaternary International* 405:78–90.

Coward, Fiona, and R. I. M. Dunbar. 2014. "Communities on the Edge of Civilization." In *Lucy to Language: The Benchmark Papers*, edited by R. I. M. Dunbar, Clive Gamble, and J. A. J. Gowlett, 380–404. Oxford: Oxford University Press.

Coward, Fiona, and Clive Gamble. 2008. "Big Brains, Small Worlds: Material Culture and the Evolution of the Mind." *Philosophical Transactions of the Royal Society B, Biological Sciences* 363:1969–79.

Cowgill, George L. 2017. "A Speculative History of Teotihuacan." In *Teotihuacan: City of Water, City of Fire*, edited by Matthew H. Robb, 20–27. San Francisco: Fine Arts Museum of San Francisco.

Cyphers, Ann. 1996. "Reconstructing Olmec Life at San Lorenzo." In *Olmec Art of Ancient Mexico*, edited by Elizabeth P. Benson and Beatríz de la Fuente, 61–71. Washington, DC: National Gallery of Art.

Cyphers, Ann, and Anna Di Castro. 2009. "Early Olmec Architecture and Imagery." In *The Art of Urbanism in Mesoamerica: How Mesoamerican Kingdoms Represented Themselves in Architecture*, edited by William L. Fash and Leonardo López Luján, 21–52. Washington, DC: Dumbarton Oaks.

De Ruiter, Jan, Gavin Weston, and Stephen M. Lyon. 2011. "Dunbar's Number: Group Size and Brain Physiology in Humans Reexamined." *American Anthropologist* 113:557–68.

Dunbar, R. I. M. 2007. "Mind the Gap: Or Why Humans Are Not Just Great Apes." *Proceedings of the British Academy* 154:403–23.

Dunbar, R. I. M. 2011. "Constraints on the Evolution of Social Institutions and Their Implications for Information Flow." *Journal of Institutional Economics* 7:345–71.

Dunbar, R. I. M. 2013. "What Makes the Neolithic So Special?" *Neo-Lithics* 2/13:25–29.

Ebert, Claire E., Mark Dennison, Kenneth G. Hirth, Sarah B. McClure, and Douglass J. Kennett. 2015. "Formative Period Obsidian Exchange along the Pacific Coast of Mesoamerica." *Archaeometry* 57 (S1): 54–73.

Estrada-Belli, Francisco. 2011. *The First Maya Civilization: Ritual and Power before the Classic Period*. New York: Routledge.

Evans, Susan Toby. 2012. "Time and Space Boundaries: Chronologies and Regions in Mesoamerica." In *The Oxford Handbook of Mesoamerican Archaeology*, edited by Deborah L. Nichols and Christopher A. Pool, 114–26. Oxford: Oxford University Press.

Fargher, Lane F., Ricardo R. Antorcha-Pedemonte, Verenice Y. Heredia Espinoza, Richard E. Blanton, Aurelio López Corral, Robert A. Cook, John K. Millhauser, et al. 2020. "Wealth Inequality, Social Stratification, and the Built Environment in Late Prehispanic Highland Mexico: A Comparative Analysis with Special Emphasis on Tlaxcallan." *Journal of Anthropological Archaeology* 58:101–76.

Fargher, Lane F., Verenice Y. Heredia Espinoza, and Richard E. Blanton. 2011. "Alternative Pathways to Power in Late Postclassic Highland Mesoamerica." *Journal of Anthropological Archaeology* 30:306–26.

Feinman, Gary M. 1991. "Demography, Surplus, and Inequality: Early Political Formations in Highland Mesoamerica." In *Chiefdoms: Power, Economy, and Ideology*, edited by Timothy Earle, 229–62. Cambridge, UK: Cambridge University Press.

Feinman, Gary M. 1995. "The Emergence of Inequality: A Focus on Strategies and Processes." In *Foundations of Social Inequality*, edited by T. Douglas Price and Gary M. Feinman, 255–79. New York: Springer.

Feinman, Gary M. 1998. "Scale and Social Organization: Perspectives on the Archaic State." In *Archaic States*, edited by Gary M. Feinman and Joyce Marcus, 95–133. Santa Fe, NM: School of American Research Press.

Feinman, Gary M. 2011. "Size, Complexity, and Organizational Variation: A Comparative Approach." *Cross-Cultural Research* 45:37–58.

Feinman, Gary M. 2013. "The Emergence of Social Complexity: Why More than Population Size Matters." In *Cooperation and Collective Action: Archaeological Perspectives*, edited by David M. Carballo, 35–56. Boulder: University Press of Colorado.

Feinman, Gary M. 2016. "Framing the Rise and Variability of Past Complex Societies." In *Alternative Pathways to Complexity: A Collection of Essays on Architecture, Economics, Power, and Cross-Cultural Analysis*, edited by Lane F. Fargher and Verenice Y. Heredia Espinoza, 271–89. Boulder: University Press of Colorado.

Feinman, Gary M. 2017a. "Re-visioning Classic Maya Polities: Book Review Essay." *Latin American Research Review* 53:458–68.

Feinman, Gary M. 2017b. "Multiple Pathways to Large-Scale Human Cooperative Networks: A Reframing." In *Feast, Famine or Fighting: Multiple Pathways to Social Complexity*, edited by Richard J. Chacon and Rubén G. Mendoza, 459–73. Cham: Springer.

Feinman, Gary M. 2018. "The Governance and Leadership of Prehispanic Mesoamerican Polities: New Perspectives and Comparative Implications." *Cliodynamics* 9 (2): 1–39.

Feinman, Gary M., and David M. Carballo. 2018. "Collaborative and Competitive Strategies in the Variability and Resiliency of Large-Scale Societies in Mesoamerica." *Economic Anthropology* 5:7–19.

Feinman, Gary M., and Linda M. Nicholas. 2013. *Settlement Patterns of the Ejutla Valley, Oaxaca, Mexico: A Diachronic Macroscale Perspective*. Fieldiana Anthropology 43. Chicago: Field Museum of Natural History.

Flanagan, James G. 1989. "Hierarchy in Simple 'Egalitarian' Societies." *Annual Review of Anthropology* 18:245–66.

Flannery, Kent V. 1968. "The Olmec and the Valley of Oaxaca: A Model for Interregional Interaction in Formative Times." In *Dumbarton Oaks Conference on the Olmec*, edited by Elizabeth P. Benson, 79–110. Washington, DC: Dumbarton Oaks.

Flannery, Kent V. 1972. "The Cultural Evolution of Civilizations." *Annual Review of Ecology and Systematics* 3:399–426.

Flannery, Kent V., ed. 1976. *The Early Mesoamerican Village*. New York: Academic Press.

Flannery, Kent V., ed. 1986. *Guilá Naquitz*. Orlando, FL: Academic Press.

Flannery, Kent V., and Joyce Marcus. 1994. *Early Formative Pottery of the Valley of Oaxaca*. Ann Arbor: Museum of Anthropology, University of Michigan.

Flannery, Kent V., and Joyce Marcus. 2000. "Formative Mexican Chiefdoms and the Myth of the 'Mother Culture.'" *Journal of Anthropological Archaeology* 19:1–37.

Flannery, Kent V., and Joyce Marcus. 2005. *Excavations at San José Mogote 1: The Household Archaeology*. Memoirs of the Museum of Anthropology 40. Ann Arbor: University of Michigan.

Flannery, Kent V., and Joyce Marcus. 2015. *Excavations at San José Mogote 2: The Household Archaeology*. Memoirs of the Museum of Anthropology 58. Ann Arbor: University of Michigan.

Fletcher, Roland. 1995. *The Limits of Settlement Growth: A Theoretical Outline*. Cambridge, UK: Cambridge University Press.

Freidel, David. 2008. "Maya Divine Kings: A Brief History of the Idea." In *Religion and Power: Divine Kingship in the Ancient World and Beyond*, edited by Nicole Brisch, 191–206. Oriental Institute Seminars 4. Chicago: Oriental Institute of the University of Chicago.

Gillespie, Susan D. 2011. "Inside and Outside: Residential Burial at Formative Period Chalcatzingo, Mexico." *Archeological Papers, American Anthropological Association* 20:98–120.

Golitko, Mark, and Gary M. Feinman. 2015. "Procurement and Distribution of Pre-Hispanic Mesoamerican Obsidian 900 BC–AD 1520: A Social Network Analysis." *Journal of Archaeological Method and Theory* 22:206–47.

Granovetter, Mark S. 1973. "The Strength of Weak Ties." *American Journal of Sociology* 78:1360–80.

Granovetter, Mark S. 1983. "The Strength of Weak Ties: A Network Theory Revisited." *Sociological Theory* 1:201–33.

Grove, David C. 1999. "Public Monuments and Sacred Mountains: Observations on Three Formative Period Sacred Landscapes." In *Social Patterns in Pre-Classic Mesoamerica*, edited by David C. Grove and Rosemary A. Joyce, 255–99. Washington, DC: Dumbarton Oaks.

Grove, David C. 2014. *Discovering the Olmecs: An Unconventional History*. Austin: University of Texas Press.

Grove, David C., and Susan D. Gillespie. 2009. "People of the *Cerro*: Landscape, Settlement, and Art at Middle Formative Period Chalcatzingo." In *The Art of Urbanism in Mesoamerica: How Mesoamerican Kingdoms Represented Themselves in Architecture*, edited by William L. Fash and Leonardo López Luján, 53–76. Washington, DC: Dumbarton Oaks.

Gunn, Joel D., William J. Folan, Christian Isendahl, María de Rosario Domínguez Carrasco, Betty B. Faust, and Beniamino Volta. 2014. "Calakmul: Agent Risk and Sustainability in the Western Maya Lowlands." *Archeological Papers, American Anthropological Association* 24:101–23.

Hansen, Richard D. 2017. "The Feast before Famine and Fighting: The Origins and Consequences of Social Complexity in the Mirador Basin, Guatemala." In *Feast, Famine or Fighting: Multiple Pathways to Social Complexity*, edited by Richard J. Chacon and Rubén G. Mendoza, 305–35. Cham: Springer.

Hedström, Peter, and Richard Swedberg. 1996. "Social Mechanisms." *Acta Sociologica* 39:281–308.

Henderson, John S., Rosemary A. Joyce, Gretchen R. Hall, W. Jeffrey Hurst, and Patrick E. McGovern. 2007. "Chemical and Archaeological Evidence for the Earliest Cacao Beverages." *Proceedings of the National Academy of Sciences* 104:18937–40.

Hill, R. A., and R. I. M. Dunbar. 2003. "Social Network Size in Humans." *Human Nature* 14:53–72.

Hill, Warren D., and John E. Clark. 2001. "Sports, Gambling, and Government: America's First Social Compact?" *American Anthropologist* 103:331–45.

Hirth, Kenneth, Ann Cyphers, Robert Cobean, Jason De León, and Michael D. Glascock. 2013. "Early Olmec Obsidian Trade and Economic Organization at San Lorenzo." *Journal of Archaeological Science* 40:2784–98.

Holland-Lulewicz, Jacob, Megan Anne Conger, Jennifer Birch, Stephen A. Kowalewski, and Travis W. Jones. 2020. "An Institutional Approach for Archaeology." *Journal of Anthropological Archaeology* 58:101–63.

Inomata, Takeshi. 2017. "The Isthmian Origins of the E Group at Its Adoption in the Maya Lowlands." In *Maya E Groups: Calendars, Astronomy, and Urbanism in the Early Lowlands*, edited by David A. Freidel, Arlen F. Chase, Anne S. Dowd, and Jerry Murdock, 215–52. Gainesville: University Press of Florida.

Inomata, Takeshi, Jessica MacLellan, Daniela Triadan, Jessica Munson, Melissa Burham, Kazuo Aoyama, Hiroo Nasu, Flory Pinzón, and Hitoshi Yonenobu. 2015. "The Development of Sedentary Communities in the Maya Lowlands: Co-existing Mobile Groups and Public Ceremonies at Ceibal, Guatemala." *Proceedings of the National Academy of Sciences* 112:4268–73.

Inomata, Takeshi, Flory Pinzón, Juan Manuel Palomo, Ashley Sharpe, Raúl Ortíz, María Belén Méndez, and Otto Román. 2017. "Public Ritual and Interregional Interactions: Excavations of the Central Plaza of Group A, Ceibal." *Ancient Mesoamerica* 28:203–32.

Inomata, Takeshi, Daniela Triadan, Flory Pinzón, and Kazuo Aoyama. 2019. "Artificial Plateau Construction during the Preclassic Period at the Maya Site of Ceibal, Guatemala." *PLoS ONE* 14 (8): e0221943.

Inomata, Takeshi, Daniela Triadan, Verónica A. Vázquez López, Juan Carlos Fernandez-Diaz, Takayuki Omori, María Belén Méndez Bauer, Melina García Hernández, et al. 2020. "Monumental Architecture at Aguada Fénix and the Rise of Maya Civilization." *Nature* 582:530–33.

Janssen, Marco A., Timothy A. Kohler, and Marten Scheffer. 2003. "Sunk-Costs Effect and Vulnerability to Collapse in Ancient Societies." *Current Anthropology* 44:722–28.

Johnson, Gregory A. 1982. "Organizational Structure and Scalar Stress." In *Theory and Explanation in Archaeology, the Southampton Conference*, edited by Colin Renfrew, Michael J. Rowlands, and Barbara A. Seagraves, 389–421. New York: Academic Press.

Joyce, Rosemary A., and David C. Grove. 1999. "Asking New Questions about the Mesoamerican Pre-Classic." In *Social Patterns in Pre-Classic Mesoamerica*, edited by David C. Grove and Rosemary A. Joyce, 1–14. Washington, DC: Dumbarton Oaks.

Kalin, Michael, and Nicholas Sambanis. 2018. "How to Think about Social Identity." *Annual Review of Political Science* 21:239–57.

Kennett, Douglas J. 2012. "Archaic-Period Foragers and Farmers in Mesoamerica." In *The Oxford Handbook of Mesoamerican Archaeology*, edited by Deborah L. Nichols and Christopher A. Pool, 141–50. Oxford: Oxford University Press.

Kennett, Douglas J., Keith M. Prufer, Brendan J. Culleton, Richard J. George, Mark Robinson, Willa R. Trask, Gina M. Buckley, et al. 2020. "Early Isotopic Evidence for Maize as a Staple Grain in the Americas." *Science Advances* 6:eaba3245.

Killion, Thomas W. 2013. "Nonagricultural Cultivation and Social Complexity: The Olmec. Their Ancestors, and Mexico's Southern Gulf Coast Lowlands." *Current Anthropology* 54:569–606.

Kosse, Kristina. 1990. "Group Size and Societal Complexity: Thresholds in the Long-Term Memory." *Journal of Anthropological Archaeology* 9:275–303.

Kostof, Spiro. 1991. *The City Shaped: Urban Patterns and Meanings through History*. Boston: Bulfinch Press.

Kowalewski, Stephen A. 1990. "The Evolution of Complexity in the Valley of Oaxaca." *Annual Review of Anthropology* 19:39–58.

Kowalewski, Stephen A. 2013. "The Work of Making Community." In *From Prehistoric Villages to Cities: Settlement Aggregation and Community Transformation*, edited by Jennifer Birch, 201–18. New York: Routledge.

Kowalewski, Stephen A., and Jennifer Birch. 2020. "How Do People Get Big Things Done?" In *The Evolution of Social Institutions: Interdisciplinary Perspectives*, edited by Dmitri M. Bondarenko, Stephen A. Kowalewski, and David B. Small, 29–50. Cham: Springer.

Kowalewski, Stephen A., and Verenice Y. Heredia Espinoza. 2020. "Mesoamerica as an Assemblage of Institutions." In *The Evolution of Social Institutions: Interdisciplinary Perspectives*, edited by Dmitri M. Bondarenko, Stephen A. Kowalewski, and David B. Small, 495–522. Cham: Springer.

Lekson, S. H. 1985. "Largest Settlement Size and the Interpretation of Socio-Political Complexity at Chaco Canyon, New Mexico." *Haliksa'i: UNM Contributions to Anthropology* 4:68–75.

Lesure, Richard G. 2008. "The Neolithic Transition in Mesoamerica? Larger Implications of the Strategy of Relative Chronology." In *The Neolithic Demographic Transition and Its Consequences*, edited by Jean-Pierre Bocquet-Appel and Ofer Bar-Yosef, 107–38. Berlin: Springer.

Lesure, Richard G., Thomas A. Wake, Alexander Borejsza, Jennifer Carballo, David M. Carballo, Isabel Rodríguez López, and Mauro de Ángeles Guzmán. 2013. "Swidden Agriculture, Village Longevity, and Social Relations in Formative Central Tlaxcala: Towards an Understanding of Macroregional Structure." *Journal of Anthropological Archaeology* 32:224–41.

Levi, Margaret. 1988. *Of Revenue and Rule*. Berkeley: University of California Press.

MacNeish, Richard S., and Antoinette Nelken-Terner. 1983. "The Preceramic of Mesoamerica." *Journal of Field Archaeology* 10:71–84.

Marcus, Joyce. 1989. "Zapotec Chiefdoms and the Nature of Formative Religion." In *Regional Perspectives on the Olmec*, edited by Robert J. Sharer and David C. Grove, 148–97. Cambridge, UK: Cambridge University Press.

McAnany, Patricia A. 2011. "Practices of Place-Making, Ancestralizing, and Re-animation within Memory Communities." *Archeological Papers, American Anthropological Association* 20:136–42.

Melis, Alice P., and Dirk Semmann. 2010. "How Is Human Cooperation Different?" *Philosophical Transactions of the Royal Society B, Biological Sciences* 365:2663–74.

Nettle, Daniel, and Robin I. M. Dunbar. 1997. "Social Markers and the Evolution of Reciprocal Exchange." *Current Anthropology* 38:93–99.

Ortman, Scott G., and Grant D. Coffey. 2017. "Settlement Scaling in Middle-Range Societies." *American Antiquity* 82:662–82.

Perry-Smith, Jill E. 2006. "Social Yet Creative: The Role of Social Relationships in Facilitating Individual Creativity." *Academy of Management Journal* 49:85–101.

Peterson, Christian E., and Robert D. Drennan. 2012. "Patterned Variation in Regional Trajectories of Community Growth." In *The Comparative Archaeology of Complex Societies*, edited by Michael E. Smith, 88–137. Cambridge, UK: Cambridge University Press.

Piperno, Dolores R., and Bruce D. Smith. 2012. "The Origins of Food Production in Mesoamerica." In *The Oxford Handbook of Mesoamerican Archaeology*, edited by Deborah L. Nichols and Christopher A. Pool, 151–64. Oxford: Oxford University Press.

Pires-Ferreira, Jane W. 1976. "Shell and Iron-Ore Mirror Exchange in Formative Mesoamerica, with Comments on Other Commodities." In *The Early Mesoamerican Village*, edited by Kent V. Flannery, 311–28. New York: Academic Press.

Plunket, Patricia, and Gabriela Uruñuela. 2012. "Where East Meets West: The Formative in Mexico's Central Highlands." *Journal of Archaeological Research* 20:1–51.

Pool, Christopher A. 2007. *Olmec Archaeology and Early Mesoamerica*. Cambridge, UK: Cambridge University Press.

Pool, Christopher A. 2009. "Asking More and Better Questions: Olmec Archaeology for the Next 'Katun.'" *Ancient Mesoamerica* 20:241–52.

Pool, Christopher A. 2012. "The Formation of Complex Societies in Mesoamerica." In *The Oxford Handbook of Mesoamerican Archaeology*, edited by Deborah L. Nichols and Christopher A. Pool, 169–87. Oxford: Oxford University Press.

Pool, Christopher A., Ponciano Ortiz Ceballos, María del Carmen Rodríguez Martínez, and Michael L. Loughlin. 2010. "The Early Horizon at Tres Zapotes: Implications for Olmec Interaction." *Ancient Mesoamerica* 21:95–105.

Pool, Christopher A., and Michael L. Loughlin. 2016. "Tres Zapotes: The Evolution of a Resilient Polity in the Olmec Heartland of Mexico." In *Beyond Collapse: Archaeological Perspectives on Resilience, Revitalization, and Transformation in Complex Societies*, edited by Ronald K. Faulseit, 287–309. Carbondale: Southern Illinois University Press.

Pruitt, Jonathan N., Andrew Berdahl, Christina Riehl, Noa Pinter-Wollman, Holly V. Moeller, et al. 2018 "Social Tipping Points in Animal Societies." *Proceedings of the Royal Society B* 285:20181282. http://dx.doi.org/10.1098/rspb.2018.1282.

Pugh, Timothy W., Evelyn M. Chan Nieto, and Gabriela W. Zygadło. 2019. "Faceless Hierarchy at Nixtun-Ch'ich', Peten, Guatemala." *Ancient Mesoamerica* 31:248–60.

Renfrew, Colin. 1974. "Beyond Subsistence Economy: The Evolution of Social Organization in Prehistoric Europe." In *Reconstructing Complex Societies: An Archaeological Colloquium*, edited by Charlotte B. Moore, 69–85. Alexandria, VA: American Schools of Oriental Research.

Rice, Prudence M. 2021. "In Search of Middle Preclassic Lowland Ideologies." *Journal of Archaeological Research* 29:1–46.

Roberts, Sam G. B. 2010. "Constraints on Social Networks." In *Social Brain, Distributed Mind*, edited by Robin Dunbar, Clive Gamble, and John Gowlett, 115–34. Oxford: Oxford University Press.

Rosenswig, Robert M. 2010. *The Beginnings of Mesoamerican Civilization: Inter-Regional Interaction and the Olmec*. Cambridge, UK: Cambridge University Press.

Rosenswig, Robert M. 2011. "An Early Mesoamerican Archipelago of Complexity." In *Sociopolitical Transformation in Early Mesoamerica: Archaic to Formative in the Soconusco Region*, edited by Richard G. Lesure, 242–71. Berkeley: University of California Press.

Rosenswig, Robert M. 2015. "A Mosaic of Adaptation: The Archaeological Record for Mesoamerica's Archaic Period." *Journal of Archaeological Research* 23:115–62.

Sanders, William T. 1972. "Population, Agricultural History, and Societal Evolution in Mesoamerica." In *Population Growth: Anthropological Implications*, edited by Brian Spooner, 101–53. Cambridge, MA: MIT Press.

Smith, Bruce D. 2012. "A Cultural Niche Construction Theory of Initial Domestication." *Biological Theory* 6:1–12.

Smith, Charlotte A. 2002. "Concordant Change and Core-Periphery Dynamics: A Synthesis of Highland Mesoamerican Archaeological Survey Data." PhD diss., University of Georgia, Athens.

Smith, Michael E. 2002. "The Earliest Cities." In *Urban Life: Readings in the Anthropology of the City, Fourth Edition*, edited by George Gmelch and Walter P. Zenner, 3–19. Long Grove, IL: Waveland.

Smith, Michael E. 2007. "Form and Meaning in the Earliest Cities: A New Approach to Ancient Urban Planning." *Journal of Planning History* 6:3–47.

Smith, Michael E. 2010. "Sprawl, Squatters and Sustainable Cities: Can Archaeological Data Shed Light on Modern Urban Issue?" *Cambridge Archaeological Journal* 20:229–53.

Smith, Michael E. 2019. "Energized Crowding and the Generative Role of Settlement Aggregation and Urbanization." In *Coming Together: Comparative Approaches to Population Aggregation and Early Urbanization*, edited by Attila Gyucha, 37–58. IEMA Proceedings, Vol. 8. Albany, NY: SUNY Press.

Stark, Barbara, L. 2017. "Figuring Out the Early Olmec Era." In *The Early Olmec and Mesoamerica: The Material Record*, edited by Jeffrey P. Blomster and David Cheetham, 288–312. New York: Cambridge University Press.

Sterelny, Kim, and Trevor Watkins. 2015. "Neolithization in Southwest Asia in a Context of Niche Construction Theory." *Cambridge Archaeological Journal* 25:673–705.

Sutcliffe, Alistair, Robin Dunbar, Jens Binder, and Holly Arrow. 2012. "Relationships and the Social Brain: Integrating Psychological and Evolutionary Perspectives." *British Journal of Psychology* 103:149–68.

Thompson, Victor D., and Jennifer Birch. 2018. "The Power of Villages." In *The Archaeology of Villages in Eastern North America*, edited by Jennifer Birch and Victor D. Thompson, 1–19. Gainesville: University Press of Florida.

Tomasello, Michael. 2014. "The Ultra-Social Animal." *European Journal of Social Psychology* 44:187–94.

Tuzin, Donald. 2001. *Social Complexity in the Making*. London: Routledge.

UN DESA (United Nations Department of Economic and Social Affairs). 2018. *World Urbanization Prospects: The 2018 Revision*. United Nations, Department of Economic and Social Affairs, New York. https://esa.un.org/unpd/wup/publications/Files/WUP2018-KeyFacts.pdf.

Wade, Lizzie. 2017a. "Kings of Cooperation." *Archaeology* 70 (2): 27–29.

Wade, Lizzie. 2017b. "Unearthing Democracy's Roots." *Science* 355:1114–18.

Watkins, Trevor. 2008 "Supra-Regional Networks in the Neolithic of Southwest Asia." *Journal of World Prehistory* 21:139–71.

Watkins, Trevor. 2017. "From Pleistocene to Holocene: The Prehistory of Southwest Asia in Evolutionary Context." *History and Philosophy of the Life Sciences* 39:22.

Wendt, Carl J. 2009. "The Scale and Structure of Bitumen Processing in Early Formative Olmec Households." *Archeological Papers, American Anthropological Association* 19:33–44.

Wellman, Barry. 2007. "The Network is Personal: Introduction to a Special Issue of Social Networks." *Social Networks* 29:349–56.

Wellman, Barry. 2012. "Is Dunbar's Number Up?" *British Journal of Psychology* 103:174–76.

Whitelaw, Todd. 1991. "Some Dimensions of Variability in the Social Organization of Community Space among Foragers." In *Ethnoarchaeological Approaches to Mobile Campsites: Hunter-Gatherer and Pastoralist Case Studies*, edited by Clive S. Gamble and William A. Boismier, 139–88. Ethnoarchaeological Series 1. Ann Arbor, MI: International Monographs in Prehistory.

Woodfill, Brent K. S., and Chloé Andrieu. 2012 "Tikal's Early Classic Domination of the Great Western Trade Route: Ceramic, Lithic, and Iconographic Evidence." *Ancient Mesoamerica* 23:189–209.

Index

costume, 255, 269, 271; attire/clothing, 20, 23, 24, 27, 29, 32–34, 291; hair/hairstyles, 25, 27–29, 256; jewelry, 20, 33, 42

craft production, 10, 77–80, 88, 89, 99, 106–108, 133, 136, 144, 146–147, 148, 154, 162, 164, 175, 186, 194, 201, 203, 206, 234, 236, 243, 251–271, 289, 293

Cuello, 257

Cuicuilco, 149, 156, 158–160, 162, 290

DeLance, Lisa, 10

differentiation, social status, 5, 7, 15, 21, 23, 35, 98, 119, 132, 135–136, 150, 163, 187, 227, 234, 241–244, 263, 271, 283, 291

divination, 42

divine kingship, 57, 78, 174, 203–204, 217, 220–221, 226, 251, 255, 292

Dos Chombitos, 257

double-line-break, 154, 156, 161, 162

Doyle, James A., 202

Dresden Codex, 97

Dunning, Nicholas, 192

Dzibilchaltun, 179, 257

E Group (E-Group), 15, 56–61, 66–67, 69–70, 72, 74, 76, 78–80, 119, 122–127, 129, 131–136, 174, 179, 184–185, 204, 206–210, 211–213, 216–221, 262, 264, 290; Cenote style, 122, 123, 127, 129, 132; Uaxactun style, 122–123

Early Mesoamerican Village (Kent V. Flannery), 281

egalitarian groups, 4, 20–21, 23, 42, 66, 70, 174, 194, 202, 251, 264, 271, 284

El Chayal, 237

El Mirador, 194, 261

El Palmillo, 107

Elson, Christina M., 99, 107

energized crowding, 285

Estrada-Belli, Francisco, 214

ethnoarchaeology, 58, 59

ethnogenesis, 12–14

exotic goods, 22, 38, 150, 154, 182–183, 186, 215, 234, 243, 293

experimental archaeology, 59, 72, 78

Fargher, Lane, 22, 293

fauna (faunal remains), 35, 38

feasting, 20, 23, 31–33, 38–42, 87–88, 90, 91, 105, 107, 108, 131, 134, 286

Feinman, Gary M., 7–8, 22, 107

fermentation, 76–77

figurines, 10, 20, 24–30, 32–33, 35–36, 42, 56, 79–80, 103, 119, 128, 130–133, 136, 151–152, 154,

159, 201, 226–245, 269, 287; anthropomorphic, 23, 25, 27, 28, 29, 89, 103, 128, 131, 133, 136, 159, 237, 239; ocarinas, 34, 36, 128, 239; Pili style, 151; supernatural, 133, 237, 239; zoomorphic, 89, 92–93, 103, 128, 131, 136, 237, 239

Foias, Antonia E., 227

Freidel, David, 194, 218

freshwater resources, 150, 265

funerary/mortuary practice, 20, 23, 29, 35–37, 42, 89, 91, 103, 106, 135, 221, 242, 289

funerary/mortuary deposits, 24, 25, 194, 281, 290

galactic polities, 203

Garber, James F., 238

gathering places, 57, 79, 136

Geertz, Clifford, 203

Gillespie, Susan D., 231

governance, 281, 289, 290–294: aggrandizing (individualizing), 15, 22, 42, 291; distributed power, 291; fiscal foundations, 293; internal versus external, 289, 290–294

greenstone, 33, 34, 69, 92, 148, 150, 154, 182, 183, 186, 187, 215, 217–219, 252, 266, 269, 270

Gremion, Daniela, 58

Grove, David C., 231

Gruta Tucil, 193

Guernsey, Julia, 26

Gulf Coast, 67, 96, 122, 156, 164, 287, 290–291, 293–294

gum brackets, 154

Harrison-Buck, Eleanor, 244

Healy, Paul F., 234, 236

hematite, 33, 34, 186

Hepp, Guy David, 5, 9, 228, 286

heterarchy, 5, 19, 21–24, 42–43, 227, 228

hierarchy (settlement), 90, 125, 126, 130, 150, 158, 170, 178–179, 192–195

hierarchy (social), 9, 20–22, 35, 40–43, 57, 68, 125, 126, 130, 174–175, 195, 227, 266, 271

Historia Tolteca-Chichimeca, 100

Holbonbek, 192–193

Holocene epoch, 19

Horn III, Sherman W., 234

household ritual, 229

households, 10, 19, 57, 80, 107, 137, 150, 174–175, 220, 229–231, 234, 257, 260–261, 270, 286, 289, 290–291

Huitzilopochtli, 35

human sacrifice, 103, 105

hunter-gatherers, 120, 135, 251, 280, 284, 285

Huntichmul, 192

About the Authors

Jaime J. Awe is associate professor of anthropology at Northern Arizona University, codirector of the Belize Valley Archaeological Reconnaissance Project, and emeritus member of the Belize Institute of Archaeology. His research and publications cover topics that span from the Preceramic period to the time of European contact, with particular focus on the rise of cultural complexity and human environment interaction in western Belize. Presently, Awe continues his active program of research and conservation, conducting regional and multidisciplinary investigations with his colleagues and students at the major Belize Valley Maya sites of Cahal Pech, Baking Pot, Xunantunich, and Lower Dover.

Sarah B. Barber is associate professor of anthropology and in the National Center for Integrated Coastal Research at the University of Central Florida. Her research focuses on the development and durability of early complex societies on the Pacific coast of Oaxaca, Mexico. Her work has been supported by the National Science Foundation, the National Geographic Society, the Historical Society, and Argonne National Laboratories, among others.

M. Kathryn Brown is the Lutcher Brown Endowed Professor in Anthropology at the University of Texas at San Antonio. She received her PhD from Southern Methodist University in 2003. Her research focuses on the rise of complexity in the Maya Lowlands and the role of ritual and ceremonial architecture in the Preclassic period. Her publications include *Ancient Mesoamerican Warfare* (with Travis Stanton), *Pathways to Complexity: A View from the Maya Lowlands* (with George J. Bey III), and *A Forest of History: The Maya after the Emergence of Divine Kinship* (with Travis Stanton).

Jeffrey S. Brzezinski is lecturer in the Departments of Anthropology and Continuing Education at the University of Colorado Boulder. His research in Mesoamerican archaeology focuses on the development and organization of early complex polities in Oaxaca, Mexico, particularly the role of religious practices in the negotiation of political authority during the later Formative period (400 BCE–250 CE). His dissertation examined the monumental architecture of Cerro de la Virgen, a hilltop site located in the lower Río Verde Valley. His research has been supported by the National Science Foundation, the University of Colorado Boulder, and the Tinker Foundation.

Ryan H. Collins is a Neukom postdoctoral fellow in the Department of Anthropology at Dartmouth College. Specializing in Mesoamerican archaeology, his research focuses on the role of ritual and identity in the development of early urbanism in the Maya area. Collins is a cofounder of the digital media project *This Anthro Life: Podcast*, hosting over one hundred episodes of content in official collaboration with the American Anthropological Association and the Smithsonian Center for Folklife and Heritage.

Kaitlin Crow has explored the world of archaeology and anthropology throughout her years in the field. She has been a scholar at Kennesaw State University, where she earned her bachelor of science degree in anthropology, at the University of Reading, where she earned a certificate in medieval archaeology, and New York University, where she received her master's degree in interdisciplinary studies with a focus on zooarchaeology. During this time, she worked for several years with the team of the Pacbitun Regional Archaeological Project (PRAP) studying the lives of the ancient Maya in Belize. With PRAP, she has presented and coauthored several chapters helping to expand the knowledge of the ancient Maya at Pacbitun.

Lisa DeLance is a lecturer of anthropology at California State Polytechnic University Pomona in California. Her research focuses on social complexity, state formation processes, gender, kinship, and negotiations of power. Her dissertation research explored correlational changes in the use of figurines and increasing complexity at Cahal Pech, Belize. Dr. DeLance is currently the project archivist for the Belize Valley Archaeological Reconnaissance (BVAR) Project.

Gary M. Feinman is the MacArthur Curator of Anthropology at The Field Museum, Chicago, IL. He has codirected long-term archaeological field programs in Oaxaca, Mexico, and Shandong, China, and has also studied in the US Southwest. His research interests include comparative studies of leadership, cooperation, and inequality, preindustrial economics, urbanism, and the complex relations between humans and environments over time. Feinman is a fellow of the American Association for the Advancement of Science and received the Presidential Recognition Award from the Society for American Archaeology. He is the founding and contact coeditor for the *Journal of Archaeological Research* and has published more than fifteen books and two hundred scholarly articles, review, and chapters.

Sara Dzul Góngora is a researcher at the Instituto Nacional de Antropología e Historia in Yucatán, Mexico. She has worked with the ceramic sequences in many different areas across the Maya Lowlands, including Calakmul, Río Bec, Uxul, Izamal, and Yaxuná. She has published extensively on ceramics in the Maya area.

Guy David Hepp is an assistant professor of anthropology at California State University, San Bernardino. He holds a BA and a PhD from the University of Colorado at Boulder and an MA from Florida State University. His research is focused on early complex societies of Mesoamerica. In 2019, Hepp published a book with the University Press of Colorado based on his dissertation. He has also authored publications regarding mortuary archaeology, paleoethnobotany, interregional interaction, radiocarbon dating, heritage politics, ceramic figurines, musical instruments, and masks.

Arthur A. Joyce is professor of anthropology at the University of Colorado Boulder. He directs long-term interdisciplinary archaeological and paleoecological research in Oaxaca, Mexico, on issues of politics, urbanism, religion, materiality, human ecology, and the Preceramic. He draws on theoretical and methodological inspirations ranging from the social sciences and humanities to the natural sciences. His publications include *Preceramic Mesoamerica* (edited with Jon Lohse and Aleksander Borejsza); *Religion and Politics in the Ancient Americas* (edited with Sarah Barber); *El pueblo de la tierra del cielo: Arqueología de la Mixteca de la Costa* (with Jamie Forde); *Polity and Ecology in Formative Period Coastal Oaxaca*; and *Mixtecs, Zapotecs, and Chatinos: Ancient Peoples of Southern Mexico*. He has held research fellowships from the American Museum of Natural History, Fulbright Foundation, Dumbarton Oaks, and the American Council of Learned Societies.

Rodrigo Martín Morales is a potter and artist from Muna, Yucatán. He is the owner of Casa Cerámica and has been experimenting with ceramic production using traditional materials from the Yucatán Peninsula for over forty years. Collaborating with archaeologists for over fifteen years, he has several academic publications.

George J. Micheletti is a PhD candidate in the Integrative Anthropological Sciences program at the University of Central Florida. Much of his archaeological work at the site of Pacbitun, Belize, has centered on the monumental architecture of the site's ceremonial plaza. His research interests focus on community ritual, geopolitical history, and political organization, with specialties in 3D modeling and remote sensing. Currently, his dissertation work has initiated an extensive periphery study at Pacbitun investigating the intra-polity origins and movement of Classic period ritual innovation and how this reflects the relationship between households of the periphery and royal elite of the epicenter.

Deborah L. Nichols is the William J. Bryant 1925 Professor of Anthropology at Dartmouth College. Educated at the Pennsylvania State University (BA, MA, PhD), the principal focus of her archaeological research is on the origins and development of early states and cities in Mesoamerica and economic and environmental anthropology. Her recent books include the *Oxford Handbook of the Aztecs and Rethinking the Aztec Economy*. She is the incoming president of the Society for American Archaeology.

Terry G. Powis is a New World archaeologist in the Department of Geography and Anthropology at Kennesaw State University, Kennesaw, Georgia. He joined the faculty at Kennesaw State University in August 2005 and is currently an associate professor of anthropology. Terry received his master's degree in anthropology at Trent University and his PhD in anthropology at the University of Texas at Austin. He is an archaeologist who conducts research both in the Maya Lowlands of Belize, Central America, and the southeastern United States. He specializes in pottery, diet and subsistence, and the evolution of complex societies. His recent research has focused on the origin of chocolate in the New World.

Zoë J. Rawski is a recent PhD graduate of the University of Texas at San Antonio, the same institution where she received her MA. Her research focuses on the role of monumental architecture in the development of hereditary inequality and divine kingship in the Maya Lowlands. More recently, her research focus has expanded to incorporate Native North American cultures, both through her previous work as a researcher at the Institute of Texan Cultures and her more recent work as a registered professional archaeologist qualified by the State Historic Preservation Office to work in the state of Oregon. Currently, she works in support of the USDA Natural Resources Conservation Service.

Prudence M. Rice taught at the University of Florida from 1976 to 1991, then moved to Southern Illinois University Carbondale, where she was associate vice chancellor for research and distinguished professor of anthropology. She retired from SIUC in 2011. She has directed field and laboratory work at Maya sites in Petén, Guatemala, and at Spanish colonial sites in Moquegua, Peru, with a special interest in pottery.

Michael P. Smyth received his PhD in anthropology from the University of New Mexico and is president of the Foundation for Americas Research (www. FARINCO.org) who. Working for over thirty-five years at the Yucatán Puuc region sites of Sayil, Chac II, and Xcoch, he is also researching the archaeology of Colombian Andean chiefdoms. He has published numerous articles on Maya storage and subsistence systems, community organization and urbanism, ethnic interactions, hydraulic chiefdoms, and human ecodynamics and is currently investigating the Preclassic settlement hierarchy and early farmers of the Xcoch hinterland.

Katherine E. South earned her PhD in anthropology at Southern Illinois University Carbondale, specializing in Maya archaeology and pottery studies. She is a research associate at the Center for Archaeological Investigations at Southern Illinois University Carbondale and an adjunct professor of anthropology at Eastern Kentucky University.

Jon Spenard has been an assistant professor of anthropology at California State University San Marcos since 2016. He is a Mesoamerican archaeologist who specializes in ancient Maya ritual landscape use. Jon received his MA in anthropology from Florida State University and his PhD in anthropology from the University of California Riverside. He has conducted cave research in Belize, Guatemala, and Mexico. In 2018, he initiated the Rio Frio Regional Archaeological Project, a landscape archaeology project investigating the Mountain Pine Ridge, Belize.

Travis W. Stanton is professor of anthropology at the University of California, Riverside. Conducting field research in the state of Yucatán since 1995, he graduated with his doctorate from Southern Methodist University in 2000. His primary research interests are in Mesoamerican archaeology (with a focus on the Maya area), state formation and collapse, ceramic technology, landscape archaeology, memory, prehistoric violence and warfare, settlement patterns, remote sensing, ethnoarchaeology, and experimental archaeology. He currently works in central Yucatán and northern Quintana Roo, Mexico.

Wesley D. Stoner uses scientific instrumentation to understand cultural behaviors of the past that would otherwise remain invisible. Techniques like neutron activation analysis, laser ablation—inductively coupled plasma—mass spectrometry (LA-ICP-MS), and thin section petrography help to trace artifacts back to the source of production, which enables archaeologists to reconstruct trade networks and sometimes migration. When applied to ceramics, those techniques also reveal the production sequence that potters used to make their craft. Wes also uses geographic information systems (GIS) and satellite-based remote sensing to identify the ancient marks that humans left on the face of earth, such as monumental constructions and agricultural intensifications. His research combines these techniques with traditional field excavation and survey to understand ancient cultures in the Americas. His long-term research focuses on the Gulf Coast of Veracruz, central Mexico, and locations in the United States.

Teresa Tremblay Wagner is an instructor at Coast Mountain College in British Columbia, where she teaches university credit courses in the arts. Teresa earned her MA and BSc in Anthropology at Trent University. She is a member of the Trent University Archaeological Research Centre, an archaeologist for a Canadian consulting firm, and a contractor for the Ontario government's archaeology program. Her current research interests focus on social change related to colonization and capitalism, particularly in the boreal forest and subarctic regions of North America.